THE
LATINO
ENCYCLOPEDIA

THE
LATINO
ENCYCLOPEDIA

Volume 5

Peyote – Spanish Americans

Editors

RICHARD CHABRÁN AND RAFAEL CHABRÁN

Marshall Cavendish
New York • London • Toronto

Published By
Marshall Cavendish Corporation
99 White Plains Road
Tarrytown, New York 10591-9001
United States of America

∞ The paper in these volumes conforms to the American National Standard for Permanence of Paper for Printed Library Materials, Z39.48-1984.

Library of Congress Cataloging-in-Publication Data

The Latino encyclopedia / editors, Richard Chabrán, and Rafael Chabrán,
    p. cm.
    Includes bibliographical references and index.
    1. Hispanic Americans—Encyclopedias. I. Chabrán, Richard II. Chabrán, Rafael
E184.S75L357 1995
973′ .0468′003—dc20   95-13144
ISBN 0-7614-0125-3 (set).   CIP
ISBN 0-7614-0130-X (vol. 5).

First Printing

PRINTED IN THE UNITED STATES OF AMERICA

Contents

CONTENTS

THE
LATINO
ENCYCLOPEDIA

Peyote: The peyote plant is a small cactus without spines. Its name comes from the Aztec *peyutl*. It grows mainly under the ground, with only a small rounded portion above the surface. This portion is cut off and dried to form a "button." These buttons, because of their hallucinatory effects when eaten, have been used in religious ceremonies among Mexican and Native American communities for more than two centuries.

The physiological impact of peyote buttons has been described as consisting of two stages. The first is an exhilarating emotional lift and the second a depression, often accompanied by hallucinations and visions.

The religious and ceremonial uses of peyote appear to have spread northward from Mexico, where its use is well documented among the Tarahumari and Huichol Indians. It first spread to nomadic groups along what is now the U.S.-Mexico border. It was taken up by Kiowa-Comanche tribal groups, then spread to many other tribes, mainly in the American Plains.

There are differences in the use of peyote, but almost universally found is a set of ceremonial rituals and observations. These ceremonies are typically held at night, throughout the night. Among the Plains tribes, tipi structures are the preferred site for ceremonies, but this varies with the particular tribal tradition. There are typically entrance ceremonies and preceremonial purification rites.

Inside the meeting place, a ceremonial fire is tended by a selected male member of the tribe, and a male presider is in charge of the entire service. Each person who enters is assigned a place, and there is often use of ritual implements that are touched, prayed with, and passed among the celebrants. Tobacco is often used ceremonially.

When the time arrives to ingest the peyote, a sack is passed around the room by the presider. Each celebrant takes a number of buttons from the sack and eats them. Average consumption is between four and twenty buttons for each person. The ceremonial fire and consumption of water are carefully monitored by selected representatives.

As morning approaches, there is a tradition of "preaching," with elders offering advice to younger people about how their lives should be lived. This leads to the ceremonial breakfast, which breaks the somber atmosphere and is considerably less formal.

Elements of this general outline vary with different tribal traditions. In general, meetings are held on occasions called by one of the members. Meetings are called most often to offer prayers for the sick or to seek healing, although other reasons have been cited.

Many of the traditions of peyote have been "Christianized," so that many observants consider themselves to be part of a wider Christian fellowship. Use of Bible verses, the appearance of the Bible itself among the ritual objects, and Christianized hymns and sermons are among the elements unique to these variants of religious peyote use.

The visibility of the Native American Church and its use of peyote have drawn it into conflict with contemporary U.S. authorities over the issue of improper use of drugs versus freedom of religious rites and expressions. Contemporary apologists for peyote use in the context of religious services have noted the importance of the peyote religious expressions in giving new meaning and devotion to peoples otherwise devastated by European contact. They argue that peyote use is genuinely religious and not abusive.

Phoenix, Arizona: Largest city in and capital of Arizona. According to the 1990 census, Phoenix was home to 194,118 people of Hispanic descent, approximately 20 percent of the city's population.

Phoenix began its boom of development in the 1860's. As more Anglos arrived with the coming of the railroad in the 1880's, the Mexican American population became proportionally smaller, and its influence decreased.

Mexican Americans became victims of DISCRIMINATION and SEGREGATION. They began to develop their own social life and customs, focused around the family and church. St. Mary's Catholic church was an important part of their communal life during the late nineteenth and early twentieth centuries. In 1910, Mexican Americans composed about 10 percent of the Phoenix population. The figure exceeded 15 percent by 1930. During the early part of the twentieth century, as Anglos gained power and wealth, most Mexican Americans stayed at the poverty level. They lived in the poorest neighborhoods and worked as day laborers or domestics.

In the 1920's, two new churches were built to serve the Hispanic population, St. Anthony's Chapel and the Sanctuario del Corazon de María. In 1921, Phoenix opened Friendly House, a facility designed to "Americanize" Spanish speakers. Friendly House's philosophy was that immigrants should be loyal to the United States but take pride in their own culture. It operated an employment bureau and relief agency, but it was not until the 1930's that it was able to make real contributions to the Mexican community, helping to improve social and economic status. Friendly House remained active into the 1990's.

In the 1940's, several events improved conditions for Mexican Americans in Phoenix, 59 percent of whom were on relief during the Depression. The Marcos de Miza housing project for Mexicans was completed, allowing many people to move out of substandard housing. New Hispanic voluntary organizations emerged, including the Latin American Club.

Following World War II, the GI Bill gave Hispanics who served in the armed services a new opportunity for education. Most, however, continued to work as laborers. Hispanic people were almost completely unrepresented in the professional ranks of the city.

Hispanics became visible in local politics in the 1970's. Rosendo Gutierrez was elected to the city council, and Alfred Gutierrez (no relation) was elected to the Arizona legislature. More organizations devoted to helping Hispanics were founded. When demands for better education and responsiveness to the minority population went unheard, Hispanics boycotted Phoenix Union High School.

Mexican Americans composed about 91 percent of Phoenix's Hispanic population in 1990. Puerto Ricans and Central Americans each made up about 1.3 percent of the population. The Hispanic influence in Phoenix is apparent in the work of Chicanos por la Causa, which assists the Hispanic community through housing, counseling, and business projects; the Arizona Hispanic Chamber of Commerce; the Arizona Mexican American Chamber of Commerce; the Hispanic Women's Conference; and other organizations. Arizona State University sponsors the Center for Latin American Studies and the Hispanic Research Center. The Movimiento Artistico del Río Salado hosts art exhibits and workshops that highlight the Hispanic culture of the region.

Photography: The medium of photography has recorded life in all its manifestations, capturing an authenticity not found in any other art form. It transcends language, cultural barriers, social constraints, and religion in its attempt to capture the human condition. It has been an important vehicle of cultural expression and self-expression among Latino artists.

History. Photography originated in France in 1839. Throughout the nineteenth century, it developed both as a science and as an art form. The first color photograph was made in 1907, and color photography was refined during the first half of the twentieth century. After World War II, it replaced black and white or monochromatic photography as the preferred medium of both amateur and professional photographers.

For many years, both critics and the general public considered photography to be a minor craft rather than an art with the stature of painting or sculpture. They saw photography as the result of a mechanical process lacking both creativity and ingenuity. During the second half of the twentieth century, however, photography became recognized as a fine art. Photographs were exhibited in museums, galleries, colleges, and universities throughout the world and sold successfully in auction markets.

The art world now recognizes photography as a powerful, creative, and virtually limitless art form. A new breed of photographers has taken photography to abstract levels with the creation of images without a camera, image manipulation, and color saturation, among other techniques. The development of new photographic techniques has generated new schools of photography that have contributed to the medium's success.

Early Latin American Photography. Among the prominent Latin American photographers, Mexican-born Manuel Álvarez Bravo (b. 1902) and Víctor Agustín Cassasola (1874-1938) have been two of the most influential in the United States. Bravo focused

---

**LATINO POPULATION OF
PHOENIX, ARIZONA, 1990**

Total number of Latinos = 345,498; 16% of population

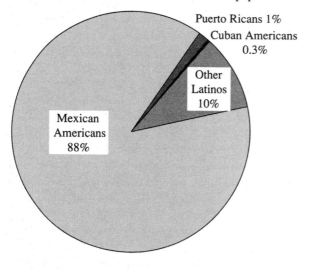

Puerto Ricans 1%
Cuban Americans 0.3%
Other Latinos 10%
Mexican Americans 88%

Source: Data are from Marlita A. Reddy, ed., *Statistical Record of Hispanic Americans* (Detroit: Gale Research, 1993), Table 111.

Note: Figures represent the population of the Metropolitan Statistical Area as delineated by the U.S. Bureau of the Census. Percentages are rounded to the nearest whole number except for Cuban Americans, for whom rounding is to the nearest 0.1%.

his work on the human condition, particularly the poor working-class people of Mexico. Later, he became a major exponent of surrealism, as evident in his strongest personal work.

Cassasola founded the first Society of Press Photographers and later the first Agency of Photographic Information. He is best remembered for his powerful, realistic images of the Mexican Revolution (1910-1921), which captured all sides of the conflict with intense drama and vitality. After the revolution, Cassasola broke away from the traditional Mexican portraiture school, devoting most of his work to women and the aftermath of war.

Another major figure has been Jack Delano (b. 1914). Delano was born in Russia but settled in the United States with his family while very young. His work captured the personal suffering and stark reality of the life during the Great Depression. Most of his work was sponsored by the federal Farm Security Administration. During the 1940's, he relocated to Puerto Rico, where he was able to capture images of the sociopolitical revolution taking place on the island.

The influence of these pioneer photographers contributed to the development of Latino photographers in the latter half of the twentieth century. Modern Latino photography is concentrated in the regions of the United States heavily populated by Latinos. In the Southwest, Mexican, Mexican American, and Chicano art has prevailed because of the area's cultural affinity with Mexico. In the East, New York City has been an important center for many internationally known art photographers from Puerto Rico, Brazil, Colombia, Spain, Chile, Argentina, and Cuba. Artists in both Florida and Puerto Rico have produced work that reflects the struggles of Caribbean communities at home as well as in the continental United States.

Ethnic and Nonethnic Approaches. Latino photography is a diverse, energetic, dramatic, and powerful creative art form. It can, but does not necessarily, reflect an ethnic definition limited to Latino issues. Marcelo Montecino (Chile) focused on the political and military conflicts of his native country during the 1970's. Sebatiâo Salgado (Brazil) has documented the economic disparities of his homeland. Adal Maldonado (Puerto Rico) captures images of Puerto Ricans adapting to life in New York City as well as photographing prominent Latin American show business personalities. The startling images of Andrés Serrano, depicting death and violence, are influenced by the contradictions of traditional Spanish Roman Catholicism.

The work of other photographers tends to depart from the ethnic element. New York artist Geno Rodríguez produces postmodernist images of belief and contemporary culture. Becky Mayer (Chile) and Marga Clark (Spain) have created haunting diptychs and triptychs of repeated images that are concerned with perception and memory. The work of Ricardo Sánchez captures images of his native New York City and its surroundings that, although resembling conventional postcard photos, reveal a questioning of the meanings of objects that are often taken for granted.

Cecilia Arboleda of Florida uses images from her native Colombia as well as neighboring Ecuador and Peru. Although she returns frequently to South America to explore its streets, houses, and human interactions, her camera does not light on the glossy images of the travel brochure or magazine. Instead, she presents a series of quiet, contemplative vignettes in precise but tonally wide-ranging black and white. When her subjects are people, they are often women and girls. Her work presents an intimacy and familiarity with her subjects, combined with high technical as well as aesthetic quality.

Chicano Photographers. Other Latino photographers specialize in the human figure. Chicano photographer Harry Gamboa, Jr., is known for his images of anxiety and erotic fantasy that represent depersonalized survival in an urban environment. To Wilfredo Castaño of Tucson, Arizona, photography is the art of constant discovery and sharing. He often blends his own poetry with his images.

Daniel Martínez of Los Angeles, California, uses holographic film to capture what he describes as the viewer's awareness of visual perspective. He believes that all social interactions depend on the complex perceptual system of the individual. His primary objective is to offer an integrated, whole-image view of urban reality.

For Patssi Valdez of Los Angeles, photography is autobiographical. Most of her early work depicts the struggles of being part of a minority group, from police brutality and racism to the hardships of living in the barrio of East Los Angeles. Later work reflects a more positive view of herself and the world around her. She attempts in her work to break negative stereotypes of Latinas.

Puerto Rican Photographers. Puerto Rico has produced several outstanding art photographers since the 1970's. Their styles are representative of the different techniques used in contemporary photography. Curiously enough, most of them tended to depart from the traditional portraiture and folk photography popular during the first half of the twentieth century.

The new school of Puerto Rican photography prefers manipulation of negatives and color, color saturation, image manipulation, texture, and printing alteration. Photographic artists try to dramatize nature as both a creative and a destructive force, and they are interested in the constant quest for human immortality. Many participants in this new school use abstract designs that force viewers to reexamine their own social reality. Among the leading members of this group are Rubén Gaztambide, Héctor Méndez Caratini, Frank X. Méndez, Frieda Medin, and Sophie Rivera.

Frank Espada, a Puerto Rican, is a master of both monochromatic realism and expressionism. Boricua College in New York City and the National Endowment for the Humanities helped sponsor his 1980 exhibit titled "The Puerto Rican Diaspora: Themes in the Survival of a People." This project documented the migration experience of more than two million Puerto Ricans who traveled to the mainland United States beginning in the early 1900's. The traveling exhibit included more than one hundred photographs of the joys, sorrows, and struggles of his people.

Latin American art photography has managed to overcome the traditional prejudices against it, both at home and abroad. Advances in photographic media technology and new aesthetic venues have combined to create a new generation of contemporary artists. Hispanic photography has become more international in outlook as the medium itself has been accepted as a fine art. Modern Latino photography is as diverse as its many practitioners. —*Angel A. Amy Moreno de Toro*

SUGGESTED READINGS:
• Espada, Frank. *The Puerto Rican Diaspora: Themes in the Survival of a People.* New York: Museo del Barrio, 1983. A brief introduction to the work of photographer Frank Espada.
• Goldman, Shifra M. "Chicano Art of the Southwest in the Eighties." *Image* 3 (1986): 41-50. A discussion of Chicano art as it attempted to define itself through the 1980's. Also surveys the development of Chicano art in the Southwest.
• Phelan, Robert J., and Ricardo Pau-Llosa. *New Traditions: Thirteen Hispanic Photographers.* Albany, N.Y.: The New York State Museum, 1986. An excellent survey for an understanding of trends in Latino photography, both in Latin America and in the United States.
• Ramos Collado, Lilliana. "La Realidad Estaba Cerca." In *Nueva Fotografía Puertorriqueña.* Río Piedras, Puerto Rico: Museo de la Universidad de Puerto Rico, 1985. A personal appraisal of what constitutes the new Puerto Rican photography.
• Rivera Rosario, Nelson. "La Nueva Fotografía Puertorriqueña: Una Exposición." In *Nueva Fotografía Puertorriqueña.* Río Piedras, Puerto Rico: Museo de la Universidad de Puerto Rico, 1985. A discussion of new trends and currents defining the scope of Puerto Rican photography.

Piazzola, Astor (b. Jan. 30, 1921, Mar del Plata, Argentina): Musician and composer. Piazzola grew up in New York City, where he learned to play the Argentine accordion, or *bandeón*, with his father. At an early age he auditioned for the legendary Argentinean tango singer Carlos Gardel, with whom he played in a film for Paramount.

Piazzola has seriously and successfully taken his instrument onto the international concert stage. After performing and arranging music for TANGO bands and orchestras in his native country, Piazzola went to Paris to study music seriously with Nadia Boulanger. There he won prizes for his compositions and also reconsidered the musical form of the tango, giving it a new harmonic twist and rhythm character, sometimes called the "new tango."

In 1976, Piazzola formed El Quinteto Tango Nuevo with bass player Héctor Console, guitarist Horacio Malvicino, pianist Pablo Ziegler, and violinist Fernando Suarez Paz. They made two well-received albums: *Tango Zero Hour* and *The Rough Dancer and the Cyclical Night*.

Piazzola's music and interpretations are famous around the world, from classical ballet and opera companies and concert halls to films, pop concert stages, theaters, and recording studios. Piazzola's original works include more than 750 compositions and more than seventy recordings.

Pico family: The Picos were a prominent family in early California history. Santiago de la Cruz Pico, the family founder of the California branch, arrived with the Juan Bautista de Anza expedition in San Francisco in 1776. With him were his wife and their seven children. The Picos eventually settled in Los Angeles in 1786.

In 1795, three of Santiago's sons were granted Rancho San José de Garcia de Simí in what is now Ventura County in Southern California, on the condition that the family continue living in the sparsely populated town of Los Angeles. The Spanish monarchy would

Pío Pico. (Security Pacific Bank Collection, Los Angeles Public Library)

make such land grants as an incentive to Spanish settlers in order to secure its territories against claims of other nations. By 1790, there were twenty-eight families in the Pueblo de Nuestra Señora la Reina de Los Angeles (now Los Angeles). In addition to the Picos, these included families with such familiar Southern California names as Sepúlveda and Figueroa.

Two other sons, José Dolores Pico (1764-1827) and José María Pico, became important members in their communities. José María's sons included Pío de Jesús Pico (1801-1894), a two-time Mexican governor of Alta California (the name by which present-day California was known in the Spanish and Mexican periods). Prior to becoming governor, Pío received a large land grant of property in Jamul, in modern San Diego County. His terms as governor were marked by ongoing political strife; his first term in 1832 lasted only thirty-two days.

During his second term, from March of 1845 to July of 1846, Pío had no treasury. José Castro, the provincial treasurer, remained in Monterey when Pío moved the capital to Los Angeles. With a lavish hand, Governor Pico presided over the final breaking up of mission properties in California. He gave away thousands of acres in land grants to friends and supporters and brought an end to the mission era, a task begun with the secularization of the missions in 1834.

During the Mexican American War (1846-1848), Andrés Pico (1810-1876), another son of José María Pico, was commander of a Mexican force at the Battle of San Pascual northeast of San Diego (December 6, 1846). His troops inflicted serious casualties on U.S. forces. On January 13, 1847, however, Andrés Pico, as commander-in-chief of the Mexican troops, made the final surrender to Colonel John C. Frémont by signing the Articles of Capitulation at Cahuenga. Andrés went on to produce coal oil in the region of Pico Canyon (named after him) near Newhall in Los Angeles County. "Old Pico," a pioneer well, was drilled there in 1876 and is now a National Historic Landmark.

Andrés Pico remained active in California politics. In 1859, as a state assemblyman, he introduced a plan—which the state legislature approved—to correct a serious representation and taxation conflict between Northern and Southern California. Pico also volunteered to raise a regiment of native California cavalry

Pico House. (Martin Hutner)

to help the North in the U.S. Civil War, but the offer was rejected.

Numerous Pico daughters and sons married into other well-known early California families, including the Alvarado, Argüello, Carrillo, and Ortega families. Salomón Pico, one of José Dolores' thirteen children, became notorious as a highwayman, reportedly to protest the U.S. occupation of California; Salomón was executed in Baja California, Mexico, for other crimes. Mount Solomon and Solomon Canyon south of Santa María, California, are so named because they were the scenes of his operations.

The many Pico siblings and cousins lost fortunes and great ranchos in costly land disputes. With the 1848 TREATY OF GUADALUPE HIDALGO, Mexico ceded California, along with other territories, to the United States. Although the treaty provided that "property of every kind" belonging to Mexicans in the ceded territories was to be "inviolably respected," conflict inevitably ensued over ownership, and land titles were in dispute for many years. The Pico family lost approximately 532,000 acres of land to which they laid claim.

The contributions of the Pico family are still evident in place names that recall their explorations and labors in early California. Among these are Pico House, a well-known Los Angeles hotel built by Pío Pico in 1870; Pico Rivera, a southeastern Los Angeles suburb; and Pico Boulevard, a major east-west Los Angeles artery.

Pietri, Pedro (b. Mar. 21, 1943, Ponce, Puerto Rico): Poet. Reared in New York City, Pietri was the second child in a family of four children. Pietri's parents died while he was still a child, and he was brought up by his grandmother. In his literature and personal life, Pietri has identified with the marginal and the downtrodden. Little more is known about Pietri's biography.

Pietri's work is quintessentially urban, and the city has figured importantly as a protagonist in his work. Pietri's poems, intended to be read aloud, have been performed in the city's cafés, community centers, and colleges.

Puerto Rican Obituary (1973), his first book, was so popular that it spawned hundreds of young street poets who imitated his style. It focuses on aspects of Puerto Rican life in New York. In *Traffic Violations* (1983), Pietri's work becomes a full-blown revolt against social convention. A prose work, *Lost in the Museum of Natural History* (1981), is a surrealistic examination of modern capitalist alienation. Pietri's unconventional, subversive poetry reflects the dark conception of the world of alienation while simultaneously raising the level of consciousness of those alienated.

Pimentel, David (b. May 24, 1925, Fresno, Calif.): Ecologist and entomologist. Pimentel received his B.S. in biology from the University of Massachusetts in 1948 and his Ph.D. in entomology from Cornell University in 1951. From 1951 to 1953, he was chief of the Tropical Research Laboratory at the U.S. Public Health Service in San Juan, Puerto Rico. In 1955, he joined the staff of Cornell. He rose from assistant professor to full professor in ecology.

Pimentel has done research in ecology, the genetics of insects and plants, environmental resource management and population, energy and land resources in the food system, ecosytems management, and pest control. From 1964 to 1966 he served on the President's Science Advising Council. He has also worked in various functions for the United Nations; the United Nations Educational, Scientific, and Cultural Organization; and the National Academies of Science.

Pimería Alta: Region that formerly covered the northern part of Spanish colonial Sonora and later the southwestern part of the state of Arizona. It extended from the Altar River in Sonora to the Gila River in Arizona, and from the San Pedro River in the east to the Gulf of California and the Colorado River in the west. During the Spanish colonial era, it was first part of the province of Nueva Vizcaya, then transferred to Sonora.

Pimería Alta was named for native tribes that inhabited the area. These included the Pima, Papago, Sobaipuri, Yuma, Cocomaricopa, Cocopa, and others.

The Kino Era. Jesuit missionary Eusebio Francisco KINO was the first European to explore, map, and settle Pimería Alta. When he arrived at Cucurpe on the San Miguel River in February of 1687, it was the most northern extension of the Spanish frontier. Kino and his companions established the mission of Nuestra Senora de los Dolores on the San Miguel as their base of operations. Within a year, several other missions were founded on the San Miguel and on the Magdalena River to the north.

In 1690, Kino and Juan María Salvatierra inspected the area from the Altar River valley north to Tumacácori on the Santa Cruz River, a tributary of the Gila. There a delegation of the Sobaipuris invited the missionaries to their towns further north, at San Xavier del Bac.

In December of 1694, Kino explored northward up the Santa Cruz River to its junction with the Gila

River. There he made contact with the Opas and the Cocomaricopas.

The next year, the Pimas on the Magdalena attacked the settlers. After the revolt was put down, Kino helped influence the natives to accept the peace settlement.

In 1696, Kino returned to the Gila area. This time he ranged eastward, following the San Pedro south to Quíburi, about seventy-five miles southwest of San Xavier del Bac. Several Apache attacks along the Pimerian frontier were repulsed by the Pimas, led by the Quiburi Captain Coro.

Another Kino exploration in 1699 followed the Gila down to its junction with the Colorado. During this trip, the missionary was given a number of blue abalone shells. Remembering having seen such shells in Baja California, he concluded that California could be reached by land and was a peninsula rather than an island, as had commonly been supposed.

In April of 1700, Kino established his northernmost mission, SAN XAVIER DEL BAC, on the Santa Cruz River near present-day Tucson. He continued exploring and mapping his beloved Pimería, making at least six trips to the Gila. Twice he reached the Yuma area, and once he went all the way to the mouth of the Colorado and into California. In his own mind, his greatest discovery was the accessibility of the California peninsula by land.

Kino wrote the Spanish government urging that Pimería Alta be used as a way station for the settlement and colonization of California. His advice was ignored because of lack of manpower and increasing attacks by the Apaches to the east of Pimería. Kino died in 1711 without realizing his dream.

Expansion and Indian Attacks. In 1736, a silver strike at Arizonac in the Altar River valley drew miners from Sonora, but the vein was small and the duration of mining brief. A revolt by the eastern Pimas and attacks by the Apaches kept Captain Juan Bautista de ANZA, commander of the Spanish military forces, busy protecting the Pimería. In 1737, he was killed

Eusebio Francisco Kino led the expedition into Pimería Alta. (Ruben G. Mendoza)

Tubac was the first Spanish military post in Arizona. (Arizona Historical Society)

fighting the Apaches, and his plans for advancing the settlement of the region northward to the Gila line had to be abandoned.

By the 1740's, civilian settlement in Pimería Alta had reached the Santa Cruz valley. The settlers located near Kino's missions. They were hit hard by the Great Pima Revolt of 1751 and by continued Apache attacks. Governor Diego Ortiz Parilla established a presidio at Tubac, the first Spanish military post in Arizona. He appointed Juan Bautista de Anza, the son of the famous frontiersman, as its commander. Anza spent much of his time campaigning against the Seris to the west and the Apaches to the east in order to make the area safe for the colonists.

In the mid-1770's, José de Galvez, visitador general of New Spain, decided that it was finally time to occupy California. Pimería Alta was to be part of that expansion. The expedition to settle San Francisco, a favorite project of Fray Junípero Serra, was to leave from Tubac under the leadership of Anza.

Soon thereafter, however, the presidio was moved from Tubac to Tucson and the land route to California was closed. The Pimería, no longer part of the Spanish

colonial route to California, remained thinly populated and isolated until the northern part passed into U.S. control with the GADSDEN PURCHASE in 1854.

—*Ray F. Broussard*

SUGGESTED READINGS:

• Bannon, John Francis. *The Spanish Borderlands Frontier, 1513-1821*. New York: Holt, Rinehart and Winston, 1970.

• Bolton, Herbert Eugene. *Kino's Historical Memoir of Pimeria Alta*. Reprint. Berkeley: University of California Press, 1948.

• Officer, James E. *Hispanic Arizona 1536-1856*. Tucson: University of Arizona Press, 1987.

• Riva Palacio, Vicente, ed. *El Vireinato: Historia de la dominacion Espanol en Mexico desde 1521 a 1808*. Vol. 2 in *Mexico a traves de los siglos*. 4th ed. Mexico City: Editorial Cumbre, 1962.

Piñata: Mexican hollow papier-mâché vessel in a whimsical form. Piñatas are used to create a festive air at many occasions in Mexico. The piñata is made of papier-mâché, usually in the form of an animal, and its hollow interior is filled with various little gifts, usually

A blindfolded girl swings at a piñata during a school festival. (James Shaffer)

candy and toys. It then is suspended, and blindfolded children take turns trying to break it with a bat. When it breaks, its contents spill onto the floor, and the children scramble for them. Piñata parties are particularly associated with Las Posadas and Christmas in Mexico and adjacent Central America.

Pincay, Laffit, Jr. (b. Dec. 29, 1946, Panama City, Panama): Jockey. Pincay, the son of a famous Panamanian rider, began his racing career as an apprentice hot-walker and groomer. After taking his first competitive mount in 1964, he enter U.S. racing in 1966. Pincay quickly rose through racing circles to become a top jockey despite a continual battle to keep his weight down. At times, he literally starved himself to maintain his ideal riding weight.

Despite these struggles, Pincay broke numerous racing records. He set records for single season earnings ($13,353,299 in 1985) and career earnings, with a total of more than $116 million. He also won the sport's richest one-race purse, $2 million, for finishing first in the 1985 Jersey Derby. Pincay was the leading money winner among U.S. jockeys for five consecutive years (1970 1974) and in 1979.

Ranking second only to Bill Shoemaker in career victories, Pincay crossed the finish line first more than seventy-eight hundred times. His most notable triumphs include three consecutive Belmont Stakes victories (1982-1984) and a first-place finish in the 1984 Kentucky Derby. Voted the sport's outstanding jockey five times (1971, 1973, 1974, 1979, and 1985), Pincay was elected to the National Museum of Racing Hall of Fame in 1975.

Pineapple: Tropical fruit. The pineapple was domesticated by American Indians in the Caribbean, Central America, and northeastern South America. The spiny tops of pineapples were used by Caribbean Indians as symbols of hospitality in welcoming visitors. The pineapple is eaten in modern Latin America in salads, cooked as an accompaniment to meats, as juice, as desserts, and even as the basis for fermented drinks, such as Afro-Brazilian *aluá* and Mexican *tepaché*. The fruit is called *piña* or *anana* in Spanish-speaking Latin America and *abacaxi* in Brazil.

Piñero, Jesús T. (Apr. 16, 1897, Carolina, Puerto Rico—Nov. 9, 1952, San Juan, Puerto Rico): Public official. Piñero held the post of governor at a transitional point in Puerto Rico's history. He had the distinction of being the first Puerto Rican to occupy the

Laffit Pincay, Jr. (AP/Wide World Photos)

position of governor. He was appointed to serve out the term of the last American governor, Rexford G. Tugwell, who retired in 1946. Tugwell recommended Piñero as his replacement to President Harry S Truman.

Piñero, a member of the Popular Democratic Party (PARTIDO POPULAR DEMOCRÁTICO), was serving as resident commissioner, a nonvoting seat in the U.S. House of Representatives. He held the post of governor from September of 1946 until January of 1949, when Luis MUÑOZ MARÍN took office as Puerto Rico's first elected governor.

Piñero, Miguel (Dec. 19, 1946, Gurabo, Puerto Rico—June 16, 1988, New York, N.Y.): Playwright, actor, and poet. Piñero, who moved to New York with his family in 1950, became involved with gangs, street crime, and drugs as an adolescent. He began writing poetry while serving time for armed robbery in New York's Sing Sing Prison, and from there he began writing plays. His 1974 play *Short Eyes*, about a child molester in prison, received an Obie and a New York Drama Critics Circle Award. Piñero adapted the play for film in 1977, including a role for himself.

Jesús Piñero was the first Puerto Rican to be governor of the island. (AP/Wide World Photos)

Miguel Piñero (right) and Marvin Felix Camillo, who directed Short Eyes *on stage.* (AP/Wide World Photos)

His other plays include *Eulogy for a Small-Time Thief* (1977), *The Sun Always Shines for the Cool* (1978), *Playland Blues* (1980), *A Midnight Moon at the Greasy Spoon* (1981), and such one-acts, skits, and revues as *Guntower*, *Paper Toilet*, *Cold Beer*, *All Junkies*, and *Straight from the Ghetto*. As an actor, Piñero played God in the off-Broadway play *Steambath*, appeared in the films *Alambrista!* (1977) and *Fort Apache, the Bronx* (1981), and had television roles on *Baretta*, *Kojak*, and *Miami Vice*. Piñero also coedited the 1975 anthology *NuYorican Poet* and published his own collection of poetry, *La Bodega Sold Dreams* (1980).

Piñon, Nélida (b. May 3, 1936, Rio de Janeiro, Brazil): Writer. Piñon was born to a Spanish father and a Brazilian mother. She was graduated from the Catholic Uni-

versity of Rio. She worked for the newspaper *O Globo* until she decided that journalism was incompatible with literature. She then worked as an assistant editor of the literary magazine *Cadernos Brasileiros*. She taught university courses in Brazil and at Columbia University in New York City.

Piñon dedicated herself full-time to creative writing in 1955, publishing more than half a dozen novels and three collections of short stories by the early 1990's. Her novels include *Guia-mapa de Gabriel Arcanjo* (1961), *Madeira feita cruz* (1963), *Fundador* (1969), *A casa da paixao* (1972), the semiautobiographical *A república dos sonhos* (1984; *The Republic of Dreams*, 1989), and *A doce cancao de Caetana* (1987; *Caetana's Sweet Song*, 1992).

In her short stories, Piñon turns away from trying to clarify spirituality to a world in which only her mate-

Francisco Pizarro. (Library of Congress)

rial and minute descriptions of the surroundings, along with fragmentary sensations and posturing of individuals, reflect the characters' state of mind. Considered one of Brazil's foremost contemporary authors of fiction, Piñon writes in a dense, often mystical, poetic language and an unconventional narrative style. Her characters are often self-conscious and obsessive.

Pinto: Chicano prison inmate. In the Chicano dialect of CALÓ, a pinto ("pinta" for a female) is a prison inmate. Many pintos are incarcerated for drug possession or gang activities; many have weak educational backgrounds. The experiences of Chicano prisoners are unique among inmates. A culture of pinto poetry and art has developed that explains the particulars of their lives and hopes. A pinto who has served his or her time in prison is sometimes referred to as a *pinto veterano* (veteran pinto).

Pipián: Sauce of tomatoes and chiles. *Pipián* is a sauce eaten by the Aztecs and still eaten in Mexico. There are two kinds, red and green. Red *pipián* is made with tomatoes and ripe chiles, while green *pipián* is made with tomatillos and green chiles. Both are thickened with ground pumpkin seeds, lending a nutty flavor. Modern usage often considers any nut-thickened Mexican-style sauce to be *pipián*. The sauce most commonly is used over fowl or fish.

Piragua: Shaved ice with fruit syrup, eaten from a paper cone. Street vendors in Puerto Rico and New York City sell these cones of shaved ice, especially during hot weather. Similar to Italian and Hawaiian shaved ice cones, *piragua* is made by scraping ice from a block, stuffing it into a wrapped paper cone, molding the top with another cone, and drizzling any of several fruit syrups over it. *Piragua* is beloved by adults and children alike. The name literally refers to a type of small canoe, alluding to the boat-shaped depression left in the block of ice after it has been shaved.

Pizarro, Francisco (1475, Trujillo, Spain—June 26, 1541, Lima, Peru): Conquistador. Pizarro sailed to Hispaniola in 1502. He participated in several expeditions of territories around the Gulf of Darien. With two partners, Diego de Almagro and Fray Hernando de Luque, he carried out two expeditions down the Pacific coast between 1524 and 1527. He collected enough gold and information about a wealthy Indian civilization, the Incas, to return to Spain and request a

capitulation. In 1531, after the capitulation had been awarded, he began his last voyage to Inca territory.

Pizarro had only about 180 men in his party, making his goal of conquest seemingly impossible. The timing, however, was excellent. Two Inca princes, Atahualpa and Huascar, had been fighting for the throne and had divided the loyalties of the people. When Pizarro arrested Atahualpa, the winner of the Inca power struggle, no troops came to Atahualpa's rescue.

Pizarro massacred many Incas and executed Atahualpa to assure his hegemony. He took over Cuzco, the major Inca city, and founded Lima as the capital of the colony. He ruled for eight years, but the riches of the empire brought the attention and competition of many other Spaniards. He killed his partner, Diego de Almagro, but Almagro's men retaliated by killing Pizarro in 1541.

Plan de Ayala (Nov. 28, 1911): Plan for land reform and confiscation of property. After Mexican dictator Porfirio Díaz was overthrown in the Mexican Revolution of 1910, Francisco Madero became the new president. He supported elections and land reform. Emiliano ZAPATA, a popular leader among the peasants, issued the Plan de Ayala in support of a far-reaching revolutionary program. Zapata and his supporters, called Zapatistas, demanded that all land be held communally as it had been in Aztec times. The present owners would be paid for their lost property unless they refused to agree, in which case it would be taken without compensation.

Madero did not accept the proposal. The plan argued that "the land belongs to everyone, like the air, the water, the light, and the heat of the sun," but only in Zapata's home state of Morelos did some *campesinos* (small farmers) get any land. This 1911 plan inspired the PLAN DE DELANO issued by California grape workers during a strike in the late 1960's. It also led to the establishment of a secret army of Zapatistas in the 1920's.

Plan de Delano (1968): Plan for economic reform. In 1968, César CHÁVEZ, head of the NATIONAL FARM WORKERS ASSOCIATION, issued a plan for economic and social reform modeled after the PLAN DE AYALA. The Plan de Ayala, written by Emiliano ZAPATA in 1911, called for giving land and food to poor farmers in Mexico. Chávez, calling himself a "son of the Mexican Revolution," called on the American government to take land from the giant agricultural interests in California and give it to migrant workers, who would

César Chávez formulated the Plan de Delano as a means of empowering farmworkers. (Library of Congress)

then grow their own food on their own farms. Chávez's goal, as was Zapata's, was "bread and justice" for the poor.

Likening his campaign to that of the Civil Rights movement and its drive for racial justice in the American South, Chávez argued that the oppressed grape pickers, most of whom were Mexicans and Filipinos, were exploited by California growers. The National Farm Workers Union sent the plan to all the barrios in the Southwest, and it became an organizing tool for oppressed peoples everywhere. "The triumph of our race depends," Chávez wrote, on the unity of "all races that comprise the oppressed."

Plan de San Diego (January-February, 1915): Plan for an uprising along the Mexico-Texas border. Early in January, 1915, Texas state troopers found a letter in the possession of Basilio Ramos, a supporter of Mexican president Victoriano Huerta. Relations between Mexico and the United States had been strained since the beginning of the Mexican Revolution in 1910. Ramos' letter outlined the Plan de San Diego, named after a small town outside of San Antonio, Texas. The plan called for a general uprising among Mexican Americans on February 20, 1915. It also called for the killing of all Anglos over the age of sixteen, except the elderly, and the creation of a Supreme Revolutionary Congress that would lead Texas back into the Mexican nation. The author of the plan was never revealed. Many Anglos believed it to be part of a general revolutionary plot to regain territory lost in the Mexican American War.

President Woodrow Wilson sent 100,000 troops to the border after rebels robbed a bank on the American side of the border. The troops remained in the area for more than a year. More than three hundred suspected Mexican agents were shot or hung by the Army and the Texas Rangers, and vigilantes killed many more. The author of the plan and whether it was genuine were never established.

Plan de Santa Bárbara: A Chicano Plan for Higher Education, El: Document providing a framework of goals and methods. This plan to achieve equity and equality in higher education for Chicanos was written in the spring of 1969 at the University of California, Santa Barbara. A group of student leaders, faculty, and staff members met to discuss work relating to Chicano studies being done on various campuses. The plan grew out of a perceived need for more Chicanos in higher levels of education and an education that re-

lated to the Chicano experience. Specifically, the plan called for recruitment of more Chicano educators and students, the institutionalization of CHICANO STUDIES PROGRAMS, formation of culturally relevant curricula, and control by Chicanos of Chicano studies programs. The planners viewed education as a way to inspire self-determination among Chicanos and to train them to develop ways to serve their community. The plan contributed in important ways to the development and further definition of Chicano studies programs on university campuses in California and elsewhere. It also helped unify various Chicano groups under one ideology that its developers called CHICANISMO. This unification resulted in the creation of the student group MOVIMIENTO ESTUDIANTIL CHICANO DE AZTLÁN (MECHA).

Plan Espiritual de Aztlán, El (March, 1969): Document proclaiming Chicano cultural identity and goals. The CHICANO YOUTH LIBERATION CONFERENCE, led by Rodolfo "Corky" GONZÁLES, met in March, 1969, in Denver, Colorado. Delegates to the conference voted to adopt *El Plan Espiritual de Aztlán*, which called for Chicanos to cooperate to achieve common goals including a revival of the legendary Aztec homeland of AZTLÁN. The document urged recognition of Chicano cultural identity, with its different components from indigenous, Hispanic, and Mexican history. The poet ALURISTA was one of the writers of the plan.

The plan document supported Chicano nationalism and a revival of cultural values as well as calling for creation of a new political party. It influenced the subsequent *El PLAN DE SANTA BÁRBARA: A CHICANO PLAN FOR HIGHER EDUCATION* (1969), which proposed creation of university courses and programs in Chicano studies. *El Plan Espiritual de Aztlán* was published in the journal *El grito del Norte* (volume 2, 1969).

Plátanos: Plantains. *Plátanos*, a starchy bananalike fruit, are eaten primarily as a vegetable. *Plátanos* were brought to the Americas by the Spanish or their African slaves. The plantain fruit is hard and starchy and is cooked much like a root vegetable. It must be cooked to become edible. Plantains thrive throughout tropical America, and they are an inexpensive ingredient. They are eaten in a variety of dishes, including soups, fritters, TOSTONES, MOFONGUITOS, TAMALES, rice dishes, sweetened and spiced cakes, and sauced desserts. Plantains are used extensively in the Caribbean, eastern Mexico, Central America, and eastern South America.

American troops entering Havana, Cuba, on January 1, 1899. (National Archives)

Platt Amendment (1902): In response to fear of foreign intervention in Cuba at the end of the SPANISH-AMERICAN WAR (1898), the Platt Amendment was added to the Cuban constitution. The amendment provided for intervention by the United States in Cuba's political and economic affairs with other nations.

As the Cuban rebellion against Spain was nearing a successful conclusion, the landed Creole elite became concerned about the prospect of a country ruled by the landless. In June, 1896, more than one hundred planters, attorneys, and manufacturers appealed to the United States for intervention. At that time, the economy of Cuba, crippled by the colonial misrule of Spain and the period of war, still held enormous potential to produce sugar and other tropical products.

Many U.S. senators held their positions at the indulgence of the large businesses that had sponsored and supported them in their respective state legislatures, which at the time chose U.S. senators. This patronage came to an end temporarily with ratification of the Seventeenth Amendment to the U.S. Constitution, which provided for direct elections. Trading in commodities was an important source of wealth and thus provided political power; as a result, intervention in Cuba was readily launched. The United States thus became embroiled in the Spanish-American War.

Spain, already losing the war, soon surrendered to the United States, and Cuba became the spoils of war instead of a worker's paradise. The United States found itself occupying a large new territory. Cuba, unlike the possessions the United States had acquired earlier, had a large population and a rich commercial potential. It was soon apparent, however, that the best interests of the United States would be served by ensuring that Cuba remained an independent nation under the benevolent eye of its "liberator."

To bring this nation under a stable government and protect it from the effects of rule by landless reformers, a constitution was created by General Leonard Wood, then commanding the occupying forces. Based on the United States Constitution, it was adopted in May, 1902, when U.S. occupation was formally ended. During the creation of this Cuban constitution, several amendments were proposed by Elihu Root, then U.S. secretary of war. One of these, the Platt Amendment, was to have profound influence on the future of Cuba.

Sponsored by Senator Orville Platt of Connecticut, the Platt Amendment established many purported safeguards for the emerging nation. The proximity of the island to the United States bred fears that Cuba's independence might make it the target for foreign intervention. Accordingly, the following provisions were added by Platt: No treaties could be made by Cuba to grant concessions to any foreign nation without the express approval of the United States, no treaties could be made that abrogated the independence of Cuba without the approval of the United States, a permanent naval base would be leased from Cuba at Guantánamo Bay, and the United States had the right to unilaterally initiate intervention in Cuban affairs.

The Platt Amendment was sweeping and many times required clarification through additional laws and debate. It held the island nation of Cuba as a virtual vassal of the United States, depending on the United States for almost every outside commercial venture. This caused strong popular feeling in Cuba against the United States. The amendment was abrogated by the Senate in 1934 as part of President Franklin D. Roosevelt's GOOD NEIGHBOR POLICY. Only the naval base at Guantánamo Bay was retained.

Plena: Puerto Rican song and dance form. The music of the *plena* is lively, accompanied almost exclusively by percussion instruments: drums, claves, MARACAS, and the *pandareta* (tambourine). The melody is supplied by voices singing humorous, satirical lyrics that poke fun at contemporary events. The *plena* originated in Ponce, Puerto Rico, in 1916 and spread across the country, becoming the last true Puerto Rican dance to do so. It rose in popularity and became a true folk dance. The *plena* was a rebellion against traditional patterns. It is the final blending of the races and cultures that characterize Puerto Rican folk music and dance.

Plunkett, Jim (James William Plunkett, Jr.; b. Dec. 5, 1947, Santa Clara, Calif.): Football player. The son of William Gutiérrez Plunkett and Carmen (Blea) Plunkett, both legally blind, Jim Plunkett was reared by his bilingual parents to speak only English so that he would be accepted by Anglo society. After an outstanding high-school career, Plunkett became the starting quarterback at Stanford University in his sophomore year. Plunkett was named an All-American and the Pacific Eight Conference's Outstanding Player as a junior. In his senior year, he led Stanford to a Rose Bowl win over Ohio State and was named Player of the Game. That year, he became the first major college player to throw for more than seven thousand yards in a career, and he was named the Heisman Trophy winner and *The Sporting News* Player of the Year.

The number-one draft pick of the New England Patriots in 1971, Plunkett earned the United Press

Jim Plunkett led the Oakland Raiders to victory in Super Bowl XV in 1981. (AP/Wide World Photos)

International American Football Conference Rookie of the Year Award. Bothered by injuries, however, he played less well over the next six seasons with the Patriots and the San Francisco 49ers and was released. Picked up by the Oakland Raiders in 1978, Plunkett saw little action until the 1980 season, when he led the team to a Super Bowl victory and was named both the Super Bowl Most Valuable Player and the Comeback Player of the Year.

In the 1983 season, Plunkett led the Los Angeles Raiders to a Super Bowl win over the Washington Redskins. He retired after the 1986 season.

Plyler v. Doe (457 U.S. 202, decided June 15, 1982): U.S. Supreme Court case regarding education. It challenged a section of the Texas State Code that allowed only citizens of the United States and legally admitted aliens to receive tuition-free education.

Plyler v. Doe arose after the state of Texas enacted a statute denying local school districts funds for the education of undocumented alien children unless the students paid a tuition of one thousand dollars per year. A class action suit was filed in the U.S. District Court for the Eastern District of Texas in September, 1977, on behalf of "certain unnamed Mexican school-aged children illegally residing in Smith County, Texas" (identified as "J. and R. Doe et al."). The defendants named were James Plyler, who was superintendent of the Tyler Independent School District, and that district's board of trustees.

The district court agreed with the plaintiffs that to deny them a free public school education was a violation of their right to equal protection of the law under the FOURTEENTH AMENDMENT to the U.S. Constitution. In handing down this decision, the court noted that even undocumented aliens are subject to the provisions of the equal protection clause. It ordered the school district not to prevent the children from enrolling in public school. On October 20, 1980, the U.S. Fifth Circuit Court of Appeals issued a ruling sustaining the district court's holding.

The state of Texas appealed the case to the U.S. Supreme Court. The case was consolidated with *In Re Alien Children* and argued on December 1, 1981, by Peter Roos of the MEXICAN AMERICAN LEGAL DEFENSE AND EDUCATION FUND (MALDEF). The National Education Association (NEA), the State Board of Education of California, the LEAGUE OF UNITED LATIN AMERICAN CITIZENS (LULAC), the Washington Lawyers' Committee, and the MEXICAN AMERICAN BAR ASSOCIATION, among other groups, lent their support to the children's side of the case. Briefs supporting the state of Texas were filed by several Texas border school districts, the Federation of Americans for Immigration Reform (FAIR), and a cadre of conservative public interest law firms.

The Court struck down the Texas statute as a violation of the equal protection clause of the Fourteenth Amendment, which provides that no state shall deny to any person the equal protection of the laws. The state of Texas argued, in part, that undocumented aliens were not persons "within its jurisdiction" and therefore were not entitled to equal treatment by the laws of Texas. The state also argued against spending public funds on children unlikely to remain productively employed in the state. The Court rejected these arguments by a vote of five to four. The majority opinion, written by Justice William Brennan, stressed the importance of education to the individual, to democracy, and to society in general.

In *Plyler v. Doe*, the Court majority seemed to hold that mere physical presence, and not legal status, within the state's borders entitled people to equality under the law. The Texas statute was judged to deny equal protection in this case because it imposed "a lifetime hardship on a discrete class of children not accountable for their disabling status." The ruling has since been narrowly construed by the Court to apply strictly to undocumented alien children in the area of public education. Many of the children directly affected by the ruling were made U.S. citizens shortly thereafter through a federal amnesty program.

Pobladores: Early Spanish settlers. In Spanish America, the general pattern for occupation of a territory followed several steps. First, the conquistadores would explore a region, then civil and religious authorities would settle the region. Once civil government and the church were established, other Spaniards would settle the region and dedicate themselves to agriculture, mining, or other activities. These last settlers were *pobladores*.

Pocho: Pejorative term for Chicanos and their language. This derogatory term refers both to Chicanos and to the nonstandard Spanish they may speak. In Mexico, the term originally meant "stupid," "small," "squat," or "discolored." *Pocho* is used by Mexicans and Mexican Americans to accuse others of becoming assimilated into Anglo culture to the point of losing loyalty to the Chicano community. The term may also imply a lack of awareness of Mexican and Mexican

American culture. *Pocho* speech refers to a combination of Spanish and English, accented Spanish, or a complete lack of Spanish. A *pochismo* is a Spanish word altered by the English language. *Pocho*, although sometimes considered an insult, is also used by the people it describes as a term of cultural identification.

Police brutality: Police officers in many areas have been accused of using unnecessary force on suspected criminals, particularly members of minority groups, including Latinos. Reports of police brutality against Latinos are increasingly common, perhaps because the incidence of brutality is rising or perhaps because Latinos are becoming more willing to report it.

Victimization results in part from discrimination and prejudice. Police officers appear to be more likely to presume that a Latino, as compared to a non-Hispanic white person, is a criminal. This assumption is particularly intense in the Southwest, where the Latino population is overwhelmingly Mexican in origin. Many Mexicans cross the United States border illegally in search of higher-paying jobs than they can find in Mexico. By their very presence in the United States, they are criminals. This large undocumented population leads police officers to suspect anyone of Mexican appearance of being a criminal. (*See* LAW ENFORCEMENT AND THE LATINO COMMUNITY.)

In all parts of the country, Latinos are considered by some to be foreigners. Many consider themselves to be a separate national group within United States culture. Many Puerto Ricans in New York City, for example, consider themselves to be Puerto Ricans rather

Various factors can contribute to discrimination against Latinos by police officers. (Lou DeMatteis)

than New Yorkers, even if they are second- or third-generation immigrants. This feeling of alienation fosters disrespect for the law, because it is the law of a country of which Latinos do not see themselves as being a part. Police officers and many Latinos thus have mutual disrespect that can vent itself in violence and brutality.

Language barriers pose other problems. As of the early 1990's, Latinos and other Spanish-speaking officers were proportionally underrepresented on most police forces. Many officers therefore did not speak the language of the community they served and were not a part of it. Such officers are less likely to empathize with community residents and more likely to misinterpret their actions as well as their language. They may resort to brutality against suspects who do not obey commands; those commands, however, may not have been delivered in a language understood by the suspects.

In the last few decades of the twentieth century, there were movements toward increasing minority group representation on police forces. These efforts may well lower the incidence of police brutality, but no end to the problem appeared likely.

Political activism: The roots of Latino political activism stretch back to England's struggles with Spain for dominance in the New World. Later, the presence of large numbers of Latinos in Florida and Texas and Spain's control of Puerto Rico and Cuba posed obstacles to U.S territorial expansion. Such conflicts created ongoing tensions between Latino and majority cultures in the United States and have led to a variety of political responses from Latino populations.

Mexican Americans. The MEXICAN AMERICAN WAR ended with the signing of the TREATY OF GUADALUPE HIDALGO in 1848. Roughly half of the total territory previously claimed by Mexico was ceded to the United States, including what are now the states of Texas, New Mexico, Arizona, and California, along with parts of Colorado and Nevada. At the war's end, approximately eighty thousand Mexican citizens living in the ceded areas became U.S. citizens; they were given the choice of remaining in their homes and obtaining U.S. citizenship by default or leaving their homes to move to what remained of Mexico. In the latter case, they were promised that they would retain land ownership, but that promise was not always kept.

Many Mexican Americans believed that the U.S. government failed to adhere to the guarantees of the treaty. One response was militant insurrection; for ex-

ample, LAS GORRAS BLANCAS (the white caps) opposed the systematic loss of land by cutting down fences and burning the property of Anglo ranchers. By the early 1900's, however, many Mexican Americans allied with the Anglo community at the urging of Mexican American elites.

Political strategies concentrated on electoral politics while ensuring that services not provided through the government would reach Latinos. *MUTUALISTAS* (mutual aid societies) were one type of political response to Anglo control. These societies, which were most important from the late 1880's to the early 1930's, provided life insurance coverage and social services in the areas of employment, health, and education; these services were not always provided in adequate measure to Mexican Americans by U.S. government agencies.

Direct resistance to U.S. government policy declined in the early decades of the twentieth century. The LEAGUE OF UNITED LATIN AMERICAN CITIZENS (LULAC), formed in 1929, typified the political efforts of the period. LULAC demanded equal access to and equal treatment from public institutions for Mexican Americans. LULAC's demands were not radical; the organization accepted existing social and political processes and clearly proclaimed its loyalty to the United States. LULAC primarily benefited middle-class Mexican Americans and generally kept its distance from newly arrived Mexican and Latino immigrants, who tended to be less affluent.

The AMERICAN G.I. FORUM, formed in 1948, initially focused on demanding government benefits for Latino war veterans but had widened its scope of political activism by the 1950's. The organization was a leader in securing basic civil rights for Latinos in the areas of education, health, employment, and housing. Started in Texas, the American G.I. Forum evolved into a national organization known for its effective leadership.

The Community Service Organization. The COMMUNITY SERVICE ORGANIZATION (CSO), formed in 1948 in Los Angeles, is another example of Latino political effort motivated by postwar optimism. Organized around the belief that local electoral power was basic to change, CSO started massive voter registration drives in an attempt to gain electoral majorities. Its membership came predominantly from the urban working class. By 1962, CSO had twenty-two chapters in California and had extended its activities to protect the civil rights of newly arrived Latino immigrants, a politically radical effort for the time. As a result of internal conflicts, however, CSO declined in influence

During the 1960's, Mexican Americans became more active politically, both by holding office and by organizing various movements. (Security Pacific Bank Collection, Los Angeles Public Library)

in the mid-1960's. By the end of the decade, CSO had become a service organization providing modest benefits to a reduced clientele. It established leadership training and citizenship classes and engaged in neighborhood beautification programs.

CSO was the impetus for other locally oriented groups. Notable were the MEXICAN AMERICAN POLITICAL ASSOCIATION (MAPA), formed in California in 1959, and the POLITICAL ASSOCIATION OF SPANISH SPEAKING ORGANIZATIONS (PASSO), formed in Texas in 1960. Both organizations concentrated on voter registration and political education.

The Chicano Movement. The CHICANO MOVEMENT, which gained momentum in the 1960's, called for ethnic unity and pride among Mexican Americans. Chicano activists rejected notions of Anglo superiority, emphasized their ancestry and heritage, and down-

played Spanish and European influences on both Mexican and Mexican American culture. Chicanos called for self-determination and community control of political, social, and economic institutions in the barrios; according to the ideological beliefs of CHICANISMO, such control was crucial if Mexican Americans were to receive equitable treatment in the United States.

The Chicano movement encompassed many groups and a variety of ideas. In northern New Mexico, the Alianza Federal de Mercedes (Federal Alliance of Land Grants), led by Reies López TIJERINA, struggled to reclaim land lost by Mexican Americans whose Spanish and Mexican land grants were not honored by the U.S. government. In Colorado, the Denver-based CRUSADE FOR JUSTICE, led by Rodolfo "Corky" GONZÁLES, protested discrimination in schools and police

Communities Organized for Public Service is one of the groups that arose to promote mainstream political involvement. (Institute of Texan Cultures)

brutality and called for the establishment of Chicano cultural programs. The Crusade for Justice, which organized barrio youths, sanitation and postal workers, and former convicts, advocated a humanist, family-oriented social consciousness. The UNITED FARM WORKERS (UFW), led by César CHÁVEZ, developed primarily as a labor organization, but its moral crusade and use of Mexican symbolism brought attention to the plight of all Mexican Americans. The UFW used marches, labor strikes, and boycotts as part of its political activism.

Chicano movement groups encompassed a broad range of philosophies and approaches, including paramilitary organizations such as the BROWN BERETS, student groups such as El MOVIMIENTO ESTUDIANTIL CHICANO DE AZTLÁN (MECHA), and explicitly political organizations such as La RAZA UNIDA PARTY (the Party of the United Race). Although these and other Chicano movement groups reflected a variety of approaches and concerns, they shared a belief that the social and political system of the United States had both ignored and discriminated against the Mexican American population. In the early 1970's, however, the Chicano movement declined as a result of government pressure and ideological differences within the movement's leadership.

Later Mexican American Movements. With the decline of Chicanismo, many Chicano movement members returned to moderate political approaches, focusing on such efforts as voter registration drives, legal challenges to electoral obstacles, and lobbying. Older organizations such as LULAC and the AMERICAN G.I. FORUM were revitalized. Social-service groups such as COMMUNITIES ORGANIZED FOR PUBLIC SERVICE (COPS) in San Antonio and the UNITED NEIGHBORHOODS ORGANIZATION (UNO) in Los Angeles became increasingly important in local Mexican American politics. Such GRASSROOTS ORGANIZATIONS tended to address such issues as teenage pregnancy, AIDS, police brutality, and the rights of workers, women, and children. Most such organizations are comprehensive, addressing varied concerns in an integrated fashion. Contemporary national organizations include the CONGRESSIONAL HISPANIC CAUCUS Institute, the Hispanic Chamber of Commerce, the Hispanic Bar Association, the MEXICAN AMERICAN LEGAL DEFENSE AND

Puerto Ricans in New York City support Antonio Pagan's campaign for a city council seat. (Frances M. Roberts)

Cuban Americans rally in New York City against Fidel Castro's control of Cuba. (Richard B. Levine)

EDUCATIONAL FUND (MALDEF), the MEXICAN AMERICAN WOMEN'S NATIONAL ASSOCIATION, the NATIONAL COALITION OF HISPANIC HEALTH AND HUMAN SERVICES, the NATIONAL COUNCIL OF LA RAZA, and the National Democratic Hispanic Caucus.

The major effect of these groups has been to influence Mexican Americans, and Latinos generally, to rethink their social, economic, and political status in the United States. Such reevaluation has produced a sharp decline in radical protest activity; the shift has been back to a politics of accommodation and moderation.

Puerto Ricans. The island of Puerto Rico became a U.S. territory in 1898 following the Spanish-American War. With the passage of the JONES ACT in 1917, Puerto Ricans became U.S. citizens, although they were not allowed to participate fully in federal social-service programs. In the 1920's and 1930's, there were steady levels of emigration from Puerto Rico to the U.S. mainland; after World War II, emigration increased substantially.

The mainland Puerto Rican population is mostly concentrated in New York City, and its political influ-ence is mostly limited to this local arena. Prior to the 1930's, New York Puerto Ricans were largely ignored by city officials. By the 1930's, however, the city's Puerto Rican community had become too large to ignore. The first Puerto Rican official from New York City was elected to the New York State Assembly in 1937.

Throughout the 1940's and 1950's, there was a virtual absence of Puerto Ricans from New York City politics. Puerto Ricans were viewed by some as a "troublesome" group because of their radical politics. Puerto Ricans had supported leftist political candidates in New York City, and many called for Puerto Rican independence from the United States. In 1950, two Puerto Rican nationalists even attempted to attack President Harry S Truman in Washington, D.C. The attempt was unsuccessful, ending in the death of one attacker, Griselio Torresola, and the arrest of the other, Oscar COLLAZO.

Puerto Rican political activism increased in the 1960's, in part as a result of the Civil Rights movement. Militancy also grew in the Puerto Rican community in the 1960's. The YOUNG LORDS, Puerto Rican militants who called themselves "socialists and revolutionaries," linked the struggle for social justice in New York with the demand for the independence of Puerto Rico. The social conditions in mainland ghettos were linked with those on the island.

Puerto Ricans forged a general political alliance with the Democratic Party in the 1970's. Most Puerto Rican political activists were moderates who worked within a mainstream political context. In the 1990's, Puerto Ricans attempted to gain greater influence in city politics by using a strategy of coalition politics, joining with African American and liberal Anglo candidates to pursue common goals.

Cuban Americans. Like Puerto Rico, Cuba was acquired by the United States following the SPANISH-AMERICAN WAR of 1898; the island was given its independence in 1902. The largest and most visible influx of Cubans to the United States followed the overthrow of Fulgencio Batista by Fidel CASTRO's revolutionary forces in 1959. The first Cuban immigrants were generally those most severely affected by Castro's political regime; they tended to be well educated, affluent, and politically conservative.

The exiles' prospects of returning to Cuba vanished with the failure of the U.S.-sponsored BAY OF PIGS INVASION in 1961. In the mid-1960's, large numbers of Cubans were airlifted to the United States. These immigrants were of middle-class origin and were provided with special resettlement programs that entitled them to food, clothing, medical care, and cash benefits. In 1980, about 120,000 Cubans, mostly of lower socioeconomic status, fled Cuba for the United States in the MARIEL BOAT LIFT. A similar exodus in 1994 was stemmed when President Bill Clinton announced that Cuban refugees would no longer receive special treatment from U.S. immigration authorities.

Political activism by Cuban immigrants has traditionally centered on the desire to overthrow the Castro regime. Prominent Cubans have thus often found common cause with U.S. anticommunists and have forged political alliances with the Republican Party. In the 1980's, as Cubans formed a political base in Miami, the scope of Cuban American political activism expanded to include such issues as BILINGUAL EDUCATION. In Florida, Cuban Americans have been successful at the local government level, electing many of their candidates to school boards, city councils, and county commissions. Cuban Americans maintain a cohesive voting bloc that has consistently enabled them to elect their generally conservative candidates.

—*David E. Camacho*

SUGGESTED READINGS:

- Barrera, Mario. *Race and Class in the Southwest: A Theory of Racial Inequality.* Notre Dame, Ind.: University of Notre Dame Press, 1979. An economic analysis of the Mexican American political experience.
- Garcia, F. Chris, ed. *Latinos and the Political System.* Notre Dame, Ind.: University of Notre Dame Press, 1988. Compares and contrasts Latino ethnic groups.
- Hero, Rodney E. *Latinos in the U.S. Political System: Two-Tiered Pluralism.* Philadelphia: Temple University Press, 1992. A history of Mexican American, Puerto Rican, and Cuban political experiences, with demographic and political data.
- National Association of Latino Elected and Appointed Officials. *1990 National Roster of Hispanic Elected Officials.* Washington, D.C.: Author, 1990. Complete state-by-state listing of Latino elected officials.
- Schaefer, Richard. *Racial and Ethnic Groups.* 4th ed. Glenview, Ill.: Scott, Foresman, 1990. Includes social histories of various Latino subgroups.

Political Association of Spanish Speaking Organizations (PASSO): Political group. PASSO was established in 1961 in Victoria, Texas, as an outgrowth of Mexican Americans for Political Action. PASSO sought to solidify Mexican American advocacy and community groups by combining their organizational skills and members.

The AMERICAN G.I. FORUM, the LEAGUE OF UNITED LATIN AMERICAN CITIZENS, and other groups were actively involved in PASSO's ambitious attempt to create a multistate organization. Gilbert Garcia was appointed as the primary organizer.

The first test of strength for PASSO came with the 1962 primary and general elections in Texas. The endorsing of candidates caused division within the organization. Voter participation in San Antonio and South Texas was disappointingly low. PASSO faded in 1964, when new political coalitions began to emerge. It attempted to spread throughout the Southwest but was important only in Texas. It lost many of its members to La RAZA UNIDA PARTY.

Political economy: Academic discipline that examines the interplay of economics and politics. In the most general sense, the economy can be defined as the system of producing, distributing, and using wealth. Politics is the set of institutions and rules by which society and economic interactions are governed. Some political economists are interested primarily in the political basis of economic actions, or how government policies affect market operations. Others are concerned with the economic basis of political action, or the ways by which economic forces mold government policies. The two orientations are complementary, because politics and markets constantly interact.

Political economy emerged as a field of study in the eighteenth century as a set of rational theories that challenged traditional beliefs. The new theories declared that governments, laws, procedures, and associations were all efficient institutions created by people to solve problems. Political economy imposed standards of empiricism, pragmatism, and utility that were in sharp contrast to such feudal ideas as the divine right of kings.

Political economy provided nineteenth century social scientists with powerful tools for research and policy analysis. For individuals as diverse as Adam Smith, John Stuart Mills, and Karl Marx, the economy was eminently political and politics was obviously tied to economic phenomena. Few scholars before 1900 attempted to describe and analyze politics and economics separately.

The first half of the twentieth century saw scholarly separation of economics and politics. Economists developed elaborate and sophisticated models of how the economy functions, and other social scientists created increasingly complex theories of political development and activity. The field of political economy enjoyed a resurgence in the 1970's as scholars became dissatisfied with the gap between abstract models and political and economic reality. For both intellectual and practical reasons, social scientists began seeking once more to understand how politics and economics interact in modern society.

Although the field of political economy developed concurrently with liberalism, it also has a Marxist variant. Karl Marx was a nineteenth century political economist and perhaps capitalism's most severe critic. Marx wrote primarily about domestic political economy, or the dynamics of economic change within a single country. He viewed political economy as necessarily conflictual, because the relationship between capitalists and workers is essentially antagonistic, with any gains made by workers being at the expense of capitalists and vice versa.

Radical scholars have used Marxist perspectives on political economy to study the Latino community. They argue that in order to understand Latino POVERTY and powerlessness, one has to understand the structure of American capitalism. Many radical scholars perceive numerous problems in the Latino community as linked to the relative absence of Latinos in the capitalist power structure.

Political organizations: Political organizations are groups with a history of advocacy and orientation to change. They are active in the electoral arena, supporting or running candidates for public office, or are involved in interest group politics and issues of public policy.

History. Formation of organizations has been an integral part of the Latino experience in the United States. Generally these organizations have had as their main purpose fostering some form of change in the environment. Historically, Latino organizational development occurred in environments of repression, poverty, and alienation. The political organizations that arose in response to these environmental factors took on different forms, including protest, political party, and pressure groups.

Protest Organizations. During the epoch of the CHICANO MOVEMENT of the 1960's and early 1970's, political organizations became more common. They were more protest-oriented and committed to change and empowerment than were their predecessors. Members of the Chicano movement, influenced by a history of resistance, took a radical approach in redefining themselves as CHICANOS rather than as Mexican Americans. Chicano protest leaders and organizations involved followers in movements tied to the Civil Rights movement, the New Left, and antiwar protests. Unlike previous political organizations, protest groups used unconventional protest strategies and tactics such as marches, demonstrations, sit-ins, boycotts, and picketing. They adhered to a spirit of CHICANISMO, or cultural pride and self-determination.

The Chicano movement produced numerous protest organizations. The most prominent included the UNITED FARM WORKERS (UFW), led by César CHÁVEZ; the CRUSADE FOR JUSTICE, headed by Rodolfo "Corky" GONZÁLES; and the Alianza Federal de Mercedes, formed by Reies López TIJERINA. These three were the leading Chicano political protest organizations during the epoch of the Chicano movement.

These three groups, in turn, influenced the formation of numerous student and youth groups. These groups included the Mexican American Student Confederation (MASC), the Mexican American Student Association (MASA), UNITED MEXICAN AMERICAN STUDENTS (UMAS), the MEXICAN AMERICAN YOUTH ORGANIZATION (MAYO), El MOVIMIENTO ESTUDIAN-

César Chávez led the United Farm Workers, which mixed labor unionism with political activism.
(AP/Wide World Photos)

TIL CHICANO DE AZTLÁN (MECHA), and the BROWN BERETS.

Through the use of unconventional methods, student protest organizations advanced a change agenda that included establishment of Chicano studies departments; the hiring of Chicano faculty, administrators, and staff; an end to the Vietnam War; and many other national, state, and community-related problems.

Political Party Organization. La RAZA UNIDA PARTY (RUP) was created in 1970 as an ethnic third party. In protest against an unresponsive two-party system, the RUP chose the electoral rather than the interest group arena as its focus. The RUP's leadership argued that Chicanos needed their own political party to achieve self-determination. Unlike protest and pressure organizations, which sought to influence policy, RUP sought to control it.

Led by José Ángel GUTIÉRREZ, one of the founders of MAYO, the party received national visibility as a result of its well-organized electoral successes in the Texas cities of CRYSTAL CITY, Carrizo Springs, and Cotulla. Party candidates were elected to several city council and school board seats.

News of the RUP's success spread throughout the Southwest. Efforts to establish the RUP were initiated in Colorado, California, New Mexico, and Arizona. Between 1970 and 1978, the RUP sought to increase Latino political representation by running candidates for public office. In 1970, several candidates, organized by the Crusade for Justice, ran unsuccessfully for state and local offices in Colorado. Throughout much of the 1970's, the party continued to run candidates for local and state offices in Texas, but few successes were achieved. In California, Arizona, and New Mexico, the RUP never achieved official party status. By the early 1980's, much of the RUP movement had disappeared, with only a few fragmentary organizing committees still functioning.

Pressure Organizations. By the mid-1970's, the Chicano movement was over. Many of the more protest-oriented organizations had disappeared or were in a state of rapid decline. More moderate political organizations emerged, with an emphasis on interest group politics. These political organizations rejected unconventional protest methods. Their strategies for change were predicated on using conventional pressure methods such as lobbying, letter writing, litigation, and voter registration.

Unlike the protest organizations of the Chicano movement, many of these pressure organizations were regional or national in scope. Examples include the NATIONAL COUNCIL OF LA RAZA (NCLR), founded in 1968 as the Southwest Council of La Raza; the MEXICAN AMERICAN LEGAL DEFENSE AND EDUCATION FUND (MALDEF), also formed in 1968; the SOUTHWEST VOTER REGISTRATION EDUCATION PROJECT (SVREP), established in Texas in 1974; and the National Association of Latino Elected Officials (NALEO), founded in 1975 (*see* NATIONAL ASSOCIATION OF LATINO ELECTED AND APPOINTED OFFICIALS).

At about this time, the protest-oriented organizations of the Chicano movement were being replaced by groups organized through Saul Alinsky's INDUSTRIAL AREAS FOUNDATION (IAF). With the support of both Catholic and Protestant churches, the IAF was instrumental in forming Latino-based poor people's organizations in some of the barrios (Latino enclaves) of Texas and California. In San Antonio, Texas, the IAF was successful in forming COMMUNITIES ORGANIZED FOR PUBLIC SERVICE (COPS) in 1974.

By the mid-1970's, the IAF's organizing efforts spread to Los Angeles, where it established the UNITED NEIGHBORHOODS ORGANIZATION (UNO). Subsequently, numerous other IAF poor people's organizations were formed in cities across Texas and California. Using the Alinsky principle of focusing on goals that could reasonably be achieved, these organizations became involved in a variety of local issues, such as high insurance rates, community redevelopment, gang violence, and crime. Strategically and tactically, they relied on a combination of pressure and protest methods. They lacked the Chicano movement's emphasis on Chicanismo.

Latina feminist-oriented pressure groups emerged during the 1970's, with many more following in the 1980's. They sought to assert the dignity, identity, and self-determination of their members, using conventional methods. Among these organizations were the COMISIÓN FEMENIL MEXICANA NACIONAL, the National Chicana Institute, National Chicana Welfare Rights, National Institute for Chicana Women, National Chicana Barrio Women's Association, Barrio Pride, NATIONAL ASSOCIATION OF CUBAN-AMERICAN WOMEN, NATIONAL CONFERENCE OF PUERTO RICAN WOMEN, National Chicana Foundation, and MEXICAN AMERICAN WOMEN'S NATIONAL ASSOCIATION.

Other Types of Organizations. Other types of organizations formed after the 1970's. Some were oriented toward programs and services, such as the Mexican American Unity Council in San Antonio, Texas; Chicanos por la Raza in Phoenix, Arizona; and the SPANISH SPEAKING UNITY COUNCIL in Oakland, California.

Reies López Tijerina mobilized activists in attempts to reclaim areas they believed were included in land grants. (AP/Wide World Photos)

Throughout the nation, numerous business and economic development organizations were formed, among them The EAST LOS ANGELES COMMUNITY UNION (TELACU), the Hispanic Chamber of Commerce, the Mexican American Grocers Association, and the Latino Business Association. These and other business groups were active in promoting Latino economic empowerment.

An array of professional organizations also emerged to advance their particular vocational interest. These included the Hispanic Bar Association, the Association of Mexican American Educators, the NATIONAL HISPANIC MEDIA COALITION, and many more.

Traditional civic action groups, such as the LEAGUE OF UNITED LATIN AMERICAN CITIZENS (LULAC), AMERICAN G.I. FORUM, and MEXICAN AMERICAN POLITICAL ASSOCIATION (MAPA), took a more assertive role toward change following the 1970's. Relying for the most part on a conventional approach, on some occasions they used protest methods in dealing with such issues as immigration, corporate responsibility, education, and political empowerment. Following the demise in Texas of the POLITICAL ASSOCIATION OF SPANISH SPEAKING ORGANIZATIONS (PASSO) and the RUP, the Mexican American Democrats (MAD) emerged and became the state's most prominent political organization. In California, partisan Latino organizations such as the Hispanic American Democrats and the Hispanic Republican Assembly proved to be transitory. By the 1990's, as a result of scarce resources, a conservative political climate, and numerous other obstacles, there were fewer active political organizations in the Latino community than there were in the 1970's.

Impact. During the 1970's and later, Latino organizations had a positive impact on the quality of life in their respective communities. In particular, political

Members of various organizations protested a 1994 House of Representatives resolution calling for the United States to lift its embargo on Cuba. (AP/Wide World Photos)

organizations of various sorts were active in addressing the many issues and social problems affecting the Latino community. Using both the electoral approach of getting supportive candidates elected and the interest group approach of influencing public policy, Latino organizations were active at local, state, national, and even international levels of politics. Numerous other types of organizations also contributed to the Latino community's general welfare. Diversity of function and roles characterized the Latino organizational experience.

The activism of the post-1970 years was not comparable to that of the CHICANO MOVEMENT. With the end of the war in Vietnam and the decline of the Civil Rights, Black Power, New Left, and antiwar movements, the Chicano movement gave way to a growing conservativism. This was evident with the dramatic decline of both protest organizations and use of unconventional direct-action strategies and tactics. The radicalism and militancy of Chicano movement organizations was superseded by interest groups that were more mainstream in their politics. Their emphasis was on working within the electoral arena in getting more Latinos elected to political office.

At the national and regional levels, protest organizations such as the Crusade for Justice, Alianza Federal de Mercedes, and RUP were replaced by interest groups as the organizational leaders of the Chicano community. MALDEF, with its emphasis on litigation, scored victories regarding legal rights in such areas as employment and education. The NCLR evolved from a programmatic consulting entity into a lobbying leader on a variety of issues. The SVREP focused its organizational activities on voter registration and other political empowerment issues. NALEO came to represent the varied interests of Latino political officeholders, concurrently emphasizing citizenship training.

Numerous state and local Latino organizations emerged, using a mixture of pressure and protest strategies and tactics. California saw the formation of several new organizations and coalitions, including the Congreso para Pueblos Unidos, Californios for Fair Representation, Institute for Social Justice, and Hermandad Mexicana. These advocacy organizations dealt with such issues as immigration, affirmative action, political empowerment, corporate responsibility, educational reform, and peace in Central America.

In the 1990's, economic crises and many social problems, including immigration, plagued the nation, posing serious challenges to existing Latino organizations. They faced insufficient resources, dependency on governmental and corporate funding, small memberships, weak leadership, growing societal hostility toward Latinos, and apathy and indifference among Latinos. *—Armando Navarro*

SUGGESTED READINGS:

• Acuña, Rodolfo. *Occupied America*. 3d ed. New York: Harper & Row, 1988. Excellent historical overview of the various organizations that developed out of the Chicano history of resistance.

• Gómez-Quiñones, Juan. *Chicano Politics: Reality and Promise, 1940-1990*. Albuquerque: University of New Mexico Press, 1990. Examines the politics, leadership issues, events, and Chicano organizations that shaped the years 1940-1990.

• Navarro, Armando. *MAYO: Avant-garde of the Chicano Movement in Texas*. Austin: University of Texas Press, 1994. An in-depth case study of the Mexican American Youth Organization and the politics of the Chicano movement and Chicano student movement of 1967-1972.

• Santiestevan, Henry. "A Perspective on Mexican-American Organizations." In *Mexican-Americans Tomorrow*, edited by Gus Tyler. Albuquerque: University of New Mexico Press, 1975. An excellent article on the development of Latino organizations.

• Skerry, Peter. *Mexican-Americans: The Ambivalent Minority*. New York: Free Press, 1993. An excellent comparative analysis of Chicano politics in Los Angeles, California, and San Antonio, Texas.

• Tirado, Miguel. "Mexican American Community Political Organization: The Key to Chicano Political Power." *Aztlan* 1 (Spring, 1970): 53-78. Analysis of the development of Latino organizations.

• Vigil, Maurilio E. *Hispanics in American Politics*. Lanham, Md.: University Press of America, 1987. Examines various aspects of Latino politics and organizations.

Political representation: Representative democracy is a system of government that gives people the opportunity to make government responsive through the election of representatives. Elected officials respond to the concerns of people by passing laws and implementing public policy measures. In their struggle for political representation and responsiveness, Latinos encounter the obstacles of barriers to voting, electoral arrangements, and lack of responsiveness within Latino constituencies.

Barriers to Voting. Voting is the most fundamental right in a representative democracy. Historically, however, some U.S. citizens have been denied this right.

PERCENTAGE OF LOCAL ELECTED OFFICES HELD BY LATINOS, 1987

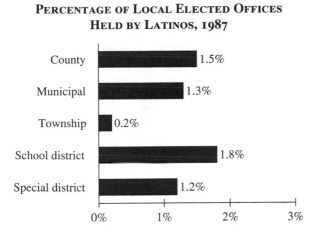

County	1.5%
Municipal	1.3%
Township	0.2%
School district	1.8%
Special district	1.2%

Source: Data are from Marlita A. Reddy, ed., *Statistical Record of Hispanic Americans* (Detroit: Gale Research, 1993), Table 833.

Voting rights initially resided in the hands of older white male property owners; by the 1820's, however, most states had dropped property qualifications for voting. Over time, the U.S. Constitution has been amended to give the right to vote to a variety of groups. The Fifteenth Amendment, ratified in 1870, gave the vote to African Americans; the Nineteenth Amendment, ratified in 1920, gave voting rights to women; and the Twenty-sixth Amendment, ratified in 1971, gave the vote to citizens eighteen years of age or older, adding to the political voice of the younger population.

Despite constitutional guarantees, a number of states and localities developed legal barriers to limit the expansion of the electorate. The most significant barriers arose in the southern states early in the twentieth century, with attempts to prevent voting by African Americans, Latinos, and poor whites. One such barrier was the poll tax, which had to be paid before a citizen could register to vote. The tax was often an insurmountable burden to those with very low incomes.

Another barrier was the literacy test, which required citizens to demonstrate their ability to read and interpret a specific document, such as the state or federal constitution. The tests could be used discriminatorily, as the questions asked to test comprehension could be varied in difficulty.

A third restrictive device was the "whites only" primary, which excluded African Americans and Latinos from electing their representatives in the primary election. These discriminatory restrictions were effectively outlawed by the VOTING RIGHTS ACT OF 1965.

The registration process can also act as a voting barrier. This process affects a citizen's right to vote in two ways. First, a citizen is required to establish legal residency in a state or local political jurisdiction. Residency requirements vary from state to state. Citizens are required to live in a state for periods ranging from six months to two years before they become eligible to register to vote. Second, some states require citizens to go to a central office in a city, township, or county to register. Some offices are open only during working hours, posing problems for those who cannot leave their jobs to register. For many citizens, the value derived from voting is lower than the costs imposed by the voter-registration system; as a consequence, many citizens are not registered and so cannot vote.

In its *1991 National Roster of Hispanic Elected Officials*, the NATIONAL ASSOCIATION OF LATINO ELECTED AND APPOINTED OFFICIALS (NALEO) reported two factors that restrict voting participation of Latinos: age and citizenship status. According to 1990 census data, approximately 38 percent of Latinos were below the age of eighteen and were thus too young to vote. About 20 percent of all Latinos of voting age were between eighteen and twenty-four years of age. That age group participates the least in electoral poli-

LATINO LOCAL ELECTED OFFICIALS, 1987

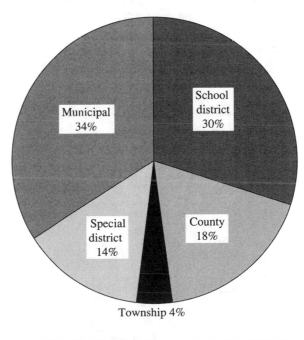

Source: Data are from Marlita A. Reddy, ed., *Statistical Record of Hispanic Americans* (Detroit: Gale Research, 1993), Table 833.

tics. A second factor reducing the voting power of Latinos is the fact that many are not U.S. citizens. In 1990, more than half of all Latinos who did not vote were ineligible to participate in the electoral process because of citizenship requirements.

Electoral Arrangements. Certain types of electoral arrangements can work to limit Latino political representation. At-large elections, in which candidates run for election throughout an entire city rather than in a specific ward or district, can dilute the voting strength of ethnic minorities concentrated in a particular section of a city. For example, a city with a population that is 30 percent Latino may have Latinos concentrated in a few neighborhoods. Even if all the registered Latinos voted for a single Latino candidate, the Latino vote would be unlikely to overcome the votes of a non-Latino voting majority. On the other hand, if such a city were divided into a number of voting districts, then Latinos would have a better chance of electing Latino candidates in districts where Latinos constituted a majority. Such an arrangement is called a ward-based or single-member-district system. Within such systems, Latinos have struggled to have district lines drawn so that at least some districts have Latino majorities.

GERRYMANDERING, the process of designing voting district boundaries so that the composition of the district is favorable to a particular political party or group, can also reduce Latino political power. Although technically illegal, gerrymandering has often been used to decrease the voting strength of ethnic groups as well as of political parties. The general strategy is to change a predominantly ethnic district into numerous smaller districts, each having a minority percentage of ethnic voters, or to draw district boundary lines so that they divide concentrations of ethnic voters into separate districts.

Latino Responsiveness. Latino candidates face some practical limitations in seeking election to office. These include the difficulty of raising campaign money, a lack of political opportunities, and an undermobilization of Latino populations.

When Latinos are elected to office, the principle of majority rule hinders these officials' ability to respond to Latino interests. Majority rule requires approval of decisions by more than half of the persons voting. In 1991, NALEO reported that Latinos holding elected offices represented less than 1 percent of all U.S. elected officials. NALEO's report further indicated a discrepancy in the ratio of Latino state populations to Latino state elected officials. For example, Texas, with a 25.5 percent Latino population, had only 7.3 percent Latino elected officials; California, with a 25.8 percent Latino population, had only 3.2 percent Latino elected officials. The eleven Latinos in the U.S. House of Representatives constituted 0.26 percent of all U.S. representatives, whereas Latinos constituted about 9 percent of the U.S. population. On every level, Latino elected officials were at a large numerical disadvantage in their attempts to respond to Latino interests through laws and public policy. —*David E. Camacho*

SUGGESTED READINGS: • Davidson, Chandler, ed. *Minority Vote Dilution.* Washington, D.C.: Howard University Press, 1989. • Garcia, F. Chris, ed. *Latinos and the Political System.* Notre Dame, Ind.: University of Notre Dame Press, 1988. • Gómez-Quiñones, Juan. *Chicano Politics: Reality and Promise, 1940-1990.* Albuquerque: University of New Mexico Press, 1990. • Hero, Rodney E. *Latinos and the U.S. Political System: Two-Tiered Pluralism.* Philadelphia: Temple University Press, 1992. • Piven, Frances Fox, and Richard A. Cloward. *Why Americans Don't Vote.* New York: Pantheon Books, 1988.

Politics, Latinos and: The term "political participation" describes activities used by people to influence the selection of political leaders or the policies they pursue. Latino political participation has been both organizational and electoral.

The Politics of Resistance (1846-1915). With the TREATY OF GUADALUPE HIDALGO (1848), Mexico lost more than half of its territory (750,000 square miles), including the areas now comprising Arizona, California, Colorado, New Mexico, Texas, and other parts of the Southwest. Mexicans living in the surrendered territory had one year to decide their fate. They were given two choices. The first was to move into territory still owned by Mexico. The second was to remain where they were and accept U.S. citizenship and sovereignty. Those who chose the latter were promised all the rights of citizens of the United States.

Between 1848 and 1915, the Treaty of Guadalupe Hidalgo became known to some as "the treaty of broken promises." Throughout the Southwest (but less so in New Mexico), Mexican Americans were politically disfranchised. Their lands were stolen, and their language and culture came under attack. Mexican Americans were subjected to segregation, became a source of inexpensive labor without access to the best jobs, and received inferior education. In general, they were impoverished and were not given access to the political process, leaving them powerless.

During this period, political participation was not encouraged. Some Mexican Americans sought to correct injustices by taking part in armed resistance. Scholars have documented the deeds of *guerrilleros* (guerrillas) and armed movements active during this period. Their form of political participation relied on the use of robbery, cattle rustling, killing, and other extralegal tactics.

Guerrilleros were particularly active in the states of California and Texas. From the 1850's to the 1870's, Joaquín MURIETA, Tiburcio VÁSQUEZ, and Juan FLORES roamed the countryside of California seeking vengeance against "gringos" for perceived injustices. In Texas, Juan CORTINA carried out raids across the U.S.-Mexico border for thirty years. This form of political participation was neutralized by U.S. law enforcement and military agencies.

In New Mexico, some Mexicans violently resisted the invasion of their territory by U.S. military forces, as illustrated by the TAOS REBELLION (1847). The use of armed resistance recurred in the 1890's, when Mexicans organized themselves into vigilante groups (among them Las GORRAS BLANCAS and La Mano Negra) for the purpose of protecting their private lands and interests.

The politics of resistance peaked in 1915 with El PLAN DE SAN DIEGO. The plan called for an insurrection that would establish an independent Mexican republic that would include the land Mexico lost to the United States in 1848. The plan failed when it was discovered and its supporters were apprehended in Texas by U.S. authorities.

Not all Mexicans decided to take a part in armed resistance. A few chose to resist oppression through electoral politics. Some members of the Mexican American elite sought to protect their interests by becoming involved in politics, challenging the hostile political environment. In California, this political participation peaked in the 1850's. During these years, Mexican Americans took part in drawing up the state's constitution and were active in local politics, primarily in Los Angeles and Santa Barbara. Statewide, only four Mexican Americans from Southern California served in the state assembly. Romualdo PACHECO of Santa Barbara was elected lieutenant governor in 1871 and served as governor in 1875 to finish the term of the former governor, who had taken a seat in the U.S. Senate. As the white population of California grew rapidly, Mexicans became powerless and disfranchised.

In Texas, Mexican American political participation was almost nonexistent. Even before the Mexican American War, Mexicans were given little chance to gain political power. A few participated in the signing of the Texas Declaration of Independence from Mexico. By 1845, a few Mexicans had served in the Texas Congress. When Texas was annexed by the United States in 1845, only one Mexican, José Antonio NAVARRO, was allowed to attend the constitutional convention. From 1846 to 1915, Mexican American political participation was limited to activity in political machines controlled by white political bosses, who encouraged Mexican Americans to participate but never put themselves at risk of losing political control. Political participation by Mexican Americans was discouraged by primary elections designed to exclude nonwhites and by poll taxes. Violence, intimidation, and persecution all were used to keep Mexican Americans from gaining political power.

New Mexico was the only exception to this political situation. Because Mexican Americans made up the majority of the state's population and had a well-organized political leadership, their level of political participation was high in comparison to that in the remainder of the Southwest. People of Mexican ancestry identified themselves more with the term HISPANIC, preferring to identify with Spain rather than Mexico. Their politics generally were oriented toward accommodation, working within the system rather than against it.

The Hispanic political elite of New Mexico was involved from 1846 to 1915 at all levels of government. Up until the 1880's, they often dominated key elective offices of the territorial legislature. They remained well represented until New Mexico became a state in 1912. Of the hundred delegates to the 1910 constitutional convention, thirty-five were Hispanic. They were an effective voting bloc and were able to make New Mexico a bilingual state.

In other parts of the Southwest, Mexican American political participation was more limited. Arizona, which was a part of New Mexico until 1863, quickly came under the political control of whites. A few Mexican Americans from Tucson were elected to the state legislature. After 1880, no one with a Spanish surname held a major elected or appointed state office.

The Politics of Accommodation (1915-1945). Between 1910 and 1921, Mexico was involved in a violent revolution that influenced the political participation of Mexican Americans. Hundreds of thousands of Mexicans crossed the border into the United States, fleeing the revolution. Some of the refugees were very politicized, in that they continued to support and participate in Mexico's various revolutionary move-

The Mexican Revolution sent hundreds of thousands of refugees to the United States and increased levels of political interest and involvement. (Institute of Texan Cultures)

ments. In 1910, the Mexican American population numbered approximately 210,000; by 1930 it had increased to some 1.3 million. This population growth helped to accelerate Mexican American political participation.

Few Mexican Americans outside New Mexico took part in the politics of accommodation. During these years, New Mexico was the only state in which Mexican Americans continued significant involvement in politics at all levels. Their vote was solicited by both Republicans and Democrats. At times, the Mexican American vote decided elections. Mexican Americans served in the state legislature, and New Mexico was the only state with a Mexican American senator, Dennis CHÁVEZ, who served from 1935 to 1962.

Mexican Americans during this period were much more active in the formation of political organizations than in electoral politics. They depended on organizations to promote unity, direction, and protection for themselves. MUTUALISTAS, or mutual benefit organizations, were first established in Texas but spread elsewhere. *Mutualistas* were self-help fraternal groups that provided social and cultural services, including life

insurance, to their members. Some *mutualistas* were indirectly political in that they drew white politicians to their events. Their political participation was limited by their nonprofit status as well as by the high percentage of membership composed of Mexican nationals.

Some examples of *mutualistas* are Club Reciproco (1870), the Sociedad Mutualista Benito Juárez (1879), and the Sociedad Ignacio Zaragosa (1881). All three were established in Corpus Christi, Texas. In 1881, the Sociedad Mutualista Miguel Hidalgo was established in Brownsville, Texas. Mexican women also joined these groups as well as forming their own, including La Sociedad Mutualista de Beneficiencia de Señoras y Señoritas (1882) and Sociedad Beneficiencia (1890). In Arizona, in 1894, the ALIANZA HISPANO-AMERICANA was organized. In California, several *mutualistas* were formed during the early 1900's. One of the most prominent was La SOCIEDAD PROGRESISTA MEXICANA (1929), which grew out of the Sociedad Ignacio Zaragosa.

Mexican Americans also participated in the formation of civic action and labor organizations. By the 1920's, the Alianza Hispano-Americana had developed from a *mutualista* into an advocacy and issue-oriented organization. In 1921, La Orden de Los Hijos de América was founded in San Antonio, Texas; in 1929, it was absorbed into the newly founded LEAGUE OF UNITED LATIN AMERICAN CITIZENS (LULAC). Both were organized by middle-class, U.S.-born Mexican Americans. At about this time, Mexican Americans began to identify with the term "Latino." Many of the new groups strongly supported assimilation, in contrast to the *mutualistas*, which espoused a cultural nationalist commitment to Mexico.

Mexican Americans also participated extensively in various labor struggles during this era. From the days of the CLIFTON-MORENCI STRIKES in Arizona (1903 and 1915) to the Great DEPRESSION, there was a tremendous growth in Mexican American participation in various union movements. In California, Mexican Americans organized their own unions, including La Union de Jornaleros Unidos (1910), Trabajadores Uni-

dos (1917), and La CONFEDERACIÓN DE UNIONES OBRERAS MEXICANAS (1928). Mexican Americans also allied with established labor unions.

During the Depression of the 1930's, Mexican Americans continued their participation in the electoral process, but often in a more limited manner. In New Mexico, they were active in both the Republican and Democratic parties. The NEW DEAL programs of the Franklin D. Roosevelt Administration brought many Mexican Americans from throughout the Southwest into the Democratic Party.

The Depression brought a resurgence of RACISM directed against Mexicans Americans. Nativists perceived Mexican Americans as taking jobs away from white workers. Consequently, 500,000 people of Mexican descent, including some who were born in the United States, were sent to Mexico. This hostile environment discouraged, but did not stop, the electoral participation of Mexican Americans.

The Alianza Hispano-Americana was an early and influential mutualista; *these members of the chapter in Tucson, Arizona, were photographed in 1896.* (Arizona Historical Society)

In 1938, in an attempt to coalesce existing organizations, the first Mexican national conference was held in Los Angeles, California. It resulted in the formation of El Congreso de los Pueblos de Habla Español. Another form of participation was military service in World War II. About 400,000 Mexican Americans served in the U.S. armed forces. World War II was important in changing the patterns of Latino political participation, as it removed some socioeconomic barriers.

The Politics of Social Action (1945-1965). The immediate postwar period was characterized by the politics of social action, meaning that Mexican Americans participated in larger numbers in both the electoral and organizational advocacy arenas. Returning war veterans, who had served as equals with white soldiers, were no longer willing to tolerate the unjust and oppressive conditions of the barrios. The postwar period also saw increased employment as well as educational and housing opportunities provided through the G.I. Bill. As they began to benefit from American citizenship, people of Mexican descent began more often to identify themselves as Mexican Americans.

Mexican Americans continued to participate in groups formed earlier but also established several new organizations oriented toward social action. These included California's Unity Leagues (1945) and COMMUNITY SERVICE ORGANIZATION (1948), and the AMERICAN G.I. FORUM (1948) in Texas.

These groups were more oriented to ACCULTURATION, as opposed to assimilation, than were their predecessors, and they were more oriented toward advocacy and politics. The Unity Leagues and the Community Service Organization (CSO) conducted voter registration drives as well as running and supporting Mexican American candidates for public office. The American G.I. Forum actively lobbied on veterans' issues and programs.

In the late 1950's, Mexican Americans became disenchanted with their lack of political influence and formed political organizations designed to change the political process. These included the MEXICAN AMERICAN POLITICAL ASSOCIATION (MAPA) in California, the POLITICAL ASSOCIATION OF SPANISH SPEAKING ORGANIZATIONS (PASSO) in Texas, and the American Coordinating Council of Political Education (ACCPE) in Arizona.

This epoch saw the beginning of shifts in party loyalty. As the Latino population diversified and expanded through emigration from Puerto Rico, Cuba, and elsewhere in Latin America, a Latino political power base began to take form. Traditionally, Mexican Americans had participated in both major political parties; however, along with Puerto Ricans, they tended more to be Democratic in their affiliation. Cubans who had fled from Fidel Castro's Cuba identified more with the Republicans.

Expansion in the Latino population facilitated increased political representation. In 1949, the Unity Leagues were successful in getting Andres Morales elected as the first Mexican American member of the Chino, California, city council. That same year, Edward Roybal, a Democrat supported by the CSO, was elected to the Los Angeles City Council (*see* ROYBAL FAMILY). After unsuccessful attempts to become lieutenant governor in 1954 and join the Los Angeles County Board of Supervisors in 1958, he was elected to Congress in 1962. In 1962, two Mexican Americans, John Moreno and Philip S. Soto, were elected to the state assembly. Mexican Americans were also elected to numerous city councils.

In New Mexico, Mexican Americans continued to flex their political muscle. Republican candidate Manuel LUJÁN lost his bid for the governorship in 1948 but was elected to Congress in 1964. Mexican American Joseph MONTOYA held the position of lieutenant governor from 1947 through 1957 and was succeeded by Tibo J. Chávez, another Mexican American. Montoya was elected to Congress in 1957 and to the U.S. Senate in 1965, after filling the seat emptied by the death of Dennis CHÁVEZ. By 1960, 40 percent of the members of the state legislature were Mexican Americans.

In Texas, in the early 1940's, Augustine Celeya was elected to Congress. Henry Barbosa GONZÁLEZ was elected to the San Antonio City Council in 1953; in 1956, he was elected to the state senate. González lost a try for the governorship in 1958 but was elected to Congress in 1961. In 1964, Kika DE LA GARZA was elected to Congress. In CRYSTAL CITY, Mexican Americans supported by PASSO were successful in winning all the seats on the city council.

Other states also saw gains in officeholding by Latinos. Two Mexican Americans served in Colorado's state legislature between 1940 and 1960. In 1956, Bert Gallegos became the first Mexican American to be elected to the Denver City Council. In Arizona in the early 1940's, C. J. Carreon served in the state legislature. With the support of ACCPE, five Mexican Americans were elected to the seven-member Miami City Council in 1962.

At the national level, Mexican Americans became involved electorally at an unprecedented level during

Joseph Montoya began serving in Congress in 1957; he is pictured during the Watergate hearings in 1973.
(AP/Wide World Photos)

the presidential candidacy of John F. Kennedy. Inspired by Kennedy, the leadership of the American G.I. Forum and LULAC formed VIVA KENNEDY CLUBS. The 1960 election, in which 85 percent of Mexican American voters supported Kennedy, gave Mexican Americans a new awareness of their voting power.

The Politics of Protest (1965-1975). By 1965, a new politics of protest began to dominate Mexican American political participation. Mexican Americans during this period continued to take part in accommodation politics, but the Civil Rights, New Left, antiwar, Black Power, and other movements introduced unconventional protest methods that were soon adopted by Mexican American groups. These methods included marches, sit-ins, boycotts, and picketing, all active forms of protest and confrontation. A new militancy, influenced by a society in turmoil, became evident in political activism.

Mexican Americans began to identify themselves as CHICANOS, rejecting assimilation and integration. They identified with CHICANISMO, predicated on the preservation of Mexican culture, language, and heritage.

From 1965 to 1975, those who identified themselves as Chicanos participated in the formation of numerous protest-oriented organizations. These included the Alianza Federal de Mercedes, led by Reies López TIJERINA in New Mexico; the UNITED FARM WORKERS OF AMERICA (UFW), headed by César CHÁVEZ in California; the CRUSADE FOR JUSTICE, led by Rodolfo "Corky" GONZÁLES; and La RAZA UNIDA PARTY (RUP), headed by José Ángel GUTIÉRREZ, in Texas. These four organizations inspired the formation of student and youth groups including UNITED MEXICAN AMERICAN STUDENTS (UMAS), the Mexican American Student Association (MASA), the MEXICAN AMERICAN YOUTH ORGANIZATION (MAYO), MOVIMIENTO ESTUDIANTIL CHICANO DE AZTLÁN (MECHA), and the BROWN BERETS.

Never before had Mexican Americans been so involved in protest activities, from school walkouts such as those in East Los Angeles in 1968 by protesters demanding establishment of CHICANO STUDIES PROGRAMS to the antiwar marches of 1969 and 1970 that involved thousands of Chicano activists from throughout what they called AZTLÁN, the Aztecs' term for their geographic point of origin, the Southwest. Puerto Ricans, likewise influenced by a society in turmoil, formed their own protest organizations, prominent among them the YOUNG LORDS. Latino activists were inspired by issues of change and power. They de-

nounced their community's impoverished and powerless condition. They struck out angrily at a system they perceived to be in need of major changes.

This anger carried over into the electoral arena. In 1970, José Ángel Gutiérrez in Texas and Rodolfo Gonzáles in Colorado contributed to the formation of La Raza Unida Party (RUP), the first major ethnic third-party movement in American politics. The RUP provided a political alternative to what was perceived to be an indifferent two-party system that did not represent the interests of Chicanos. It was committed to Chicano self-determination, empowerment, and CHICANISMO.

In Texas in 1970, the RUP scored electoral victories in Crystal City, Cotulla, and Carrizo Springs. After suffering political defeats in Texas and Colorado and not gaining official party status in other states, by 1978 the RUP had all but disappeared. During its brief existence, it served to motivate many poor and middle-class Chicanos into participating in electoral politics.

Traditional social action efforts coexisted with the more aggressive politics and leaders of the CHICANO MOVEMENT. Several new regional and national organizations were formed: the Southwest Council of La Raza (1968), renamed in 1972 as the NATIONAL COUNCIL OF LA RAZA (NCLR); the MEXICAN AMERICAN LEGAL DEFENSE AND EDUCATION FUND (1968); the SOUTHWEST VOTER REGISTRATION EDUCATION PROJECT (1975); and the NATIONAL ASSOCIATION OF LATINO ELECTED AND APPOINTED OFFICIALS (1975). Through the use of conventional methods such as lobbying, litigation, voter registration, and education, these four organizations further increased Latino political participation.

The Latino population, during this era, continued to increase rapidly as a result of rapid immigration and high birth rates. Levels of political participation at the national level did not keep pace. After a high in 1960, the Latino vote dropped in the 1964, 1968, and 1972 presidential elections. Latinos also began to vote in a less homogeneous manner. In 1968, Democrat Hubert Humphrey received 87 percent of the Latino vote and Republican Richard Nixon received 11 percent. In 1972, Democrat George McGovern received 60 percent of the Latino vote to Nixon's 30 percent.

In local and state elections, Latinos continued to make substantial gains. Latino representatives in state legislatures increased in number. In 1974, Jerry APODACA was elected governor of New Mexico and Raúl CASTRO became governor of Arizona. Both were Democrats. At the local level, numerous Latinos were

Jerry Apodaca was elected governor of Arizona in 1974. (AP/Wide World Photos)

elected to city councils and school boards. Latino political efforts were enhanced by the cumulative effects of the 1965, 1970, and 1975 VOTING RIGHTS ACTS, which decreased barriers to voting and in some areas stipulated ballots printed in Spanish.

The Era of Self-Interest (1976-1990's). By the mid-1970's, the Chicano movement was essentially over. With the end of the war in Vietnam and the decline of radical groups, the nation experienced a shift toward more conservative politics.

The 1960's had produced a counterculture that challenged the nation's economic and political structures. The late 1970's and 1980's saw an increasing emphasis on "I" rather than "we." This ideology rejected protest and returned to accommodation politics. This was especially true during the Ronald Reagan and George Bush administrations (1981-1993). A growing apathy, complacency, and indifference toward political participation replaced the militant activism of the 1960's.

Latinos adopted a more conservative posture to their politics, and many adopted the prevalent self-interested attitudes. Organizationally, this change was reflected in the decline of protest organizations and in the resurgence of older civic action groups such as MAPA, LULAC, and the American G.I. Forum. Groups that

took strong stands tended to use conservative approaches to their causes.

Not all groups ceased using confrontational protest methods. Some organizations, such as COMMUNITIES ORGANIZED FOR PUBLIC SERVICE (COPS) in San Antonio, Texas, and the UNITED NEIGHBORHOODS ORGANIZATION (UNO) in Los Angeles, California, continued to use a combination of conventional and protest politics.

During this era, Latino population growth continued to affect political participation. In 1980, Latinos numbered some 14 million; by 1990, the Latino population had increased to about 22 million, or about 9 percent of the U.S. population. Immigration from Mexico and Latin America and high birth rates were large factors in the increase. This demographic transformation resulted in gains in the number of representatives in state legislatures and other political bodies.

Gains were made in states outside the Southwest. By 1991, Florida, with a large Cuban population, had eleven Latino legislators. New York, with a large Puerto Rican population, had seven. According to the 1993 National Roster of Hispanic Elected Officials, Latinos constituted about 1 percent of all elected public officials.

During the 1990's, Latinos continued to make important political gains. Amendments to the Voting Rights Act in 1982 provided legal grounds for litigating *Gomez v. City of Watsonville* (1987) and *GARZA V. COUNTY OF LOS ANGELES, CALIFORNIA BOARD OF SUPERVISORS* (1990). These two decisions affected creation of a fairer political redistricting process in 1991.

Increases in political representation were evident in California, where the number of Latino state legislators increased from seven in 1991 to eleven in 1994. Increases in the number of Latino legislators were evident in most states with large Latino populations. The number of Latinos in Congress increased from eight in the early 1980's to eighteen in 1994.

It was at the local level that Latinos made most of their political gains. In 1982, Federico PEÑA was elected mayor of the city of Denver, Colorado. He and Henry Gabriel CISNEROS were the only two Latino mayors of large cities; later, both would be named to President Bill Clinton's cabinet. In communities from California to New York, the number of Latinos on city councils and school boards continued to increase.

Latino political gains resulted in large part from an increase in the number of eligible Latino voters. The SOUTHWEST VOTER REGISTRATION EDUCATION PROJECT, the Midwest/Northeast Voter Registration Education Project, and numerous other groups registered

VOTING PATTERNS AMONG ADULT LATINOS, 1976-1988

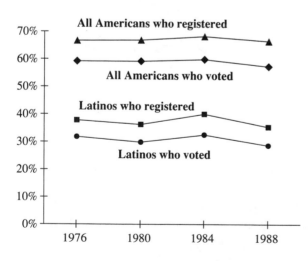

Source: Data are from Bureau of the Census, *Statistical Abstract of the United States: 1992* (Washington, D.C.: Bureau of the Census, 1992), Table 435.

Note: In assessing these data, the lower rates of Latinos eligible to vote should be considered. Percentages are for self-reported behaviors.

Federico Peña served as mayor of Denver, Colorado, before becoming secretary of transportation. (AP/Wide World Photos)

Latinos increasingly support the Republican Party. (AP/Wide World Photos)

large numbers of voters. In 1980, there were approximately 3.1 million Latinos registered. By 1986, the number had increased to 4.2 million, and by 1994 the figure exceeded 5 million. Latinos became more heterogeneous in their political affiliation, with Latino Republicans dramatically increasing in number. In state and national elections, it was not uncommon to have 30 to 40 percent of Latinos voting Republican. This change in party affiliation has been attributed in part to an increase in the size of the Latino middle and upper classes, mostly business and professional people. In the 1992 presidential election, approximately 70 percent of Latinos voted as Democrats. Latino affiliation with the Democratic Party continued to result from the perception that the Democratic Party better represented Latino socioeconomic interests. In 1993, 92 percent of Latino public officials were Democrats. Increasingly, by the 1990's, Latinos were perceived as a potentially powerful voting bloc.

Conclusion. Latino political participation has been cyclical and subject to clashes of political cultures, values, beliefs, and attitudes. The political culture of the United States is strongly based on democratic principles and a theory of popular sovereignty, limited government, individualism, and equality. That of Latinos, however, was shaped by authoritarianism, distrust of government, violence, and poverty.

In the 1990's, Latino politics underwent a transition as a result of several forces. These included an increase in the size of the Latino population; a resurgence of nativism and anti-immigrant sentiment; a re-emergence of Latino CULTURAL NATIONALISM, activism, and use of protest methods; and increasing ethnic and racial tensions that created a more hostile political environment. These forces, along with a national economic crisis, challenged America's political culture, institutions, and laws.

The struggle to increase Latino political participation in the 1990's was impeded by several obstacles. These included a large undocumented population; relatively low rates of citizenship; the relative youth of the Latino population; inability to raise money to maintain organizations and support Latino candidates; lack of strong, broad-based political organizations; dif-

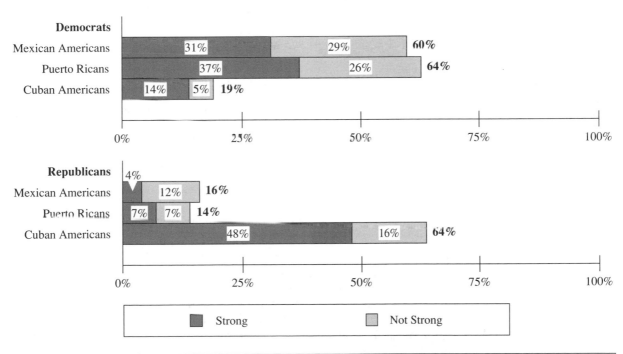

PARTISANSHIP AMONG LATINO CITIZENS, 1989-1990

Source: Data are from the Latino National Political Survey, which polled a representative sample of 1,546 Mexican Americans, 589 Puerto Ricans, and 682 Cuban Americans in forty metropolitan areas in 1989-1990. See Rodolfo O. de la Garza et al., *Latino Voices: Mexican, Puerto Rican, and Cuban Perspectives on American Politics* (Boulder, Colo.: Westview Press, 1992), Table 8.24.

Note: Choices for political affiliation were "Strong Democrat," "Not strong Democrat," "Closer to Democrat," "Independent/other," "Closer to Republican," "Not strong Republican," and "Strong Republican."

ficulty in recruiting viable candidates for public office; apathy and indifference; infighting and divisions within the Latino community; unwillingness of non-Latinos to support Latino efforts for change; and a socioeconomic environment that included increasing poverty, social problems, and political alienation.

—*Armando Navarro*

SUGGESTED READINGS:

• Acuña, Rodolfo. *Occupied America: A History of Chicanos*. 3d ed. New York: Harper & Row, 1988. Excellent overview of the events, organizations, and leaders shaping the evolution of Chicano history.

• Garcia, F. Chris, ed. *Latinos and the Political System*. Notre Dame, Ind.: University of Notre Dame Press, 1988. Contains several articles that focus on a variety of topics related to the Latino political experience.

• Gómez-Quiñones, Juan. *Chicano Politics: Reality and Promise, 1940-1990*. Albuquerque: University of New Mexico Press, 1990. Examines the diverse forces influencing the development of Chicano politics.

• Navarro, Armando. *MAYO: Avant-garde of the Chicano Movement in Texas*. Austin: University of Texas Press, 1994. Examines the politics of the Chicano movement, focusing on a case study of MAYO's organizing activities in Texas between 1967 and 1972.

• Skerry, Peter. *Mexican Americans: The Ambivalent Minority*. New York: Free Press, 1993. Provides a comparative study of Chicano politics in San Antonio, Texas, and Los Angeles, California.

• Vigil, Maurilio E. *Hispanics in American Politics: The Search for Political Power*. Lanham, Md.: University Press of America, 1987. Provides a profile of Latino politics and its various aspects.

• Villarreal, Robert E., and Norman G. Hernandez, eds. *Latinos and Political Coalitions: Political Empowerment for the 1990s*. New York: Praeger, 1991. Includes various articles that touch on the diverse aspects of Latino empowerment efforts.

Pollo: Chicken. Chickens are an Asian species and came with the Spanish to the Americas, where they became popular immediately. In Mexico, turkeys had been domesticated before arrival of the Spanish, and many turkey dishes were converted to use chicken. Elsewhere, chickens replaced ducks, doves, and wild fowl. Most chickens in Latin America range freely and are more flavorful than the industrially raised chickens of the United States.

Pompa, Gilbert (Oct. 1, 1931, Devine, Tex.—April, 1990, Washington, D.C.): Government official.

Pompa, a Mexican American, completed his undergraduate and his law studies at St. Mary's University in San Antonio, Texas, by 1958. He began his career in public service as assistant city attorney in San Antonio (1960-1963). He then served as assistant district attorney in Bexar County (1963-1967).

Pompa joined the Community Relations Service of the U.S. Department of Justice as a field representative in 1967. He worked his way up the ranks from assistant director, to deputy director, to acting director, and finally to director in 1978. Pompa's tenure with the Justice Department was marked by distinguished service during incidents at Wounded Knee, South Dakota, and Attica State Prison in New York. He was a member of various law enforcement and Latino community organizations.

Ponce, Mary Helen (b. Jan. 24, 1938, Southern California): Writer. Born and reared in the San Fernando Valley of California, Ponce, the youngest of ten children, grew up among first- and second-generation Mexican Americans who in the 1940's adopted Southern California as their home. She chose to document this era in her writing. Ponce earned a B.A. and an M.A. in Mexican American studies from California State University at Northridge and a second master's degree in history from the University of California at Los Angeles.

Ponce's writing presents everyday experiences and rituals in a simple manner. She allows her characters to reveal themselves without excessive detail. Her fiction explores such issues as bilingualism, biculturalism, and acculturation. Aside from numerous essays and journalistic pieces, her major publications include two books of short stories, *Recuerdo: Short Stories of the Barrio* (1983) and *Taking Control* (1987). She also wrote *The Wedding* (1989), a novel documenting the life of a young working-class Chicana woman in Southern California in the 1940's and 1950's. Ponce's strength as a writer lies in her ability to transform Mexican and Chicano daily life into a universal experience.

Ponce de León, Juan (1460, León, Spain—1521, Havana, Cuba): Explorer. Ponce de León is believed to have first traveled to the New World in 1493, with Christopher Columbus. He returned to Spain but in 1502 again sailed for the New World. He played a significant role in the occupation of Puerto Rico, but the political environment at the time quickly ended his position as governor of Puerto Rico, granted in 1509.

Juan Ponce de León. (Library of Congress)

In 1512, Ponce de León obtained the capitulation to explore and settle the island of Bimini. Other travelers had told him that Bimini had a fountain that provided eternal youth. His expedition to Bimini took off in 1513. The expedition landed on the mainland, somewhere near present-day St. Augustine, Florida. Ponce de León named the land FLORIDA because of its luscious vegetation and because the landing occurred on Palm Sunday, or *Pascua Florida* in Spanish. The native population was hostile and forced the Spaniards to retreat.

Ponce de León traveled to Spain to obtain the Crown's capitulation for Florida. After this, he re-turned to the New World but was requested to crush an Indian rebellion in Puerto Rico. He settled there, and it was not until 1521 that he organized a new expedition to Florida. Again Indians attacked. Ponce de León was wounded, and the expedition returned to Cuba. A few days after arrival, Ponce de León died of his wounds. Ponce, Puerto Rico, was named in his honor.

Ponce de León, Michael (b. July 4, 1922, Miami Fla.): Printmaker. Ponce de León has said that in his formative years as an artist he was influenced by the works of the 1930's and 1940's. He has created relief prints with his own press, using special papers and pressure. He has stated that art is a confrontation between artist, equipment, and material, and he has combined elements of sculpture, painting, cinematography, and music in works such as *Countertrust*. His prints often include photographs and often are inspired by film, music, or theater.

Ponce de León spent his formative years in Mexico City. As a child he planned to be an architect, but he began drawing while in his early teenage years. After service in the U.S. Air Force during World War II, he began submitting drawings and cartoons to national magazines. His work appeared in such publications as *The Saturday Evening Post*, *The New Yorker*, and *American Legion*. He studied with the Art Students League and began teaching for that group in 1978. He also has taught at Pratt Graphic Center in New York, New York. His work is in the Museum of Modern Art and the Metropolitan Museum of Art in New York, New York, as well as in the Smithsonian Institution.

Poniatowska, Elena (b. May 19, 1932, Paris, France): Writer. The heir to a rich Polish spiritual and cultural tradition, Poniatowska was born in Paris, where her father was a director of a large company. Her mother, Paula Amor Iturbe, was a Mexican national. Poniatowska began her education in Vouvray on the Loire and in Cannes. She continued her primary studies at the Liceo Franco Mexicano in Mexico. She attended Eden Hall in Philadelphia for her secondary education.

Poniatowska returned to Mexico to start a career in journalism on the newspaper *Excelsior* in 1954. In 1955, she went to *Novedades*. She became a Mexican citizen in 1969.

Poniatowska achieved widespread recognition as a writer with the publication of what remain among her best-known journalistic works: *Hasta no verte, Jesús mío* (1969) and *La noche de Tlatelolco* (1971; *Massacre in Mexico*, 1975). Other notable works are *Querido Diego, te abraza Quiela* (1978; *Dear Diego*, 1986) and *Gaby Brimmer* (1979, with Gabriela Brimmer). She has also published *De noche nienes* (1979), a collection of short stories, and *La "flor de Lis"* (1988), a novel. Poniatowska is considered by many to be the most prestigious female writer in Mexico of the late twentieth century.

Popé's Revolt (August, 1680): Indian revolt. Spanish colonial leaders experienced a rare defeat in Popé's Revolt. Fleeing to El Paso, the Spanish colonists lived in exile for twelve years, until they were again able to secure control of New Mexico.

After conquering central Mexico, Spaniards moved northward, hoping to find a new region as rich as Mexico. In the area that includes modern-day New Mexico, the Spanish conquerors found several groups of Indians living in towns, or pueblos. They also encountered the more nomadic Apache Indians. A relatively small number of bureaucrats, priests, and soldiers secured Spanish control over the region. The new rulers established a system of tribute, or taxation, and imposed the Christian religion on the Pueblo Indian inhabitants.

An Indian named Popé, of the Tewa Pueblos, chafed under Spanish rule, especially after his punishment for following a religion not recognized by the mission priests. Popé fled to Taos, where he confided in a small number of followers, saw apocalyptic visions, and began to organize a revolt against the Spanish. The two chief complaints of the revolutionaries were the heavy Spanish tribute and suppression of Indian religion.

Beginning on August 10, 1680, Apache and Pueblo Indians attacked isolated missions and ranches, killing Spaniards and destroying the buildings. Governor Antonio de Otermín called the remaining Spaniards together for their own protection at Santa Fe. An Indian siege of Santa Fe began on August 15 and ended nine days later with the flight of the surviving Spaniards to El Paso.

For twelve years, the Pueblo and Apache Indian groups enjoyed complete control of the former Spanish colony. The unity that had allowed them to defeat the Spanish, however, was short-lived, and the various groups of Indians soon acted on their ancient rivalries.

Despite three major Spanish efforts to reconquer New Mexico, Indian control continued. The Spanish reconquest finally came in 1692, under the leadership of Governor Diego de VARGAS. Soon, new contingents of Spanish priests, soldiers, families, and bureaucrats arrived in Santa Fe to begin rebuilding the Hispanic colony.

Historians disagree about the impact and meaning of Popé's Revolt. Writers of Indian ancestry emphasize the solidarity of the various Indian groups and stress the popular nature of the uprising against the Spaniards. Other historians, largely of Anglo background, believe that Popé and his lieutenants were an elite angry at their own loss of power; these writers deny that Popé's Revolt was a popular uprising. These writers also claim that many important leaders of the revolt were mixed-race individuals (mulatto and MESTIZO), so that the revolt was not a simple aboriginal revolt against the outsiders. At any rate, the aftermath of Popé's Revolt secured New Mexico for the Spanish, paving the way for the development of an area that has remained one of the most Hispanic regions in the United States.

Popol Vuh: Mayan religious text. Written in the Quiché Maya language of Guatemala, the Popol Vuh is the great epic of Mayan civilization, mixing mythology with legends and history. It contains a creation myth and a dynastic history of the Mayan ruling class. It was written in the sixteenth century in the Quiché language, but using Spanish letters. The myths it contains were probably formulated at the beginning of the Christian era.

Francisco Ximénez, a Spanish priest, discovered the Popol Vuh in the eighteenth century. He copied it and translated it into Spanish. It has become a major source of information about the ancient Maya.

Population distribution, trends, and demographics: The Latino population in the United States, projected to reach fifty-nine million by the year 2030, has grown increasingly diverse. Latinos have settled in every state. According to the 1990 U.S. Census, there were more than twenty-two million people of Hispanic origin living in the United States, representing 9 percent of the U.S. population. Because of the high rate of growth and lower-than-average socioeconomic status of the Latino population, Latino demographics are watched closely by social scientists, community leaders, politicians, educators, and the media.

Background. The defining characteristic of Latinos is that they represent a mixture of Spanish, indigenous, and to a degree, African peoples and cultures in the Western Hemisphere. The mixing process began about five hundred years ago with the explorations of Christopher Columbus and the European settlers who followed.

The presence of Latinos in the United States has been officially documented by the government since the early nineteenth century. In 1820, there were 344 people who identified Mexico, the Caribbean, or Central or South America as their last residence, according to the Immigration and Naturalization Service (INS). Since that time, many factors have contributed to changing the nature of the U.S. Latino population.

Latinos came to live in the United States through conquest and immigration. Events in U.S. expansion during the nineteenth century, including the LOUISIANA PURCHASE (1803), the purchase of Florida (1821), the annexation of Texas (1845), the MEXICAN AMERICAN WAR (1846-1848), and the SPANISH-AMERICAN WAR (1898), resulted in large numbers of Latinos being absorbed into the United States or its territories. Equally important were events in the nations of origin, including the MEXICAN REVOLUTION (1910-1921), the CUBAN REVOLUTION (1959), and civil strife in the Central American nations of El Salvador and Nicaragua during the late 1970's and the 1980's. These events dictated in large measure the relationship between specific Latino groups and the United States.

Mexican Americans were the first Latino subgroup with a large presence in the United States. The TREATY OF GUADALUPE HIDALGO, which ended the Mexican American War, ceded northwestern Mexico to the United States. This area included what became the states of Texas and California as well as parts of New Mexico, Arizona, Colorado, Utah, and Nevada. About seventy-five thousand Mexicans in the ceded territories became American citizens by conquest.

The situation was different for the Cuban American population, particularly those who immigrated after 1959. Of the almost 740,000 Cubans who arrived in the United States between 1820 and 1989, 82 percent arrived after 1961. Cuban immigrants during the early 1960's received special refugee status because they were fleeing the newly formed communist government under Fidel CASTRO.

Like Cuba, Puerto Rico came under American rule with the TREATY OF PARIS (1898), which ended the Spanish-American War. The JONES ACT of 1917 conferred U.S. citizenship on Puerto Ricans and obligated them to serve in the U.S. armed forces.

It has only been since 1930 that segments of the U.S. Latino population have been identified and counted in a separate category in the census (*see* CENSUS, TREATMENT AND COUNTING OF LATINOS IN THE). In 1980, census respondents who identified themselves as "Spanish/Hispanic" could select Mexican, Puerto Rican, Cuban, or "other Hispanic"as their background. Ten years later, data on approximately thirty additional Hispanic subgroups was tabulated by the Bureau of the Census. During this same ten-year period, the Latino population grew seven times as fast as did the rest of the nation. The Hispanic population grew not only in numbers but also in diversity. Increased Central and South American immigration broadened the boundaries of the Latino experience and expanded areas of settlement to every state.

The three largest Hispanic subgroups, according to the 1990 census, were Mexican Americans (61.2 percent), mainland Puerto Ricans (12.1 percent), and Cuban Americans (4.8 percent). The residents of the

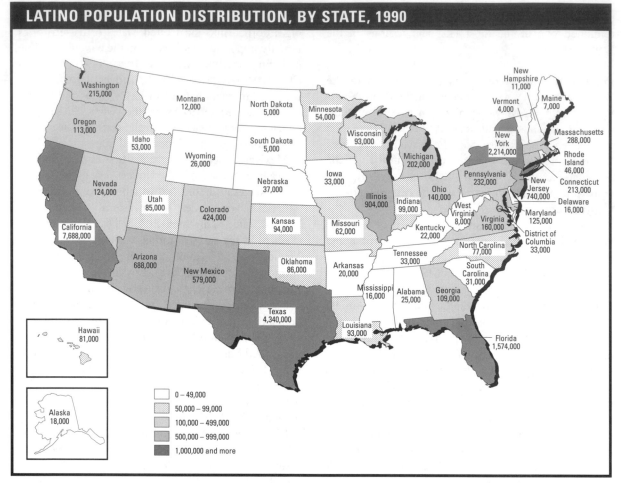

LATINO POPULATION DISTRIBUTION, BY STATE, 1990

Washington 215,000
Oregon 113,000
Montana 12,000
North Dakota 5,000
Minnesota 54,000
New Hampshire 11,000
Vermont 4,000
Maine 7,000
Idaho 53,000
South Dakota 5,000
Wisconsin 93,000
Michigan 202,000
New York 2,214,000
Massachusetts 288,000
Rhode Island 46,000
Wyoming 26,000
Nevada 124,000
Utah 85,000
Colorado 424,000
Nebraska 37,000
Iowa 33,000
Illinois 904,000
Indiana 99,000
Ohio 140,000
Pennsylvania 232,000
New Jersey 740,000
Connecticut 213,000
Delaware 16,000
West Virginia 8,000
Maryland 125,000
California 7,688,000
Kansas 94,000
Missouri 62,000
Kentucky 22,000
Virginia 160,000
District of Columbia 33,000
Arizona 688,000
New Mexico 579,000
Oklahoma 86,000
Arkansas 20,000
Tennessee 33,000
North Carolina 77,000
South Carolina 31,000
Texas 4,340,000
Mississippi 16,000
Alabama 25,000
Georgia 109,000
Louisiana 93,000
Florida 1,574,000
Hawaii 81,000
Alaska 18,000

0 – 49,000
50,000 – 99,000
100,000 – 499,000
500,000 – 999,000
1,000,000 and more

Source: Population data are from Marlita A. Reddy, ed., *Statistical Record of Hispanic Americans* (Detroit: Gale Research, 1993), Table 92.

Commonwealth of Puerto Rico, although U.S. citizens, were counted in a separate census.

Population Distribution. In 1990, Latinos could be found in every state of the Union, from the 4,000 recorded in Vermont to the 7.6 million residing in California. The highest concentrations, however, were in ten states. Nearly nine of every ten Hispanics lived in California, Texas, New York, Florida, Illinois, New Mexico, Arizona, New Jersey, Colorado, or Massachusetts. Latinos represented 38 percent of New Mexico's residents and 25 percent of the state populations of both California and Texas. Arizona's Hispanics composed 18 percent of the state's population, and both New York and Florida had enough Latinos to make up 12 percent of their respective populations.

Five states recorded increases of at least 100 percent in their Latino populations from 1980 to 1990. Rhode Island and Nevada had the largest increases with 132.2 percent and 130 percent respectively. Massachusetts'

Latino population increased by 103.9 percent, New Hampshire's by 102.8 percent, and Virginia's by 100.7 percent. Seven states experienced decreases in their Latino populations during the same ten-year period: Alabama (26 percent), Kentucky (19 percent), Louisiana (6 percent), Mississippi (35 percent), South Carolina (8 percent), Tennessee (4 percent), and West Virginia (33 percent).

Mexican Americans made up close to 80 percent of California's Latino population in 1990. The second-highest category (18 percent) was "other Hispanic," partly an indication of increased immigration from Central America. Cubans made up less than 1 percent and Puerto Ricans 1.6 percent of California's Latinos. Hispanics were close to 40 percent of the population of Los Angeles, 20 percent of San Diego residents, and 26 percent of San Jose's population.

In Texas, Mexican Americans represented almost 90 percent of the state's Hispanic population. The "other

Hispanic" category accounted for 9 percent. Puerto Ricans were about 1 percent of the state's Latino population, and Cuban Americans were less than one-half of 1 percent. In Houston, 27 percent of the city's 1.7 million people were Latinos, while in Dallas, the figure was 20 percent. Latinos were 55 percent of San Antonio's residents and 70 percent of El Paso's population.

New York, with its 2.2 million Latinos, hosted the largest mainland concentration of Puerto Ricans. Numbering close to 1.1 million in 1990, Puerto Ricans composed 49 percent of New York's Latino population. Another 43 percent were categorized as "other Hispanic." The Dominican American population in New York City has grown so quickly that researchers have noted that Santo Domingo, the capital city of the Dominican Republic, had only a slight numerical edge in its population of Dominicans. New York City was the destination of record for 60 percent of the 24,858 Dominicans who immigrated to the United States in 1987. Mexican Americans made up only 4 percent of New York's Latino population, while 3 percent were

Cuban American. Latinos represented 24 percent of New York City's residents.

The largest concentration of Cuban Americans can be found in Florida, where they represented 43 percent of that state's 1.5 million Hispanics in 1990. The INS reported that of the 28,916 Cubans who immigrated to the United States in 1987, 77 percent selected Florida as their destination. The next largest segment (31 percent) of Florida's Latino population was "other Hispanic," including relatively large numbers of Dominican Americans and Colombian Americans. Puerto Ricans represented 15 percent and Mexican Americans 10 percent of the state's Latino population.

Mexican Americans represented 70 percent of all Latinos in Illinois, while Puerto Ricans, the next largest group, accounted for 16 percent. Another 13 percent were "other Hispanic," and 2 percent were Cuban. Almost 20 percent of Chicago's 2.8 million residents were Latino. Two major Latino subgroups, Mexican Americans and Puerto Ricans, successfully converged on that city. Chicago's Fourth Congressional District, with a heavily Mexican American population, elected

The large Mexican American presence in Texas shows in the state's cultural life. (James Shaffer)

a Puerto Rican to Congress in 1992. Congressman Luis Gutierrez enjoyed the distinction of being the first Latino from the state of Illinois elected to the U.S. House of Representatives.

Puerto Ricans in New Jersey were the largest Latino subgroup, representing 43 percent of the state's Hispanic population in 1990. "Other Hispanics" followed a close second, composing 41 percent. This state saw a 50 percent increase in its Latino population between 1980 and 1990. The Bergen-Passaic metropolitan area was listed as a common destination for Dominican immigrants during 1984 and 1987. Four major cities in New Jersey had sizable Latino concentrations: Paterson (40 percent), Elizabeth (39 percent), Newark (26 percent), and Jersey City (24 percent). Cuban Americans made up 11 percent of New Jersey's Hispanics, and Mexican Americans represented another 4 percent.

Mexican Americans represented almost 90 percent of Hispanics in Arizona in 1990. "Other Hispanics" were the next largest group at almost 9 percent. Arizona experienced a 56 percent increase in its Hispanic population between 1980 and 1990. This jump moved Arizona up to seventh from eighth in the ranking of states with the largest number of Latinos. Almost 30 percent of Tucson's population was Latino, and Hispanic residents of the state's largest city, Phoenix, represented 26 percent of its population.

New Mexico is the state with the highest percentage of Latinos, almost 40 percent in 1990. This segment of the population grew by only 21 percent between 1980 and 1990. New Mexico changed places with Arizona on the scale ranking states with the highest numbers of Hispanic residents. Nearly 35 percent of the population of Albuquerque was Latino. Of New Mexico's Hispanic residents, 56 percent were Mexican American and 42 percent were classified as "other Hispanics," among whom were large proportions of Salvadorans and Guatemalans as well as HISPANOS whose families had been in the area for centuries.

Colorado's Hispanic population increased by nearly 25 percent between 1980 and 1990. Two-thirds of the state's Latinos were Mexican Americans, with "other Hispanics" composing 31 percent. Major groups of immigrants included people from Peru, El Salvador, Guatemala, and Colombia.

Massachusetts replaced Michigan in 1990 as the state with the tenth largest Hispanic population. Puerto Ricans composed 52 percent of the state's Hispanic population. The increase in the number of Latino residents since 1980 was dramatic and resulted in large part from an influx of Dominicans and Central Americans. Hispanics represented 10 percent of the residents in both Boston and Lowell, as well as 17 percent of Springfield.

Demographics. Latinos in the United States tend to be younger than other Americans. Census figures indicate that in 1991, the median age for all Americans was 33 years, while for Hispanics, it was 26 years. There was variance among Latino subgroups for this statistic. Puerto Ricans were the youngest, with a median age of 20.4 years. Cuban Americans registered the highest median age, at 39.9 years. "Other Hispanics" had the next highest median age, registering 31 years, while Central and South Americans showed a median age of 27.9 years.

According to 1990 census figures, non-Hispanic people were much more likely than Latinos to be elderly. Approximately 5 percent of Latinos were at least 65 years of age or older, compared to 13 percent of the rest of the population.

Nativity. The 1990 census figures revealed that 64 percent of Latinos were born in the United States. Almost 10 percent were foreign-born, naturalized citizens. The remaining 26 percent were foreign-born and not citizens. Nearly two-thirds of Central Americans in the United States fell into this latter category, as did more than half of the South Americans and Dominicans. Because the process of becoming an American citizen takes several years, it is not surprising that more recent immigrants have a lower rate of naturalization compared to groups such as Cuban Americans, 65 percent of whom were naturalized.

Participation in the Political Process. According to census data, 13.7 million Latinos were eligible to vote in the 1990 elections. Less than one-third, however, registered to vote. Voter participation was strongest among older Latinos. About half of eligible Hispanic voters who were fifty years of age or older registered, compared to 25 percent of Latinos between the ages of eighteen and thirty-four. (*See* POLITICS, LATINOS AND.)

The ten states with the largest concentrations of Latinos had differing percentages of registered voters in 1990, ranging from a low of 25 percent in California to a high of 51 percent in New Mexico. New Mexico had more Hispanic elected officials (672) than did California (617), but both were overshadowed by Texas, with almost 2,000. Texas had 40 percent of its 2.6 million eligible Latinos registered for the 1990 elections. Colorado, with almost 43 percent of its 231,000 eligible Latinos registered to vote, had more than 200 Hispanic elected officials. Although Arizona

Latino politicians face the challenge of low rates of voter registration and voting among Latinos. (Frances M. Roberts)

had a relatively low percentage of eligible Hispanic voters registered (28.9 percent), it had more than 280 Hispanic elected officials.

New Jersey had about one-third of its eligible Latinos registered to vote. In 1992, Robert Menendez became not only the first Latino to be elected to the House of Representatives from that state but also the first Cuban Democrat to serve in Congress.

Educational Attainment. A comparison of census data from 1970, 1980, and 1990 indicates that impressive gains have been made by Latinos regarding EDUCATION AND ACADEMIC ACHIEVEMENT. Nearly 50 percent of all Hispanics aged twenty-five and older were at least high school graduates in 1990. Twenty years earlier, the figure was 32 percent. The percentage of Latinos in the same age group who had earned a bachelor's degree nearly doubled between 1970 and 1990, reaching 9 percent.

Encouraging as these gains are, Latinos had not yet closed the gap separating their achievements from the educational levels of non-Hispanics. In 1990, 77 percent of non-Hispanics aged twenty-five and older were high-school graduates, and 20 percent had a bachelor's degree. The Latino high-school dropout rate was 29 percent in 1990 and had not improved significantly since the 1970's.

Among the various Latino subgroups, South Americans showed the highest percentages of high school graduates (70 percent) and persons with bachelor's degrees (close to 20 percent). In 1990, Cuban Americans ranked second in both categories, with 56.8 percent high school graduates and 16.6 percent having a bachelor's degree. Puerto Ricans showed 53.4 percent high school graduates and nearly 10 percent with a bachelor's degree. Dominican Americans had the lowest percentage of high school graduates (42.6 percent), while Mexican Americans had the lowest percentage of bachelor's degrees (6.2 percent) and the highest proportion of poorly educated adults.

Employment and Income. Census data show that the UNEMPLOYMENT rate of Latinos dropped from 16.5 percent in March, 1983, to 7.8 percent in 1989. This period coincided with the end of one economic recession and the beginning of another. The unemployment rate for Latinos rose to nearly 12 percent in 1993. These changes reflected the overall pattern of unemployment rates.

Latinos have improved in educational achievement, but gaps remain in comparison with non-Hispanics. (Impact Visuals, Loren Santow)

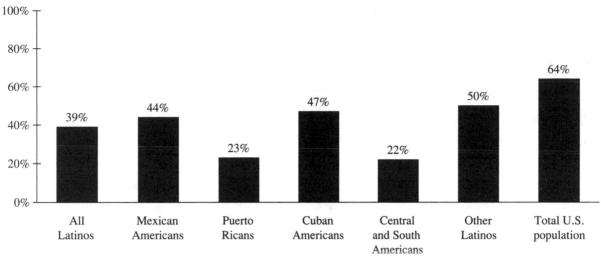

HOME OWNERSHIP AMONG LATINOS, 1991

Source: Data are from Marlita A. Reddy, ed., *Statistical Record of Hispanic Americans* (Detroit: Gale Research, 1993), Table 561. Original data are from U.S. Bureau of the Census, *Current Population Reports: The Hispanic Population in the United States: March, 1991* (Series P-20, No. 455) (Washington, D.C.: Government Printing Office, 1991), pp. 16-17.

The percentage of Latinos living in poverty declined from nearly 30 percent in 1982 to 26 percent in 1989. Like the unemployment rate, POVERTY among Hispanics rose in the early 1990's, exceeding 29 percent by 1992.

In 1990, 28 percent of Latino males aged sixteen years or older were employed in the category of operators, fabricators, and laborers. This was the highest percentage for Latinos among the occupational categories. For both Hispanic (39 percent) and non-Hispanic (45 percent) females in the same age range, the category of technical, sales, and administrative support positions provided the most jobs. (*See* OCCUPATIONS AND OCCUPATIONAL TRENDS.)

In New York City, more Latinos (22.6 percent) were employed in services in 1990 than in any other census employment category. Manufacturing employed the highest percentages of Hispanics in both Los Angeles (26.5 percent) and Chicago (nearly 39 percent). Higher percentages of the Latino populations of Miami (25 percent) and San Antonio (26 percent) were employed in the census employment category of trade than in any other.

The real (adjusted for inflation) median money income of Latinos rose by slightly more than 11 percent between 1982 and 1989. The median household income of Latinos was about three-fourths that of non-Hispanics. Household incomes of $50,000 or more

were reported by 25 percent of non-Hispanic households but only 13 percent of Latino households. Among the Hispanic subgroups, nearly 20 percent of Cuban American households, 19.4 percent of "other Hispanic" households, and 15 percent of Central and South American households reported incomes at this level. Less than 12 percent of both Mexican American and Puerto Rican households reported incomes of $50,000 or more. (*See* INCOME AND WAGE LEVELS.)

The median family income for all Americans in 1990 was $35,225. For Latinos, the median family income was a full $10,000 less than that amount. Among Latino subgroups, Dominican Americans had the lowest median family income ($19,726), while Cuban Americans had the highest ($32,417).

More than 20 percent of Latino families lived below the poverty level in 1990. This compared to less than 10 percent of non-Hispanic families. Most affected by poverty were Dominican American families (33 percent), Hispanic children (18.4 percent), Latinas (27 percent), and the elderly (24 percent).

Family Patterns. Almost 70 percent of all Latino families in 1990 were maintained by married couples, including 76 percent of Cuban American families and 73 percent of both Mexican American and South American families. The lowest percentages of married-couple families were found among Puerto Ricans (56 percent) and Dominican Americans (50 percent). Central American families had the highest percentage of families headed by a male with no wife present (14 percent). Dominican Americans registered the highest percentage (41 percent) of female-headed households, followed by Puerto Ricans (36 percent).

Income levels were lower for female-headed households. Puerto Rican families headed by women had the lowest average income ($8,912), followed by Dominican American families of the same type, with an income of $9,724. Similar Cuban American households fared much better, with an average income of $19,511.

Trends. Projections to the year 2050 made by the Bureau of the Census indicate that Latinos will continue to grow not only in numbers but also as a percentage of the nation's overall population. The Hispanic population is expected to reach 88 million (nearly four times the 1990 figure) and will represent 60 percent of the U.S. population by the middle of the twenty-first century. This growth is expected to occur by virtue of natural increases rather than immigration.

The difference in median age between Latinos and non-Hispanic whites will widen according to these projections. In 1990, the median age for Hispanics was 25.4 years. The figure for non-Hispanic whites was 34.8 years. By the year 2050, the median age for Hispanics was projected to be 32.1 years, while for non-Hispanic whites the estimate was 54.2 years.

It remains unclear whether such population growth can translate into increased political and social influence for Latinos in the twenty-first century. One determining factor may be the extent to which members of various subgroups identify collectively as "Latinos" or "Hispanics" rather than as Mexican Americans, as Cuban Americans, or as members of various other national-origin groups. Data collected for the LATINO NATIONAL POLITICAL SURVEY in 1989 and 1990 suggest that native-born Latinos are more likely to accept such pan-ethnic labels than are members of the immigrant generation.

Latinos are often defined as a single entity by the media, government, and the rest of American society. This will become increasingly true as they come to see

The relatively large average size of Latino families contributes to the low median age of Latinos. (Unicorn Stock Photos, MacDonald Photography)

U.S. LATINO POPULATION, 1988

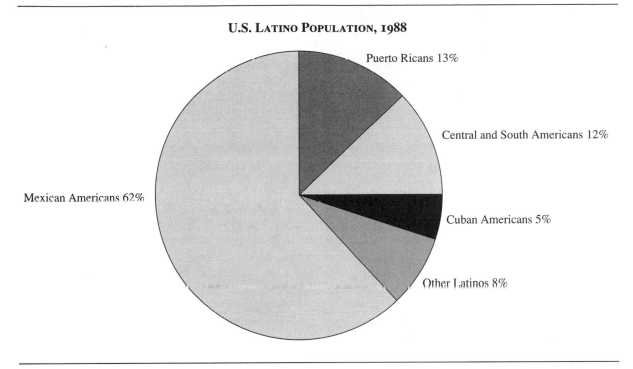

Puerto Ricans 13%

Central and South Americans 12%

Cuban Americans 5%

Other Latinos 8%

Mexican Americans 62%

Source: Data are from Frank L. Schick and Renee Schick, comps. and eds., *Statistical Handbook on U.S. Hispanics* (Phoenix, Ariz.: Oryx Press, 1991), p. 7.

interests in common beyond the boundaries of their subgroups. Research appears to support the feasibility of developing a collective Latino identity in the twenty-first century.   —*Cecilia M. Garcia*

SUGGESTED READINGS:

• Boswell, T. D., and J. R. Curtis. *The Cuban American Experience: Culture, Images, and Perspectives.* Totowa, N.J.: Rowman and Allanheld, 1984. Describes the development of the Cuban community in the United States.

• Chavez, John R. *The Lost Land: The Chicano Image of the Southwest.* Albuquerque: University of New Mexico Press, 1984. Traces the image that Mexican Americans have of the Southwest and of themselves from the early history of the region through the late twentieth century.

• De la Garza, Rodolfo O., Louis DeSipio, F. Chris Garcia, John Garcia, and Angelo Falcon. *Latino Voices: Mexican, Puerto Rican, and Cuban Perspectives on American Politics.* Boulder, Colo.: Westview Press, 1992. Examines political attitudes and values of the three largest Hispanic subgroups, based on findings from the Latino National Political Survey.

• Portes, Alejandro, and Rubén G. Rumbaut. *Immigrant America: A Portrait.* Berkeley: University of California Press, 1990. Analyzes the ways in which

immigrants interact with and affect such aspects of American life as the economy, neighborhoods, politics, and national identity.

• Reddy, Marlita A., ed. *Statistical Record of Hispanic Americans.* Detroit: Gale Research, 1993. A massive volume of statistical information, much of it derived from census data.

• Sanchez Korrol, Virginia. *From Colonia to Community: The History of Puerto Ricans in New York City, 1917-1948.* Westport, Conn.: Greenwood Press, 1983. Traces the experiences of New York's Puerto Rican community from the beginnings of American citizenship through the second significant migration to the mainland.

Porter, Liliana (b. Oct. 6, 1941, Buenos Aires, Argentina): Artist. Porter has exhibited her works around the world. Among her many awards are a first prize at the Latin American Graphic Arts Biennial in 1986 and a first prize at the VIII Latin American Print Biennial in San Juan, Puerto Rico, in 1986.

Porter studied at the School of Fine Arts in Buenos Aires. After a brief stay in Mexico, she arrived in New York, New York, in 1964 and studied printmaking at the Pratt Graphic Art Center. Her work has been exhibited at the Museum of Modern Art in New York and the

Museo de Bellas Artes in Caracas, Venezuela, as well as in other major museums.

With José Guillermo Castillo and Luis Camnitzer, Porter founded the New York Graphic Workshop. Her work of the 1960's has been described as minimalist. During the 1970's, her paintings and prints began to put real and painted objects together to reveal the ambiguous nature of reality. Porter has also been active politically in opposition to dictatorships in the Southern Hemisphere.

Portes, Alejandro (b. Oct. 13, 1944, Havana, Cuba): Educator. Portes is known for his interpretations of Spanish-language culture, particularly Cuban culture, to the United States. He has studied urban culture in both the United States and developing countries. His research examines the sources of poverty and inequity, particularly in less developed countries. His work has helped to dispel myths about immigrants and emigration from Mexico. He has written extensively on immigration to the United States from Mexico and other Latin American areas as well as on labor markets and urban conditions.

Portes attended the University of Havana from 1959 to 1960 and the Catholic University of Argentina in 1963. He earned his B.A. at Creighton University in 1965, then his M.A. (1967) and Ph.D. (1970) at the University of Wisconsin-Madison. Portes lectured in sociology at the University of Wisconsin-Madison during the 1969-1970 academic year, then joined the faculty of the University of Illinois at Urbana for the following year. In 1971, he became an associate professor of sociology at the University of Texas at Austin. In 1975, he took a position as professor of sociology at Duke University. During his career, he has been a guest researcher, visiting professor, and speaker in Chile, Brazil, and Colombia.

Portillo Trambley, Estela (b. Jan. 16, 1936, El Paso, Tex.): Writer. Portillo Trambley received a B.A. in English in 1956 and an M.A. in English in 1978 from the University of Texas at El Paso. In 1979, she began working for the Department of Special Services of the El Paso public schools. Portillo Trambley served as chairperson of the English department at the El Paso Technical Institute and as drama instructor, producer, and director at El Paso Community College for five years. In 1972, she won the Quinto Sol Award, a prestigious literary honor.

Portillo Trambley's most important works include her collection of short stories titled *Rain of Scorpions*

and Other Writings (1975) and the drama *The Day of the Swallows* (1971). She also wrote the script for a musical comedy called *Sun Images* (unpublished, 1979) and composed eleven of its songs. She has written a number of plays, including *Sor Juana and Other Plays* (1983), and two novels, *Woman of the Earth* (1977) and *Trini* (1986). Portillo Trambley's fiction is permeated by an uncompromising concern for the equality and liberation of women from the antiquated social norms of society. She is the first Chicana to have published a widely distributed book of short stories.

Porto Rican Brotherhood of America: Civic organization. The Porto Rican Brotherhood of America was founded in the early 1920's. It organized and documented Puerto Rican political, cultural, civic, and social issues in New York City. The brotherhood protected the rights of Puerto Ricans in race riots during the late 1920's. The Brotherhood published the social and demographic characteristics of Puerto Rican communities to dramatize the conditions faced by Puerto Ricans.

Portolá, Gaspar de (c. 1723, Balageur, Spain—1784, Mexico): Soldier and explorer. Portolá was a Spaniard of noble birth who entered the Spanish army in the 1730's. In 1767, as a captain, Portolá was sent to California as its governor. Upon arrival, one of his first actions was to assume the command of an expedition aimed at securing Spanish claims to ALTA CALIFORNIA and establishing missions throughout the area. Portolá also founded the cities of SAN DIEGO and Monterey.

To accomplish those ends, Portolá commanded a two-year expedition that began in 1769. Its members included Jesuit missionary Father Junípero SERRA. The rigorous journey began in Lower California and first established a mission at San Diego. It proceeded on to explore, but not settle, territory including the Bay of Monterey. In May of 1771, Portolá and his followers returned to the Monterey Bay area to found both the mission of Carmel and the city of Monterey. From 1777 to 1784, Portolá was the governor of the Mexican city of Puebla. He was succeeded by Jacobo de UGARTE Y LOYOLA and ordered back to Spain. Portolá is believed to have returned to Mexico and to have died there, but some historians report his death as occurring in Spain.

Posadas, Las: Las Posadas is the re-creation of Joseph and Mary's search for lodgings and a place for Mary to give birth to the Christ Child. Las Posadas celebrations

San Antonio, Texas, has a large procession for Las Posadas. (Bob Daemmrich)

are held on various scales throughout Latin America and in the United States. Typically, a procession, led by children carrying a small litter with clay figures of Mary and Joseph, winds through a town stopping at houses to ask for lodging.

In San Antonio, Las Posadas is held in conjunction with the Fiesta de las Luminarias (fiesta of the lights) and involves a procession on the Paso del Rio, San Antonio's famous Riverwalk.The procession starts at the Mansion del Rio Hotel and winds along the candle-lit Riverwalk to Armeson River Theatre in La Villita, the 250-year-old Spanish quarter that was reconstructed and preserved beginning in 1939. It is led by mariachis; children dressed as Mary, Joseph, angels, and shepherds; and a choir group singing Christmas songs in both English and Spanish. The ceremony concludes with a PIÑATA party in the Plaza Juarez in La Villita featuring *folklórico* dancing and music.

Posole: Hominy, or corn treated with lime to release its outer hull. The outer hull of corn is tough and hard, and it can cut the gums and cause indigestion. To remove it, ancient American Indians devised a technique of boiling corn kernels in water with lime added. The hull loosened and was washed away with the lime water, leaving *posole*, also known as hominy. *Posole* is particularly important in modern Mexican and Central American cuisine, where it is used in soups and stews. Ground *posole* becomes MASA, the basis for corn tortillas and ANTOJITOS.

Poster art: As one of the most representative expressions of urban life, poster art was embraced by many artists in the United States, including many of Latin American background. Poster art often is made using a silkscreen process. Silkscreen is an ideal medium for producing broad, flat images of highly saturated color, the aesthetic of the commercial poster.

The Silkscreen Process. A silkscreen or serigraph is a stencil print, made by one of three methods: cut stencils, which are made from paper or translucent film; blockout, in which the design is drawn or painted directly onto the screen with glue or lacquer, which then blocks the flow of ink; and the photographic method, in which stencils are made with photographic film and areas shielded from light during exposure dissolve in water. The photographic method can reproduce designs with photographic accuracy and can be used to reproduce photographs themselves.

To create a silkscreen, the printmaker first cuts an image in a sheet of paper or plastic film. Removing the cutaway areas creates a stencil, the open spaces of which are the shapes that will print. The stencil is then placed on a screen made of silk or other thin cloth stretched to a frame, and a piece of paper is placed under the frame. The printmaker pulls ink across the screen with a thin rubber blade, squeezing ink through the open areas of the screen onto the paper underneath. The screen is raised, and the image appears on the paper.

History. The poster as an art form originated in France in the mid-nineteenth century and quickly became an effective means of mass communication. During the early part of the twentieth century, posters were the preferred art form of the German expressionists, the Dadaists, the cubists, and the Russian constructivists, among others. The poster was used to express political freedom, promote liberty, and advertise both cultural events and products. Poster art flourished more in urban industrial societies than in rural settings. As a result, it tends to reflect the mood, conflict, syncretism, intricacy, and diversity of city life.

The Cuban Poster. Cuban poster art had its origins in the pictorial avant-garde movements of the 1920's. During the 1930's, many Cuban avant-garde artists were recognized in Chicago, New York City, and San Francisco. Among these artists were Fidelio Ponce de León, René Portocarrero, and Wilfredo Lam. Although Lam is considered primarily as a painter, he was a pivotal force behind the development and diffusion of Cuban poster art.

During the 1960's, the CUBAN REVOLUTION was expressed both at home and throughout the world through political posters. Millions of people recognized and identified with the spirit of the Cuban Revolution through the well-known poster of Ernesto "Che" GUEVARA, one of the heroes of the revolution.

In 1981, a new school of younger artists opened a collective show in Havana under the title "Vol. I." This show challenged the prevailing strictures regarding art of the 1970's. The artists demanded a reaffirmation of the Cuban national identity as well as a new socialistic realism. The next movement, *los Novísimos,* comprised younger artists who have been characterized as satirical and critical, but also as having adapted to the dictates of institutional art without betraying the symbolic content of their reality.

Some of the best Cuban silkscreen artists of the 1990's are Glexis Novoa Vian, Carlos Rodríguez Cárdenas, and Ciro Quintana Gutiérrez, all born in the early 1960's. Novoa Vian's work has been described as similar to political propaganda slogans on billboards but devoid of meaning. He has tried to capture ironies regarding art, culture, and politics. Rodríguez Cárdenas' work deconstructs the stereotyped slogans that inundate Cuban society, making the slogans problematical and using them to analyze aspects of SOCIALISM. Quintana Gutiérrez describes reality as "an unreachable fiction, forever controlled by images." His texts capture the essence of Cuban art of the late twentieth century.

Beginning in the 1980's, Cuban poster art and the plastic arts experienced a renaissance. Art critic Luis Cammitzer has argued that Cuban art in the late twentieth century has been a model for Latin America and for breaking out of the centuries-old cycle of dependence on the metropolitan centers, in which the colonies were literally the raw materials of the "developing" process.

The Mexican American Poster. Mexican American graphic arts were shaped most directly by David Alfaro SIQUEIROS (1896-1974), one of Mexico's greatest mural craftsmen. Although Siqueiros devoted most of his work to *arte público* (public art), he also created poster art. Most Mexican American artists have benefited from Siqueiros' thematic and technical approach to poster art in particular and plastic arts in general.

Some well-known Chicano graphic artists are Carlos Almaraz, Ricardo FAVELA, Juanishi V. Orozco, Gregorio Rivera, and Patssi Valdez. Almaraz was commissioned by the city of Los Angeles to design its bicentennial poster (1981) and its Olympic poster (1984). He has described his art as frightening, disturbing, anxiety provoking, universal, and tragic. Favela prefers to use his art to promote community organization around issues and to advance Chicano causes. His work reveals the vision of enhancing the cultural roots of Chicano urban life. Orozco's posters convey his commitment to understanding Chicano culture and emphasize its indigenous foundation. His work has been exhibited and published throughout the United States, Mexico, Latin America, and Europe. Rivera's work reflects his commitment to visual literacy and socialization around new media for informational, educational, and cultural programming. His work, which attempts to integrate the arts with communication technologies, has been exhibited in galleries and museums in more than twenty countries. Valdez has

Mass-produced posters decorate the walls of a United Farm Workers office. (Impact Visuals, Thor Swift)

excelled in graphic arts and photography. Her work attempts to break stereotypes about Mexican and Latin American women. It depicts the daily injustices and experiences of being a member of a minority group struggling to make a living in the barrio of East Los Angeles.

The Puerto Rican Poster. The Puerto Rican poster originated during the nineteenth century, when it was used to advertise social and cultural events in the island's major cities. The first modern poster was produced in 1927 for the San Juan Carnival festivities. During the 1940's, the University of Puerto Rico held the first Puerto Rican poster exhibit. This exhibit, which addressed health-related issues, was also shown at the Riverside Museum in New York City.

Although there was an early interest in the production and dissemination of the poster, it was not until the Department of Education established the Taller Cinema y Gráfica (cinema and graphic workshop) in 1946 that the Puerto Rican poster emerged as a serious art form. Irene Delano, Edwin Roskan, and Robert Gwathney developed that national center for the production of silkscreens. A few years later, the workshop became an independent agency under the auspices of the Department of Education, and its name was changed to the División de Educación de la Comunidad (division of community education). The agency brought several talented artists together, attracting several back to the island.

The division's poster production soon became engaged with the sociopolitical revolution of the new Popular Democratic Party (PARTIDO POPULAR DEMOCRÁTICO), headed by Luis MUÑOZ MARÍN. Posters were used to express the government's programmatic commitment to the masses because they could be produced rapidly and cheaply, without large expenditures on equipment. Most of the poster production in Puerto Rico during this period reflected the need to bring information on health, housing, hygiene, and schooling to the country's rural areas. In addition, urban communities were informed of such cultural activities as concerts, theatrical presentations, and art exhibits.

The establishment of the Institute of Puerto Rican Culture in 1955 brought together a group of young and energetic artists. The institute's commitment to the cultural history of Puerto Rico was diffused throughout the island through posters, which commemorated local and national historical events, heroes, and cultural activities.

The success of the institute's graphic arts department opened the doors to the establishment of other independent workshops. Two graphic arts workshops were founded at the University of Puerto Rico in the 1960's, one attached to the Social Sciences Research Center and under the direction of Rafael Rivera Sosa, the other under the Cultural Activities Program and directed by Carlos Marichal. In the latter, artists such as Nelson Sambolín, Ernesto Álvarez, and Luis Maisonet made significant contributions. Other independent workshops such as Taller Alacrán, Taller Bija, Taller El Caño, and Visión Plástica also produced excellent posters.

The aesthetic aspect of the Puerto Rican poster transcended its propagandistic purpose, and it remained a true work of art. Lorenzo HOMAR, considered "the master of masters" of the Puerto Rican poster, has emphasized the importance of typography and placing of letters on posters as an integral part of the graphic design. His *Ballets of San Juan* is an excellent example of this trend. Another master of the poster is Rafael Tufiño. Most of his designs praise the national heroes of Puerto Rico and Latin America. His posters are rich in color, tradition, and personal feelings. Antonio Maldonado's work shows a unity of composition and effective images. Eduardo Vera Cortés' posters are saturated in rich colors and feature patriotic images and popular themes. His designs convey their graphic meaning with great eloquence. Antonio MARTORELL, founder of the Taller Alacrán, exhibits technical mastery in the manner in which both color and lettering are blended.

Mainland Puerto Ricans. The Puerto Rican poster was introduced in the United States in the late 1960's in the context of the Puerto Rican independence and the Young Lords movements. The issues of Puerto Rico's political status and the jailing of Independence Party leader Pedro ALBIZU CAMPOS provided much of the subject matter for Puerto Rican graphic artists living in New York City. Puerto Rican art took two roads, one devoted to protest art (the war in Vietnam, social injustice, discrimination, racism) and another devoted to nationalistic art, celebrating the Puerto Rican identity and national heritage. Most of the art produced by Puerto Rican artists born in New York had a nationalistic subject matter, with an emphasis on rich color, movement, and dramatic lettering. Carlos Irizarry, a printmaker trained in New York, experimented with the development of photo silkscreen as an alternative to the traditional silkscreen technique.

Another pivotal force in the development of poster art in the continental United States was the Civil Rights movement. At the center of this movement was a rejection of the metaphor of the MELTING POT in favor of the concept of MULTICULTURALISM. As part of the struggle for recognition of the validity of their culture, Puerto Rican artists successfully brought their art back to their communities. They believed that art had to be made relevant to the common people, not only to the educated elite, the traditional patrons of the arts.

In 1974, a group of community activists established the Taller Areyto in Boston, Massachusetts, under the direction of actress Myrna Vázquez and Cristina Corrada, a former student of Irene Delano. José Delgado also established a workshop, Taller Tamíz, which produced an impressive collection of highly refined commercial and political posters and serigraphs.

The poster, because of its visual qualities and impact, has remained one of the preferred artistic media in the continental United States and throughout Latin America. It has been one of the most acclaimed art forms throughout the Americas.

—*Angel A. Amy Moreno de Toro*

SUGGESTED READINGS:
• Benítez, Marimar, ed. *Exposición retrospectiva de la obra de Lorenzo Homar*. Ponce, Puerto Rico: Museo de Arte de Ponce, 1978. An excellent study of the development of poster art in Puerto Rico through the perspective of one of the masters of the medium.
• Goldman, Shifra M. "Chicano Art of the Southwest in the Eighties." *Imagen* 3, no. 1-2 (1986): 42-50. A brief introduction to the state of Chicano fine arts in the United States.
• Rivera, Gregorio, and Edward Chávez. "Introduction, Arte Chicano: Window on the Hemisphere." *Imagen* 3, no. 1-2 (1986): 1-10. An overview of Chicano fine arts throughout the United States during the 1980's.
• Stermer, Dugald. *The Art of Revolution: Ninety-six Posters from Cuba*. London: Pall Mall Press, 1970. An early overview of the state of the Cuban revolutionary fine art poster. Includes a moving article by journalist Susan Sontag.
• Tío Fernández, Elsa. "Content and Context of the Puerto Rican Poster." In *The Poster in Puerto Rico, 1946-1985*. San Juan, Puerto Rico: SK&F, 1985. An excellent overview of the historical development of the Puerto Rican poster both on the island and in the continental United States.
• Weiss, Rachel, ed. *The Nearest Edge of the World: Art and Cuba Now*. Brookline, Mass.: Polarities, 1990. An excellent overview of the development of art in Cuba during the 1980's and 1990's.

Potatoes and sweet potatoes: American starchy roots. Although not closely related, potatoes and sweet potatoes are starchy roots and are used similarly in Latin American cooking. Both are native to the Americas, the sweet potato to the tropical lowlands of Central and South America and the potato to the Andean highlands. Potatoes are used sporadically in all Latin American cuisines, but they reach their pinnacle in Peru, where virtually any meal might feature one of the dozens of varieties in one of myriad dishes. Sweet potatoes are commonly used throughout Latin America, where they are eaten alone, made into desserts, used to accompany meats and poultry, or glazed.

Pottery and ceramics: Peoples of the Americas have used clay to make useful and decorative items since ancient times. The potter's wheel, introduced by Spaniards in the 1500's, drastically improved the possibilities of working with clay. Compared to those of other continents, the pottery and ceramics of South America are notably decorative and diverse.

Pottery. Mesoamerica discovered pottery before 1500 B.C.E. It was the single most necessary and important invention of the Preclassic period.

The Maya made pots for the storage and preparation of food and to contain their various necessities of life. They also made cache vessels and incense burners for sacrificial and ceremonial purposes. The form, technology, and decoration of Mayan pottery helps to determine relative dating of objects throughout the Preclassic era. Pottery is the central focus of archaeological research. It suggests how people lived and worshipped, and its frequent inclusion in burial sites tells of expectations in the afterlife.

Pottery was the greatest of pre-Columbian crafts. Ancient pottery utensils that are still used include the COMAL, which is a flat, round griddle for heating tortillas; a MOLCAJETE bowl, which has a roughened bottom for grating chili peppers and similar foods; and *pichanchas*, or colanders, for straining corn. Techniques and decorative styles are in some places as enduring as the form and function of the object.

Early artifacts were frequently fired indoors in the embers of a cooking stove. Potters needed very little equipment. They excavated clay and brought it home, dried it in the sun, and laboriously ground it into a powder. Next, it was mixed with water until the proper consistency was achieved, then kneaded by hand or trampled with bare feet. Large pots were made by coiling clay into long tubes and pressing the tubes together.

When Spaniards brought the spinning potter's wheel, techniques, aesthetics, and quality changed. Vessel walls became more contoured and evenly shaped. After a piece is shaped on the wheel, it is laid in the sun to dry, because going directly to the furnace would crack a pot. Then it is fired for about thirty minutes in a kiln. The hardened and brittle object is then left with its bricklike texture or is glazed and painted. Motifs of flowers, leaves, snakes, animals, and colorful lines have adorned pots for centuries.

Molds have been employed since pre-Conquest times. In this technique, flat sheets of clay are pressed onto or over a mold to be shaped. Rough or uneven areas are smoothed by hand or with a cloth.

Ceramics. Between 3000 and 2100 B.C.E., potters at Valdivia in Ecuador and Puerto Houmiga in Colombia were making ceramics. The Maya made elaborate ce-

ramic objects that served as offerings in burial sites. Painted ceramics help archaeologists to identify groups and distinguish them from others. The style of a ceramic piece may denote status in the community hierarchy and is a significant tool for scholars studying the patterns and symbols left by ancient cultures.

The introduction of Christian themes was a significant factor in the evolution of Latino ceramic figurines. After the SPANISH CONQUEST, representations of native gods were supplanted by images of the Virgin, saints, devils, and angels.

Twentieth century Mexican and Mexican American/ Hispanic figural ceramists often portray popular folk heroes such as Pancho VILLA and Emiliano ZAPATA, or clever mischievous animals from traditional fables. Sacred folk religious personages are depicted as well as memorable people from history or myth. Other fig-

A potter's wheel from the mission of San José de Tumacácori in Arizona. (Ruben G. Mendoza)

Hand-painted pottery remains popular in tourist-oriented locations. (Robert Fried)

ures depict men and women engaged in traditional activities that suggest the daily rhythm of village or city life: the tortilla maker, the bullfighter, the town drunk, the breast-feeding mother and child, the soldier, the nightclub dancers, the quarreling lovers, and the young bride and groom, as well as musicians, politicians, horsemen, and market vendors. The masked and costumed partygoer of the nineteenth century is often found among ceramic figurines.

In addition to sacred and secular scenes involving people, many ceramic figurines represent realistic or imaginary animals. Animals sometimes are depicted tricking people, such as a dog with ripped fabric in his mouth and a frightened man in a tree. Other ceramic objects take their inspiration from popular symbols or folktales, such as the intertwined eagle and snake, the kissing doves, and the gorgeous mermaid.

Ceramic items are made with tools and materials similar to those used in pottery. For more intricately shaped figures, two or more types of clay are often mixed to create the desired texture, porosity, and pliability. Then the mixed clay is submerged in large tanks of water to separate out the impurities. Each piece is thrown on a wheel or formed completely by hand or with delicate tools. It dries and hardens in an unventilated room. The piece is then baked once before being decorated over a base of white glaze. Although all colors of the spectrum are used, blues and yellows often predominate. *—Beaird Glover*

SUGGESTED READINGS: • Body, Elizabeth. *Popular Arts of Spanish New Mexico*. Santa Fe: Museum of New Mexico Press, 1974. • Graham, Joe S., ed. *Hecho en Tejas: Texas-Mexican Folk Arts and Crafts*. Denton: University of North Texas Press, 1991. • Kolb, Charles C., and Louana M. Lackey, eds. *A Pot for All Reasons: Ceramic Ecology Revisited*. Philadelphia, Pa.: Laboratory of Anthropology, Temple University, 1988. • Marken, Mitchell W. *Pottery from Spanish Shipwrecks*. Gainesville: University Press of Florida, 1994. • Panyella, August, ed. *Folk Art of the Americas*. New York: Harry N. Abrams, 1981. • Sayer, Chloë. *Arts and Crafts of Mexico*. San Francisco: Chronicle Books, 1990.

Pous, Arquímides (d. April, 1926, Mayagüez, Puerto Rico): Actor and playwright. Pous was a popular Cuban blackface comedian of the 1920's. In 1921, he organized the Compañía de Bufos Cubanos at New York's Leslie Theater. He created more than two hundred OBRAS BUFAS CUBANAS, social satires that strongly attacked racism in contemporary society, explored Afro-Cuban culture, and incorporated elements of Afro-Cuban music and religious belief. His works included *Pobre Papá Montero, Los mulatas de Bombay, El tabaquero, Amor tirano, La loca de la casa, La honradez de un obrero, La boda de Papá Montero, El velorio de Papá Montero, La clave de oro, El muerto vivo,* and *La huelga de hambre.* In addition to performing and writing in the live theater, Pous also was a recording artist with Columbia Records. In 1926, he was killed in a boating accident in Puerto Rico.

Poverty: By almost any measurable standard, Latinos tend to be economically disadvantaged. The Bureau of

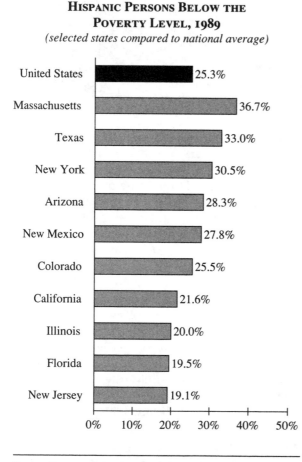

HISPANIC PERSONS BELOW THE POVERTY LEVEL, 1989

(selected states compared to national average)

State	Percent
United States	25.3%
Massachusetts	36.7%
Texas	33.0%
New York	30.5%
Arizona	28.3%
New Mexico	27.8%
Colorado	25.5%
California	21.6%
Illinois	20.0%
Florida	19.5%
New Jersey	19.1%

Source: Bureau of the Census, *1990 Census of Population and Housing: Persons in Poverty by Race for U.S. States* (Washington, D.C.: Government Printing Office, 1993), Figure 32.

the Census reports that economic gains many Hispanics made in the 1980's were eroded by the recession in 1990 and 1991. Although three-quarters of Latino families lived in relative comfort in American society in 1992, one in every four Latino families—and almost two of every five Latino children—were poor. Nearly 30 percent of Hispanics lived in poverty in 1982. The proportion declined to 26 percent in 1989 but had climbed back to nearly 30 percent by 1992. Employed Latinos are far more likely than other Americans to be among the working poor. The rate of poverty among Latinos in general grew far more rapidly in the late twentieth century than that of non-Hispanic whites or African Americans.

Generalizations about Latino poverty, especially in urban areas, refer essentially to two subgroups, Mexican Americans and mainland Puerto Ricans, who together account for roughly three-fourths of all Latinos living in the United States. Cuban Americans have the lowest poverty rate among Latino subgroups. For example, in 1990, poverty rates were 38 percent for Puerto Ricans, 25 percent for Mexican Americans, 22 percent for Central Americans and South Americans, and 14 percent for Cuban Americans.

There are also regional differences in Latino poverty rates. Among the ten states with the largest Latino populations, Massachusetts had the highest Latino poverty rate (37 percent) and New Jersey had the lowest (19 percent), followed closely by Florida and Illinois (20 percent). Latinos in Texas and New York had poverty rates of 33 percent and 31 percent, respectively.

Families in Poverty. Latino families are more likely than non-Latino families to live in poverty. In 1982, 27 percent of Latino families lived below the poverty level, compared to about 11 percent of non-Latino families. A decade later, the poverty rate for Latinos remained unchanged. According to census data, the median income of Hispanic households in 1992 was $22,859, about 69 percent of the median income of non-Hispanic white households. Latino children (those under eighteen years) also were more likely to be living in poverty: 40.7 percent of Latino children lived in poverty in 1991 compared to 19.6 percent of other children. Poverty is particularly likely for children who live in families with only one parent, especially if the parent is a single female.

Latino married-couple families with children have higher poverty rates than similar black or white families. In 1990, 21 percent of such Latino families were poor, compared to 14 percent of married-couple black

Two-parent households have a lower rate of poverty than do single-parent households. (Lester Sloan)

families and 7 percent of such white families. Although the income disparity between white and black married-couple families has lessened over time, the gap between white and Latino married-couple families has widened. Latino married-couple family income was 69 percent of white married-couple family income in 1990, down from 76 percent of white married-couple family income in 1981.

The dramatic rise in single-parent families has contributed to poverty in the Latino community. In 1990, about one-third of all Latino families were headed by a single parent, the great majority maintained by a woman. Comparable figures for single-parent families were 60 percent for blacks and 23 percent for whites. Between 1980 and 1990, the number of Latino single-parent families increased at annual rates greater than those for white or black families (7 percent, compared with 3 percent for whites and 4 percent for blacks).

Reasons for the high poverty rate among Latinos include discriminatory practices in the labor force, undereducation, concentration in low-paying jobs, early childbearing, and single-parent families. Many of these factors are interrelated. For example, having children

early makes it more difficult for young parents to continue their education, acquire job skills, and hold higher-paying jobs. These difficulties are compounded for single parents who have more pressures related to childcare. Generally speaking, higher economic status is correlated with the presence of two parents in the household.

Colonialism and Conquest. Among the historical explanations and contributing factors for poverty in the Latino community are colonialism, discrimination, and immigration.

Latinos in the United States trace their origin or descent to Spain and Portugal or to Mexico, Puerto Rico, Cuba, and other countries of Latin America. The Spanish settled North America long before the English, and many Latinos are descended from individuals who became U.S. citizens as a result of conquest during the mid-1800's. The United States invaded Mexico under the banner of MANIFEST DESTINY. After the MEXICAN AMERICAN WAR (1846-1848), land that was once part of Mexico (Texas, California, most of Arizona and New Mexico, and parts of Colorado, Utah, and Nevada) became territory of the United States.

POVERTY RATES FOR SELECTED LATINO GROUPS, 1990

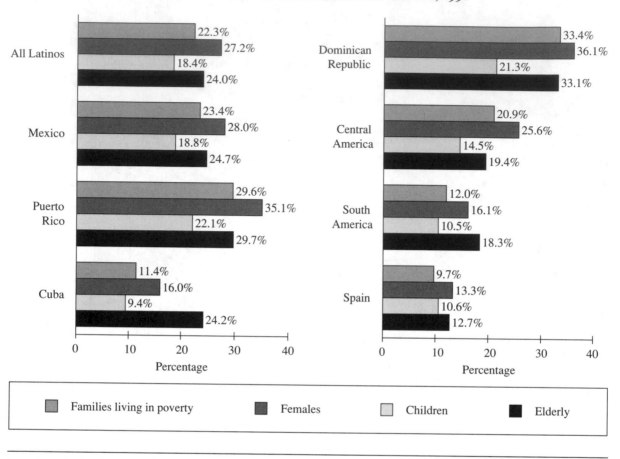

Source: *We the American . . . Hispanics* (Washington, D.C.: U.S. Bureau of the Census, 1993), Figure 16, p. 9.
Note: Groups are identified by country or region of background.

Although they were promised property rights by the TREATY OF GUADALUPE HIDALGO (1848), many Mexicans were forced off their property.

The poverty of many contemporary Mexican Americans can be traced to their history of colonialism and relationship to the United States. They were exploited on a large scale for both their land and their labor. In the Southwest of the 1820's and 1830's, there is evidence of relative equality and cooperation between Mexicans and Anglos, but this was soon to change. By the 1830's in Texas, conflict had already arisen over the role of the Mexican government. Many Texans, both Mexican and Anglos, favored a type of government not unlike the system of the United States. The Mexican government's 1829 decision to abolish slavery was unpopular with the many Anglos who migrated to Texas, many of whom were slave-owning cotton growers from the South.

In an effort to control the Texan dissidents, the Mexican government sent in its army. The dissidents responded by creating, for a short time, an independent nation. This encouraged Anglo migration from the United States. Anglo demands for land in Texas resulted almost overnight in gross social and economic inequalities between Mexicans and Anglos. Outnumbered by a ratio of five to one, most Mexicans were quickly deprived of their land, either by force or by American law.

As Mexican Americans were being displaced from their land by whites during the latter half of the nineteenth century, whites in the Southwest were developing an economic system built around mining, large-scale agriculture, and railroad transportation. These activities are highly labor intensive and depend on a large labor supply. Mexican Americans became the most important source of such labor. By the early twentieth century, Mexican American laborers were in a position only marginally better than that of slaves. They were generally restricted to low-paying, low-status jobs with long hours and poor living conditions. Anglos commonly believed that Mexican Americans were incapable of work other than unskilled labor or farm work. Many farmworkers spent the off-seasons in the city, working at low-skill jobs and living in the barrios. By the World War II period, a majority of Mexican Americans lived in urban areas, still in relative poverty.

Colonialism played a different role in the history of Puerto Rico and Cuba, with different implications for Latinos from those countries. Puerto Rico gained independence from Spain in 1898 but entered into a free association with the United States as a commonwealth. The United States continued to exert tremendous control over land, capital, and business enterprise on the island, angering those Puerto Ricans who favor independence. Although Puerto Ricans are U.S. citizens, they have no voting power in the U.S. Congress. Hundreds of thousands of Puerto Ricans began to migrate to the mainland in the 1940's for economic reasons but found that conditions were not much improved for them in American barrios. They remain the poorest of Latino subgroups.

Cuba, also a former Spanish colony gained by the United States in 1898, declared its independence in 1902. The socialist revolution of Fidel CASTRO in 1959 was in part an effort to rid the country of economic domination by U.S. interests. Shortly thereafter, the United States instituted an economic blockade against Cuba and cut off diplomatic relations. Large waves of political and economic refugees from Cuba fled to the United States beginning in the 1960's. Although Cuban Americans as a group are less likely than other Latinos to live in poverty, there are many poor people among later waves of Cuban exiles.

Discrimination. Another historical reason for Latino poverty is DISCRIMINATION. Colonialism often leads to an attitude of superiority of the colonizers toward the natives, which manifests itself in prejudice and discrimination. Such discrimination may take the form of violent expressions against the colonized people. After Mexican Americans were deprived of their land in the Southwest, racist practices continued. Lynching and murders of Mexican Americans by Anglos became so common in California and Texas that the Mexican ambassador formally protested such mistreatment in 1912. This brutality, in addition to their increasing poverty, led many Mexican Americans to a deep sense of alienation, distrust, and enmity toward the people who had taken their source of sustenance.

Discrimination can occur in more insidious and subtle ways when one group of people is exploited by another. Many times what starts out as a pact that seems beneficial to both parties may result in the deprivation of resources and civil liberties, contributing to deepening poverty and despair.

A case in point is the BRACERO PROGRAM. Because of the labor shortage during World War II, the U.S. government made an agreement with the Mexican government to supply temporary workers, known as braceros, for American agricultural work. The temporary workers were recruited by the United States from poorer central and southern areas such as Guanajuato, Michoacán, and Guerrero. The braceros wanted to come to the United States for the higher wages offered there. Some remained in the country, swelling the ranks of migrant farmworkers who follow the harvest of seasonal crops such as orchard fruits, melons, and truck vegetables. This nomadic lifestyle, with irregular school attendance for farmworkers' children, perpetuates a pattern of undereducation with serious consequences for their economic well-being. Migrant workers are among the poorest of the working poor in the United States.

Other flashpoints of discrimination have helped impoverish Latinos. These include prejudicial treatment of black Puerto Ricans and Cuban Americans, and the stereotyping of Mexican immigrants as illegal aliens, regardless of their actual status.

Immigration. Immigration to the United States often represents a move up to the land of opportunity. Many immigrants from Latin American countries, however, have not realized their dreams of improved economic status, particularly when they measure themselves by the cost of living in the United States or in terms of the American Dream.

Cuban Americans, the third largest Latino subgroup, arrived in great numbers shortly after the victory of the socialist revolution in Cuba in 1959. Many were prominent professionals and businesspeople in their native land and continued to prosper in the United States. The city of Miami owes its prosperity, to a large extent, to the early Cuban immigrants. These immigrants received refugee resettlement aid from the U.S. government and also brought their wealth and business skills. Later waves of Cuban immigrants were not so fortunate. In 1980, the MARIEL BOAT LIFT included many unskilled people who have had difficulty finding work in the United States.

At least 100,000 Puerto Ricans arrived in the mainland United States in 1944 as a result of OPERATION BOOTSTRAP, a program started by the Puerto Rican government. Puerto Rico wanted to reduce unemployment on the island, and the United States needed workers as a result of its wartime labor shortage. At the height of the program, 100,000 workers migrated each year to work in agriculture and canning operations, service industries, and manufacturing. These Puerto Ricans were, for the most part, unskilled, semiskilled, or skilled workers as opposed to professionals. Later arrivals fell into similar patterns. Lack of professional and technical skills, together with racial and ethnic discriminatory practices, helps explain why Puerto Ricans have the highest poverty rate of all Latinos.

Immigration can be especially difficult for Latinos who come to the United States lacking not only education and job skills but also knowledge of English. Language barriers make a new situation even more foreign and alienating. The high rate of immigration and the tendency to concentrate in Spanish-speaking barrios contribute to the high rate of limited English fluency among Latinos (39 percent in 1990). The problem is serious for schoolchildren, who may receive insufficient training in English or be mislabeled as "slow" because of their lack of English proficiency. These children tend to be the first to drop out of school, thus preventing further educational development to help them acquire marketable skills.

Low Educational Attainment. The causes of Latino poverty in the past led to a perpetuation of poverty in parts of the Latino community today. A root cause of contemporary poverty among Latinos is undereducation, which in turn leads to or is associated with concentration in low-paying jobs, early childbearing, and single-parent families. (*See* EDUCATION AND ACADEMIC ACHIEVEMENT.)

The average educational levels among Latinos are well below those of non-Latino whites. Latino children face special challenges in school if their parents are poorly educated, their families are poor, and their households primarily speak Spanish. Poor children

Skills in technology improve a worker's chances of finding a job with a high salary. (Impact Visuals, Mark Ludak)

often live in areas with schools that have substandard programs and facilities. Adding to problems of high dropout rates among Latino youth, many immigrants from Latin America arrive in the United States with only an elementary-level education.

In 1990, half of Latinos over twenty-five years of age had at least finished high school, compared to about three-quarters of non-Latinos, according to census data. Poverty rates are substantially higher among Hispanics who lack a high school diploma. The poverty rate for Latino household heads aged twenty-five and above who did not complete high school rose from 25.3 percent in 1978 to 36.3 percent in 1987. In 1990, more than one of every three Latino heads of household without a high school diploma lived in poverty. (*See* DROPOUTS AND DROPOUT RATES.)

Latinos with little education were at a far greater disadvantage in the late twentieth century than they were before World War II. More jobs require higher educational levels and an understanding of high technology, such as computers. The number of jobs for unskilled workers has declined with increasing automation, computerization, international competition, and the relocation of U.S. factories to other countries. These trends have had the most devastating impact on minorities, such as Latinos, who have been heavily concentrated in manufacturing jobs.

Problems in the Workplace. Latinos are more likely than other Americans to be among the working poor. This is a reflection of low education levels as well as discrimination in the workplace. It can also be traced to the undocumented status of some Latino immigrants, who have trouble finding stable or well-paying jobs. In large cities such as Los Angeles, both legal and undocumented Latinos work in the underground economy as housekeepers, nannies, gardeners, and day laborers who are paid in cash and have no benefits or job security. Latinos are also overrepresented in low-status, poorly paid employment such as in the hotel and restaurant service industries and agriculture.

Employment discrimination continues to be a cause of poverty among Latinos. Social researchers Alejandro PORTES and Cynthia Truelove have argued that high unemployment among mainland Puerto Ricans and low wages among Mexican Americans can be traced to economically motivated discriminatory practices on the part of employers. In the Northeast, employers avoid Puerto Rican workers in order to exercise their preference for the more easily exploitable labor of more recent immigrants, such as Dominicans and Colombians, and undocumented persons. In the Southwest, employers prefer Mexican American workers precisely because they represent the most exploitable labor force in that region.

According to the dual market theory, racial and ethnic minorities are intentionally relegated to the "secondary" sector of the labor market. This sector is characterized by unstable work with low pay and little room for advancement. Once started in this sector, workers tend to develop habits and attitudes that further erode their prospects for better employment.

The Culture of Poverty. The "culture of poverty" is another reason that is often cited for persistent poverty among Latinos. Anthropologist Oscar Lewis coined this term to refer to a way of life developed among some poor people in rural or urban slums. Lewis and other social scientists observed certain interrelated social, economic, and psychological traits among poor people of diverse racial and ethnic backgrounds in industrial, capitalist societies. Among these characteristics are rapid initiation into adulthood, the prevalence of female-headed households, and competition for limited goods.

Lewis argued that such cultural characteristics enable people to adapt to difficulties arising from poverty, while also making it harder for them to escape poverty. In this way, poverty is passed from generation to generation. By the time children are six or seven years old, they have usually absorbed the basic values and attitudes of the subculture of poverty. They may not be psychologically equipped to take full advantage of changing conditions or increased opportunities that may occur. Young poor Latinos are especially at risk of continuing in this culture of poverty because of their high dropout rate.

Some social researchers have criticized this theory for its tendency to "blame the victim," finding fault with the individual rather than with aspects of the system such as discrimination. Further, when poor people are blamed for their poverty, there is less effort on the part of institutions to rectify their policies and practices that contribute to poverty.

Another explanation of poverty among Latinos and other minorities relates to the availability of government assistance (welfare). Charles Murray has argued that the liberalization of welfare laws during the 1960's made work less beneficial, thus serving to encourage low-income people to avoid work and marriage in order to reap government benefits. He believes that poverty stopped decreasing at about the same time that social spending and the proportion of female-headed households began to increase. For example,

Barrios like this one in New York City offer affordable housing and can provide a network of support. (Hazel Hankin)

Puerto Ricans, who have the highest rate of participation in welfare programs among Latinos, also have higher proportions of families headed by women.

Coping with Poverty. Latinos may draw on aspects of the culture of poverty to adapt to their marginal position in a class-stratified, highly individuated, capitalist society. Carrying on this culture represents an effort to cope with feelings of hopelessness and despair about ever achieving success in the larger society. Through the culture of poverty, some Latinos find their own solutions to problems not addressed by existing institutions and agencies.

Other ways of coping with poverty involve dependence on family and community. Some Latinos rely on strong extended families for job referrals, financial support, and shared housing. It is often believed that the relatively low rate of homelessness among Latinos can be traced to the tendency of families to take care of their own, even with limited resources. Many Latinos live, by choice or by necessity, in barrios, surrounded by other Latinos. The barrio often provides a network of support amid a familiar language and culture. It also serves as an affordable first home for numerous immigrants. (*See* BARRIOS AND BARRIO LIFE.)

For some Latinos, migration is a way of life that is necessary in order to survive. For example, Puerto Ricans commonly shuttle back and forth between the mainland and the island according to the availability of jobs (*see* CIRCULAR MIGRATION). Mexican workers who cross the border illegally and are apprehended and returned to Mexico may soon become economically desperate enough to enter the United States again in search of work. Migrant farmworkers must follow the crop harvest from state to state if they are to feed their families. Although poor Latinos stay on the move in order to stay out of the direst poverty, migration also creates problems, such as undereducation of children, that perpetuate poverty.

Still more ways of coping with poverty include illegal activities, such as drug dealing, gang warfare, and theft. These strategies may be used by people who see no hope of acquiring what they want or even need for their daily sustenance.

Conclusion. The explanations provided above attempt to explain the causes and persistence of poverty among Latinos. Although not exhaustive, they are among the most influential arguments in contemporary public debate on poverty. Taken individually, they each have limitations in accounting for a complex phenomenon. Taken together, however, along with data on social indicators, these theories may lead to an understanding of the problem and potential solutions. If Latino poverty is ever to be addressed adequately, expanded employment opportunities, increased wages, security for those unable to work, and promotion of higher levels of human capital attainment are major public policy imperatives.

—*Maria Wilson-Figueroa*

SUGGESTED READINGS: • Conover, Ted. *Coyotes: A Journey Through the Secret World of America's Illegal Aliens.* New York: Vintage, 1987. • Farley, John E. *Majority-Minority Relations.* 2d ed. Englewood Cliffs, N.J.: Prentice Hall, 1988. • *Hispanic Americans Today.* Washington, D.C.: U.S. Department of Commerce, Bureau of the Census, 1993. • Miranda, Leticia, and Julia Teresa Quiroz. *The Decade of the Hispanic: An Economic Retrospective.* Washington, D.C.: National Council of La Raza, Policy Analysis Center, 1990. • Moore, Joan, and Raquel Pinderhughes. *In the Barrios: Latinos and the Underclass Debate.* New York: Russell Sage Foundation, 1993. • Morales, Rebecca, and Frank Bonilla. *Latinos in a Changing U.S. Economy: Comparative Perspectives on Growing Inequality.* Newbury Park, Calif.: Sage Publications, 1993. • Shorris, Earl. *Latinos: A Biography of the People.* New York: W. W. Norton, 1992. • Sotomayor, Marta. *Empowering Hispanic Families: A Critical Issue for the '90's.* Milwaukee: Family Service America, 1991.

Pozo y Gonzáles, Luciano "Chano" (Jan. 7, 1915, Havana, Cuba—Dec. 2, 1948, New York, N.Y.): Musician. Pozo's musical roots can be traced to Nigeria. His artistic collaboration with musician Dizzy Gillespie began in 1947, when he participated in a concert at Carnegie Hall. This concert marked the first time that a serious attempt had been made to fuse elements of jazz and Latin music. Together, Pozo and Gillespie altered the history of jazz. They made several recordings, including well-known versions of "Manteca," "Cubana Be, Cubana Bop," and "Afro-Cuban Suite."

Gillespie's memoirs *To Be or Not to Bop* (1979) contain anecdotes about his close musical friendship with Pozo and their common interests in Latin music. Gillespie made Pozo, a percussionist, a hero of the early "Cubop" movement. Pozo's virtuosic cross-rhythmic playing and singing style were admired by all who heard him perform. Pozo was murdered in a bar in Harlem, New York.

Prado, Pedro (Oct. 8, 1886, Santiago, Chile—Jan. 31, 1952, Viña del Mar, Chile): Writer. Prado completed his secondary studies at the prestigious Instituto Nacional of Santiago and then enrolled at the Esquela de Ingeniería of the University of Chile. He never completed his university studies, but he did practice as an architect, distinguishing himself as the designer of the building later occupied by the United States Consulate in Santiago.

As a poet, Prado is usually considered a postmodernist. In his initial books he used free verse. His most lasting poetry, however, was written in sonnet form and collected in *Camino de las horas* (1934) and *No más que una rosa* (1946). Prado is sometimes referred to as one of the finest sonnetists in the Spanish language. A book published in 1949 under the title *Viejos poemas inéditos* is a forerunner of Pablo Neruda's *Viente poemas de amor y una canción desesperada* (1924).

Of Prado's published novels, two are most representative of his narrative art at its best: *Alsino* (1920) and *Un juez rural* (1924). Considering the whole of his work in the context of Latin American literature of the first half of the twentieth century, Prado must be considered one of the greatest prose writers of the modernist movement.

Prado, Pérez (Nov. 13, 1922, Matanzas, Cuba—Dec. 4, 1983, Mexico City, Mexico): Pianist, arranger, and bandleader. Prado began his career playing the piano and organ in cinemas and nightclubs in Havana, Cuba. In the 1940's, he joined the Orquesta Casino de la Playa as a pianist. This was the true start of his successful musical career.

Between 1942 and 1948, Prado became a popular arranger for the local mambo-style bands. He is credited in large part with making this dance form as popular as it was.

Seeking better musical opportunities, he moved to Mexico and recorded for RCA Mexico City Studios. These recordings were targeted to the Latin market in the United States, but soon "Mambo No. 5" and "Caballo Negro" picked up crossover sales. The MAMBO craze in the United States reached its peak in the mid-1950's, and although there were many other Latin mambo musicians, Prado was the best known because he made his music arrangements more accessible to large non-Latin American audiences.

Prado's 1955 mambo "Cherry Pink and Apple Blossom White" is considered his most original and biggest crossover hit. This song, together with other hits including "Patricia" (1958), "Guaglione" (1958), and "Patricia Twist" (1962), earned for him the title "el rey del mambo," or "king of the mambo."

Pérez Prado. (AP/Wide World Photos)

Pregnancy and prenatal care: Pregnancy is divided into three periods, or trimesters, of three months each for health care purposes. Prenatal care is defined as health treatment, prevention, and education during pregnancy.

According to U.S. Census reports, during 1990, 16.8 percent of all Hispanic births were to teenage mothers. This was higher than the 10.9 percent for whites but less than the 23.1 percent for African Americans. Puerto Ricans had the highest rate among Latinos at 21.7 percent; Mexican Americans were next at 17.7 percent. The rate was lowest for Cuban Americans at 7.7 percent. Education, economic factors, and availability of birth control contributed to the wide differences in rates of teenage pregnancy.

Prenatal care data also show diversity. During the first trimester, 77.7 percent of pregnant white women received prenatal care. The rates were 60.7 percent for African Americans and 60.2 percent for Hispanics. Among Hispanics, rates were 57.8 percent for Mexican Americans, 63.5 percent for Puerto Ricans, and 84.8 percent for Cuban Americans. The differences in rates may result in large part from differences in availability of care for low-income groups. Some reports suggest that Hispanic women often discontinue prenatal care visits when they feel healthy and that they are accustomed to using medical professionals for crisis intervention rather than for preventive care.

The percentages of Hispanic mothers who did not begin prenatal care until the third trimester or had no care were higher than for whites and blacks. The differences were probably related to economic factors.

When teenage pregnancy rates and prenatal care rates are correlated with low birth weights, some surprising differences are noted. Rates of low birth weight are lower than expected for all Hispanic groups except Cuban Americans. For example, black and Hispanic mothers had similar proportions receiving prenatal care, but only 6.1 percent of Hispanic babies had low birth weights, compared to 13.3 percent of black babies. The rate of low birth weights for Puerto Ricans was higher than for other Latino groups. The reasons for the difference are not clearly understood but may include cultural factors such as diet and family support.

Hispanic women have a surprisingly low rate of low birth weight babies considering their relative lack of prenatal care. Prenatal care is of utmost importance for all women, however, especially those with underlying health conditions. Early diagnosis of health problems in the mother is an essential part of prevention of health problems in babies. Prenatal care also provides

PERCENTAGE OF BABIES BORN TO WOMEN WHO RECEIVED EARLY PRENATAL CARE, 1986

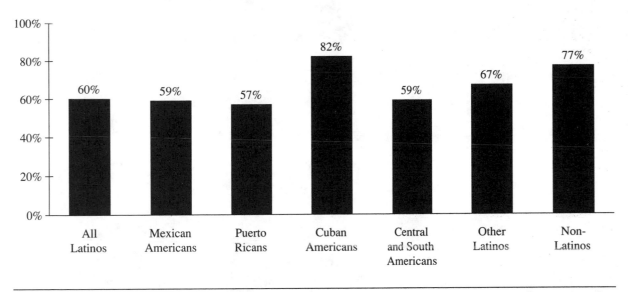

Source: Data are from Marlita A. Reddy, ed., *Statistical Record of Hispanic Americans* (Detroit: Gale Research, 1993), Table 460.

a good opportunity for education of mothers about proper care for themselves and for their babies.

Prejudice. *See* **Discrimination, bigotry, and prejudice against Latinos**

Premio Quinto Sol: National award. The Premio Quinto Sol is a national award for the best book of Chicano literature. It was established in 1970 under the sponsorship of QUINTO SOL PUBLICATIONS. The first independent Chicano publishing house in the United States, Quinto Sol Publications was established by Octavio ROMANO-V., cofounder of *El Grito: A Journal of Contemporary Mexican-American Thought*. The first writer to receive the award was Tomás Rivera, for his *. . . y no se lo tragó la tierra* (1971; *. . . and the Earth Did Not Part*, 1971). Other recipients include Rudolfo ANAYA and Rolando HINOJOSA. The prize was awarded for the last time in 1974.

Presbyterian church: The Presbyterian church offered Latinos in the southwestern United States their first real alternative to Catholicism. The greatest influence of the church was in the late 1800's. Within two years of Texas' declaration of independence from Mexico in 1835, the Cumberland Presbyterians had organized the Texas Presbytery. Soon the Presbyterian church moved westward and established its first stronghold among Latinos.

The Catholic ministers of northern New Mexico charged high fees for weddings, funerals, and baptisms. People who could not afford to pay the exorbitant rates were forced to do without these ceremonies. When Presbyterians arrived and offered the same services at lower prices, many people adopted the Protestant Presbyterian faith.

The Presbyterians realized their opportunity to convert the Latinos of the vast Southwest. Progress was slow at first. Latinos saw the newcomers as being pushy and brash, impersonal, and legalistic; the Presbyterians thought the Latinos were lazy, superstitious, poor, and ignorant. As an added difficulty, the New Mexicans did not appreciate or value Protestantism or the English language.

Presbyterians set up a mission in New Mexico, then developed an extensive school system with plaza schools and two high schools—one for men and one for women. They also built a college in Del Norte, Colorado.

Between 1867 and 1890, the Presbyterians founded forty-seven schools, thirty-seven of which were still open in 1890. They were more successful than Methodists, Baptists, and other Protestant faiths because they built schools first and organized congregations later. While the Presbyterians were building so many schools, they built only thirteen churches.

By 1910, there were eleven hundred Presbyterians in New Mexico. The Catholic church then reemerged,

Latinos attend a Pentecostal revival in Washington, D.C. (Impact Visuals, Shia Photo)

and many new Pentecostal churches entered the scene. The Pentecostal church appealed to people on the margins of American society who had little or no control of their destinies. The revival, instrumental in their services, involved emotional, unrestrained, uninhibited behavior. This symbolized the plight of the dispossessed people who lived on the American frontier.

In the same way that Presbyterians had given Latinos what they needed in the late 1800's, the Pentecostals ministered to their needs in the early 1900's. The Presbyterian church began to decline.

Presbyterians closed many schools before 1920. They then reorganized and began to do more medical and community service work. Their efforts produced a slight recovery in Presbyterian membership.

During the Depression of the 1930's, many Latinos returned to Mexico from the Southwest, hurting the Presbyterian church's membership. World War II further eroded its membership.

By the 1950's, Presbyterian missions were being built in the eastern sector of the United States for Puerto Ricans. In the Southwest, the influence of the Presbyterian church declined. Latinos were not getting adequate funding for church development or for scholarships for minority students, nor were they included in the decision-making processes that would affect them.

Presidio system: Important frontier institution of the Spanish colonial era in northern Mexico and the American Southwest. Initially a military installation, the presidio later implied a loose military, imperial, and civil relationship in a fortified settlement. From its beginning as a simple garrisoned fort, the presidio evolved to become the center of a civilian town, a market for the produce of neighboring ranches and farms, and an agency for an Indian reservation.

The first presidios were established by Viceroy Martín Enríquez during the 1570's to protect highways and mining communities. For example, he situated five presidios along the highway from Mexico City to the silver mines in Zacatecas. Between 1580 and 1600, the last two decades of the Chichimeco War, at least fifteen other presidios were added. These early presidios were often small garrisons of four or five armed men.

As Indian tribes became a growing threat, military protection increased to two dozen or so men on active duty under a commanding officer. In succeeding years, the number of men at a presidio increased to about fifty, depending on need. As other European nations threatened to extend their reach in North America, the presidio gained importance in ensuring Spanish occupation and retention of the southwestern region.

The presidio at Monterey, California, about 1791. (Museum of New Mexico)

Architecturally, presidios resembled their prototypes in Spanish Morocco, with walled enclosures, commanding towers, and embrasures for cannons, all designed to defend and protect Spanish civilization and Christianity from surrounding alien and "pagan" influences. Although presidios were often plagued by inadequate equipment and poorly trained garrison soldiers, making them inefficient means of defense, they did a remarkable job of securing the advance line of occupation.

Intermittent hostility between the Spaniards and the Indians characterized most of the seventeenth century. As a result, at least seven presidios were established in the highlands of New Vizcaya (at Guanacevi, Guazamota, Santa Catalina, and Cerrogordo), in the Pacific Slope (Montesclaro), and in the newly organized province of Nuevo León (Cerralvo and Cadereita). To cope with the spreading hostility caused by the Pueblo Revolt of 1680 in New Mexico, the Spaniards again relied on presidios. El Paso del Norte was created in 1683; El Pasaje, El Gallo, and Conchos in 1685; Casas Grandes in 1686; Janos about 1691; Fronteras in 1692; and Tucson in 1776. Fear of French incursions made Spain turn to Texas and establish presidios at San Juan Bautista (1703), San Antonio (1718), Los Adaes (1721) opposite the French post of Natchtoches, and La Bahía (1722). The threat of Russian occupation and maritime invasions of European nations encouraged establishment of presidios in Alta California. Major presidios were established at San Diego, Monterey, and San Francisco, but these presidios were aimed at forestalling invasion rather than protecting settlements against Indian attack.

Prida, Dolores (b. Sept. 5, 1943, Caibarién, Cuba): Writer. In 1961, Prida left Cuba with her family and settled in New York. She studied at Hunter College with a major in Spanish American literature. Between 1960 and 1970 she was an international correspondent for Collier-Macmillan International. She then worked as an assistant editor for Simon and Schuster's international dictionary. She edited a Spanish-language daily newspaper, then worked as an arts and sciences editor in London. She continued that work in New York, for *Visión* as well as for several other literary publications.

Her first play, *Beautiful Señoritas* (pb. 1991), was produced in New York in 1977. In 1980, she presented *La era latina*, a bilingual musical comedy cowritten with Victor Fragoso. Aside from her many plays, which have been performed in New York, Puerto Rico, Venezuela, and the Dominican Republic, Prida has also published poetry, including *Treinta y un poemas* (1967) and *Women of the Hour* (1971), and cowritten a full-length screenplay, *The Spring of the Tiger*. Prida's poetic and dramatic production are related in their use of bilingualism and in their attempt to present the problems of women in contemporary society.

Primer Congreso Mexicanista (September, 1911): Meeting to discuss cultural and social advancement. In mid-September, 1911, Texas newspaper editor Clemente Idar called for a conference of Mexican American leaders from around the United States to address problems of discrimination, lynching, and the decline of Hispanic culture and language in the United States. The call came after a series of violent attacks, including several lynchings and murders, against Mexicans in the Rio Grande Valley. The victims were supporters of the Mexican Revolution; Anglo farmers in the area were afraid they were spreading radical ideas among migrant farmworkers.

The Primer Congreso Mexicanista, held in Laredo, Texas, had representatives from across the Southwest, but a majority of the delegates came from Texas. They created the Gran Liga Mexicanista, which stressed cultural nationalism and downplayed economic issues. Liga president Idar raised money to support presentations of Spanish-language plays and music. The group promoted lectures on Mexican history and called for celebration of traditional Mexican holidays. A woman's auxiliary, the Liga Femenil Mexicanista, was also founded. Financial problems resulted in short lives for both groups.

Primer Encuentro Nacional Hispano (1971-1977): Meetings of Hispanic Catholic leaders. The *encuentro* consisted of a series of meetings called by the National Conference of Catholic Bishops, Office of the Secretariat of Hispanic Affairs. Hispanic Catholic leaders met in an "encounter" in Washington, D.C., to work within the Roman Catholic church in support of political and social rights for the poor, of whom many were Latinos. The church, it was decided, should be on the side of the oppressed, fighting discrimination and improving opportunities in employment and education. A center to protect the rights of UNAUTHORIZED WORKERS was established, and programs of BILINGUAL EDUCATION were begun.

Priests and lay Catholics had to fight traditional attitudes of fatalism, or accepting things as they are, that afflicted the Latino community and convince people that things could get better through united community action. The *encuentro* brought many Latino bishops and priests from across the United States together for the first time. Many became influential leaders in the campaign for social justice for the residents of barrios.

Prinze, Freddie (June 22, 1954, New York, N.Y.—Jan. 28, 1977, Los Angeles, Calif.): Actor. Son of a Puerto Rican mother and Hungarian Jewish father, Prinze referred to himself as a "Hungarican." He grew up in the Washington Heights section of Manhattan and studied ballet and drama at New York City's High School for the Performing Arts. There, he delighted audiences by transforming the character of a Jewish repairman in Neil Simon's *Barefoot in the Park* into a Puerto Rican.

Becoming aware of his penchant for provocative, ethnic-based comedy, Prinze began appearing as an amateur at New York's stand-up comedy clubs. After making appearances on *The Jack Paar Show* and *The Tonight Show*, Prinze in 1974 was given the starring role in the television series *Chico and the Man*, in which he played a streetwise, smart-talking Chicano youth working for a bigoted garage owner in East Los Angeles. The program was an immediate success, moving quickly into the top ratings bracket. Prinze and costar Jack Albertson were praised for their individual comic abilities and their smooth collaboration. The show also became a target of activists offended by stereotypical, anti-Hispanic views freely espoused by Albertson's character. In 1977, Prinze died at the age of twenty-two in a shooting accident that may have been a suicide.

Proposition 187: California ballot initiative. On November 8, 1994, 59 percent of California voters cast approval of Proposition 187, a controversial ballot initiative regulating provision of government services to undocumented residents of the United States. The day after the election, Superior Court Judge Stuart R. Pollak ordered that the initiative's ban on providing elementary, secondary, and postsecondary education to undocumented persons be blocked. That ruling came in response to lawsuits filed by the Los Angeles Unified School District and other school boards and individuals.

Although California's Proposition 187 addressed all undocumented residents, Latinos, particularly Mexican Americans, most strongly resisted the measure. (Tony Cuevas)

In mid-November, U.S. District Judge W. Matthew Byrne, Jr., issued a temporary restraining order halting implementation of all portions of the ballot measure except sanctions against the sale and use of fraudulent citizenship documents. In December, as that restraining order was about to expire, U.S. District Judge Mariana R. Pfaelzer prohibited most key provisions of the ballot initiative from being implemented until a trial was held to determine the constitutionality of the initiative.

In her ruling, Pfaelzer noted that the measure's education, law enforcement, social welfare, and health care bans raise constitutional questions and practical issues. Included among the practical issues is that undocumented persons would be prohibited from obtaining free immunizations and other nonemergency care. This might put undocumented persons at a higher risk for illness as well as exposing other people to greater risks from contagious diseases.

Pfaelzer barred implementation of a portion of the measure that would require law enforcement officials to verify the legal status of any person arrested, then to notify those suspected of being in the country illegally that they must acquire legal status or leave the country. Also blocked were requirements that educators, social workers, and health administrators ask the people they serve about residency status and report suspects to the police. Pfaelzer did not block a portion of the initiative that would exclude illegal residents from public colleges and universities, but that section was already stalled because of a separate lawsuit.

Perhaps the most controversial portion of the initiative pertained to public education. If implemented, the initiative in effect would overturn the Supreme Court decision in *PLYLER V. DOE*. In that case, the Court had ruled that undocumented children in Texas were entitled to a free public education.

Also at issue was California's right to regulate provision of social services, many of which are provided through federal funding. Some federal programs base funding on the number of clients served; if Proposition 187 were found to be constitutional and implemented, California thus could face reductions in federal funds of as much as $15 billion. Critics of the proposition questioned whether California could assert the right to regulate provision of some programs, because the federal government has already set eligibility criteria. In addition, portions of the proposition appear to establish a state program for regulating immigration. Regulation of immigration is clearly defined as a power of the federal government.

California contains about 40 percent of the estimated 3.4 million undocumented residents of the United States. Some political analysts have suggested that California voters wanted to send a message to the federal government that illegal immigration is a problem deserving of attention. They therefore voted for Proposition 187 as a means of communication, not because they believed it was the best solution or was even likely to be implemented. Campaigning for the proposition created the impression that undocumented residents would be cut off from receiving welfare payments; in fact, they already were ineligible.

Although Proposition 187 applies to all undocumented residents, Latino rights groups provided the strongest opposition to the measure. A large part of California's population of undocumented residents is Latino, and campaigning for and against the proposition centered on illegal immigration across the Mexican border.

Prostitution: Although prostitution is considered a criminal activity in most parts of the country, the laws are not always enforced. Prostitution, especially in large cities, is most often practiced in areas where murder, robbery, and other serious crimes are common; police attention focuses on these crimes rather than on prostitution.

Arrests made and surveys of populations indicate that Latinos engage in prostitution in numbers far out of proportion to their representation in the population. Part of the reason is economic. Latinos as a group are among the poorest people in the United States, and Latinos figure disproportionately among those living in poverty.

Prostitution requires no formal education and little command of the English language. It can pay well, and where it is illegal, it is not subject to taxes. Prostitutes may collect welfare and other government benefits. Prostitution attracts undocumented residents because there is no employer to demand proof of citizenship.

Drug use is also a factor. Illegal drugs are expensive, and an addiction cannot be financed with welfare checks. Drug use is believed to lead to a large proportion of crimes, particularly among the poor. A young woman is much less likely to be successful at robbery or violent crime than is a man; prostitution is relatively safe.

Prostitution is one of a number of "victimless" crimes that have long been a subject of controversy. Many people believe that if a man wishes to pay for sex and a woman wishes to engage in sex for payment, this should not be a concern of law enforcement.

(Women make up an overwhelming percentage of prostitutes and men an overwhelming proportion of clients.) Others, however, have pointed out the dangers of spreading disease. This concern intensified with the emergence of AIDS, which is far more prevalent among minorities than in the population as a whole.

Some attempts have been made to educate people about the dangers involved in unsafe sex. Those at the low end of the economic scale, the most likely to resort to prostitution as a means of support, also tend to be the least educated. A common view among sociologists is that prostitution can be eliminated or seriously reduced only if the economic problems leading to it are more effectively addressed.

Protestantism: A major form of Christianity, Protestantism derives from groups that separated themselves from the Roman Catholic church beginning in the sixteenth century, particularly in Central and Northern Europe and in England.

Principal Features and Groups. Although Protestants can hold a wide variety of beliefs, common ones include the use of the Bible as the only source of authority, salvation through faith alone, the priesthood of all believers, and, in most cases, the elimination of the cult of the saints and the Virgin Mary. Major Protestant denominations include Episcopalians, Presbyterians, Baptists, Methodists, Lutherans, and various Pentecostal groups.

History and Profile Among Hispanics. The fact that Catholicism was the official religion of Spain and its empire in Latin America explains the relative insignificance of Protestantism among Latin Americans for most of the last five hundred years. Even at the beginning of the twentieth century, there were only a few Protestant churches (especially Episcopalian, Presbyterian, and Methodist) in Latin America.

Mexicans living in what became the American Southwest were among the first Latin Americans to interact at a significant level with Protestants, and particularly with Protestant Anglo settlers in Texas. The end of the Mexican American War in 1848 provided a new impetus for the work of Protestant missionaries, who sometimes saw the conversion of Mexican Americans as an initial step toward the conversion of Mexico to Protestantism.

Protestants believe in the Bible as the sole religious authority. (Gail Denham)

This Methodist church in the Olvera Street district of Los Angeles, California, has a predominantly Latino congregation. (Martin Hutner)

One of the first missionaries to work with Mexican Americans was Melinda Rankin, a New England Presbyterian. Ambrosio Gonzalez, the first recorded convert in New Mexico, was gained by the Methodist Episcopal Church in the 1850's. Reies López TIJERINA (Pentecostal) and Rodolfo "Corky" GONZÁLES (Presbyterian) have been among the most notable Protestant Chicano political leaders in recent decades. Some surveys estimate that about 15.5 percent of Mexican Americans born in the United States are Protestant, compared to 8.4 percent of those immigrating from Mexico.

Protestantism made its first significant inroads into Puerto Rico after the United States gained control of the island in the aftermath of the SPANISH-AMERICAN WAR of 1898. By around 1910, Protestants had some fifteen missionary societies, 120 churches, and 326 missions in Puerto Rico. These developments have influenced the rise of Protestantism among Puerto Ricans who have moved to the mainland, particularly since 1950. Some scholars estimate that 15 percent of Puerto Ricans in New York are Protestant, with Pentecostal varieties being dominant. Other surveys estimate that 20.7 percent of Puerto Ricans born on the U.S. mainland are Protestant.

Although Episcopalians were active in Cuba in the middle of the nineteenth century, Protestantism in Cuba became significant after the Spanish-American War. Many Cubans who moved to the United States converted to Protestantism and returned as missionaries to Cuba. Some scholars estimate that 5 percent of the Cuban population was Protestant by the beginning of the Fidel Castro regime in 1959. The Castro revolution had a negative effect on Protestants but did not eliminate them completely. Many exiles established Protestant churches in the United States, especially in Miami. About 14 percent of Cuban Americans are Protestant.

Although some studies cite a strong continuity in Catholic affiliation among Latinos in some local areas (for example, Austin, Texas), Andrew Greeley estimates that some sixty thousand persons per year shift from Catholicism to Protestantism. The rate of Latino conversion to Protestantism is highest among Puerto Ricans. The Southern Baptist Convention alone has an estimated fifteen hundred Hispanic congregations and adds about 150 per year. According to polls, about 18 percent of Hispanics are Protestant. About 2 percent of Hispanics are Baptists, 2 percent are Methodists, and 5 percent belong to the Christian Church (Disciples of Christ).

The general profile of Hispanic Protestants provided by Greeley shows an average yearly income of about $25,000, compared with $19,000 per year for Catholic Hispanics. Hispanic Protestants have an average education of 10.8 years, while Hispanic Catholics average 10.4 years. Second-generation Protestants have an average income of $27,000 per year and have an average education of 11.3 years.

Reasons for "Protestantization." There is no single reason for the shift to Protestantism. Many Mexican immigrants to the United States brought anticlerical sentiments acquired in Mexico. Hispanics in the United States often felt alienated from an American brand of Catholicism that was not willing to adjust to their cultural distinctiveness. Protestant churches were often willing to train and provide Hispanic ministers for Hispanic congregations, even while trying to "Americanize" them. Becoming a Catholic priest can be a lengthy process, but Protestant ministry and leadership can be achieved relatively quickly. Switching to Protestantism also may be part of assimilation to American culture, which is perceived to be predominantly Protestant. Moreover, Protestants may use aggressive methods of proselytizing that cater to social needs.

Trends. Although Protestantism among Latinos in the United States is not monolithic, many scholars see the movement away from Anglo denominational hierarchies as a significant trend. The Assemblies of God and other denominations have large Spanish divisions managed almost entirely by Hispanic ministers. Some churches have always been exclusively in the hands of Latinos (for example, the Puerto Rican Assembly of Christian Churches). Increasing participation by women is expected in most denominations. Central and South American immigrants, particularly from Honduras and Guatemala, may add significantly to the proportion of Hispanic Protestants in the United States.

Latino Protestants are also affecting Catholic policy, and two principal paradoxical responses have resulted from this influence. One is a counteroffensive to stop the shift to Protestantism, reflected in the National Pastoral Plan for Hispanic Ministry approved by the U.S. bishops in 1987. The other response is a type of ecumenism that acknowledges the future vitality of Hispanic Protestantism and stresses common interests among Latinos of various religious traditions.

—Hector Ignacio Avalos
SUGGESTED READINGS: • Crocker, Ruth Hutchinson. "Gary Mexicans and 'Christian Americanization': A Study in Cultural Conflict." In *Forging a Commu-*

nity: The Latino Experience in Northwest Indiana 1919-1975, edited by James B. Lane and Edward J. Escobar. Chicago: Cattails Press, 1987. ● De la Garza, Rodolfo, et al. *Latino Voices: Mexican, Puerto Rican, and Cuban Perspectives on American Politics*. Boulder, Colo.: Westview Press, 1992. ● Gallup, George, and Jim Castelli. *The People's Religion: American Faith in the Nineties*. New York: Macmillan, 1989. ● Gonzalez, Justo L. *Mañana: Christian Theology from a Hispanic Perspective*. Nashville, Tenn.: Abingdon, 1990. ● Greeley, Andrew. "Defection Among Hispanics." *America* 159 (July 30, 1988): 61-62. ● Sandoval, Moises. *On the Move: A History of the Hispanic Church in the United States*. Maryknoll, N.Y.: Orbis Books, 1990.

Public Law 78 (1951): Law extending the BRACERO PROGRAM. Also known as the Migratory Labor Agreement of 1951, this legislation was proposed in Congress to allow for the importation of bracero workers from Mexico. Its sponsors claimed to be acting to meet the increased need for workers in the wake of the Korean War and the continuing demand for agricultural workers in the Southwest. The secretary of labor was directed to certify this need for workers; to arrange for recruiting, transportation, and processing of workers; and to assist in negotiating contracts between workers and employers. The department was also authorized to enforce compliance with contract provisions.

Although many labor organizations and Mexican American social organizations protested the lack of guarantees for workers, the law was renewed until 1964, when it was allowed to lapse. Employers also had become dissatisfied with the provisions of the program. Both sides were in favor of the adoption of laws that would make it easier for temporary laborers to find jobs in the United States.

Pueblo: Township or village. Patterned after the Spanish town model, this type of settlement influenced the early pattern of settlement and urban growth of Mexican American communities in the United States. Many cities and areas in the Southwest that were first settled by Mexicans follow patterns quite different from those of areas occupied by other groups. Following the Spanish pattern, these communities were organized around central plazas, which later became business districts. Other settlements copying the pueblo model began as agricultural labor communities.

Puente, Tito (Ernesto Antonio Puente; b. Apr. 20, 1923, New York, N.Y.): Percussionist and bandleader. Born to Puerto Rican parents, Puente studied the piano as a child. He later studied composition, orchestration,

Tito Puente. (Hazel Hankin)

and piano at the Juilliard School of Music and the New York School of Music.

Around 1936, he joined the Noro MORALES orchestra and started his professional career. In the 1940's, Tito and his band Picadilly Boys started touring and recording for RCA.

Dance Mania (1958) is still considered one of the finest among Puente's more than one hundred albums. As an arranger, composer, producer, and showman, Puente has reached the highest position among American musicians. Many of his works have become classics.

In the 1960's, Puente wrote PACHANGAS and *bugalús*, and in the 1970's and 1980's he became directly involved with the SALSA movement. He has won numerous awards, including a Grammy, and he celebrated his one hundredth album with *The Mambo King: 100th LP* in 1991. The quality of his work and his collaborations with some of the greatest American and Latin musicians should not be underestimated.

Puerto Rican Association for Community Affairs: Cultural preservation group. Founded in 1953 under the name Hispanic Young Adults Association, the association had a 1994 membership of about 150, a staff of 100, and an annual budget of $5 million. Its main objective is to preserve Puerto Rican language, history, art, and culture. The group also works to develop self-esteem among Puerto Ricans and create awareness of self inside and outside the Puerto Rican community. Another goal is to develop leadership potential within the Puerto Rican community and advocate for human rights and civil liberties.

The organization works toward its objectives in various ways, including sharing resources with other Puerto Rican organizations in the United States and a foster parents and adoption program (Criemos Los Nuestros) designed to provide services to Puerto Rican and other Latino children. During the early 1990's, the group operated an emergency boardinghouse to protect children during temporary crisis situations, a day care center with a bilingual and bicultural curriculum, and after-school programs. It also sponsored day care services for homeless families and provided medical, dental, and psychiatric services as well as an alternative high school for dropouts.

Puerto Rican Bar Association: Professional association. Founded in 1957, this group of Puerto Rican and Hispanic attorneys is also known as Asociación de Abogados Puertorriqueños. As of 1992, membership was approximately three hundred. The group was founded with the goals of increasing opportunities for Puerto Rican and Hispanic attorneys and encouraging Hispanic youngsters to seek careers in the legal professions. It offered scholarships to promising Hispanic students. The organization had committees on educational issues, judiciary issues, and scholarships.

Puerto Rican Community Development Project (New York, N.Y.): Program to aid the Puerto Rican community. The project was established in about 1964 by Antonio PANTOJA, a Puerto Rican intellectual and activist. It was proposed by the National Puerto Rican Forum, an organization formed to deal with Puerto Ricans' poor economic condition in New York City. The project sought to improve the education levels, income, family life, culture, and organizational strength of the New York Puerto Rican community through an organization created and administered by Puerto Ricans. For each program designed, it created a separate board of directors to maximize community participation. Some project officials were bothered by this bureaucracy and other conflicts in policies and goals, leading to internal problems. In spite of this, the project continued and was important both in organizational history in the Puerto Rican community and for having started several programs that still serve the community, such as ASPIRA.

Puerto Rican Dance Theatre: Dance company and school. This dance company was founded in 1970 by dancer Julio Torres, a Puerto Rican New Yorker. Torres combined African and flamenco styles with classical techniques to produce a unique genre of dance. He founded two Puerto Rican Dance Theatre schools in New York City, in Manhattan and the Bronx. The Manhattan school continued into the 1990's. The company has trained thousands of young students recruited from Latino neighborhoods at auditions. It offers classes in Latin dance as well as ballet and performs at schools, theaters, and other venues.

Puerto Rican diaspora: The word "diaspora" comes from a Greek word that means "scattered." More than 40 percent of the more than six million people identifying themselves as Puerto Ricans in 1990 lived outside their homeland.

The origins of the Puerto Rican diaspora can be found in social and economic changes taking place in Puerto Rico as it became part of an expanding world market during the nineteenth and early twentieth cen-

Puerto Rican children, many of them recent immigrants, play in a community center in New York City in 1953. (AP/Wide World Photos)

turies. Because of population growth and expansion of commercial agriculture during the last two decades of the nineteenth century, Puerto Ricans migrated off the island. Some went to Cuba and the Dominican Republic to work on sugar plantations; others traveled to other parts of Latin America and to the United States. This migratory movement was to become a fixture of the Puerto Rican experience.

In 1898, the United States and Spain fought in the SPANISH-AMERICAN WAR, giving rise to another chapter in the history of the Puerto Rican diaspora. Puerto Rico, which had been a colonial possession of Spain for four hundred years, was ceded to the United States as a result of the negotiations that followed Spain's defeat. These negotiations led to the signing of the TREATY OF PARIS, which placed Puerto Rico under the colonial control of the United States. By the JONES ACT of 1917, Puerto Ricans were made citizens of the United States, with the right to travel freely to the mainland.

The United States installed a military government on the island that immediately effected dramatic economic and social reforms. Many of these reforms, such as devaluation of the peso and limitations on Puerto Rico's external trade, created severe economic problems for some of the island's agricultural producers. An economic crisis devastated the coffee-growing regions of Puerto Rico's central mountain region, leading to a massive exodus of peasants to the United States, Mexico, Colombia, Ecuador, and Hawaii.

The next period of massive immigration took place after World War II, when the Puerto Rican sugar industry suffered a dramatic decline. At the same time, the local government promoted and facilitated the immigration of Puerto Ricans to the United States as an escape valve for economic and population pressures.

NEW YORK CITY has been the traditional destination for Puerto Ricans moving to the United States. The advent of inexpensive air travel made moves easier. In addition, if things did not work out, or if they became homesick, immigrants knew that they could afford to return home, making the decision to move easier. From the primary base in New York City, the mainland population of Puerto Ricans spread, partially with encouragement and assistance from federal government programs. By the end of the twentieth century, Puerto Ricans were dispersed across the United States, from Hawaii to New York and from Florida to Illinois.

Puerto Rican Legal Defense and Education Fund (PRLDEF): Nonprofit civil rights organization. The PRLDEF was founded in 1972 to protect and promote the legal rights of Puerto Ricans and other Latinos. It also provides guidance and financial assistance to Latinos interested in careers in the legal profession. Located in New York City, the PRLDEF in the early 1990's had a staff of approximately twenty people.

The PRLDEF was founded by such distinguished individuals as Jorge L. Batista, Victor Marrero, and César A. PERALES with the purpose of providing advocacy and community educational programs for Latino communities. Its primary objective is to ensure equal protection under the law through advocacy and litigation, by challenging DISCRIMINATION in the areas of education, employment, health, housing, political participation, and women's rights.

The PRLDEF has successfully argued landmark cases, several of which have reached the United States Supreme Court. In 1972, its lawsuit *Aspira of New York v. Board of Education of the City of New York* helped obtain the right to BILINGUAL EDUCATION for Latino children with limited English proficiency in what is known as the Aspira Consent Decree. *Pabón v. Levine* (1976) helped to secure the right of Puerto Ricans to have unemployment insurance services and materials, such as hearings and claims forms, in the Spanish language. Cases such as these filed by the PRLDEF have played an important role in shaping language-based national origin discrimination rulings.

The PRLDEF's lawsuits against the New York City police, fire, and sanitation departments have resulted in expanding the representation of Latinos in civil service jobs in those departments. The PRLDEF has defended the availability of low-income housing for Latinos and has challenged discriminatory practices against Latinos in public and private housing projects.

The Voting Rights Project of the PRLDEF has worked successfully toward increasing the number of Latino elected officials at the federal, state, and local levels in the Northeast. For example, the organization filed lawsuits and complaints with the U.S. Department of Justice against gerrymandering, the practice of strategically dividing voting districts to favor a particular political party or English-speaking residents. Through its internships, mentoring programs, Law School Admissions Test (LSAT) preparatory classes, and scholarships, the PRLDEF also has played a pivotal role in dramatically expanding the number of Latino and other ethnic minority attorneys in the Northeast.

Puerto Rican migration: Puerto Rican immigration to the United States has its roots in events that began unfolding in Puerto Rico at the end of the nineteenth century. Since that time, emigration has been almost a defining characteristic of the Puerto Rican experience. Although most people moved in search of improved economic opportunities, emigration became an unavoidable event in the lives of many Puerto Ricans.

Introduction. Puerto Rican emigration is among the largest displacements of people in recent history. More than 44 percent of all Puerto Ricans lived in the United States toward the end of the twentieth century. According to the U.S. Bureau of the Census, in 1990, 2.7 million Puerto Ricans resided on the mainland, and 3.5 million resided on the island. Although a majority of the Puerto Ricans on the mainland lived in the state of New York, there were communities of Puerto Ricans all across the nation. This massive uprooting of so many Puerto Ricans from their homeland had its roots in the nineteenth century.

Events in the late nineteenth century marked the character of Puerto Rican emigration in the following decades. Puerto Ricans increasingly became superfluous in their homeland and became part of a floating population that circulated back and forth between Puerto Rico and the urban areas of the United States. This CIRCULAR MIGRATION also included a displacement to new geographic areas such as the West and the Southeast of the United States, where the Puerto Rican presence historically had been rather limited.

Reasons for Migration. During the last twenty years of the nineteenth century, particularly around the 1880's, Puerto Ricans for the first time emigrated off the island in large numbers to find work. Many of the emigrants before that time had left because they were politically persecuted, were slaves who escaped to other islands, or were Spaniards who returned to their

Puerto Rican immigrants brought their culture to the mainland; this Puerto Rican restaurant offers island specialties as part of the expanding service economy. (Don Franklin)

country after retirement from business. During the 1880's, the island's sugar economy was experiencing a downturn, and many workers found themselves without work. Some went to the neighboring island of Santo Domingo to work on the sugar plantations; others went to Cuba, Panama, Venezuela, Guatemala, Brazil, and the United States, especially New York City.

Since the last part of the nineteenth century, most Puerto Ricans who have left their island have done so because of lack of employment and other economic opportunities. Dramatic changes that Puerto Rico experienced in the 1880's, in 1898, after World War II, and in the 1990's all prompted large emigrations.

In 1898, because of political and economic differences, Spain and the United States fought the SPANISH-AMERICAN WAR. Spain was defeated and, as a result, Puerto Rico became a colonial possession of the United States. Under the U.S. government, the economy of the island was geared toward the massive production of sugar and tobacco, and coffee suffered a dramatic decline. As a result, many coffee farmers lost their farms and many coffee workers lost their jobs. Many of them immigrated to the United States, Mexico, Colombia, Ecuador, and Hawaii.

During the early decades of the twentieth century, NEW YORK CITY became a magnet for large numbers of unskilled, semiskilled, and skilled workers. The city was growing and could absorb these workers in newly created jobs. It has been estimated that by the 1920's the Puerto Rican population of New York City had increased to 45,000. Many of the early immigrants were male and white; many had more craft skills than the average island worker.

Migration After World War II. Early immigrants were the pioneers for thousands of Puerto Ricans who immigrated to New York after World War II. The postwar period saw the second and largest of the emigration movements of Puerto Ricans. Emigration resulted in part from a crisis in the agricultural sector and also because emigration was promoted by the island's government. From 1950 to 1970, more than 600,000 persons left the island for the United States. This figure represented about one-fourth of the island's population in 1950.

While Puerto Ricans continued to arrive in New York, the city changed from an industrial hub to a services center. Many Puerto Ricans lost their jobs and experienced increasing levels of poverty. Between 1970 and 1980, more people returned to Puerto Rico than left, a process called return migration. Poverty and crime rose within the mainland Puerto Rican com-

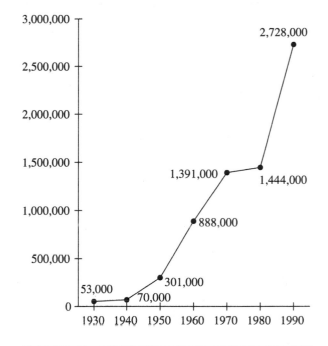

PUERTO RICAN POPULATION IN THE CONTINENTAL UNITED STATES, 1930-1990

Source: Data are from "Puerto Ricans," in Stephan Thernstrom, ed., *Harvard Encyclopedia of American Ethnic Groups* (Cambridge, Mass.: Harvard University Press, 1980), Table 1, p. 860; and Marlita A. Reddy, ed., *Statistical Record of Hispanic Americans* (Detroit: Gale Research, 1993), Tables 25 and 26.
Note: Numbers are rounded to the nearest 1,000.

munity, and racial prejudice against Puerto Ricans reached high levels. The same people who had been received with open arms by the city in the 1950's now were received with hostility. Toward the end of the twentieth century, Puerto Ricans were migrating back and forth between the United States and Puerto Rico, also displacing themselves from the East to other areas of the nation. —*Victor M. Rodriguez*

SUGGESTED READINGS:

• Dietz, James L. *Economic History of Puerto Rico.* Princeton, N.J.: Princeton University Press, 1986. One of the most authoritative economic histories of Puerto Rico. Its analyses of the nineteenth and twentieth centuries are the best sections.

• Flores, Juan, ed. *Divided Arrival: Narratives of the Puerto Rican Migration, 1920-1950.* New York: Centro de Estudios Puertorriqueños, Hunter College, City University of New York, 1987. Helpful collection of histories and stories of the emigration process by emigrants themselves.

• History Task Force, Centro de Estudios Puertorriqueños. *Labor Migration Under Capitalism: The Puerto Rican Experience*. New York: Monthly Review Press, 1979. Early attempt to provide an overall view of the process of immigration of Puerto Ricans to the United States. Good review of the migration literature.

• Maldonado-Denis, Manuel. *The Emigration Dialectic: Puerto Rico and the U.S.A.* New York: International Publishers, 1980. Places the Puerto Rican emigration process into a theoretical perspective.

• Rosario Natal, Carmelo. *Exodo Puertorriqueño: Las Emigraciones al Caribe y Hawaii: 1900-1915*. San Juan, Puerto Rico: Author, 1983. Insightful study about Puerto Ricans who immigrated to the sugar plantations of Hawaii.

Puerto Rican nationalism: As a result of its long history as a colony, Puerto Rico has a well-developed tradition of nationalism. Nationalist political movements have attempted, without success, to bring full independence to the island. Although Puerto Rico remained subject to U.S. jurisdiction in the 1990's, there was a vibrant national pride among Puerto Ricans both on the island and on the U.S. mainland. A substantial number of Puerto Ricans continued to share nationalist aspirations for an independent Puerto Rico.

The Legacy of Colonialism. Puerto Rico is one of the world's oldest colonies. Ever since the Spanish colonized the island in the early sixteenth century, the island's destiny has been controlled by foreigners. Little changed in this respect when, in the SPANISH-AMERICAN WAR (1898), the Spanish were driven out by U.S. forces and a military governor was installed. Puerto Rico became an "unincorporated territory" of the United States, much to the resentment of those Puerto Ricans who dreamed of independence. The FORAKER ACT (1900) set terms of government on the island, and the JONES ACT (1917) made Puerto Ricans U.S. citizens by birth.

In the 1920's, Puerto Rican politics entered a new era with the founding of the Nationalist Party. Pedro ALBIZU CAMPOS became the party's president in 1930, and under his leadership, Puerto Rican nationalism emerged into prominence as a radical force demanding immediate and unconditional independence. By 1933, Albizu Campos had already come to reject electoral strategies. Influenced by the Irish independence struggle, he advocated increasingly militant strategies. He believed that nationalism represented "the nation organized for the rescue of its sovereignty."

In late 1935, a nationalist rally at the University of Puerto Rico led to violent street confrontations in which three nationalists were murdered by police forces. Albizu Campos vowed revenge, and four months later, a North American police chief was slain by nationalist forces on the island. Two nationalists subsequently arrested for the murder were shot while in police custody, allegedly because they tried to escape, and the cycle of violence escalated.

Albizu Campos and other nationalists were arrested and brought to the United States, where they were convicted of seditious conspiracy in 1936. Nationalists' activities intensified on the island following the imprisonment of their leaders. On Palm Sunday of 1937, police fired on a nationalist demonstration in Ponce, leaving twenty-one people dead and more than one hundred wounded in what became known as the Ponce Massacre.

From World War II to the 1960's. During World War II, the Nationalist Party refused to support the Allied war effort because of the mandatory draft of Puerto Ricans into the U.S. armed forces. This position led to the imprisonment of hundreds of nationalists. Albizu Campos was not released from U.S. federal imprisonment until 1947, when he returned to Puerto Rico and resumed organizing. At the same time, the United States began to move toward greater autonomy for Puerto Rico, including the popular election of a Puerto Rican governor. The Nationalist Party abstained from participation in all such activities, organizing a boycott of the first governor's election in 1948; ultimately, 42 percent of Puerto Ricans did not participate. The Nationalists steadfastly refused to recognize the legitimacy of U.S.-sponsored reforms and continued to advance militant demands for full independence.

At the end of October, 1950, a Nationalist insurrection took place on the island, proclaiming the formation of the Second Republic of Puerto Rico in the town of Jayuya. The revolt, which became known as the Grito de Jayuya, held out for seventy-two hours, leading to twenty-one nationalist casualties and ten police and National Guard deaths. Two days later, two Puerto Rican nationalists attacked the Blair House in Washington, D.C., then the temporary home of President Harry S Truman. Only one of the nationalists, Oscar COLLAZO, survived the attack. He was subsequently imprisoned in the United States.

In the aftermath of the Jayuya uprising and the Blair House attack, several thousand Puerto Ricans were arrested on suspicion of sharing nationalist sympathies. A new Puerto Rican constitution was drafted and

Oscar Collazo received a death sentence for his attempted assassination of President Harry S Truman. (AP/Wide World Photos)

adopted by the end of 1952. It officially designated the island as a "freely associated state." The response of the Nationalist Party was issued on March 1, 1954, when four nationalists—Irving Flores, Lolita LEBRÓN SOTO, Rafael CANCEL MIRANDA, and Andrés FIGUEROA CORDERO—entered the visitors' gallery and opened fire upon the House of Representatives, wounding five members of Congress before being captured.

Nationalism and Puerto Rican Independence. Nationalist ideology, which places an intense love for the island at the forefront of any political agenda, is closely associated with calls for the full independence of Puerto Rico. The United States has consistently regarded Puerto Rican nationalism as a subversive cause and has frequently displayed its displeasure by harsh means designed to repress the movement's influence.

From the 1960's to the 1980's, various clandestine organizations were formed to combine militant nationalist currents with revolutionary Marxism. Armed actions were carried out on U.S. military and corporate sites by groups such as Los Macheteros (EPB) on the island and the FUERZAS ARMADAS DE LIBERACIÓN NACIONAL (FALN) on the U.S. mainland. At the same time, highly politicized cultural centers developed in

Rafael Cancel Miranda, Andrés Figueroa Cordero, Lolita Lebrón Soto, and Irving Flores (left to right) following their arraignment on charges of felonious assault with intent to kill. (AP/Wide World Photos)

virtually all the large Puerto Rican communities on the U.S. mainland, including New York City, Chicago, Philadelphia, and Hartford, Connecticut.

A newspaper poll conducted in Puerto Rico in the late 1980's showed that a majority of Puerto Ricans living on the island viewed armed, clandestine nationalists as patriots rather than as "terrorists." Sympathy for imprisoned Puerto Rican nationalists remained pronounced within Puerto Rican communities on the U.S. mainland as well as on the island. In the 1990's, the chief of the U.S. Federal Bureau of Investigation asserted that Puerto Rican revolutionary nationalism was the "Achilles' heel" of U.S. national security.

—Richard A. Dello Buono

SUGGESTED READINGS: • Dello Buono, Richard A. "State Repression and Popular Resistance: The Criminalization of Puerto Rican Independistas." *Humanity and Society* 15 (February, 1991): 111-131. • Fernandez, Ronald. *Los Macheteros: The Wells Fargo Rob-*bery and the Violent Struggle for Puerto Rican Independence. New York: Prentice Hall, 1987. • Lopez, Jose E., ed. *Puerto Rican Nationalism*. Chicago: Editorial Coqui, 1977. • Samoiloff, Louise Cripps. *Human Rights in a United States Colony*. Cambridge, Mass.: Schenkman Books, 1982. • Suarez, Manuel. *Requiem on Cerro Maravilla: The Police Murders in Puerto Rico and the U.S. Government Coverup*. Maplewood, N.J.: Waterfront Press, 1987.

Puerto Rican studies programs: Puerto Rican studies programs and departments, located primarily in universities and colleges in the northeastern United States, offer a wide range of courses in the social sciences and humanities and explore the history and the contemporary experiences of Puerto Ricans in the United States and in Puerto Rico.

History. July 9, 1969, is often cited as the founding date of the discipline of Puerto Rican studies. On that date, the Board of Higher Education of the City University of New York (CUNY) issued a policy statement announcing its support of African American and Puerto Rican studies programs in the university and constituent colleges. This official proclamation came on the heels of a protracted student and community struggle on many campuses throughout the City University of New York, which in its curriculum had neglected the Puerto Rican reality.

The founding of Puerto Rican studies programs and departments on campuses in the City University of New York and in other universities in the Northeast and Midwest gave rise to a new, interdisciplinary way of looking at the experience of Puerto Ricans in the United States and Puerto Rico. The courses that developed in succeeding decades reflected a wide range of disciplines, and such courses spread to the curricula of most Puerto Rican studies programs and departments. Most programs offer courses that explore the history of Puerto Rico from the pre-Columbian period to the present, the creative literature of the island, and the literature produced by U.S.-based or "NUYORICAN" writers. Programs invariably include courses that explore the development of the Puerto Rican community in the United States, from the earliest concentrated settlements, or barrios, to the diaspora of Puerto Ricans throughout the United States. Puerto Rican music, art, and ever-changing cultural expressions are also studied in many programs. Courses examining economics, religion, politics, health, mental health, education, labor, migration, and the media reflect Puerto Rican studies' ongoing commitment to teaching and examining the life of the community from a variety of perspectives.

The Expanding Vision of Puerto Rican Studies. When Puerto Rican studies programs were first established, Puerto Ricans constituted the single largest Latino ethnic group in the Northeast. During the 1980's and 1990's, however, there was a significant increase of non-Puerto Rican Latino immigrants throughout the nation. In direct response to these demographic changes, a number of programs and departments broadened the content and expanded the titles of their course offerings to include the concerns and issues of other Latino groups. In some instances, Puerto Rican studies programs have included specific courses on Dominicans and other Latin American communities in the United States. This shift clearly reveals an approach that is more inclusive and comparative.

Some departments and programs have acknowledged the changes in their curriculum by formally expanding their departmental names. For example, the City College of New York, one of the longest-running Puerto Rican studies departments in the CUNY system, was renamed the Department of Latin American and Hispanic Caribbean Studies. This program encompasses the original Puerto Rican studies major concentration, a Latin American area studies sequence, and courses on Dominicans and other Latino groups in the United States. Northeastern University in Massachusetts has a Latino, Latin American, and Caribbean studies program, and Rutgers University in New Jersey has a Department of Puerto Rican and Hispanic Caribbean Studies. Brooklyn College, one of the oldest and largest departments in the CUNY system, continues to support a Department of Puerto Rican Studies and also maintains a Latino Studies Institute. Other programs and departments of Puerto Rican studies have recognized the importance of retaining Puerto Rican in their departmental titles but have modified their curricula in response to demographic shifts.

In addition to degree-granting academic programs, research centers and institutes exist for the study of Puerto Rican culture. The oldest, El Centro de Estudios Puertorriqueños, is housed at Hunter College (CUNY). The MAURICIO GASTON INSTITUTE FOR LATINO COMMUNITY DEVELOPMENT AND PUBLIC POLICY at the University of Massachusetts at Boston and the Center for Latino, Latin American, and Caribbean Studies at the State University of New York at Albany also conduct research on the Puerto Rican reality in the United States and in Puerto Rico. The INSTITUTE FOR PUERTO RICAN POLICY in New York is a self-supporting community research organization. The Puerto Rican Studies Association for Research, Advocacy, and Education affords scholars the opportunity to participate in a professional organization that is dedicated to the promotion and integration of the interdisciplinary research, praxis, and community empowerment of Puerto Ricans in Puerto Rico, the United States, and elsewhere. —*Jesse M. Vazquez*

SUGGESTED READINGS:

• *Explorations in Ethnic Studies: The Journal of the National Association for Ethnic Studies* 11 (January, 1988). This special issue provides a close look at the historical beginnings, contemporary challenges, and future prospects for ethnic studies in the twenty-first century.

• Stevens-Arroyo, Antonio M., and Maria Sanchez, eds. *Towards a Renaissance of Puerto Rican Studies: Ethnic and Area Studies in the University Education.* Highland Lakes, N.J.: Atlantic Research and Publications, 1987. Includes a number of chapters based on papers presented at the first international Puerto Rican Studies conference.

• Vazquez, Jesse M. "Embattled Scholars in the Academy: A Shared Odyssey." *Callaloo* 15 (Fall, 1992): 1039-1051. Explores the challenges facing Puerto Rican and other ethnic studies scholars.

• Vazquez, Jesse M. "A Re-Examination of the Founding Principles of Puerto Rican Studies: Ethnic Studies and the New Multiculturalism." *Impart: Journal of Openmind* 1 (1993): 65-76. Draws a critical comparison between the founding principles of Puerto Rican and other ethnic studies programs and the emerging multicultural movement in American universities.

Puerto Rican Traveling Theater: Theater group. This theater was founded in 1967 by actress Miriam COLÓN. It is a bilingual, professional theater group producing works by Puerto Ricans and other Latino writers. It performs these plays for a diverse audience. The group runs four programs, three of which are offered for no charge. These programs are the annual summer tour, offering a free play throughout New York City and parts of New Jersey; a training unit offering free theater training to limited-income young adults; playwriting assistance for Latino writers; and the Mainstage Season, which showcases new and old Latino works in the company's converted-firehouse theater in New York City. The theater group also performs internationally.

Puerto Rican Week Festival (Philadelphia, Pa.): Sponsored by the Council of Spanish Speaking Organizations, Inc., since 1964, the Puerto Rican Week Festival has annually attracted upwards of 100,000 visitors to downtown Philadelphia for the various festival events. Performances by Puerto Ricans, Cuban Americans, and members of other Hispanic groups dominate the activities and attractions, which include Latino food, music, and dance; folk arts; costumes and crafts; and traditional and nontraditional games.

Preceding the Puerto Rican Week Festival, which is held the last week in September, the smaller Festival del Barrio, started in 1979, is held in the 2700 block of North Fifth Street during the last week of August. It is predominantly Puerto Rican in tone, reflecting Philadelphia's fairly large Puerto Rican community. The Festival del Barrio features traditional music, dance, folk arts and crafts, foodways, games, art exhibits, and folk costumes.

Puerto Ricans: Puerto Ricans who live on the mainland of the United States are the second largest Latino subgroup. The majority of this Latino group speaks Spanish and has a distinctive culture that is derived from Spanish, African, and Indian roots.

Introduction. Many Puerto Ricans, like many Mexican Americans, came to be associated with the United States when their homeland was annexed as a result of a war. In 1898, Spain and the United States fought the SPANISH-AMERICAN WAR. As a result of Spain's defeat, PUERTO RICO became a colonial possession of the United States. This meant that most of the important decisions that affected the lives of Puerto Ricans living on the island were made by the U.S. government.

All Puerto Ricans are citizens of the United States. According to the U.S. Bureau of the Census, in 1990, 2.7 million Puerto Ricans resided on the mainland and 3.5 million resided on the island. The use of English is more common among those Puerto Ricans who live on the mainland of the United States. The majority of the Puerto Ricans on the mainland live in the state of New York, but there are communities of Puerto Ricans all across the nation.

Early History and Culture. Before the arrival of Europeans in Puerto Rico, a group of indigenous people, popularly called Taino, inhabited the island. They are believed to have migrated from the Orinoco Valley and the coasts of what today are the South American nations of Guyana and Venezuela. They are believed to have arrived at different times beginning about 2,300 B.C.E.

The Taino called the island of Puerto Rico Borinquen. Today, many Puerto Ricans call themselves Borinqueños or BORICUA as a reference to BORINQUEN, the Taino name for the island. The Taino developed a simple agriculture based on the cultivation of tobacco, peppers, corn, and yucca. The Taino also depended on hunting, fishing, and gathering fruits for their sustenance. They used cotton for cloth and built *hamacas* or hammocks (a hanging canvas placed between two trees) in which to sleep.

Taino lived in family units. Women are believed to have been very important in this culture, and a number of Taino chiefs were women. Taino practiced what social scientists call animism, the belief that spirits inhabit the natural world. They believed that supernatural powers controlled nature, and they performed rituals and ceremonies to protect themselves from these supernatural powers. Their culture also relied on a ceremony called the *areito*, in which stories were told about great battles and the supernatural powers of the world.

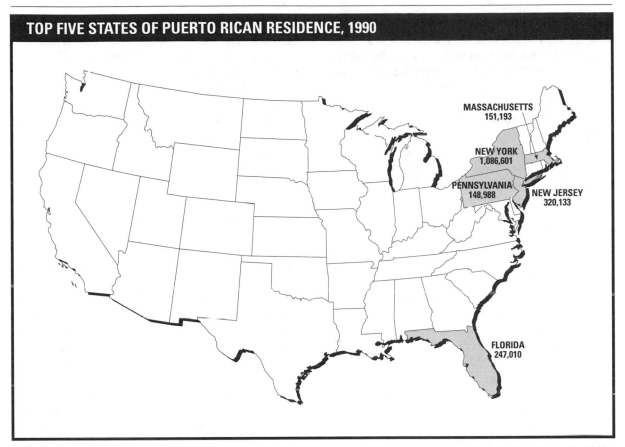

TOP FIVE STATES OF PUERTO RICAN RESIDENCE, 1990

MASSACHUSETTS
151,193

NEW YORK
1,086,601

PENNSYLVANIA
148,988

NEW JERSEY
320,133

FLORIDA
247,010

Source: Population data are from Marlita A. Reddy, ed., *Statistical Record of Hispanic Americans* (Detroit: Gale Research, 1993), Table 106.

Arrival of Europeans. In 1493, during his second trip to the Americas, Christopher Columbus arrived at Borinquen. The Taino received the Europeans with hospitality and curiosity. The Spaniards who first settled on the island were interested in mining the island's abundant gold. Many of the settlers, hoping to become wealthy quickly and return to Spain, promoted rapid exploitation of mines. Many of the natives were forced to work in the gold mines.

The Taino were not used to working in the mines, nor were they used to the diseases that commonly afflicted Europeans. Measles and chickenpox had been unknown among the Taino. Because they had not developed resistance to European diseases, many Taino died in epidemics. As hard work and diseases started killing the Taino, many of them became dissatisfied with their relationship to the Spaniards. In 1511, the first native uprising against the Europeans in the Americas occurred in PUERTO RICO. The Taino were defeated eventually, and gradually they became absorbed by the growing Spanish population of the island. It is believed that many left the island but that

others went into the mountains of the interior and mixed with the local poor white peasants. The Taino culture also became a part of the developing Puerto Rican culture.

After the year 1520, the production of gold on the island declined. In the following two hundred years, Puerto Rico's economy increasingly shifted toward agriculture. The island started producing ginger, sugar, and hides. Because of the need for labor for the growing production of sugarcane, out of which sugar is produced, many Africans were brought to work on the plantations as slaves. SLAVERY in Puerto Rico was not abolished until 1873. Africans brought with them a rich culture that affected the culture of the island.

Puerto Rican Culture. By the time of the SPANISH-AMERICAN WAR of 1898, Puerto Ricans had developed a culture that was distinct from Spanish culture. Although they spoke Spanish, many of their traditions, religious practices, foods, dances, and musical forms represented a style unique to people in the Spanish Caribbean. Although the majority of the population was formally Roman Catholic, church attendance was not extensive. Before the nineteenth century, priests were scarce. The spiritual needs of people were met in various ways that included the use of less formal religious practices. Some of these practices and rituals came from the Africans, and some took the form of a practice called SANTERÍA. Santería was a mixture of Christian beliefs and beliefs from African religions.

Many of the names of cities, neighborhoods, and mountains are derived from Taino names. For example, the word "hurricane," the name of the storms that often afflict the Caribbean, is derived from the Taino name *Juracán*, one of their powerful deities. Many of the ingredients used in Puerto Rican cooking are derived from African, Taino, and Spanish sources. One indigenous dance, the bomba, was developed by Africans in Puerto Rico. The *PLENA* is a mulatto musical form. The *DANZA* is mainly Spanish-influenced. In reality, none of these is a pure African or Spanish form. Although *danzas* are considered to be the most Spanish, upper-class musical expression, some of the most famous *danza* writers were black or mulatto. The *BOMBA* and *plena*, on the other hand, are sung in Spanish. There is also peasant music, which derives inspiration from all of Puerto Rico's cultural groups and heritages. Puerto Rican culture is an example of a melting pot culture.

During the nineteenth century, many Puerto Ricans on the island differentiated between those from Spain and those from Puerto Rico. Some even wanted to create an independent republic like the United States. On September 23, 1868, a number of island residents responded to El GRITO DE LARES, taking up arms against the Spanish government in Puerto Rico and declaring Puerto Rico an independent nation. This republic was short-lived, because the rebellion was quickly controlled. The *grito* and rebellion represented the shared feeling of many Puerto Ricans that they are a separate culture and nationality.

Puerto Rican Migration. When the United States obtained Puerto Rico following the Spanish-American War, many Puerto Ricans were glad to be free from what they considered Spanish oppression. Under the new U.S. military government, the economy of the island was geared toward the massive production of sugar and tobacco. During the last part of the nineteenth century, coffee production in PUERTO RICO had increased dramatically. Coffee was produced mostly in the mountains of the island's interior, and sugar was cultivated in the coastal lowland valleys. Under the U.S. government in Puerto Rico, coffee suffered a dramatic decline. One reason for this was that Puerto Rico's coffee was more expensive than Brazilian coffee, which had become popular in the United States. A second reason was that Puerto Rico's coffee was not allowed to enter the United States free of taxes. Many coffee farmers lost their farms, and many coffee workers lost their jobs. Many of them immigrated to the United States, Mexico, Colombia, and Ecuador; some traveled as far as Hawaii to work in the growing sugar economy of that U.S. territory.

Puerto Rico Under U.S. Control. During the early years under U.S. rule, Puerto Ricans were governed by a military government. In 1900, under the FORAKER ACT, Puerto Rico had a civilian government. In 1917, the JONES ACT made Puerto Ricans citizens of the United States. It was not until 1947, however, that Puerto Ricans were able to elect their first Puerto Rican governor. None of the previous governors named by the president of the United States had been Puerto Rican.

During the first twenty years of U.S. control, sugar became Puerto Rico's dominant crop. Sugarcane fields extended throughout the island. Many of the island's sugar mills belonged to United States investors, but others were owned by Puerto Ricans. Thousands of workers labored in the sugarcane fields and factories, and on the docks and railroads, processing, transporting, cutting, and packing so that sugar could reach the nation's markets. These workers, together with those in the tobacco factories, became the foundation of a large and important labor movement on the island. This labor movement went on to create the Socialist Party, the first political party in the island's history with a primarily working-class membership.

Workers were influenced by European social philosophers who had proclaimed a social revolution in which workers would be the leaders. Many of them believed that a better society, without poverty or oppression, could be created if workers became the leading force of society. This aspiration was never fulfilled, because the party became like any other political party, focusing on practical, everyday issues. Out of this social movement, however, developed a movement supporting political rights for women.

Women, in the early part of the twentieth century, were not allowed to vote and enjoyed few legal or civil rights. Some women, such as Luisa CAPETILLO, a feminist labor leader, became involved in a struggle to emancipate women. They wanted women to enjoy the same rights as men. After women received the right to vote, this movement suffered a decline. During the 1980's it resurfaced as women again struggled to gain their rightful place in Puerto Rican society.

STATISTICAL PROFILE OF PUERTO RICANS, 1990

The Latino Population

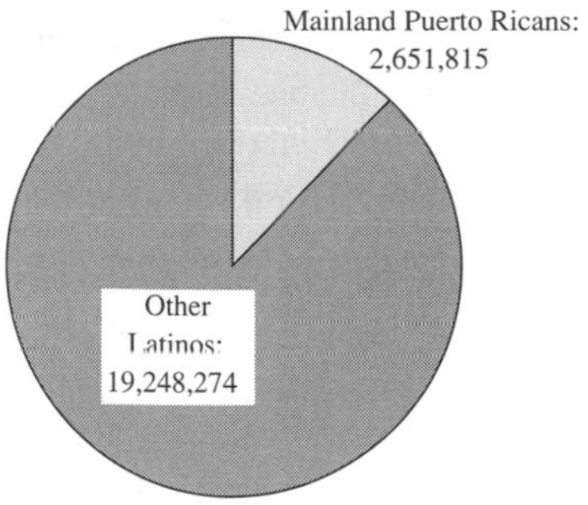

Mainland Puerto Ricans: 2,651,815

Other Latinos: 19,248,274

Nativity*

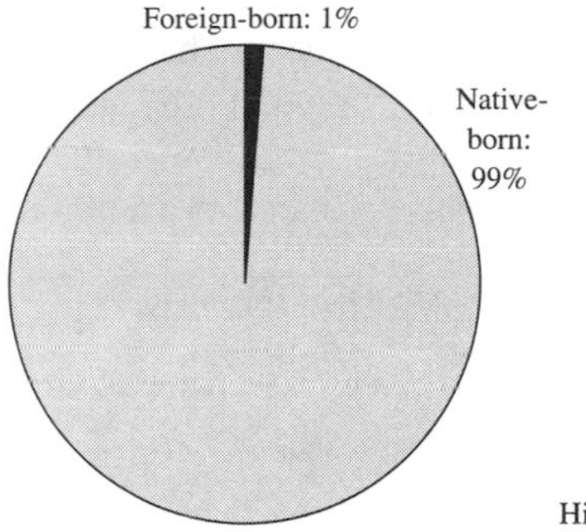

Foreign-born: 1%

Native-born: 99%

Schooling Completed
(persons 25 years of age or older)

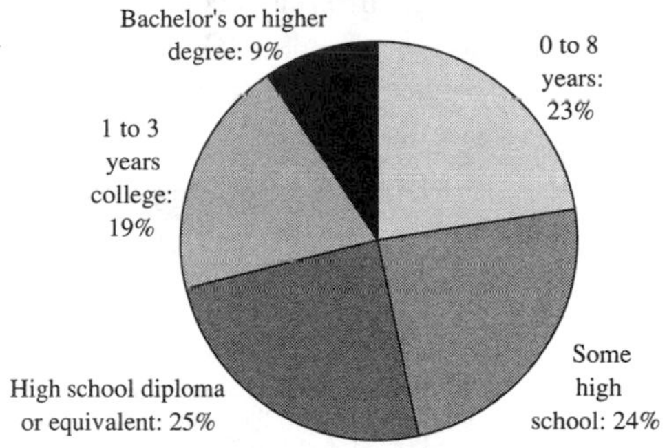

Bachelor's or higher degree: 9%

1 to 3 years college: 19%

0 to 8 years: 23%

Some high school: 24%

High school diploma or equivalent: 25%

English Language Fluency
(persons 5 years of age or older)

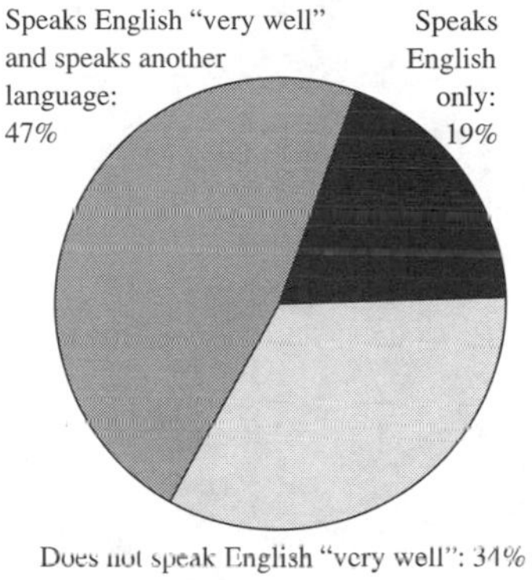

Speaks English "very well" and speaks another language: 47%

Speaks English only: 19%

Does not speak English "very well": 34%

Labor Force Status
(persons 16 years of age or older)

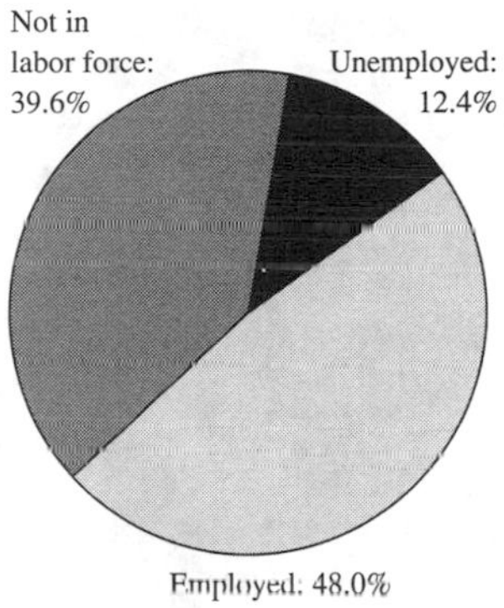

Not in labor force: 39.6%

Unemployed: 12.4%

Employed: 48.0%

Occupation

Median household income: $21,056
Per capita income: $8,403
Percentage of families in poverty: 29.6%

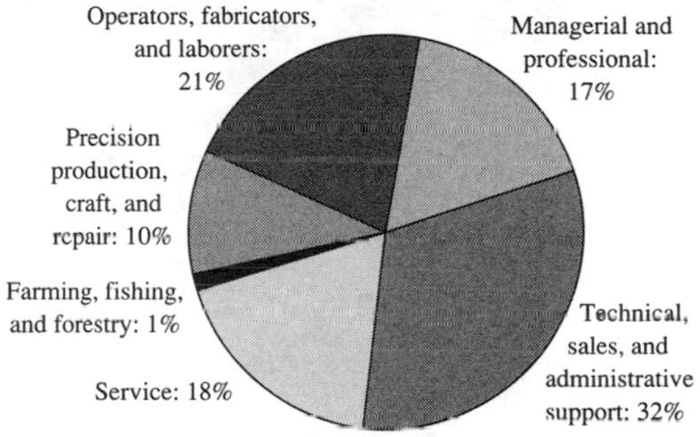

Operators, fabricators, and laborers: 21%

Managerial and professional: 17%

Precision production, craft, and repair: 10%

Farming, fishing, and forestry: 1%

Service: 18%

Technical, sales, and administrative support: 32%

Family Type

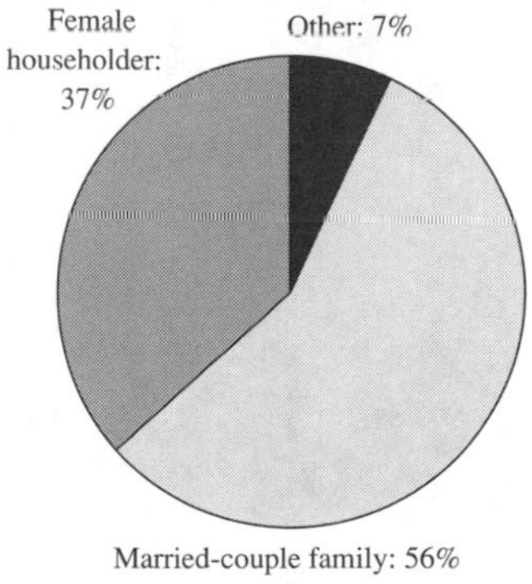

Female householder: 37%

Other: 7%

Married-couple family: 56%

Household Size
(number of persons)

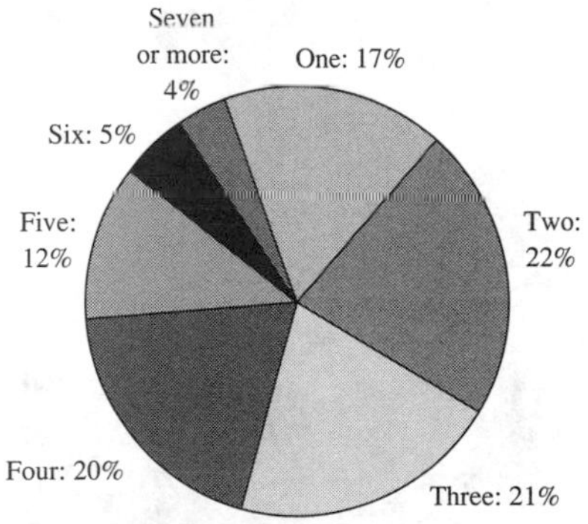

Seven or more: 4%

One: 17%

Six: 5%

Five: 12%

Two: 22%

Four: 20%

Three: 21%

Age (median = 25.5 years)

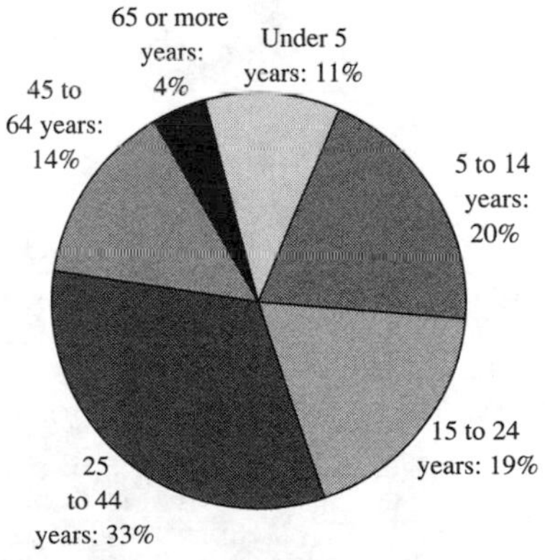

65 or more years: 4%

Under 5 years: 11%

45 to 64 years: 14%

5 to 14 years: 20%

25 to 44 years: 33%

15 to 24 years: 19%

Source: Bureau of the Census, *Census of 1990: Persons of Hispanic Origin in the U.S.* (Washington, D.C.: Bureau of the Census, 1993), Tables 1-5.

Note: All figures and percentages are based on a sample, rather than 100 percent, of the Latino population, as done in reports from the Bureau of the Census.

*"Foreign-born" means born in neither the United States nor Puerto Rico.

Puerto Ricans have tended to be interested in politics. As soon as the United States took over control of the island and started extending its political institutions into Puerto Rican society, people became involved in the system. Political parties, which had functioned precariously under Spanish rule, became massive because of the larger number of Puerto Ricans who could vote. The island's parties have had varying ideas regarding Puerto Rico's relationship to the United States. This status debate concerns whether Puerto Rico should remain a U.S. commonwealth, seek independence, or seek U.S. statehood. (*See* PUERTO RICO — STATUS DEBATE.)

One important characteristic of the Puerto Rican people has been their strong pride in their native culture. Partly as a result of finding themselves ruled by a large, powerful nation, the United States, Puerto Ricans have held onto their culture as a way of surviving

A settlement house in East Harlem, New York City, offers sandwiches and milk to Puerto Rican youngsters, many of whom were part of the large influx of Puerto Ricans during the 1940's. (AP/Wide World Photos)

both on the island and in large communities within the United States.

Industrialization and Migration. After World War II, the elected government of Puerto Rico followed in the footsteps of previous United States-appointed governments. Because the island's sugar industry was experiencing a crisis, partly because U.S. tax laws that had benefited it previously had been changed, the island embarked on a program of industrialization. This program, which had begun under Rexford G. Tugwell—the last appointed governor of Puerto Rico (1941-1946)—first tried to create a national industry in Puerto Rico. After the war, the program was geared at enticing U.S. investors to establish manufacturing plants across the island. This program was popularly called OPERATION BOOTSTRAP.

In 1952, Puerto Ricans voted to create a constitution that created the Commonwealth of Puerto Rico. A commonwealth relationship with the United States meant that the island would rule itself in internal matters such as police, internal security, the local economy, and crime. The United States would still be in charge of national defense, international relations, and commerce. Many Puerto Ricans were not satisfied with this new relationship. In 1950, a group of Puerto Rican nationalists had led an armed rebellion to protest the process. The rebellion was crushed, and many of its participants were sent to jail.

This period saw a crisis in the agricultural sector and promotion of migration by the island's government. These factors prompted the second, and largest, Puerto Rican migration. Between 1950 and 1970, more than 600,000 persons left the island for the United States. This figure represented about one-fourth of the island's population in 1950. The island continued industrializing while exporting people to work on the mainland.

One reason for this migration was that although jobs were created in manufacturing, more jobs were eliminated in agriculture. The Puerto Rican government promoted migration as a safety valve to avoid creating greater problems of poverty and social conflict in PUERTO RICO. Between 1970 and 1980, however, more people returned to Puerto Rico than left. This raised concerns that emigration might not continue to solve the problem of insufficient job creation. Puerto Rican migration during the last decades of the twentieth century was a circular process: While some Puerto Ricans left, many others returned after spending time on the mainland.

During the 1990's, the island experienced the effects of the world recession, which again increased the number of emigrants. During that period, however, a larger proportion of emigrants consisted of young, college-educated professionals, some of whom were recruited from the island's universities. Also during the 1990's, more Puerto Rican students chose to attend universities on the mainland, and many remained in the United States after graduation.

Although most Puerto Rican immigrants initially went to work in agriculture and manufacturing in the eastern part of the United States, increasing numbers settled in the Southeast and the Southwest. According to the U.S. Census of 1990, New York had the largest population of Puerto Ricans, with more than a million, followed by Florida (240,673), Illinois (147,201), Connecticut (140,143), and California (131,998).

Debate concerning the island's future political status led to a referendum in 1993, in which the majority of the voters decided to retain the existing relationship with the United States with minor reforms.

Life in the United States. For early immigrants to the United States, the cold, racial prejudice, and poor housing and working conditions contradicted expectations. Many worked in agriculture, sewed in the garment industry, worked in textiles, or manufactured toys or umbrellas in light industrial concerns, saving money and establishing themselves in their new community.

NEW YORK CITY attracted the bulk of Puerto Rican immigrants, as there was an established Puerto Rican community there, along with employment opportunities. By the 1920's, the Puerto Rican population of New York City had increased to about 45,000. In 1923, an organization called the Hermandad Puertorriqueña was organized in the city to help working-class Puerto Ricans and to engage in politics and education concerning Latin America and the United States' role abroad, especially in Puerto Rico and the Caribbean. Many of the early immigrants were male, were white, and had more craft skills than the average island worker.

Migration After World War II. The advent of inexpensive air transportation after World War II encouraged immigration. Previous immigrants had traveled in ships across the Atlantic Ocean. The voyage was relatively expensive and time-consuming, and early immigrants therefore did not expect to make many, if any, visits back to the island. Inexpensive air travel made immigration less risky, because it was less expensive and because reverse migration became a feasible option.

The first Puerto Rican immigrants to settle in New York City were well received, for the most part. Their

An annual parade in New York City shows support for Puerto Rico and the desire of many for its independence. (Hazel Hankin)

labor was needed in many of the city's industries, and they were willing to work at some of the less pleasant and the lower-paying jobs. Affordable public housing was made available. The immigrants established themselves in stable working-class communities. Some began the progression up the economic ladder, opening businesses and buying homes.

As their numbers increased, Puerto Ricans gradually created communities with their own businesses, churches, and social clubs. Some Puerto Ricans joined Hispanic protestant congregations; others remained Catholic and attended Masses in Spanish; others joined social clubs. Some social clubs were based on their members' town of origin. People who had migrated from the same town organized social and cultural events at which they remembered their hometown and celebrated Puerto Rican holidays.

In the 1950's, about 80 percent of all employed Puerto Ricans worked in blue-collar and service occupations. Like earlier immigrants, they had greater skills and more education than those who remained on the island. Although many increased their earnings on the mainland, their jobs were often of a lower status than the ones they had held in PUERTO RICO.

Increasingly, Puerto Rican women joined the labor force during the 1950's. The majority were employed in factories, and a smaller number performed clerical work in businesses and offices. About forty percent of all women were in the labor force in the United States, a larger proportion than in Puerto Rico.

In the late 1950's and early 1960's, many younger and more rural immigrants began arriving in the United States, many with contracts to work in the agricultural fields. During this period, the economy of New York City also experienced a shift.

Puerto Ricans in the 1980's and 1990's. Industry was the mainstay of the U.S. economy for many years. In the last decades of the twentieth century, however, the economy shifted away from manufacturing and toward services. Some service jobs required high levels of education and training; others required few skills. The service economy became split between high-paying and low-paying jobs, with fewer in the middle. One reason for this was that the U.S. economy increasingly was linked to the global economy. Many formerly high-paying industrial jobs were sent to other nations where salaries were lower.

One effect of this process, which some have called the globalization of the economy, was that the function of cities changed. Many jobs in large cities of the United States in the 1990's were part of the service sector of the economy, such as international and national communications, advertising, financial services, and banking, education, and government. Most of these jobs required high levels of education and training, which negatively affected groups such as Puerto Ricans who migrated to these large urban industrial centers. Entry-level jobs at decent wages became increasingly difficult to find, particularly for workers not fluent in English.

The media and the entertainment industry have portrayed negative images of Puerto Ricans. Some people who did not know Puerto Ricans personally assumed that these images, reflecting high rates of gang membership, unemployment, drug use, and poverty, applied to all Puerto Ricans. Puerto Ricans therefore encountered these stereotypes as obstacles to success and acceptance.

Puerto Rican Influences. The phenomenal growth of SALSA music in the United States and its revival on the island showed a strong, vibrant Puerto Rican culture among the communities that spanned the United States. Although many Puerto Ricans learned English, most did not forget Spanish. As Clara RODRÍGUEZ noted in *Puerto Ricans: Born in the U.S.A.* (1989), 91 percent of Puerto Ricans in New York spoke Spanish at home. This proportion was higher than for any other Latino group in the city. Fewer Puerto Ricans than any other Latino group indicated that they could not speak English well. Other surveys have shown that Puerto Ricans on the mainland have not forgotten their island: Among all the Latino subgroups, they showed the highest level of interest in the politics of their homeland. This has not meant a withdrawal from politics in the United States, however. In 1992, three Puerto Ricans were elected to the U.S. Congress, among them

Puerto Rican musicians present a demonstration in Washington Heights, an area of New York City in which many students are Dominican Americans. (Hazel Hankin)

the first Puerto Rican congresswoman. Those elected in 1992 were José Serrano and Nydia Velázquez from New York and Luis Gutierrez from Chicago.

Sociodemographic Profile. The Puerto Rican population in the United States in 1990 was a very young one. The median age (the age of the person in the middle, if the ages of all people are put in order) for non-Hispanic whites was 35.2 according to the 1990 U.S. Census. The median was 26.9 years for Puerto Ricans. Only Mexican Americans, with a median of 24.4 years, were younger than Puerto Ricans. These statistics imply that Puerto Ricans will have higher birth rates than average and that their population on the mainland will continue to grow. Latinos constituted more than 9 percent of the U.S. population in 1990, and Puerto Ricans composed almost 11 percent of that subtotal.

POVERTY has been a powerful force affecting Puerto Rican families. In 1991, Puerto Ricans had the highest family poverty rate of all Latinos, at 35.6 percent. Children experienced poverty to the greatest extent. In 1991, 57.9 percent of all Puerto Rican children lived in poverty. Combined with the number of Latino children who attended segregated, underfunded schools, this statistic painted a bleak picture. One study conducted in the early 1990's found that 73.4 percent of all Latino children attended schools with student bodies composed primarily of minority students. This percentage was higher than for black children.

Changes in the national economy in the 1980's and early 1990's affected Puerto Ricans dramatically. In 1991, only 56.7 percent of all Puerto Ricans sixteen years of age or older were in the labor force; the comparable proportion was 66.3 percent for non-Hispanic whites. There were, however, positive signs for the future. Of all employed Puerto Ricans on the mainland, 49 percent were in managerial, professional, technical, sales, and administrative support positions. These positions carry higher status and often pay more than many industrial occupations. This proportion exceeded that for Mexican Americans and almost matched that for Cuban Americans, long considered to be the most economically successful Latino subgroup. Median household income for Puerto Ricans in 1990 was lower than for any other Latino subgroup. Puerto Ricans had a median household income of $21,056, compared to $23,694 for Mexican Americans and $27,741 for Cuban Americans.

Changes in the Puerto Rican community on the mainland seemed to mirror those in the nation as a whole during the last decades of the twentieth century. These changes were creating a split society of the poor, the affluent, and a declining middle class. This process was a challenge to the Puerto Rican community as it struggled to find a social space within a multicultural United States. —*Victor M. Rodriguez*

SUGGESTED READINGS:

• Dietz, James L. *Economic History of Puerto Rico.* Princeton, N.J.: Princeton University Press, 1986. Probably the most authoritative economic history of Puerto Rico. Its analyses of the nineteenth and twentieth centuries are the best sections of the book.

• Flores, Juan. *Divided Borders: Essays on Puerto Rican Identity.* Houston: Arte Público Press, 1993. A good collection of essays exploring the various roots of the cultural identity of Puerto Ricans. The author is probably the most authoritative contemporary voice on Puerto Rican cultural identity.

• History Task Force, Centro de Estudios Puertorriqueños. *Labor Migration Under Capitalism: The Puerto Rican Experience.* New York: Monthly Review Press, 1979. Attempts to provide an overall view of the process of migration of Puerto Ricans to the United States. Good review of the migration literature.

• Meléndez, Edwin, and Edgardo Meléndez, eds. *Colonial Dilemma: Critical Perspectives on Contemporary Puerto Rico.* Boston: South End Press, 1993. A collection of articles by Puerto Rican specialists in the political, economic, and social issues regarding relations between Puerto Rico and the United States.

• Rodríguez, Clara E. *Puerto Ricans: Born in the U.S.A.* Boston: Unwin Hyman, 1989. A comprehensive attempt to provide a historical, sociological, and cultural understanding of Puerto Ricans in the United States and their historical roots.

Puerto Rico: The Commonwealth of Puerto Rico is the fourth largest island in the Caribbean Sea. Its citizens, though they speak Spanish, are citizens of the United States because of the island's commonwealth relationship with the United States. They have the highest per capita income in that area of the Spanish-speaking world.

Introduction. Puerto Ricans of the late twentieth century were confronted by cultural concerns. Were they Latin Americans or tied to the culture of the United States? Could they achieve a cultural blend incorporating the best of both worlds? How Puerto Ricans arrived at this dilemma is an interesting historical lesson.

Settlement. Christopher Columbus first explored the coast of the island on November 19, 1493. He was accompanied by the young nobleman Juan PONCE DE LEÓN, who is said to have exclaimed, "¡Que puerto rico!" ("What a rich port!") upon first seeing San Juan's harbor. The island was at first called San Juan, with the port named Puerto Rico. Having received permission to colonize the island in 1508, Ponce de León and his companions encountered about thirty thousand native Arawaks living there. The Arawaks, who are also known as Taino, called their land Borinquen. They were prosperous and contented before European contact, but EPIDEMICS of imported European diseases reduced their number to about four thousand by 1515. They had disappeared almost completely by the year 1600.

Evidence of native culture can still be found in scattered locations. One of these is the Caguana Indian Ceremonial Park, west of Utuado. This site dates from around A.D. 1100 and contains ten Taino ball courts and small monoliths with petroglyphs. The setting, amid limestone haystacks and lush green vegetation, is truly spectacular.

The Tibes Indian Ceremonial Center, at the edge of Ponce on Route 503, is more developed. Dating from A.D. 300, it contains a burial ground, seven ball courts, two plazas, a good museum, and a replica of a Taino village. The site was discovered in 1975, after runoff from a heavy rain exposed parts of the stone foundations.

Although some black slaves were imported during the colonial period to provide labor on sugarcane plantations, most Puerto Ricans are primarily of Hispanic origin. A rich source of information about rural colonial life is the Hacienda Buena Vista, at kilometer 16.8 on Route 10, north of Ponce. This hacienda dates from 1833, was converted into a coffee plantation and corn mill in 1845, and continued to operate until 1937. It was restored by Fideicomiso de Conservación de Puerto Rico.

Spain ceded Puerto Rico to the United States in 1898. Since that time, cultural influences from the United States have been strong, but much of the indigenous culture remains. The cultural heritage of the people is particularly evident in their architecture. Ornate and beautiful colonial structures often sit side by side with modern office buildings. These sharp contrasts are typical of the hybrid culture of modern Puerto Rico, which mixes old and new, Hispanic and English.

El Morro, in old San Juan, Puerto Rico. (Hazel Hankin)

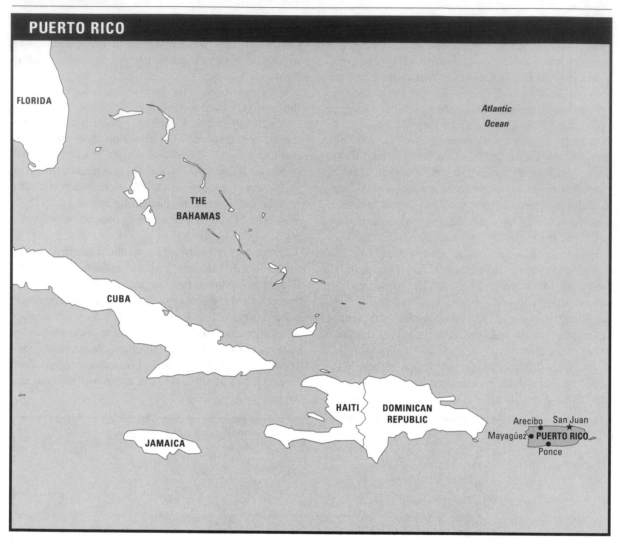

PUERTO RICO

Land and Resources. Puerto Rico is one of the four islands that form the Greater Antilles in the Caribbean Sea. It lies about one thousand miles southeast of Miami, Florida, between the island of Hispaniola and the Virgin Islands. It is roughly rectangular in shape, extending about 35 miles from north to south and about 105 miles east to west. It has about thirty-four hundred square miles of land area, making it larger than the state of Delaware but smaller than Connecticut. Vieques and Culebra, small islands off the eastern coast, are Puerto Rican possessions. The Puerto Rico Trench, just to the north of the island, is one of the deepest parts of the Atlantic Ocean, more than twenty-eight thousand feet deep.

Landforms. Puerto Rico has very little flat land. It is ringed by a narrow coastal plain, and a mountain range runs the width of the island from west to east. This range is known as the Cordillera Central in the western part of the island and the Sierra de Cayey in the east. The highest peak within it, Cerro de Punta, reaches about forty-four hundred feet above sea level. Part of this mountainous backbone is composed of old, long-inactive volcanic mountains. Limestone rocks cover large areas as well.

Limestone erosion in tropical regions frequently results in surface features such as haystacks and sinkholes; Puerto Rico has many of both. Weathered limestone terrain with features of this sort is called karst topography. A number of spectacular haystacks can be seen along the road west of Utuado near La Caguana archaeological site. Just to the north, the main antenna at the Arecibo radio-telescope observatory occupies a giant sinkhole. The topography of Puerto Rico includes some of the most important caves in the Western Hemisphere. One of the more spectacular sites is the Río Camuy Cave Park, near Lares. Río Camuy runs underground for part of its course, forming what is said to be the third largest subterranean river in the world.

Coastal landforms make up an important part of the landscape of any island. Fine sandy beaches dot Puerto Rico's periphery. Apart from those at the major hotels, one of the best for swimming is located at Luquillo, east of San Juan. Popular beaches for surfing include Pine Grove Beach in Isla Verde and Surfer Beach at the former Ramey Air Force Base in the northwest corner of the island. Beautiful coral reefs and cays lie close offshore in many places, offering opportunities for snorkelers and scuba divers. Phosphorescent Bay, on the southwest coast, is home to a minute form of marine life that gives off a spectacular ghostly glow on moonless nights.

Climate. Four major factors affect Puerto Rico's climate. First, the island's location in the tropics produces warm to hot temperatures throughout the year. Second, the surrounding ocean supplies plenty of moisture. Third, the prevailing northeast trade winds (often referred to as the "Weather Machine of the Caribbean") carry this moisture to the island. Fourth, the central mountain range forces the wind to release much of its moisture on north-facing slopes, in a process called orographic precipitation.

Temperatures generally range from the low 70's to the mid-80's, in degrees Fahrenheit. Temperatures are at the low end of this range during the Northern Hemisphere winter. Places along the northern and eastern coasts are comfortable even during the summer months because of cooling breezes coming off the ocean.

Rainfall varies depending on the season and location. Most precipitation falls during the months from May to October, with the heaviest rains coming after June. San Juan, Puerto Rico's capital and its largest city, on the northeast coast, receives about sixty inches of rain each year. Nearby mountain slopes are drenched by nearly double that amount. The city of Ponce, on the southwestern coast, receives only about thirty-six inches of rainfall per year.

Puerto Rico lies within the Caribbean hurricane belt. The island is occasionally hit with a storm that causes heavy damage. For example, in 1989 Hurricane Hugo left six people dead and twelve thousand homeless, causing millions of dollars in damage.

Natural Vegetation. The island's climatic patterns are reflected in its natural vegetation. North-facing mountain slopes are covered with a lush, green, dense montane rain forest, but a sparse subtropical scrub woodland covers the southwestern coast. Natural vegetation on much of the island has been changed by human activity. Some of the rain forest in the northeast has been preserved in the Caribbean (El Yunque) National Forest, near Luquillo. Approximately 240 varieties of trees have been identified in the twenty-eight thousand acres of El Yunque. The tall trees form a solid green canopy sixty feet above the ground, darkly shading the forest floor. Bromeliads, orchids, and other epiphytic plants are numerous, as are parasitic plants such as the *liana* (vine). The entire forest is a bird sanctuary, home to the Puerto Rican parrot.

Outside the rain forest, coastal mangrove swamp can be found at Piñones Forest, east of San Juan, and on the southern coast near Salinas and Jobos Bay. Smaller areas of swampland exist elsewhere on the island.

Fauna. Guánica Forest, west of Ponce, has a large variety of bird species, some of which are endangered. This unique scrub forest has been declared an international biosphere reserve by the United Nations Educational, Scientific, and Cultural Organization (UNESCO). Manatees, turtles, and migrating ducks can be found at Jobos Bay. The unique two-toned call of the *coquí*, an inch-long green tree frog, is common throughout Puerto Rico. The little animal is popular among the people and can be regarded as one of Puerto Rico's national symbols.

Soils. Puerto Rico's soils are moderately fertile. Highly weathered reddish oxisols are found in most parts of the island. The red color is caused by the accumulation of aluminum oxide and iron oxide during the weathering process. With careful management, the soil can be productive for farming. The regions with the best soils have all been deforested at one time or another. Some of the low alluvial areas along the southern coast contain saline soils. Evaporation of moisture from the soil exceeds rainfall in that area during most of the year. Residents have taken advantage of this by constructing salt evaporation ponds.

Drainage. Because of its heavy annual rainfall, Puerto Rico has many rivers, especially on the northern side of the island, but all are short and none are navigable. Several have been dammed for hydroelectricity production.

Natural Resources. Puerto Rico has no significant mineral resources. The fine harbor at San Juan and the protected anchorage at Guánica Bay on the southwestern coast provide excellent access to the sea, however, making trading off the island easier. The island's pleasant climate, beautiful sandy beaches, rolling mountains, and lush green vegetation may prove to be its most valuable natural resources because they attract tourists.

Demography. Puerto Rico's population was estimated at 3.6 million in 1993. It was expected to reach 4.2 million by the year 2010. The island's 1.1 percent annual rate of natural population increase is one of the lowest of any Spanish-speaking country. Approximately three-fourths of all Puerto Ricans on the island live in the crowded towns and cities. The population density of more than one thousand per square mile is well above that of the United States as a whole and even higher than that of Japan.

Puerto Ricans are very mobile, and tens of thousands migrate between the mainland United States and the island each year. Net arrivals in the United States from Puerto Rico averaged thirty-two thousand per year between 1980 and 1988. As of 1990, about two million Puerto Ricans lived on the U.S. mainland, mostly in the Northeast, in the vicinity of New York City. In fact, more Puerto Ricans lived in New York City than in San Juan, and the residents of New York City have taken on their own name, NUYORICANS. Economic conditions have a major effect on the number of Puerto Ricans who decide to travel in each direction.

Language and Religion. Spanish has been the official language of Puerto Rico since March 4, 1991, and was the language in most common use long before that. English, however, is widely understood. More than 90 percent of all Puerto Ricans are Roman Catholics.

Education and Health. A well-developed system of free public education has reduced illiteracy to about 10 percent of the population. Public school classes are taught in Spanish; English is taught as a foreign language in Puerto Rican schools. The University of Puerto Rico (with major campuses in Río Piedras and Mayagüez) and Inter-American University (in San Germán) are two leading institutions of higher education. Puerto Ricans as a whole enjoy good health. Life expectancy as of 1990 was seventy-one years for males and seventy-eight years for females.

Music. Puerto Ricans consider music to be an important part of their cultural heritage. The MERENGUE and SALSA, which have spread to other countries, are favorites, but the sedate DANZA is the traditional national music. It is a slow, romantic, sentimental music

The University of Puerto Rico campus at Río Piedras. (Hazel Hankin)

that originated in Europe and is designed for ballroom dancing. Juan Morel Campos (1857-1896) was one of the most prolific of all *danza* composers, with more than five hundred published compositions.

The PLENA is a musical tradition with African origins. It was introduced to Puerto Rico by a couple from Barbados who settled in Ponce early in the 1900's. This is typical call-and-response music with a chorus led by a soloist, the *inspirador*. The four-line stanzas are calypso-style commentaries on everyday life, while the rhythm is distinctly African. Manual A. Jiménez ("Canario") is the best-known composer and performer of the *plena*. Few black people live in Puerto Rico. The largest concentration is in the town of Loíza Aldea; its annual Feast of Santiago in July is the best place to hear their music, the BOMBA.

Peasant farmers (*jíbaros*) in the hilly and mountainous interior sing and dance the *seis*, whose varied forms originated in Spain. This music is played with guitars such as the CUATRO (small, with four strings) accompanied by the GÜIRO (scraper), *pandereta* (tambourine), MARACAS, and *bomba* (drum). People of the interior also practice the custom of singing beautiful AGUINALDOS (carols) at Christmas. Baltazar Carrero is one of the best-known interpreters of mountain music. The Museo de la Música Puertorriqueña in Ponce is a rich source of information on Puerto Rican musical forms.

Writing. One of the favorite subjects of Puerto Rican writers is the *jíbaro*, a peasant farmer called a *campesino* elsewhere in Latin America. Manuel Alonso Pacheco was one of the first and best-known authors to portray the life of these rural people. His *El gíbaro: Cuadro de costumbras de la isla de Puerto-Rico* (1849; the peasant: sketch of the customs of the island of Puerto Rico) is a mixture of romanticism and *realismo costumbrista*, a style of writing in a realistic manner about people and their customs. Manuel ZENO GANDÍA's series of four novels, *Crónicas de un mundo enfermo* (chronicles of a sick world), which appeared between 1896 and 1925, are a chronicle of the economic misery of the Puerto Rican people and of immigration to New York City. *La Guaracha del Macho Camacho* (1976; *Macho Camacho's Beat*, 1980), by Luis Rafael SÁNCHEZ, reflects modern times, centering on a traffic jam in San Juan.

Economic Development. Puerto Rico was known as the "poorhouse of the Caribbean" in the 1930's. The average cane worker earned only $250 a year. During the 1940's, the island began its transformation into a modern industrial economy. The "OPERATION BOOT-STRAP" economic development program of Governor Luís MUÑOZ MARÍN, the island's first elected governor (1948-1964), spurred the rate of growth. The Economic Development Administration, known widely as FOMENTO, was created in 1950 to oversee development efforts. Its efforts continued into the late twentieth century. The island's innovative tax concession program has been studied by economists the world over. By 1990, the economy of the island had advanced sufficiently to give Puerto Rico a per capita annual income of about $6,000, the highest in the region among Spanish-speaking countries.

Agriculture. The modernization of farming in Puerto Rico began with the Rural Land Classification Program, an inventory of resource and land use undertaken by geographers between 1949 and 1951. Although farming employs less than 7 percent of the work force and sugar is no longer the driving force of the island's economy, agriculture is still important. Milk is the farm product that ranks first in value; meat, chickens, and eggs are close behind.

Traditional export crops do not contribute as much to the economy as in the past. Fields of sugarcane are still found in the coastal lowlands, and coffee farms are concentrated in the western and central parts of the highlands. Farmers raising coffee in the highlands generally take care to shade the coffee plants with taller trees so as to produce the best quality coffee possible. Tobacco continues to be a valuable specialty crop in the eastern highlands around Caguas. Some of it is grown in the shade of white muslin sheets. Most of it is used for cigar filler (the interior part of the cigar). A few farms specialize in pineapples or coconuts.

Puerto Rico is a food-deficit region, importing about $1 billion worth of food each year as of the early 1990's. Although Puerto Rico had the highest income among Spanish-speaking countries of the region in the early 1990's, the comparison was with poor relations. Nearly half of the Puerto Rican people depended on food stamps. Reliance on imported food has caused a change in the Puerto Rican diet, with traditional favorites such as taro and sweet potatoes declining in popularity.

Manufacturing. Widespread availability of cheap hydroelectricity, an attractive ten- to thirty-year tax exemption, and a well-educated work force have proved attractive to U.S. companies. Almost every town of appreciable size in Puerto Rico has at least one factory.

The island is the world's largest producer of rum. Factories manufacturing textiles, clothing, electronic

Groups including the National Congress for Puerto Rican Rights lobby on behalf of Puerto Ricans living on the mainland.
(City Lore, Martha Cooper)

items, pharmaceuticals, and consumer goods such as ballpoint pens have joined the rum factories. Oil refineries, using imported petroleum, and petrochemical plants are relatively recent arrivals on the island.

Approximately twenty-five hundred manufacturing concerns could be found within the commonwealth in the early 1990's. About half were located in the San Juan metropolitan area. Most of the companies were owned by U.S. corporations, and about 70 percent of the income from manufacturing on the island flowed back to the mainland. Despite this flight of capital, manufacturing accounted for 20 percent of Puerto Rico's total income.

The Puerto Rican government has attempted to attract capital-intensive industries that pay higher wages. One response by industrialists has been to recruit Puerto Ricans to train low-paid workers in new factories established in the Dominican Republic. Puerto Rico thus faced the dilemma of wishing to attract business but not at the expense of accepting low wages for its workers.

Puerto Rico's industrialization has provided the government with money for an extensive program of slum clearance, expressway construction, and port development. The government has made extensive efforts to revitalize the slums of San Juan. The Isla Verde airport in San Juan, another government project, is modern and attractive.

Tourism. During the early 1990's, Puerto Rico was the second-most-popular destination for tourists in the Caribbean, after the Bahamas. Most tourists stayed in hotels or resorts in the San Juan area. San Juan has also become a popular stop on the Caribbean cruise ship circuit, and many cruise ships use San Juan as their home port. Visitors pumped more than $600 million into the economy annually; tourism thus was a growth industry of critical importance to the Puerto Rican people.

In addition to the beaches, casinos, floor shows, tennis, and other attractions that the major hotels and resorts have to offer, Puerto Rico has many diversions for tourists, including fine colonial architecture and fortifications to visit in old San Juan. San Felipe del Morro, built in 1591 to guard the harbor entrance, is another popular tourist destination. Sport fishing and the racetrack at El Comandante attract others. Several hotels have championship golf courses.

Government. Puerto Rico was a colony of Spain until 1898, at which point it became a territorial possession of the United States. The constitution of 1952 established Puerto Rico as a commonwealth. Some critics maintain that Puerto Rico still has a colonial relationship with the United States, but it is officially described as a "self-governing commonwealth freely associated with the United States." Several plebiscites have been held to determine the island's political status (*see* PUERTO RICO—STATUS DEBATE). Voters favoring continuation of the current arrangement have won each time, although those voting for statehood came close to winning in 1993. The independence movement has never won more than 10 percent of the vote. A small guerrilla group, the Macheteros, demands complete separation from the United States.

The Popular Democratic Party (PARTIDO POPULAR DEMOCRÁTICO), which favors commonwealth status, saw its candidate, Rafael Hernández Colon, serve as governor from 1988 to 1992. The New Progressive Party, which favors statehood, won the governorship in 1992 with its candidate, Pedro Rossello.

Puerto Ricans became U.S. citizens in 1917, with passage of the JONES ACT. They may move freely between the island and the mainland. Once on the mainland, they are free to vote in any U.S. election once they satisfy residency requirements, but they cannot vote in federal elections while living on the island. Puerto Ricans on the island do not pay U.S. federal income tax on income earned from Puerto Rican sources.

The island elects its own governor and has done so since 1948. The governor's residence is the oldest continuously occupied executive mansion in the Western Hemisphere. The legislative branch of the Puerto Rican government is composed of a Senate and a House of Representatives. Puerto Rican voters send a nonvoting representative to the U.S. House of Representatives.

As of the early 1990's, about 30 percent of all income in Puerto Rico originated in Washington, D.C., much of it in the form of food stamps and other assistance programs. Military installations provided a channel for some of this spending. As U.S. citizens, Puerto Ricans were eligible for U.S. military service, and the United States has taken advantage of Puerto Rico's strategic location by building military installations there.

Important Cities and Other Points of Interest. San Juan is Puerto Rico's capital and largest city. Blessed with an excellent harbor on the northeastern coast, it is the island's leading manufacturing center, port city, tourist destination, and cultural mecca. The 1990 census reported a population of 437,735. Nearby Bayamón had a population of 220,262, and Carolina was home to 177,806. The beautiful colonial structures and narrow streets of Old San Juan, intermixed with outstanding art galleries, are worth an entire day to see. Other points of interest include the financial district in Hato Rey, the University of Puerto Rico campus in Río Piedras, and the botanical garden at the Agricultural Experiment Station.

Puerto Rico had about seven thousand miles of paved roads in 1990, making the automobile an efficient means of traveling across the island. Roads are maintained reasonably well but tend to twist and turn in the interior.

Ponce is one of Puerto Rico's largest cities. It is located on the southern coast and is connected to San Juan by the Autopista las Américas expressway. It is also a major manufacturing center, and many goods flow through its port. The Plaza las Delicias houses a cathedral and red-and-black fire station, built for a fair in 1883. Guánica Bay, to the west, is now the site of a large industrial complex. It was the site of the first U.S. troop landing on the island during the Spanish-American War.

Mayagüez, with a 1990 population of slightly more than one hundred thousand, is at the western end of the island. A market and service center, it is the site of a large beer brewery, the Tropical Agricultural Research Station, and a botanical garden, all of which are situated next to one of the campuses of the University of Puerto Rico.

Conclusion. Puerto Rico has a long history of ties with the United States. Its residents, citizens of the

FACTS AT A GLANCE

Capital: San Juan

Area: 3,515 square miles

Population (1990): 3,522,037

Percentage living in urban areas: 67

Status: U.S. commonwealth since 1952

United States by birth, are an important part of the Latino community. Many take advantage of the right to unrestricted travel to the U.S. mainland, and as of 1990 nearly half of Puerto Rico's citizens had chosen part-time or full-time residency on the mainland. This linkage with the United States presented a dilemma for Puerto Ricans as they struggled to maintain a national culture while taking advantage of the opportunities available through interaction with the United States.

—*James N. Snaden*

SUGGESTED READINGS:

• Fernandez, Ronald. *The Disenchanted Island: Puerto Rico and the United States in the Twentieth Century*. New York: Praeger, 1992. Analysis of the relationship between the two.

• Hanson, Earl P. *Transformation: The Story of Modern Puerto Rico*. New York: Simon & Schuster, 1955. A survey of economic development and cultural change.

• Landy, David. *Tropical Childhood*. New York: Harper & Row, 1965. A sociological study of cultural transmission and learning in a Puerto Rican Village.

• López, Adalberto, and James Petras. *Puerto Rico and Puerto Ricans*. New York: Halstead Press, 1974. A collection of studies in history and society.

• Palm, Risa, and Michael E. Hodgson. *Natural Hazards in Puerto Rico*. Boulder, Colo.: Institute of Behavior Science, 1993. Fascinating research by geographers.

• Picó, Rafael. *The Geography of Puerto Rico*. Chicago: Aldine, 1974. The best geography of Puerto Rico by the island's most famous geographer.

• Robinson, Kathryn. *The Other Puerto Rico*. Santurce, Puerto Rico: Permanent Press, 1987. A guidebook designed for those who really want to get to know the Puerto Rican people.

• Wagenheim, Kal. *Puerto Rico: A Profile*. New York: Praeger, 1970. A journalist's view of the island, its people, and their culture.

Puerto Rico—status debate: The island of Puerto Rico has been known as the Freely Associated State of Puerto Rico since 1950. Despite various attempts to change Puerto Rico's political status, it remained subject to U.S. jurisdiction in the 1990's. The debate over Puerto Rico's future status was stalemated after an indecisive 1993 referendum on options of maintaining the status quo, statehood, or independence.

Evolution of Puerto Rico's Status. When the Spanish were driven from Puerto Rico in 1898 at the end of the SPANISH-AMERICAN WAR, the island came under U.S.

military rule. Puerto Ricans were not formally consulted when civilian rule was restored by the 1900 FORAKER ACT, which declared that Puerto Rico "belonged to but did not form part of the United States." The U.S. Congress gained control over Puerto Rico's trade and taxation structures, and U.S. federal courts won jurisdiction over the island's judicial system. Washington had effectively made Puerto Rico its colony, but because U.S. law prohibits ownership of colonies, the term "colony" has always been avoided in official discourse.

In 1917, the JONES ACT provided for a popularly elected island legislature and U.S. citizenship for all Puerto Ricans. The island's governor, however, remained directly appointed by the U.S. president, who, along with Congress, retained complete veto power over decisions made in Puerto Rico. Unsettled political tensions created by the Jones Act simmered for thirty years.

In 1947, President Harry S Truman announced his support for a popularly elected governor in place of

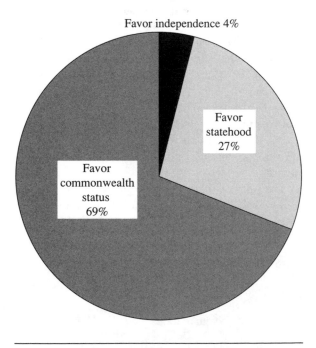

OPINIONS OF MAINLAND PUERTO RICANS ON THE STATUS QUESTION

Favor independence 4%

Favor statehood 27%

Favor commonwealth status 69%

Source: Data are from the Latino National Political Survey, which polled a representative sample of 589 Puerto Ricans in forty metropolitan areas in 1989-1990. See Rodolfo O. de la Garza et al., *Latino Voices: Mexican, Puerto Rican, and Cuban Perspectives on American Politics* (Boulder, Colo.: Westview Press, 1992), Table 7.28.

Demonstrators from the Puerto Rican Socialist Party demand independence for the island while they march in a parade in New York City. (Hazel Hankin)

appointed executives. The Elective Governor Act was passed later that year, transferring a significant amount of local administrative power to the island and leading to the first freely elected governor in 1948.

Puerto Ricans saw fit to elect Luis MUÑOZ MARÍN, an advocate of Puerto Rican independence. Eager to court Washington's support, he proposed a compromise formula whereby Puerto Rico would "freely enter" into a "compact" of political association with the United States. In 1950, U.S. law was changed to allow Puerto Rico its own constitution, subject to congressional approval, and an islandwide referendum was slated to ratify the new status arrangement known as the "freely associated state" of Puerto Rico.

The referendum was greeted with a boycott by the Puerto Rican Independence Party (PIP), an abortive uprising organized by the Nationalist Party, and even an assassination attempt in Washington, D.C., against President Truman by Puerto Rican nationalists. Pro-independence forces resented the new "partnership" with the United States, seeing it as acquiescence to colonialism. Only 65 percent of registered voters on the island participated in the vote. Three-quarters of these voters opted for the free association status. The new Puerto Rican constitution was subsequently drafted and approved.

The 1967 Referendum. Political debate over Puerto Rico's status persisted in the years following this apparent resolution, until even the governor finally conceded that the simple ratification of the island's new status had denied Puerto Ricans the choice of any alternative. In 1960, Muñoz Marín convened a status commission, and in 1967, a "decisive" popular vote was designed to resolve the issue. Puerto Ricans would now have three options from which to choose: statehood, a more autonomous commonwealth, or independence.

This U.S.-style referendum still fell short of decolonization procedures established by the United Nations because it failed to transfer power to the island prior to the vote. Consequently, most *independentistas* refused to participate and instead advocated a boycott. Fully one-third of registered Puerto Rican voters ultimately abstained from participation. Of votes cast, 60 percent favored a more autonomous commonwealth, and most of the remainder opted for statehood.

Once again, an imperfect plebiscite failed to resolve decisively the status issue. With abstention high, no specific status option managed to win a majority of Puerto Ricans. Complaints were made that the respective referendum options had not been well defined and that the process remained tainted because the real power to implement the "consultation" remained in Washington.

The 1993 Referendum. On February 9, 1989, before a joint session of the U.S. Congress, President George Bush conceded that Puerto Rico's political status remained an unresolved issue. The leadership of the pro-statehood New Progressive Party, the pro-commonwealth Popular Democratic Party, and the Puerto Rican Independence Party issued a joint response, declaring that Puerto Ricans deserved the formal opportunity to choose their political status.

Like most preceding Republican administrations, the Bush Administration supported statehood and judged the time ripe for annexation. U.S. political elites, however, have always been divided over Puerto Rico's status because of their multiple interests in the island. In the 1990's, some favored the status quo because federal tax exemptions allowed the island to net large profits for U.S. corporations. Also significant were several key military bases and testing fields that made Puerto Rico an important asset for the Pentagon, one that would likely be threatened by independence.

Those supporting the statehood option believed that massive federal subsidies for Puerto Rico were too costly, particularly since Puerto Ricans were exempt from federal income tax. Those opposing statehood noted that a fifty-first state would create two new Senate seats and reallocate seats in the House of Representatives from other states. Puerto Rico would also raise numerous social policy issues if it became the first overwhelmingly Spanish-speaking state.

From the Puerto Rican side, pro-statehood forces emphasized the benefits of winning greater representation in the U.S. federal government, such as higher levels of federal subsidies. Supporters of the free association arrangement asserted that the economic benefits of statehood would be offset by increased taxes and the threat to the cultural integrity of Puerto Rico, particularly its Spanish-speaking heritage. Moderate proindependence forces called for a gradual transition to independence, with close ties to the United States maintained in accordance with the mutual interests of both countries.

After lengthy debate, a referendum remarkably similar to the 1967 vote was held on November 15, 1993. Although the advocates of the "freely associated state" option once again prevailed, a far narrower margin of 48 percent edged ahead of the 46 percent in favor of statehood and the 4 percent in favor of independence. Given the extremely close results and the fact that most *independentistas* boycotted the vote, many analysts considered the issue of Puerto Rico's political status still unresolved in the mid-1990's.

—*Richard A. Dello Buono*

SUGGESTED READINGS: • Carr, Raymond. *Puerto Rico: A Colonial Experiment.* New York: Vintage Books, 1984. • Lopez, Adalberto, ed. *The Puerto Ricans, Their History, Culture, and Society.* Cambridge, Mass.: Schenkman, 1980. • Melendez, Edgardo. *Puerto Rico's Statehood Movement.* New York: Greenwood Press, 1988. • Melendez, Edwin, and Edgardo Melendez. *Colonial Dilemma: Critical Perspectives on Contemporary Puerto Rico.* Boston: South End Press, 1993. • Morales Carrion, Arturo. *Puerto Rico: A Political and Cultural History.* New York: W. W. Norton, 1983.

Puig, Manuel (Dec. 28, 1932, General Villegas, Argentina—July 22, 1990, Cuernavaca, Mexico): Writer. Puig was born in the province of Buenos Aires, where he spent his infancy and received his elementary education. In 1946 he was sent to the city of Buenos Aires to an American boarding school. He had begun learning English in 1942 in order to enjoy more thoroughly the American films he and his mother saw every afternoon.

In 1950, Puig enrolled in the School of Architecture of the University of Buenos Aires. He soon shifted to philosophy. He attended a film school in Italy, then left for Paris and London. At this time, Puig began writing film scripts.

Once back in Argentina, he began working as an assistant director in the Argentine movie industry. In 1965, he completed his first novel. *La traición de Rita Hayworth* (*Betrayed by Rita Hayworth*, 1971) was published in Buenos Aires in 1968. The next year, *Boquitas pintadas* (*Heartbreak Tango: A Serial*, 1973) became an instant best-seller. Puig's other novels include *El beso de la mujer araña* (1976; *Kiss of the Spider Woman*, 1984), *Pubis angelical* (1979; English translation, 1986), *Maldición eterna a quien lea estas páginas* (1980; *Eternal Curse on the Reader of These Pages*, 1982), and *Sangre de amor correspondido* (1982; *Blood of Requited Love*, 1984). Puig's innovative language and narrative technique, his juxtaposition of illusion and reality, and his revolutionary perspective make him one of the foremost contemporary writers in Latin America.

Punche: Variety of tobacco. Related to thorn apple, or *datura*, *punche* is a variety of tobacco that can be used for regular smoking and as a medicinal herb (*see* HERBAL MEDICINE). Mexican folk healing prescribes, for example, ground *punche* mixed with lard to be placed on the chest to cure a cold; pulverized *punche* mixed with the juice of the gum plant, *yerba de buey*, is tied over the kidney area to cure kidney problems. FOLK MEDICINE also prescribes chewing *punche* to aid digestion and to treat toothaches. It is also believed that smoking *punche* stimulates obese people to spit out body fat.

Purim, Flora (b. Mar. 6, 1942, Rio de Janeiro, Brazil): Singer, lyricist, and musician. Purim grew up in a musical family and studied the piano with her mother. Years later, while she was studying percussion, she met musician Airto MOREIRA, whom she later married.

Flora Purim. (AP/Wide World Photos)

Purim performed in São Paulo and Rio de Janeiro with the group Quarteto Novo, which included Hermeto Pascoal and Airto Moreira. In the late 1960's, she moved to the United States, where she played, toured, and recorded with Stan Getz's Latin jazz group (1968), Duke Pearson (1969-1970), Gil Evans (1971), and George Duke.

Both Purim and Moreira then joined Chick Corea's quintet Return to Forever. They performed on the album *Light as a Feather* (1972) and *Return to Forever* (1973).

In 1974, Purim recorded her first solo album, *Butterfly Dreams*. Her musical style is a fusion of Brazilian, jazz, pop, and other idioms. She considers her voice to be her principal musical instrument. She has developed wordless singing, using electronic devices to distort, change, or duplicate sounds as needed in order to team up with such instruments as the flute, soprano sax, guitar, and trombone. Purim won the *Down Beat* critics' poll in 1974 and went on tour in Japan, the United States, and Europe. In 1976, Purim formed her own group.

Queiroz, Rachel de (b. Nov. 17, 1910, Fortaleza, Brazil): Writer. Although many of her novels include Rio de Janeiro as part of their backdrop, it is northeastern Brazil that is an indelible source of inspiration for Queiroz's portrayals of women who search for an understanding of their role in life and society. Her first novel, *O Quinze* (1930), describes the disastrous drought of that year in her native state of Ceará.

Queiroz's other novels include *O Caçador de Tatu* (1967), *João Miguel* (1932), *Caminho de Pedras* (1937), and *As Três Marias* (1939; *The Three Marias*, 1963), which presents the constant frustrations faced by protagonists who attempt to come to grips with sexual inequality, provincial life, lack of education, their roles as mothers and wives, their own sexual feelings, and their hopes for some form of self-realization. In *Dôra, Doralina* (1975; English translation, 1984), the author draws her protagonist as a woman who eventually is free to feel independent, sexually fulfilled, and responsible.

Queiroz has won a permanent place in Brazilian literature. From her beginnings as one of the creators of the "novel of the Northeast" in the 1930's, she has been particularly successful in creating characters who reflect her deep understanding of the situation of Brazilian women.

Quelite: Edible weed found in Mexico and Central America. The word *quelite* derives from the Aztec *quilitl*, a generic name for edible greens. In Mexico and Central America, it is a common name for spinach and all sorts of herbaceous plants added to salads. Among some of the species of *quelite* one finds the stinky *quelite*, *chenopodium foetidum*; the wild *quelite* from the Sonora and Sinaloa regions, *amaranthus polygonoides*; and the ash-colored or common *quelite*, *chenopodium mexicanum*. The colloquial expression *tener cara de quelite* (to have a *quelite* face) means to have a pale and greenish complexion.

Quena: Andean open notched flute. *Quenas* were first made of animal, bird, or human bone; clay or gourd; or metals such as gold and silver. They have five or six finger holes and a thumb hole. Modern *quenas* are made of cane and are longer, usually from ten to twenty inches in length. *Quenas* produce a two-octave chromatic scale and are played almost exclusively by men, both as solo instruments and in small ensembles including other *quenas* and drums. They originated in Peru before the year 200 B.C.E., spread later to Bolivia, and now can be found in Chile, Argentina, Ecuador, Colombia, Venezuela, and elsewhere.

Querétaro, Protocol of: Clarification of the TREATY OF GUADALUPE HIDALGO. After members of the U.S. Senate amended the provisions of the Treaty of Guadalupe Hidalgo, which ended the Mexican American War, this protocol was composed. It resulted from discussion between American diplomats and Mexican officials regarding the reasons why the Senate had unilaterally made such alterations to the peace treaty. The Treaty of Guadalupe Hidalgo had been ratified by the Mexican government before the protocol was drawn up; subsequently, questions arose as to whether the language and provisions of the protocol superseded provisions made in the peace treaty. Because neither government ever officially recognized or ratified the protocol as a diplomatic agreement, the United States countered these later questions by asserting that the protocol served as an explanatory document only and did not change any of the provisions of the Treaty of Guadalupe Hidalgo.

Quesada, Eugenio (b. 1927, Wickenburg, Ariz.): Artist. Quesada studied mural painting with Jean Charlot, a pioneer of Mexican muralism. He devoted himself to murals in the figurative tradition, mixing Hispanic and Native American elements. Commenting on ethnic art, Quesada noted that the Native American (Indian) element surges to the fore in art during times of political unease.

Quesada was educated in Arizona, California, and New York. He began teaching at Arizona State University in 1972 and has had numerous exhibitions of his work in Mexico and Arizona. He has studied important murals in Mexico and developed great respect for them, but much of his work is on the smaller scale of standard-size paintings.

Quesadilla: Tortilla folded over cheese and heated. *Quesadillas* in northern Mexico usually are minimalist, consisting of a cooked tortilla with cheese, heated on a dry griddle and folded over. Further south, they become more complicated. There, they usually are made from *MASA* patted into tortilla shape, folded over cheese and seasonings, especially *EPAZOTE* and CHILES, sometimes potatoes, *CHORIZO*, squash blossoms, and corn fungus. Outside of northern Mexico, *quesadillas* may be cooked on a dry griddle or sautéed in a little lard. They are an *ANTOJITO*, eaten primarily for snacks or light meals.

Quetzalcóatl (Kukultán): Deity. Quetzalcóatl was the supreme deity of the Toltecs and other groups in Mesoamerica in pre-Columbian times. Various stories and explanations surround him, based on both legend and historical truth. The name Quetzalcóatl comes from the Nahuatl words *quetzal* (a bird found in the jungles of Central and South America and considered sacred to many groups of people) and *cóatl* (snake); thus, he had the form of a feathered serpent. In pre-Columbian mythology and religion, birds represent the intangible force of wind, and snakes represent the tangible force of the earth. Quetzalcóatl brings together these opposite forces. A second explanation of Quetzalcóatl is that he was a white man, perhaps Scandinavian, who introduced new wisdom and arts to the Toltecs and served as their ruler for a period of time. During this time, Toltec civilization flourished and spread, and human sacrifice and wars of conquest were both abolished. All explanations credit Quetzalcóatl as the discoverer of corn and the bearer of culture; all state that he left the Toltecs to sail back to his homeland, Venus. When Hernán CORTÉS arrived in the Americas, he was perceived to be Quetzalcóatl. The Maya, conquered by the Toltecs, called Quetzalcóatl by the name of Kukultán. Today, Quetzalcóatl is a national symbol of Mexico.

Quinceañera: Mexican coming-of-age ceremony for a girl on her fifteenth birthday. The *quinceañera* is practiced throughout Mexico and in much of the adjacent United States, as well as in some other parts of Latin America. On a girl's fifteenth birthday, her parents sponsor a gala event that can include prayers at church, a formal dinner, a reception, and a dance. The *quinceañera* denotes that a girl has reached social adulthood and is a major event in her life. *Quinceañeras* often involve formal gowns, rented facilities, musical performances, and catered meals, and they can be very expensive.

Quinn, Anthony (Anthony Rudolph Oaxaca Quinn; b. Apr. 21, 1915, Chihuahua, Mexico): Actor. Quinn arrived in Hollywood at the age of four. He began his acting career in 1936 in the play *Clean Beds*. Notable performances in his lengthy stage career include starring roles in a 1961 production of *A Streetcar Named Desire* and a 1983 production of *Zorba the Greek*.

Quinn's film career spans half a century and more than 175 films, including *The Last Train from Madrid* (1937), *Blood and Sand* (1941), *Guadalcanal Diary* (1943), *Irish Eyes Are Smiling* (1944), *Back to Bataan* (1945), *Seven Cities of Gold* (1955), *The Man from Del Rio* (1956), *The Guns of Navarone* (1961), *Lawrence*

A depiction of the legend of how the Aztecs chose the location of their capital city. (Institute of Texan Cultures)

The quinceañera *marks a Latina's transition into social adulthood.* (James Shaffer)

Anthony Quinn has starred in numerous films and also found success as a writer and artist. (AP/Wide World Photos)

of Arabia (1962), *Behold a Pale Horse* (1964), *The Secret of Santa Vittoria* (1969), *Mohammed: Messenger of God* (1976), *The Children of Sanchez* (1978), *The Greek Tycoon* (1978), and the 1985 television movie *Onassis: Richest Man in the World.*

Quinn received Academy Awards for his supporting performances in *Viva Zapata!* (1952) and *Lust for Life* (1956). Quinn has also been a successful writer and artist. His paintings, sculptures, and serigraphs have been exhibited in the United States, France, and Mexico.

Quiñones, Wanda Maria (b. New York, N.Y.): Artist. Quiñones works in batik inspired by Colombian and Caribbean motifs. She has created various costumes, banners, slide presentations, and demonstrations as well as a logo for the television series *Visiones.*

Quiñones has exhibited widely at venues featuring Latin American art, including El Museo del Barrio in New York. She has held classes in crafts for older people and taught art workshops for children for the Board of Education of New York City and workshops at the Taller Boricua. She holds a B.A. from Adelphi University and also attended the Fashion Institute of Technology and Albany State University.

Quinto Sol Publications: Chicano publishing firm active in the 1960's and 1970's. In 1967, Octavio I. ROMANO-V., an anthropologist and behavioral sciences professor at the University of California, Berkeley, joined forces with cofounder Hermínio Ríos to publish an influential magazine called *El Grito: A Journal of Contemporary Mexican-American Thought.* Soon thereafter, they established Editorial Quinto Sol, the first national Chicano publishing house, which achieved great success at the height of the Chicano movement.

Quinto Sol's goal was to analyze and counter the academic and media stereotype of Mexican Americans as docile, nonliterate, nonintellectual, and nonartistic. Romano-V. believed that great talent existed in the Chicano community but lacked a public forum for expression. Although Quinto Sol addressed negative issues of stereotypes and discrimination, its purpose extended to creation of new Chicano literature and art. Honoring the richness of Chicano language, Quinto Sol published literature in various languages and dialects, including English, Spanish, a mixture of the two, and CALÓ, a street dialect.

Quinto Sol was Chicano-owned and was operated independently, with Romano-V. and Ríos serving as editors. From 1967 to 1972, Quinto Sol published about twenty volumes of *El Grito*, which included the

works of 135 authors. The quarterly publication featured scholarly articles, fiction, art, and poetry. The journal circulated throughout the United States and in several other countries, becoming the first and largest contemporary source of Chicano thought.

During these years, Quinto Sol published many books, most of which have become classics in Chicano literature. The first was *El Espejo* (the mirror), an anthology of Chicano creative writing published in 1969. It underwent several printings because of its popularity. In the same year, Quinto Sol created the PREMIO QUINTO SOL, a $1,000 prize for a Chicano literary piece. The first winner was Tomás RIVERA, a professor at the University of Texas at Austin, for his short story collection entitled *. . . y no se lo tragó la tierra* (1971; *. . . and the Earth Did Not Part*, 1971). The award established Rivera as a premier Mexican American writer. The 1971 prize winner was Rudolfo A. ANAYA, for his book *Bless Me, Ultima*, considered one of the finest works of Chicano literature. Also published in 1971 was *Voices: Readings from El Grito*, a volume of selections from the journal. Other writers published by Quinto Sol include Rolando HINOJOSA and poet ALURISTA.

Quinto Sol stopped publishing in 1974. In 1976, it re-emerged as Tonatiuh International (also established by Romano-V.) and launched a new journal, *Grito del Sol.* In the same year, Romano-V. legally merged Tonatiuh and Quinto Sol to form Tonatiuh-Quinto Sol International, Inc., also based in Berkeley, California. The company continued to publish Chicano works into the 1990's and printed a newsletter, *TQS News.*

Quirarte, Jacinto (b. Aug. 17, 1931, Jerome, Ariz.): Artist and art historian. Quirarte began his career as an artist. He is the author of *Mexican American Artists* (1973), published in Austin at the University of Texas Press. He was one of the first art historians to devote sole attention to Mexican American artists and to try to incorporate them into the art canon.

Quirarte earned a B.A. (1954) and M.A. (1958) from San Francisco State College, then a Ph.D. at the National University of Mexico (1964). From 1964 to 1966, he was director of cultural affairs for the Centro Venezolano Americano in Caracas, Venezuela. He spent a year teaching at Yale, then in 1967 took a position as art historian at the University of Texas at Austin. In 1972, he moved to the University of Texas at San Antonio, where he was dean of fine and applied arts until 1978. He developed new departments of art and music as well as a graduate art program.

R

Racism: Racism is both the belief that race genetically determines the limits of intelligence and character and the practice of discriminating against individuals because of their race. Racist ideas and practices have been common throughout human history. In the sixteenth century, the Spanish jurist Juan Ginés de Sepulveda argued that American Indians were inferior beings who were naturally suited to serving Europeans as slaves. In the nineteenth century, popular writers such as Joseph Gobineau and Houston Stuart Chamberlain ascribed cultural and psychological values to discrete races, and the doctrine of Social Darwinism was often interpreted as giving scientific justification for positions of dominance and subordination in race relations. In the United States, SLAVERY and Jim Crow segregation have been conspicuous examples of racist ideology; in the twentieth century, South Africa's system of apartheid and Nazi Germany's concept of Nordic supremacy have been among the most notorious examples.

Racism should be distinguished from ethnocentrism, a term that connotes prejudice or DISCRIMINATION based on ethnicity or culture. Moreover, racism is not the same as classism, or prejudice based on socioeconomic status. In fact, race, culture, and class overlap so frequently that, often, no distinction is made among the three factors in the popular perception of group differences; in racist societies, cultural and socioeconomic traits are commonly ascribed to inherent differences among races. There is evidence that ethnocentrism and classism are more universal than is racism.

In the United States, discrimination against Latinos has often had a racial component, but it has also often been based on notions of ethnocentrism and classism. This is because Latinos are heterogeneous in their racial makeup: They may be descendants of Europeans, Africans, American Indians, MESTIZOS, or numerous combinations.

It is generally acknowledged that racist ideas in Latin America have been less rigid than in the United States, at least since the abolition of slavery in Brazil and Cuba in the 1880's. Latin American countries have not had systems of enforced segregation and have minimized the idea of "pure race" by recognizing the existence of mixed races, especially mestizos and mulattoes. Spokespersons for Latin American countries sometimes claim that their societies do not discriminate on the basis of race, but Indians and members of other subordinate groups usually refute such claims. Still, it has been possible for individuals of non-European ancestry to hold political power in Latin America.

Many sociologists emphasize that racism normally involves institutional patterns of subordination and dominance. When there is a history of racial oppression, groups in privileged positions tend to perpetuate attitudes and stereotypes that operate to the disadvantage of subordinate groups, even after laws mandate equal opportunity. In the United States and elsewhere, this has been a major justification for AFFIRMATIVE ACTION programs, which allow preferential treatment to promote groups that have faced historical discrimination. Some theorists of the institutional perspective argue that it is impossible for those of subordinate races to practice racism, but even these theorists do not deny that such individuals may be prejudiced and may practice discrimination.

Radio Bilingüe (founded 1976): Radio network. The nonprofit California network has a mission of improving life for and sustaining the cultural identity of farmworkers in the San Joaquin Valley.

With the significant backing of a grant from a Catholic charity, radio station KSJV-FM was launched in Fresno, California, on July 4, 1980. It transmits a variety of music programs in addition to information related to health, education, immigration, civic action, and the arts.

Radio Bilingüe is supported primarily by donations from community members, businesses, and some foundations. It reaches across central California via KSJV and two retransmitting stations in Bakersfield and Modesto. In southern California, some of the network's programs are also aired by affiliate KUBO-FM, which began broadcasting from El Centro in April, 1989, and produces some of its own independent programming.

One of the distinctive features of this network is the operational and programming support it receives from innumerable volunteers who produce diverse music and public service programs in English, Spanish, and bilingual formats. As of 1994, Radio Bilingüe was the largest noncommercial producer of Spanish-language and bilingual programs.

Radio Bilingüe's news service, Noticiero Latino, is dedicated to providing information on and interpreta-

Latinos may suffer from racism and associated prejudice related to socioeconomic status. (Impact Visuals, H. L. Delgado)

tion of events in the United States, Latin America, and the Caribbean that are related to Hispanics in the United States. Radio Bilingüe also sponsors Viva El Mariachi, a music festival that serves as an important fund-raiser for the network.

Radio Martí (founded 1983): Radio station. Radio Martí operates continuously, offering news, entertainment, and music. The station was created by the administration of President Ronald Reagan in an effort to break what it called Fidel CASTRO's monopoly on information in Cuba. The station transmits from Voice of America facilities on Florida's Marathon Key at a frequency of 1180 kilohertz. Its counterpart, TV Martí, was jammed by Cuban authorities since its first broadcast in 1990, preventing most Cubans from seeing it. The programs of Radio Martí have gained a large audience.

Radio Martí has a statutory obligation to ensure "balanced and accurate" programming, but because it was created as a propaganda arm of the United States government "to promote the cause of freedom in Cuba," that objective has been difficult to meet. Conflicting objectives have created tensions among anti-Castro hardliners and liberals on the station's staff.

Congress funded Radio and TV Martí at $21 million in the fiscal year 1994 spending bill for the Voice of America. Of that appropriation, $7.5 million was to be withheld until supporters could prove that Cubans were receiving information. On June 15, 1993, President Bill Clinton announced that Radio Liberty, Radio Free Europe, the Voice of America, Worldnet TV and Film, and Radio and TV Martí would merge into the U.S. Information Agency under a seven-member board of governors.

Radio Noticias (founded 1983): News provider. Radio Noticias began as a division in Spanish of United Press International, a wire service transmitting news around the world. From its base in Washington, D.C., Radio Noticias distributed its seven-minute hourly news program to forty-two affiliated stations, from 6 A.M. to 9 P.M., Monday through Friday. As of June 27, 1994, Radio Noticias went off the air.

The Columbia Broadcasting System's HISPANIC RADIO NETWORK, which became known as CBS Americas, joined forces with United Press International to provide hourly newscasts in Spanish to listeners in the United States and Latin America. These broadcasts began on June 27, 1994. With this addition of regular news broadcasts, CBS Americas became a full-service network, providing affiliates with round-the-clock programming consisting of news, sporting events, entertainment, and public affairs broadcasts.

Railroad workers: U.S. railroads relied on Mexican workers by 1880. The importation of Mexican labor, combined with industrial opportunities for dispossessed heirs to land grants, led to a growth of Mexican American communities throughout the United States. As industrial development grew or faltered during the twentieth century, the use of Mexican railroad workers became a political issue involving racism and discrimination.

Mexicans began to displace members of other ethnic groups in some industries, such as railroads in the industrial Southwest, during the late nineteenth century. Although workers of Irish and Asian descent provided labor for the first transcontinental railroad, the majority of track throughout the region was laid by Mexican workers. Because railroads provided linkages to population centers, Mexican communities began to emerge in places such as Kansas City, Missouri, and CHICAGO, ILLINOIS, as well as in communities of the Southwest.

The Mexican government of Porfirio Díaz (1876-1911) considered labor to be an exportable commodity, and many of the approximately thirty-five thousand workers who left Mexico between 1880 and 1900 went to work on U.S. railroads. American railroad entrepreneurs constructed many Mexican railways and began to recruit workers for American lines.

A rapid increase of Mexican MIGRANT LABOR around the beginning of the twentieth century combined with land dispossession in New Mexico to add to the labor force. By 1908, almost 100,000 Mexicans were in the U.S. labor market. As World War I limited European immigration, restrictions such as the head tax and literacy requirements were dropped for Mexicans. The restrictions were later reimposed, but the worth of Mexican labor had been established.

The Atchison, Topeka and Santa Fe Railroad and the Southern Pacific made the most extensive use of Mexican labor, but the Pennsylvania Railroad and the Baltimore and Ohio also recruited in the early 1920's. Most estimates gauge that 70 to 90 percent of track workers were Mexican. In 1930, that percentage translated into more than seventy thousand workers.

Mexican workers were usually limited to the most difficult and the poorest paying positions on the railroads during the first half of the twentieth century. American labor organizations contributed to the lim-

Latinos formed a vital component of the labor force laying railroad tracks. (Museum of New Mexico, Emil Bibo)

ited opportunities for Mexican workers. Railroad unions refused membership to Mexicans during World War II; as a result, most Mexicans worked primarily as track repair or maintenance laborers, supervised by Anglos.

Mexican workers often lived in boxcars as they worked track. Their families followed, and COLONIAS and BARRIOS began to spring up from discarded boxcars, though some railroad companies built homes and rented them to Mexican families. The Mexican community in Sylvis, Illinois, joined two railroad cars to construct its first church. An urbanization process began everywhere railroads ran, all across the United States. Carey McWilliams, in *North from Mexico: The Spanish-Speaking People of the United States* (1948), reported that there were still thirty or forty boxcar communities in Los Angeles County in the 1940's.

During World War II, Mexican nationals worked for thirty-two railroads under the BRACERO PROGRAM. The Southern Pacific petitioned for braceros in this nonagricultural segment. In the spring of 1942, the Railroad Retirement Board began supervision of Mexican railroad workers. The program ended in April, 1946.

Ramírez, Henry M. (b. May 29, 1929, Walnut, Calif.): Politician, administrator, and educator. Ramírez was an outspoken community leader who encouraged Latinos to increase their participation in politics and society so as to improve their lives. As chairman of the federal Council on Opportunities for Spanish-Speaking People, he strove to foster awareness and understanding of the issues and problems of Spanish-speaking people in the United States.

His parents fled Mexico after the Mexican Revolution (1910-1921), and Ramírez grew up in California in a Pomona barrio, one of eleven children. Ramírez's father lost his job on the railroad after an injury, and the family became migrant agricultural workers. Ramírez spent some of his early years as a PACHUCO, or street gang member, but went on to receive his A.B. in 1952 from St. John's College in Camarillo, California.

After several years of study for the priesthood, Ramírez left the seminary to obtain a Ph.D. from Loyola University, then taught foreign languages in Whittier, California. Drawing on his early experiences as a pachuco, he created a program called "New Horizons" in the 1950's. This school-based program to encourage

Raul Ramírez plays against Harold Solomon in the semifinals of the 1976 U.S. Pro Tennis Championships. (AP/Wide World Photos)

barrio students not to drop out was still operating in the 1990's.

Ramírez moved to Washington, D.C., in 1968 to become the director of the Mexican American Studies Division of the U.S. Commission on Civil Rights. As chairman of the Council on Opportunities for Spanish-Speaking People in the 1970's, Ramírez worked for three years to secure the appointment of other qualified Mexican Americans to positions of power in the federal government. Ramírez then became a business consultant based in Washington, D.C.

Ramírez, Joel Tito (b. June 3, 1923, Albuquerque, N.Mex.): Artist. Ramírez's work focuses on the landscapes and history of his native New Mexico, emphasizing the changing colors of the area. His works are in various media, particularly oil, and are held in public collections across New Mexico and in private collections across the United States. His works have been commissioned by large corporate clients including Ford Motor Company, Paramount Pictures, and Texas International Airlines.

Ramírez is primarily self-taught as a painter, though he attended the University of New Mexico in 1949 and 1960. His work has been influenced by Rufino Tamayo's use of color and by the strong contrasts of light and shade employed by such artists as Tamayo, Diego Velázquez, Francisco Goya, and Maxfield Parrish. He is particularly concerned with how surfaces are transformed by light and how he can show this in the colors he uses.

Ramírez, Raul Carlos (b. June 20, 1953, Ensenada, Mexico): Tennis player. Mexico's foremost open-era player, Ramírez developed his tennis game while attending the University of Southern California (USC), where he and doubles partner Brian Gottfried were an almost unbeatable combination. Ramírez's speed and volleying ability helped him to have a long professional career that included seventeen singles and sixty-two doubles titles. Ramírez reached the quarterfinals at Wimbledon and at the U.S. and French Opens, and he won the Italian Open in 1975. He represented Mexico in Davis Cup competition from 1971 to 1983.

Ramírez, Ricardo (b. Sept. 12, 1936, Bay City, Tex.): Catholic bishop, scholar, and educator. After his graduation from Bay City High School in 1955, Ramírez attended the University of St. Thomas in Houston and earned his bachelor's degree in 1959. Determined to enter the priesthood, he attended St. Basil's Seminary

in Toronto, Canada, and was ordained in 1966. Ramírez went on to complete a master's degree program at the University of Detroit in 1968 before serving as a missionary for the Basilian fathers in Mexico between 1968 and 1976. From 1973 to 1974, he studied at the East Asian Pastoral Institute in Manila, the Philippines.

In 1976, Ramírez returned to Texas and worked at the MEXICAN AMERICAN CULTURAL CENTER (MACC) in San Antonio, where he taught courses in cultural anthropology. He also served as the executive director of MACC from 1976 to 1981 and taught courses at Our Lady of the Lake University in San Antonio during the late 1970's. In 1981, he published a book titled *Fiesta, Worship, and Family*, which focused on the culture of and challenges facing the Mexican American family. Ramírez was named as auxiliary bishop of the newly created archdiocese of Las Cruces, New Mexico, in 1982. Known for his scholarship in the field of Mexican American family life, Ramírez has served as a religious adviser to many groups in Texas and New Mexico and has been active as a civic leader.

Ramirez, Sara Estela (1881, Progreso, Coahuila, Mexico—Aug. 21, 1910, Tex.): Poet and political organizer. After graduating from the Ateneo Fuentes, a teachers' school, Ramirez entered the United States in 1898 to teach Spanish to Tejano children in Laredo, Texas. Soon after her arrival, she began publishing poems and poetic essays. Much of her writing was romantic in nature, but much of it was political.

Ramirez's works appeared in two Laredo newspapers, *El Demócrata Fronterizo* and *La Crónica*. In 1901, she founded a literary journal, *La Corregidora*.

In her political writings, Ramirez strongly supported the PARTIDO LIBERAL MEXICANO and its leader, Ricardo FLORES MAGÓN. She was one of his official representatives and worked closely with other feminist revolutionary organizers in Texas. She urged women to take active roles and demanded that feminist issues be part of the revolutionary agenda. She is remembered as an early Chicana feminist and union activist as well as an outstanding poet.

Ramos Otero, Manuel (b. 1948, Manatí, Puerto Rico): Writer. Ramos Otero was born in the small town of Manatí on the northern coast of Puerto Rico. He moved to Río Piedras, a suburb of San Juan, when he was seven years old. There he received his primary education in parochial schools. He began a lifelong interest in writing at the age of fourteen.

After graduation from the University of Puerto Rico in 1968, with a degree in sociology, he moved to New York City to study film and theater. In 1970, he formed his own theater workshop, which put on experimental Puerto Rican drama for the next three years. In 1969 he earned his M.A. in Spanish and Latin American literature from New York University. He pursued a doctorate at the same institution. He has taught at La Guardia Community College.

In 1976, Ramos Otero founded a small press, Editorial Libro Viaje. The press published several books of poetry and Ramos Otero's strikingly experimental novel *La novelabingo* (1976). Ramos Otero's fiction and poetry deal with such issues as homosexuality, the passage of time, the forces of modern technology, solitude, national and ethnic consciousness, and the nature of fiction.

Ranchera music (*canción ranchera*): Type of CANCIÓN of Mexican origin. Ranchera music is in duple meter. Its accompaniment is typically performed by a *con-junto mariachi* exhibiting all the traits of the CORRIDO style. The lyrics can be either patriotic, about *soldaderas* (soldiers), or about a man abandoned by a woman. Subjects are portrayed stereotypically but completely devoid of pathos, as in the Mexican SON. Ranchera music originated in the early twentieth century, and it was spread during the MEXICAN REVOLUTION (1910-1921), a historical event with which ranchera music is often associated.

Ranchos and rancho life: Ranching was the primary industry in the Southwest from Spanish colonial times until the mid-nineteenth century. The history of the southwestern Spaniard and Mexican, as well as all of the Southwest, is strongly tied to the rancho.

Ranching was introduced to the Southwest during periods of Spanish and Mexican rule. The Spanish government granted large parcels of land to individuals for ranchos. The climate of the Southwest proved favorable to ranching activities, so ranching grew into the region's main industry. Ranchos continued to ex-

The enormous King Ranch in Texas was pieced together from smaller ranches. (Institute of Texan Cultures)

pand during the Mexican period of rule in the Southwest, from 1821 until the middle of the nineteenth century. During that period, the Mexican government distributed vast amounts of land previously held by Spanish missions to an elite group of Mexicans. These grants were extremely large, frequently fifty thousand acres or more. As a result of these immense grants, the ranching industry of the Southwest reached its peak.

During the second half of the nineteenth century, several factors led to a decline in the ranching industry. Beginning in 1848, mineral discoveries brought an influx of non-Latinos to the Southwest. These settlers resented Mexican ownership of such large expanses of prime land. Although obligated under previous agreements to recognize Mexican landholdings (*see* TREATY OF GUADALUPE HIDALGO), the United States responded to pressure from whites by requiring Mexicans to officially prove ownership of their lands. Many Mexican landholders had difficulty proving ownership of their land as a result of the inexact means by which land had been divided by the Mexican government. As a result, numerous Mexican landowners either lost their land or were forced to sell off landholdings to pay the legal expenses incurred to prove ownership. This shift of ownership, combined with other factors such as drought and the development of the MINING industry, led to the demise of the rancho.

Cattle ranching dominated work life on the rancho. The rancho's main commercial products were cattle hides and tallow. Cattle were slaughtered for beef, the food staple on the rancho. Labor on the rancho was provided by Mexicans and American Indians, with men serving as *VAQUEROS* (cowboys) and women serving as domestic workers. In exchange for these services, workers received basic living provisions.

Ranchos were famous for providing hospitality and entertainment for friends and relatives. Parties were abundant. Singing and dancing were passions on the rancho, with weddings and other celebrations lasting for several days. The social highlight of rancho life was the annual RODEO. During the rodeo, cattle that roamed freely over neighboring ranches were segregated, calves were branded, and families celebrated for several days with dancing, horsemanship, gambling, and other activities.

Ranchos are an important part of Spanish and Mexican history in the United States and had an important impact on the development of the Southwest. Spaniards and Mexicans introduced ranching practices, such as cattle roundups and the use of horned saddles, still part of ranching in the American West.

Raya, Marcos (b. 1948, Irapuato, Guanajuato, Mexico): Muralist. Raya is a politically explicit muralist associated with the Pilsen neighborhood (Little Mexico) and the Casa Aztlán community center of CHICAGO, ILLINOIS. Raya participated in painting Chicago's Benito Juárez High School mural with Jaime Longoria, Malú ORTEGA Y ALBERRO, José Oscar Moya, and Salvador VEGA. He also participated in painting *Homage to Diego Rivera* (1972), a tribute to RIVERA's *Man at the Crossroads*. Raya painted over and changed some of Raymond PATLÁN's work at Casa Aztlán after a fire in the mid-1970's necessitated repairs. Some of the changes resulted from artistic debates between the painters.

Raya made a formal effort to link Mexican American and Mexican muralism and has taken up the torch of the Casa Aztlán branch of the Pilsen school. He met with famous Mexican muralist David Alfaro SIQUEIROS to establish a link between Mexican American and Mexican muralism. (*See* MURAL ART.)

Raza, La: The symbolic Spanish term literally means "the race" yet does not reflect narrow ethnocentricity. The term has been used to promote ethnic cultural pride, political cohesiveness, and a positive identity among Latinos in the United States and beyond. It was often invoked during the heyday of the Chicano movement in the late 1960's and 1970's. The proponents of the rebirth of community pride implied by the expression looked for positive links between their heritage and their present situation.

The concept of La Raza was firmly based in the history of both Spanish speakers and pre-Columbian populations who contributed in many ways to the Hispanic tradition in the Americas in the nineteenth and twentieth centuries. La Raza was traced back to the impressive archaeological remains of highly developed pre-Columbian civilizations, including those of the Aztecs and the Maya, giving new meaning to Latino peoples who had come from Indian stock (*see* AZTEC CIVILIZATION; MAYAN CIVILIZATION). By accentuating the ethnic and cultural blend that underlay the emergence of Latinos in both North and South America, promoters of La Raza placed as much importance on Indian roots as on more immediately obvious Hispanic influences. Hence, MESTIZO ("mixed") origins and ethnic identity were given positive value, replacing previous denigrations of *indio* (Indian) origins.

By emphasizing the common heritage of all Hispanic people in the Western Hemisphere, supporters of

The concept of La Raza is a recognition of unity and has figured into collective actions such as labor disputes. (Impact Visuals, Bette Lee)

La Raza play down national boundaries between Spanish speakers. This widening of the sense of common heritage has served the broad ethnic cause of La Raza in the United States, which has received substantial numbers of migrants and immigrants from a variety of Latin American countries.

Some proponents of La Raza tend to criticize the term "Latino" for allowing European qualities (Latin-based Spanish) to predominate over deeper American roots to which both Latin and "Anglo" branches were later grafted. They also disapprove of labels such as "Mexican American" and "Cuban American," which suggest that peoples of Hispanic origin in the United States have somehow attached themselves to the culturally and politically dominant host culture. Latinos, they argue, are actually more American than members of the dominant culture of European origin.

The term "La Raza" has inspired a generation of Chicano and Latino writers, artists, and musicians, and it figures in the names of a number of publications and community centers. Whether heard in a political speech, a poem, or the casual banter of commercial radio, the use of "La Raza" is a call to unity.

Raza Unida Party, La (founded Jan. 17, 1970): La Raza Unida Party was one of the important forces during the civil rights struggles of Latino people during the Civil Rights movement.

The CHICANO MOVEMENT, which occurred alongside the Civil Rights movement, was a political, social, and cultural effort to improve general social conditions for Latinos. Latinos tended to view both the Democratic and Republican parties with distrust, so it was natural that a new political party should emerge that professed to provide an alternative political voice for Latinos. One of La Raza Unida Party's goals was to reconfigure the American political system to give more emphasis to Latino leadership.

La Raza Unida's efforts have been described as militant in nature, and the party has been viewed as an arm of the Chicano movement. Although it was motivated by political needs, that movement incorporated plays, poems, and music into its activities, utilizing the ethnic characteristics of Chicano culture.

During the 1960's, a tremendous disparity often existed between the mainstream American culture and the cultures of Chicano groups throughout the Southwest. Segregation in education and housing was common at the time of the BROWN V. BOARD OF EDUCATION decision (1954). This landmark decision changed the nature of education of Latino children in America for years to come and spurred efforts to achieve political and social empowerment.

La Raza Unida Party began in 1970 through the efforts of José Angel GUTIERREZ, whose organizational strategies helped to elect Latinos to the school board and city council in CRYSTAL CITY, TEXAS. The party soon established itself nationwide. In June of 1972, representatives from eight states (Washington, Nebraska, Texas, Idaho, Colorado, Michigan, California, and Illinois) held the party's first national convention to discuss the party's philosophy and explore strategies to use in bargaining with the Democratic and Republican parties in local and national elections.

During its peak years, La Raza Unida Party had some effect on major elections. For example, Ramsey Muñiz received more than 214,000 votes in the 1972 Texas gubernatorial election. This constituted only 6.28 percent of the vote but perhaps affected the results: The Democratic candidate defeated the Republican by less than 3 percent of the vote.

By the late 1970's, the party had lost much of its strength and began exerting less influence on elections, though candidates continued to win local offices. The party helped in 1977 to defeat an immigration reform plan proposed by President Jimmy Carter.

La Raza Unida Party campaigned heavily in the 1974 elections in Crystal City, Texas. (AP/Wide World Photos)

La Raza Unida Party helped to involve Latinos in the American political system. Historians have argued that an intensified political awareness on the part of Latinos is the party's true legacy.

Reapportionment: The process by which new electoral districts are created. The U.S. Constitution requires that every state legislature redraw boundaries of congressional districts every ten years to reflect changes in population shown by the census. The number of seats in the U.S. House of Representatives is not fixed by the Constitution but has been established at 435 by federal law. Every state initially is given one seat in the House, in accordance with Article 1, Section 1 of the Constitution. A formula based on the principle of equal proportion produces "priority numbers" on the basis of each state's population. Additional seats are apportioned on the basis of these priority numbers until all seats have been allocated.

The principle of equal proportion is an effort to conform to the Constitution and the "one person, one vote" guideline established by the Supreme Court in the case of *Wesberry v. Sanders* (1964). Further court rulings have required that congressional district populations be comparable in population size, within 1 percent of the average district population in the state. Following the census that takes place every ten years, congressional seats are redistributed to reflect changes in population so that each member of the House of Representatives represents an approximately equal number of constituents. Other electoral districts, such as those pertaining to local offices, are subject to similar constraints on redistricting.

Although federal laws and court decisions have established guidelines for congressional reapportionment, the determination of boundaries of congressional districts is left to the states. State legislatures most often take on the task, although some states have nonpartisan commissions that participate in the process.

The redistricting process is inherently complex because of the need to establish districts that are nearly equal in population size while taking into account other demographic factors, such as economics and rural or urban character. The process is further complicated by political variables.

Political parties play an important part in the redistricting process. Each party sees reapportionment as a way of improving its position. The party in control has an inherent advantage in the process. The minority party must challenge, sometimes through the courts, what it sees as inequitable practices.

Since the 1960's, members of minority groups have perceived reapportionment as a way to correct traditional representational imbalances. This position was enhanced by enactment of the VOTING RIGHTS ACT OF 1970, which prohibited creation of congressional districts that would dilute minority voting strength. In 1982, Congress extended the act to prohibit voting practices, regardless of their intended purpose, that result in discrimination. Such changes gave Latinos the tools to correct traditional representational imbalances through the legal process.

Latinos and African Americans have used the Voting Rights Act successfully to challenge redistricting plans that diluted their voting power. For example, as a result of a court challenge in the case of *GARZA V. COUNTY OF LOS ANGELES, CALIFORNIA BOARD OF SUPERVISORS*, the boundaries of the five Los Angeles County supervisorial districts were redrawn to allow consolidation of Latino voting power. Gloria MOLINA was elected in 1992 as the county's first Latino supervisor, representing the "Latino" district.

Rebolledo, Tey Diana (b. Apr. 29, 1937, Las Vegas, N.Mex.): Writer. Rebolledo has served as editor of *Las mujeres hablan: An Anthology of Nuevo Mexicano Writers* (1988) and on the editorial board of ARTE PÚBLICO Press. In 1989, she was designated as an eminent scholar by the New Mexico Commission on Higher Education.

Rebolledo is the author of numerous scholarly articles. In one stream of research concerning *abuelos* (grandmothers), she refutes the claim that differences between generations become larger with differences in age. She has studied the bonds that Hispanic girls form with their grandmothers and notes that girls often discuss important issues with their grandmothers because their mothers are too close to make such conversations comfortable.

Rebolledo received a B.A. degree (1959) from Connecticut College, an M.A. (1962) from the University of New Mexico, and a Ph.D. (1979) from the University of Arizona. She has taught at the University of North Carolina at Chapel Hill, the University of Nevada at Reno, and the University of New Mexico.

Rebozo: Traditional large Mexican shawl. The *rebozo* is a large rectangular shawl traditionally worn by middle-class and working-class Mexican women, particularly in the central region of the country. The *rebozo* is worn over the shoulders and is sometimes used to cover the head. Made of fine cotton, wool, or silk,

Women in this photo taken at the La Mota Ranch in Texas are wearing rebozos. (Institute of Texan Cultures)

the most elegant ones are embroidered with gold or silver thread. Puebla, Oaxaca, and Michoacán are known for the quality of their *rebozos*, but the finest are said to be the silk *rebozos* from Santa María del Río, in the state of San Luis Potosí.

Rechy, John Francisco (b. Mar. 10, 1934, El Paso, Tex.): Novelist. The son of Roberto Sixto Rechy and Guadalupe Flores, Rechy earned a B.A. at Texas Western College in El Paso and then attended the New School for Social Research in New York City. He has taught creative writing at the University of California, Los Angeles; the University of Southern California; and Occidental College. He also has given seminars at Yale University and Duke University.

Rechy published several journalistic pieces in *Evergreen Review* during the early 1960's. One of them formed the basis of his first novel, *City of Night* (1963), his best-known and most original and controversial work. It describes the cold, violent, and loveless depths of urban American homosexual life. The author attempted in three remarkably similar subsequent novels—*Numbers* (1967), *This Day's Death* (1969), and *The Vampires* (1971)—to reproduce the shocking success his first book had created. *The Fourth Angel* (1972) marked a departure for him. It was followed by *The Sexual Outlaw: A Non-Fiction Account, with Commentaries, of Three Days and Nights in the Sexual Underworld* (1977), *Rushes* (1979), *Bodies and Souls* (1983), and *Marilyn's Daughter* (1988). Rechy's power as a novelist lies in the brute lyricism with which he depicts the raw lives of characters on the margins of society.

John Rechy. (AP/Wide World Photos)

Reclamation Act (1902): Law regulating water use. Also known as the Newlands Act in honor of Francis Newlands, a conservationist and congressional representative from Nevada who sponsored the bill, this legislation provided that the federal government oversee the construction and maintenance of dams and irrigation canals in the Southwest. This construction led to enormous growth of agriculture in the Southwest and to increased demand for agricultural labor. The demand for labor in turn resulted in the huge influx of Mexican immigrants to this region during much of the twentieth century.

REFORMA: The National Association to Promote Library Services to the Spanish Speaking (founded 1971): Educational association. REFORMA was founded as the National Association of Spanish Speaking Librarians at the 1971 convention of the American Library Association. Arnulfo Trejo, a primary force behind the founding, served as the first president. The group developed its constitution and adopted REFORMA as part of its name the following year; the change to the current name came in 1981.

REFORMA has been active in library education and in improving library and information services for the approximately twenty-two million Spanish-speaking and Hispanic people in the United States. It has supported various curricular efforts aimed at improving library service to Latinos. Local chapters across the country work autonomously to achieve local objectives. REFORMA has actively sought to promote the development of library collections that include Spanish-language and Hispanic-oriented materials, recruitment of bilingual and bicultural library professionals and support staff, development of library services and programs that meet the needs of the Hispanic community, establishment of a national information and support network among individuals who share the association's goals, dissemination to the Hispanic population of information about the availability and types of library services, and lobbying efforts to preserve existing library resource centers serving the interests of Latinos.

Refugee Act of 1980: Federal legislation. The Refugee Act of 1980 changed how the United States defined and dealt with foreign-born refugees. Refugee status was no longer defined to include only those individuals who were fleeing from Communist political regimes. The new definition allowed the admission of many Central Americans, who were desperate to escape the political violence that had made life in their native countries almost impossible. Under the terms of this act, they were able to seek legal status as refugees in the United States.

Refugees and refugee status: Since its founding, the United States has been a haven for refugees fleeing persecution based on their religion, political beliefs, or ethnic or social status. In the second half of the twentieth century, a large number of refugees arrived from Latin American nations, especially Cuba, Haiti, El Salvador, Nicaragua, and Guatemala. The term "refugees" refers to persons who cannot live in their home country because of a well-founded fear of persecution there.

The Law and Refugee Status. Prior to World War II, U.S. immigration law treated refugees like any other immigrants. Congress passed the Displaced Persons Act in 1948 and the Refugee Relief Act in 1953. These two laws allowed more than half a million European refugees to come to the United States in the chaos of the postwar period and during the rise of Communist states in Eastern Europe. Congress also passed a number of special acts in the 1950's, allowing the influx of certain specified refugee groups, such as participants in the failed 1956 uprising in Hungary.

The IMMIGRATION AND NATIONALITY ACT OF 1952 gave the attorney general the power to "parole" aliens who faced likely persecution if they returned to their home countries. The IMMIGRATION AND NATIONALITY ACT OF 1965 defined a new status of "conditional entrant" to the United States, for refugees from Communist or Middle Eastern states. Although neither parole nor conditional entrant status was equivalent to permanent residency, it could lead to permanent ASYLUM if the applicant was likely to be persecuted if returned to the home country. Under these two laws, the United States admitted a large number of refugees, such as Lebanese citizens fleeing the civil war in their home country, persons who had been involved in the 1968 Czechoslovak revolt, and almost half a million Cubans who shunned the regime of Fidel CASTRO.

Congress approved the Refugee Act in 1980, formally separating refugee immigration from other kinds of immigration. The limit for regular immigration to the United States was set at 270,000, but refugees were not to be counted toward this ceiling. The REFUGEE ACT OF 1980 also canceled the earlier requirement that one must have come from the Middle East or from a Communist state to be recognized as a refugee. The 1980 law was also notable for offering a clear definition of a refugee: any person outside his or her home country who could not return because of a well-founded fear of persecution there. This persecution could be based on religion, nationality, race, or membership in a group, including a political party. The act calls on the president to set the number of refugees to be admitted each year, after consultation among congressional and executive branch leaders.

The U.S. government has recognized several priority levels in the admission of refugees. The high-priority categories include persons facing loss of life if refugee status is denied, former U.S. government employees, and those with close family members already in the United States. Those who have worked for U.S. firms, who face persecution because of their identification with the United States, or who face religious persecution also can receive priority status.

In the second half of the twentieth century, the United States admitted more than two million refugees. As might be expected, the country of origin of the refugees has varied from year to year. In the 1950's, admissions from Eastern Europe were at high levels. In the 1970's and 1980's, refugee arrivals from Southeast Asia and Latin America assumed new importance. Each year, the federal government sets the limit on numbers of refugees to be admitted. In 1993, for example, in consultation with congressional leaders, the president set the refugee admission limit at 132,000.

Federal Courts and Refugee Status. In 1987, the Supreme Court handed down a landmark decision in the case of *Immigration and Naturalization Service v. Cardoza-Fonseca*. Luz Marina Cardoza-Fonseca had come to the United States from Nicaragua and over-

The Rodriguez family fled Cuba by boat in 1965 because the parents wanted their children to be free. (National Archives)

stayed her visa. When the IMMIGRATION AND NATU-RALIZATION SERVICE (INS) initiated deportation proceedings, Cardoza-Fonseca applied for asylum. She explained that her brother was prominent in the anti-Sandinista movement, and although she herself was not, she feared persecution because of his prominence. Cardoza-Fonseca lost her case before an immigration judge, but the Ninth Circuit Court of Appeals reversed that decision, and the U.S. Supreme Court upheld the actions of the circuit court. The Supreme Court ruled that the INS interpretation of statutes was too strict and was not in line with Congress' "more generous intent." When the Refugee Act specified a well-founded fear of persecution, it did not mean that the asylum seeker must prove persecution was "more likely than not."

In the case of *Orantes-Hernandez v. Thornburgh* (1990), a Salvadoran asylum seeker won refugee status after being turned down in the regular course of his application. Orantes-Hernandez stated in federal court that INS agents often tricked Salvadorans into signing a voluntary departure document by implying that the only two choices were to sign the document or face deportation proceedings. Even if a Salvadoran detainee spoke of torture at home, the INS employees did not mention the possibility of asylum unless the detainee used the precise words, "I want political asylum." As a result of Orantes-Hernandez's victory in the Ninth Circuit Court, the INS revised its regulations, ruling that an application for asylum should be given to any alien who expressed a fear of persecution at home.

Controversy over U.S. Policy. Over the years, the INS and other executive branch offices have faced withering criticism for their handling of refugee issues. Nowhere has this been clearer than in the history of Haitian asylum seekers. For several decades, the United States supported a brutal dictatorship in Haiti. In December, 1990, Haiti held its first free and demo-

Salvadoran refugees faced difficulties in gaining political asylum, and many tried to protect their identities because they feared reprisals from the Salvadoran government. (Impact Visuals, Lonny Shavelson)

The United States occupied Haiti in 1994 as a means of restoring Jean-Bertrand Aristide to the presidency. (AP/Wide World Photos)

cratic election, electing Jean-Bertrand Aristide as the new president. Aristide's election was followed by a military coup. In the tense political situation that followed, many Haitians took to boats and sought refuge in the United States. Very few of these so-called "boat people" were granted asylum. U.S. activists speaking for the Haitians argued that the U.S. government had a longstanding policy of refusing asylum to Haitians, no matter what the conditions were on the island. They pointed out that of the boat people who took to the seas following Aristide's exile, fewer than 1 percent were granted asylum. Meanwhile, asylum seekers from some Asian nations saw their applications approved at a rate of 90 percent.

The State Department responded that Haitians were fleeing bleak economic prospects, not political persecution. The economic hardship, in fact, was made worse by a U.S.-supported boycott of the island nation. Two groups, the U.S. Committee for Refugees (USCR) and the Lawyers Committee for Human Rights (LCHR), complained bitterly about U.S. policy, and their complaints improved the situation for many Haitians.

Previously, noted the LCHR, the official interviews of asylum seekers lasted only a matter of minutes. The INS claimed that each applicant for asylum was asked a minimum of seventeen questions, but these seventeen included as separate questions name, address, occupation, date of birth, and similar bits of information. Even persons who spoke of family members being killed and persons who had been imprisoned by the government were sent back to Haiti. The USCR kept a vigil over the detention camps used for Haitian refugees, such as those located in Florida and at Guantánamo Naval Base. The health and safety conditions in these detention centers were abysmal, the USCR charged; in the face of its allegations, conditions for detainees improved somewhat.

Nothing made the concerns of USCR and LCHR clearer than the appearance of Cuban boat people at the same time that HAITIAN BOAT PEOPLE were attempting to make their way to U.S. shores. In April, 1991, the Coast Guard intercepted boats containing four hundred Cubans. The Cubans were escorted to a warm welcome in the United States, where their applications for asylum seemed to face good prospects. In

FEDERAL FUNDING OF REFUGEE RESETTLEMENT PROGRAMS, 1977-1992

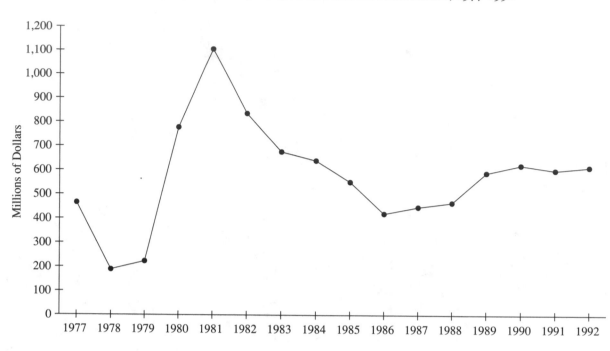

Source: Data are from Office of Refugee Resettlement, *Refugee Resettlement Program: Report to Congress, 1992* (Washington, D.C.: Department of Health and Human Services, 1993), Table 19.

the same month, the Coast Guard prevented hundreds of Haitians from even approaching U.S. shores.

During the 1980's, upheaval in several Central American countries led to an influx of asylum seekers into the United States. Once again, their reception depended more on the nuances of American foreign policy than on the merits of each individual applicant's case. For example, refugees from Nicaragua were typically greeted with open arms, because U.S. foreign policy stressed the evils of the Sandinista administration in that country. On the other hand, refugees from the turmoil in El Salvador and Guatemala had a substantially lower rate of approval of their asylum applications because the U.S. government supported the governments in power in those nations.

Changes in U.S. Refugee Policy and Procedures. In 1990, both Amnesty International and the LCHR marked the tenth anniversary of the REFUGEE ACT OF 1980 by pointing out the law's inadequacy and calling for reforms. Among the criticisms of the act was the allegation that those who won their bids for asylum were well educated and relatively wealthy; poorer applicants received little guidance and were much less likely to secure refugee status. The two organizations

also argued that the politics of foreign relations, rather than a strict system of justice, governed the refugee process.

INS figures showed that of applicants from the Soviet Union between 1983 and 1990, 77 percent were successful in winning asylum. The comparable figure for applicants from El Salvador and Guatemala (both strife-torn countries with great danger to certain groups of people) were 3 percent and 2 percent, respectively.

Once again, the complaints made by refugee advocacy organizations led to fruitful changes. By late 1990, several new policies were in place. The INS began appointing asylum officers to hear the cases of individual applicants; if the asylum officer ruled against the claim, the applicant could have a second chance before an immigration judge. The new procedures also allowed acceptance of an applicant's testimony without corroboration in many cases and dropped the requirement that an applicant prove that he or she personally was already in danger of persecution. Instead, the asylum seeker needed to prove only that persons in similar circumstances had been persecuted in the past. The regulations also called on INS employees to steer would-be asylum seekers to community groups that agreed to help them.

The U.S. government's policy of accepting refugees is a humanitarian program that prevents injustices and even loss of life. As numerous groups have pointed out, however, the policy itself sometimes includes injustice, as when the government singles out certain groups of people for help in preference to analogous groups from different countries. Nevertheless, the U.S. asylum program has been a godsend to almost three million refugees. In areas ranging from Los Angeles to Houston, and from Miami to New York City, strong communities of refugees have been established, bringing a wealth of human talent to the United States.

—*Stephen Cresswell*

SUGGESTED READINGS:

• Glazer, Nathan. *Clamor at the Gates: The New American Immigration.* San Francisco: ICS Press, 1985. Essays on a number of immigration topics, including refugees and asylum seekers. Focuses on issues of the 1970's and 1980's.

• Landes, Alison, Betsie B. Caldwell, and Mark A. Siegel, eds. *Immigration and Illegal Aliens: Burden or Blessing?* Wylie, Tex.: Information Plus, 1993. A strong introduction to an array of immigration issues, well documented with current statistics. Two chapters deal with refugee issues specifically.

• Loescher, Gil, and John A. Scanlan. *Calculated Kindness: Refugees and America's Half-Open Door, 1945 to the Present.* New York: Free Press, 1986. A thoughtful and opinionated historical analysis of the limitations of U.S. refugee policy since World War II.

• Maidens, Melinda, ed. *Immigration: New Americans, Old Questions.* New York: Facts on File, 1981. A good selection of articles treating controversial issues of immigration. One-third of the articles are devoted to refugees.

Religion: The identity of a people is symbolized by their religion. Roman Catholicism and Protestantism, the first and second largest religions among Latinos, reflect the unique identity of the Latino people.

A people's religion provides meaning, purpose, and community for their lives. Religious symbols are talked about, celebrated, and institutionalized. The Latino people have nothing that functions in this way for all of them; there are, however, a number of symbol systems, or religions, associated with Latinos.

Religious Antecedents. The first religions were those associated with the homelands of the Latino people. The various regions of the Americas and Europe each had a religion native to that particular region. Remnants of these "native" Latino religions sometimes remain in the symbols of later Latino religions. This is an important concept because even in international religions such as Roman Catholicism, religious symbols are sensed differently as they become part of various people's lives and history. An example of the many layers of meaning in one symbol can be seen in the Virgin of Guadalupe.

The Virgin of GUADALUPE is at one level Mary, the mother of Jesus. At the same time, she is obviously a young Indian maiden. She is also the mother-goddess Tonantzin of the Aztecs, with the moon as part of the image of the Virgin of Guadalupe and her apparition occurring on the hill of Tepeyac, Tonantzin's former sanctuary. The Virgin of Guadalupe was the image of revolution placed on the banner of Miguel HIDALGO Y COSTILLA in 1810. These are only a few of the meanings of the Virgin of Guadalupe.

Many religious symbols partake of the same multilayered representations. Religious symbols never have only one meaning. Thus, in the discussion that follows, it must be remembered that various symbols—whether expressed as words, ritual actions, moral imperatives, or institutional frameworks for religious life—have meanings reflective of their past history and present function.

Membership in Latino Religions. As of the early 1990's, Roman Catholicism was the dominant religion of Latinos. Of the 466 million people living in Latin America, 406 million were Catholic and 17 million Protestant. (*See* CATHOLIC CHURCH AND CATHOLICISM.)

Latinos in the United States were estimated to be 78 percent Catholic and 17 percent Protestant. Of the Catholics, 23 percent attended church regularly. Of the 97 million Catholics in North America, half were Latinos. The fastest growing Latino religion was Pentecostal Christianity.

Statistics such as these represent educated guesswork. Different meanings attach to membership in a religion. Roman Catholics, for example, are usually seen as members of their church when they are baptized as infants; Evangelical protestants are considered members when, as adults, they are converted (born again) and baptized. There is also guesswork as to the number of members, as methods of counting memberships differ. The typical contact for membership is the head of the local parish or congregation. In a typical overworked parish, a request by mail or telephone for membership statistics does not receive the highest priority. When provided, these estimates often reflect the hopes

RELIGIOUS AFFILIATIONS OF LATINOS

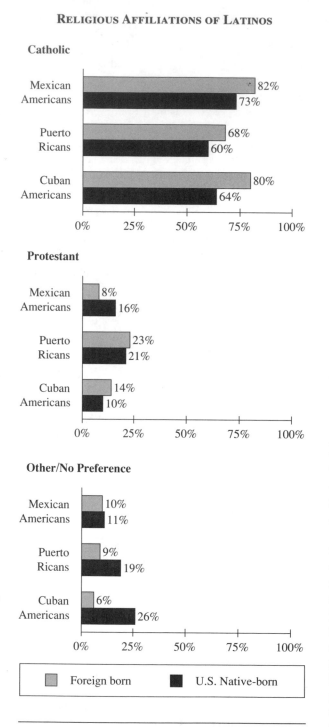

Catholic

Mexican Americans — 82% / 73%

Puerto Ricans — 68% / 60%

Cuban Americans — 80% / 64%

0%   25%   50%   75%   100%

Protestant

Mexican Americans — 8% / 16%

Puerto Ricans — 23% / 21%

Cuban Americans — 14% / 10%

0%   25%   50%   75%   100%

Other/No Preference

Mexican Americans — 10% / 11%

Puerto Ricans — 9% / 19%

Cuban Americans — 6% / 26%

0%   25%   50%   75%   100%

Foreign born   U.S. Native-born

Source: Data are from the Latino National Political Survey, which polled a representative sample of 1,546 Mexican Americans, 589 Puerto Ricans, and 682 Cuban Americans in forty metropolitan areas in 1989-1990. See Rodolfo O. de la Garza et al., *Latino Voices: Mexican, Puerto Rican, and Cuban Perspectives on American Politics* (Boulder, Colo.: Westview Press, 1992), Table 2.23.

of the pastor rather than the actual number of members. Further complications arise from the understanding of church membership held by the person providing statistics. For example, some Catholic priests consider only those who regularly attend Mass and contribute financially to the church as regular members. If the membership inquiry is made to the individual Latino, then there is the presumption that she or he is telling the truth about religious preference and membership in a country where good citizenship is often identified with church membership and being a Catholic is identified with one's heritage. These are serious reasons to read religious membership statistics as educated guesses. There is little doubt, however, because of historical origins and present statistics, that Roman Catholicism is the religion of at least three-fourths of Latinos.

Latino Roman Catholic Christianity. Roman Catholicism is an international religion with its origins in Judaism as preached and practiced by Jesus. Although it originated in and is "native" to Israel, it quickly spread to other parts of the world, particularly Greece and Rome. As it spread, it adapted to the surrounding culture and adopted many symbols found in the stories, ideologies, beliefs, rituals, moral norms, and institutional forms of the culture. To the original symbols of Israel were added those of Greece and Rome; onto the original meanings of all these symbols were projected the meanings found in the message and actions of Jesus. Just as Mary, the Jewish mother of Jesus, has various meanings when pictured as the Mexican Virgin of Guadalupe, early Roman Catholic symbols had many meanings dependent upon their Jewish, Greek, and Roman culture or context.

By the time Roman Catholicism began to be a major force in Latino life, it had already undergone significant change. As it continues to be a force in Latino life, it continues to change. There are more than one billion Catholics scattered over the globe. They are organized in a hierarchical system of bishops, with the bishop of Rome, the pope, as the legal and symbolic force of unity. Although their beliefs are summarized in the ancient creeds they proclaim each Sunday, subsidiary beliefs, in the saints and the VIRGIN MARY for example, have played important roles throughout their history. With other Christians, they affirm the Sermon on the Mount and the Ten Commandments as central moral imperatives. Papal positions on questions of sexual morality and economic justice were controversial during the late twentieth century.

Sacraments are important to Catholics. These include baptism, confirmation, Eucharist (Mass), orders,

Worshippers stop before a figure of the Virgin Mary in the Stations of the Cross. (Impact Visuals, Fred Chase)

marriage, anointing of the sick, and reconciliation. For many Latinos, the baptism of an infant is the means to membership in the church. One's first Communion is not when one first attends church but when one first eats the bread and drinks the wine symbolizing Jesus' body and blood. This usually happens at the age of six or seven and is often highlighted by parties and gifts given outside the official ceremony of the Mass, in which Communion is an essential part.

"Orders" is the sacrament through which men are ordained to be bishops, priests (presbyters), or deacons in the Catholic church. Many other individuals have important roles in the Catholic institution but are not ordained. Sisters or nuns, women leading lives dedicated to God and the people, are vital to the existence of the contemporary church institution but are not ordained. Anointing of the sick is still called extreme unction or last rites by some Latinos. Since VATICAN II, the emphasis in this sacrament has been on the ritual of healing rather than on the ritual of dying. Reconciliation is called "confession" or "penance" by some Latinos.

When compared to other world religions, Roman Catholicism is very materialistic. Its foundational principle is that God acts through and in material reality. Thus God became an actual human being in Jesus. This is the doctrine of the incarnation. God is present in certain rituals (sacraments) to bring people closer to God through rituals associated with food, oil, marriage/sex, and water. God is present in the hungry, the naked, and those in prison. God is also present, according to Catholics, when they gather in God's name. This Catholic principle is found in many aspects of Roman Catholicism. In the past, it enabled Roman Catholics to adapt to various cultures. In the present, it prevents adaptation, because God became identified with the stylized symbols of God's presence.

This tension between past adaptation and present stultification is found in any interpretation of the Roman Catholic symbol system. It is usually described as the division between the revisionists and the progressives. The revisionist point of view sees contemporary Roman Catholicism in terms of its history between 1545 and 1965. This has been called "the tradition."

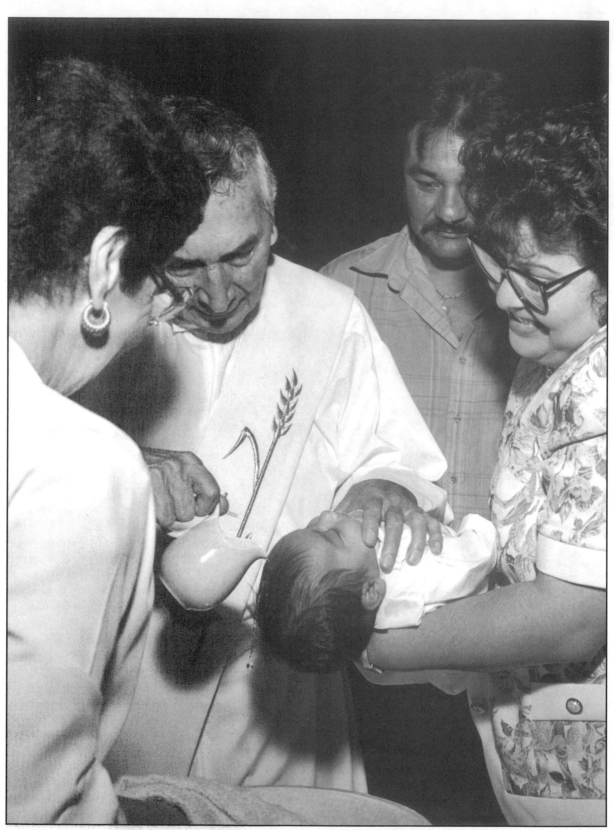

Baptism is an important ritual of the Roman Catholic church. (James Shaffer)

The progressive point of view looks to the beginnings of Christianity (the tradition) and forward to the year 3000. It acknowledges Vatican II as the pivotal reform event shaping interpretation of the past and hope for the future. Vatican II was an ecumenical council of the Catholic church that met between 1962 and 1965. It changed many things in the Catholic church. For Latinos, the most important changes were the language of worship and the emphasis on local cultures. This was a change from the pre-Vatican II church, which was becoming more centralized nationally and internationally.

For Latino progressives in North America, Vatican II was seen as an opportunity to make the church viable among a people who had a history of abandonment by church officials. This abandonment had been initiated in 1773, when the pope commanded the Jesuits to abandon their missions in the New World. It was sustained by the antirevolutionary fervor of South American bishops in the nineteenth and twentieth centuries. It was confirmed by the pope's refusal to acknowledge the Hispanic character of the dioceses formed in the new American territories as a consequence of the TREATY OF GUADALUPE HIDALGO (1848).

Once New Mexico, Arizona, Texas, and California became territories of the United States, the pope transferred their responsibility from Mexican bishops to new bishops whose principal concern was the European Catholics pouring into these territories. The first Hispanic bishop in the United States was Patricio Fernández FLORES, ordained a bishop in 1970. Non-Hispanic bishops, most of whom were Irish, viewed Latino Catholicism as a pale imitation of true (Irish) Catholicism. The Irish bishops wanted the Latinos to be quiet, go to church every Sunday, obey their priests, and pray to St. Patrick. The Latinos wanted someone who could understand their language as well as their customs. The progressives in the United States saw Vatican II as an opportunity to emphasize God's presence in the brown of the Virgin of GUADALUPE as well as in the white of Mary and the Immaculate Conception.

Popular Religion and Roman Catholicism. Many customs are identified with Latino Catholicism. Most of these reflect the original religions of native lands and the Latino understanding of Roman Catholicism. It must be remembered that until recently the institutional church seldom has been able to offer clear, consistent, personal, and understandable instruction to Latinos. Customs, or popular religion, sustained Latinos when church officials did not minister to them and when they had to struggle to survive in an alien culture.

Because one's identity is tied up with one's family in the Latino culture, one's family is constitutive of one's religion. The almost universal absence of priests who spoke Spanish, in combination with the central role of the family, resulted in many of the Latino religious practices centering on the home and the family. The same emphasis the Irish Catholic placed on the Sunday Mass is placed on the Latino Catholic's religious practices learned and exercised in the family.

Many Latino homes have a home altar. It is usually a simple affair, perhaps an altar set on a television set or a small table in the bedroom. It may have on it a picture or statue of Christ, the Virgin, or some saint, along with a vase filled with flowers. It may be a simple gathering of pictures and candles or include elaborate hand-embroidered cloths, incense, holy water, and other objects seen as appropriate to honor God and the saints. The home altar brings God's presence to the home. Prayers are said before it by some families. Sometimes when a request is denied, the statue or the picture of the respective saint is turned to the wall. At the home altar, God acts through material things to be present to God's people.

Pictures and statues of the home altar vary depending on the country of origin of the American Latino. Our Lady of Guadalupe and Our Lady of San Juan de los Lagos are common among Mexican Americans, Our Lady of Providence among Puerto Ricans, La Caridad del Cobre among Cuban Americans, and Altagracia among Dominicans. Many women have a statue of Our Lady of Sorrows because suffering is so much a part of their lives.

The Virgin, under various titles and meanings, is extremely important to Latinos. To men, she is the understanding, forgiving, and interceding mother; to women, she is the mother, sister, or daughter who suffers with them. To both, she is the symbol of home, homeland, and people.

In addition to the Virgin, one may also find pictures or statues of Jesus Christ. The various images of Jesus generally reflect the Latino's country of origin. Images include El Cristo Negro de Esquipulas (Guatemala), El Señor de los Milagros (Colombia), and Cristo El Salvador (El Salvador). Images that cut across national boundaries are those of the Sacred Heart and El Niño de Atocha. Both the focus on the suffering of Jesus—in the bleeding, wounded, and suffering Jesus of the Sacred Heart—and the innocence and resourcefulness of El Niño symbolize the concerns of many Latinos.

Together with Jesus and his mother Mary on home altars are the saints. These usually reflect those who

Home altars, on a smaller scale than this altar from Mission Santa Barbara in California, bring religious images into the home. (Ruben G. Mendoza)

were honored by one's village. Some of these are associated with the early missionaries of the Franciscan order, Saint Francis of Assisi and Saint Anthony of Padua. Saint Joseph, Saint Christopher, and, among Cuban Americans, Saint Lazarus and Saint Barbara are popular. Many honor St. Martin of Porres. Saint John the Baptist is the patron saint of Puerto Ricans.

Honor to the Virgin, Jesus, and the saints goes beyond the home to the celebrations surrounding feast days. A feast day celebration is a mixture of sacred and secular: the celebration of Mass, a procession, dancing, music, drink, and food. The yearly celebration of feast days is reflected in the pilgrimages to famous sites of these same saints. Pilgrimages are common to Our Lady of Guadalupe (Mexico City), Our Lady of San Juan de los Lagos (Jalisco, Mexico), and the shrine to La Caridad del Cobre (Coral Gables, Florida).

Often a pilgrimage includes gifts to Mary, the saint, or Jesus in gratitude for a favor granted to the petitioner. These are photos, baby shoes, letters of thanks, charms, or crutches. One finds these gifts at various shrines and pilgrimage sites.

There is much more to Latino popular religion, such as the importance of Ash Wednesday, the celebration of QUINCEAÑERA, the PENITENTES, and the *pastorela*. This religion has symbol systems reflecting many different meanings and that are responded to differently by other Roman Catholics. Many non-Latino Catholics see these as quaint customs, some Latino clergy see these as superstitions to be suppressed, and many Latinos see these as their religion, as contrasted to that of the clergy, especially the Anglo clergy, who understand neither Latino language nor Latino life and culture.

Progressives and revisionists respond differently to this popular religion. Progressives, though wanting to deepen the cultural impulses of popular religion, attempt to bring it into the church. The Sunday celebration, Mass, incorporates some of the festive atmosphere of the feast day and pilgrimage. Church buildings have begun to reflect the images found on home ALTARS. Such incorporation, however, is a challenge to popular religion because it attempts to bring it into the sacredness of the church rather than respect the holiness of the home. There is certainly a tension between popular religion and the progressive viewpoint.

Revisionists are convinced that the popular religion is a threat to true Catholicism, represented by what they see as the uniformity of doctrine, sacrament, morals, and hierarchal church power. Extreme revisionists believe that the loss of Latinos to Protestantism is a result both of the celebration of the sacraments in Spanish rather than the international church language of Latin and of the church becoming more concerned with preserving the past culture found in quaint customs than with adapting to real life, which means becoming part of the mix that is North American life.

Whether the revisionist or progressive point of view is correct in analysis and consequent shaping of the Latino Roman Catholic church, the fact is that Roman Catholicism is a vital part of Latino culture.

Latino Protestant Christianity. Some Latinos use other religions to give direction, meaning, purpose, and community to their lives. Second to Catholic Christianity is Protestant Christianity. Latino protestants immigrate to the United States, as do Latino Catholics. There also seems to be a significant increase of converts from Catholicism to Protestantism among Latinos in the United States.

PROTESTANTISM in Latino countries is of three types: that which grew out of the immigration following the first revolutions; that which is dependent on missionary efforts (for example, in Cuba and Puerto Rico intense American Protestant missionary efforts followed the Spanish-American War), and churches

The quinceañera *celebration is a Latino contribution to Catholicism.* (James Shaffer)

that grew out of the conversion of an individual Latino. When Latino protestants move to North America, they carry their religion with them. Some report a sense of alienation from the Anglos and from their compatriots. Others feel more at home in the United States because of its Protestant atmosphere.

The most influential Latino Protestant religion is Pentecostalism. Some estimates claim it constitutes 70 percent of the estimated eighteen million Latin American Protestants. Its increase in the United States is demonstrated in Southern California, where there were only 320 Protestant Latino congregations in 1970 but 1,450 in 1990.

Pentecostalism is Evangelical Protestant Christianity in its most intense form. It emphasizes the experience of the Holy Spirit and life with those who share this experience. Pentecostalism offers a person the intimacy of experiencing Jesus, one's coreligionists, and community. Such intimacy is a secure port in the storm of shifting jobs, cultures, and economic problems. Pentecostalism offers one the opportunity of contacting God without the clergy's stultifying ritual and without educational background. God is there in the Bible, personal experience, and the preaching of one's pastor. One may respond to God with joy. Services can feature loud, effusive music and offer the opportunity to shout out one's feelings about God and the world. The Pentecostal church is highly supernatural in its approach to Christianity. Miracles abound and surround its members.

Christian Pentecostalism has many similarities to the basic thrusts of Latino popular religion. It is closely knit, like the family. It acknowledges being surrounded by the supernatural, as evidenced in the home altar. It offers a place of shared suffering, as found in the images of Mary, Jesus, and the saints. The trend of Latinos becoming Pentecostal Christians will be interesting to observe.

Other Elements of Religious Life. Outside Latino Catholic and Protestant Christianity exist elements of religious practice that, though not necessarily providing a way of life with direction, purpose, meaning, and community, certainly influence those dynamics. Examples include *yerberias* of the Mexican American and *BOTÁNICAS* of Latinos of Caribbean descent. These are herb shops selling a variety of medicinal herbs and

Botánicas *sell a variety of items used in religious practices.* (Impact Visuals, Allan Clear)

other items suggested by the folk healer, or *curandero* (*see* CURANDERISMO; YERBERO).

The *curandero* deals with both the physical and the spiritual, good and evil. The *curandero* removes spells, casts spells, helps one acquire good luck, and heals illness. Some *curanderos* practice SPIRITISM. Spiritists claim to be able to contact the world of the spirits and bring knowledge of the present, future, or past. Some *curanderos* are spiritualists who act as channels for Jesus, Mary, and the saints to perform healings as well as to provide aid in facing the vicissitudes of life. One famous spiritualist is Fidencio, whose followers display images of the Sacred Heart of Jesus and the Virgin of Guadalupe that use Fidencio's face in place of those of Jesus and the Virgin.

Santería. SANTERÍA is a religion that developed among Caribbean, especially Cuban, Latinos. It is a mix of Catholic Christianity, the religion of the Yoruba slaves from Africa, Spiritism, and the regional imperatives of the Caribbean. Large numbers of practitioners exist in Miami and Tampa, Florida; New York, New York; and San Juan, Puerto Rico. From Cuban and Puerto Rican missionaries, it has spread to other Latino groups.

Santería, the way of the saints, is a set of practices that help a follower to live his or her life more fully. A *santero* or *santera* is an initiate of Santería. They believe that God determines everyone's life before birth. If one is to have a good life, one must accommodate oneself to her or his fate rather than fight it. To deal with one's fate, one should enlist the aid of the *orishas* (gods, spirits, or saints). After initiation into the religion, one establishes a special relationship with an *orisha*, who comes to live in a container in the *santero*'s house. Many *orishas* have special colors that become the color of the *santero*. The *orisha* needs food to exist, and it is the duty of the *santero* to provide it. It is also the duty of the *santero* to provide a sacrifice when necessary.

The most dramatic rituals performed in Santería are those called *bembes*, *guemileres*, or *tambores*. The sound of drums entices the *orishas* to dance and sing with the *santeros*. The result is a possession of the *santeros* that causes wild dances, speeches, and advice. Such possession is both a reminder of what has happened and what will happen with total initiation into the group. The ceremonies marking complete initiation into Santería conclude with the *orisha* being enthroned in the head of the *santero* and becoming a permanent part of her or his personality.

—*Nathan R. Kollar*

SUGGESTED READINGS:

- Gonzalez-Wippler, Migene. *The Santería Experience*. Englewood Cliffs, N.J.: Prentice-Hall, 1982. A first-person account of the author's experience with Santería in New York City.
- Lafaye, Jacques. *Quetzalcóatl and Guadalupe*. Translated by Benjamin Keen. Chicago: University of Chicago Press, 1976. Defends the idea of Guadalupe as the national myth and symbol of Mexico.
- Martin, David. *Tongues of Fire: The Explosion of Protestantism in Latin America*. Cambridge, Mass.: Blackwell, 1990. A sociological examination by a Pentecostal into the increase of Pentecostalism among Latinos.
- Sandoval, Moises. *On the Move: A History of the Hispanic Church in the United States*. Maryknoll, N.Y.: Orbis Books, 1990. An important review of Latino colonial history in the United States by an author sensitive to the need to recognize Latino culture.
- Steele, Thomas J. *Santos and Saints: The Religious Folk Art of Hispanic New Mexico*. Santa Fe, N.Mex.: Ancient City Press, 1982. A description of the role of popular religion in the art of Mexican Americans.
- Stevens Arroyo, Antonio M. *Prophets Denied Honor*. Maryknoll, N.Y.: Orbis Books, 1980. A documented history of tensions between Catholic Hispanic clergy and Catholic Anglo-American priests.
- Sylvest, Edwin E., Jr. "Religion in Hispanic America Since the Era of Independence." In *Encyclopedia of the American Religious Experience*, edited by Charles Lippy and Peter Williams. 3 vols. New York: Charles Scribner's Sons, 1988. A survey of Roman Catholicism and Protestantism in the Latino community. Contains an excellent bibliography.

Religion, Mesoamerican: An artifact dated to 10,000 B.C.E. by archaeologists is the earliest evidence that humans in Mesoamerica understood the idea of an afterlife. Uncovered in 1870 by ditch diggers at Tequíxquiac, in the Valley of Mexico, the artifact is a large vertebra fragment of an extinct llama, carved to resemble the head of a doglike animal such as a coyote or wolf. Dogs were buried with the deceased to act as guides for the soul in its journey through the underworld. This artifact is significant because it was carved approximately 7,500 years before artworks associated with the earliest village-type settlements appeared in Mesoamerica. These "village" artworks revealed obvious religious functions associated with agricultural activities. Many small female-shaped clay figurines, rep-

Huitzilopochtli, the hummingbird wizard, was an Aztec god who told the Aztecs where to locate their capital city. (Library of Congress)

resenting fertility, were scattered in agricultural fields to ensure a plentiful harvest.

The Search for Meaning. Formal religion in Meso-america is reflected in the artworks described above. The Tequíxquiac figure led to an understanding that the human search for an existence beyond the earthly carnal one requires the mind to "jump" into a world beyond the limits of ordinary experience. This tran-scendental act allows investigation of cosmological (space-time relationships of the universe) phenomena.

Cosmological quests were central in the religious beliefs of the MAYAN and AZTEC CIVILIZATIONS. Clay fertility figures illustrate the human quest to control nature. The human mind functions best in a world that is predictable and within the limits of ordinary experi-ence; in such a world, one can investigate physical cause-and-effect phenomena. Experiential quests were

also central in the religious beliefs of the Mayan and Aztec civilizations.

The two religious principles of search for another type of existence and for means to control nature em-ployed concepts that accomplished similar goals. For example, the sun and the moon as cosmological bodies represented the opposites of day and night. Each of these planetary bodies was assigned a divine personal-ity and magical powers that required the support of humans. Thus the Mayan god Kínich Ahau (face of the sun), the solar diety, was opposed by and did battle with Zotzilha Chimálman (bat god), the god of dark-ness, symbolizing the eternal conflict of day and night. In similar manner, the Aztec god Huitzilopóchtli (hummingbird wizard), the war and sun god, was op-posed by and did battle with his sister Coyolxaúhqui (she with golden bells), the moon goddess. He defeated her by decapitating her. He then flung her head into the sky, where it became the moon.

In both the Mayan and Aztec civilizations, neither of a pair of deities could be allowed to dominate the other because the result would unbalance the cosmology of the universe. If an imbalance did occur, then everything, including humans, would cease to exist. To prevent this, humans devised rituals and ceremonies designed to appease these warring deities. Thus, the sacrificial ritual in which a pulsating human heart was removed from an individual and immediately offered to the sun god was intended to give that god sustenance and strength to do battle with the forces of darkness (in this case, the moon).

Life and Death. The experiential ideas of spring and winter symbolize the opposites of life and death. These seasons manifest themselves in annual cycles and were assigned divine personalities and magical powers requiring the support of humans. Thus the Aztec god Xípe (our Lord the flayed one), god of spring, seedtime, and planting, was opposed by and did battle with Xólotl (double, monster dog), the god of the North and winter, symbolizing the eternal conflict of life and death.

In the spring, newly planted seeds provide food to humans and give the countryside a green mantle. Priests wore the flayed skin of a person to represent Xípe's sacrifice of having himself skinned alive at the precise moment that the corn seed loses its skin as the young plant begins to burst forth. This act gives strength to the corn plant as it struggles to maturity at harvest time.

Opposed to the life-giving powers of Xípe stands Xólotl, who pushes the sun down into the darkness of the night and thus prevents the sun's beneficial warmth from stimulating the corn seed to sprout. The Mayan world had gods whose functions, and rituals associated with them, paralleled those of the Aztecs. Ah Puch (death god) and his companions, the dog, moan bird, and owl, were opposed by Yum Káax (corn god), lord of the harvest.

The conceptual understanding of death was represented by the image of the dog; the conceptual understanding of life was represented by images and ideas associated with fertility, such as the sun, corn, spring, harvest, and growth. In the psyche of the Mesoamerican mind, it did not matter if one was operating on a cosmological or experiential level. The Mesoamericans understood that the natural and cosmological forces influencing their lives had opposing personalities requiring constant appeasement. The opposing personalities, known as dualities, were phases of either life or death and needed to be kept in check. The function of rituals was to minimize the conflict of these dualities so that the eternal rhythm of life would be ensured. —*Moisés Roizen*

SUGGESTED READINGS: • Burland, C. A. *The Gods of Mexico.* New York: Putnam, 1967. • Carrasco, David. *Religions of Mesoamerica: Cosmovision and Ceremonial Centers.* San Francisco: Harper & Row, 1990. • Durán, Diego. *Books of the Gods and Rites and the Ancient Calendar.* Translated and edited by Fernando Horcasitas and Doris Heyden. Norman: University of Oklahoma Press, 1971. • León-Portilla, Miguel. *Native Mesoamerican Spirituality.* New York: Paulist Press, 1980. • *Popol Vuh: The Sacred Book of the Ancient Ouiché Maya.* Translated by Delia Goetz and Sylvanus G. Morley from the Spanish translation by Adrián Recinos. Norman: University of Oklahoma Press, 1950. • Schele, Linda, and David Freidel. *A Forest of Kings: The Untold Story of the Ancient Maya.* New York: William Morrow, 1990. • Sejourne, Laurette. *Burning Water: Thought and Religion in Ancient Mexico.* New York: Grove Press, 1960.

Religious art: Religious art is the aesthetic representation of sacred images. Art, religion, family, community life, and the environment were all one for the early Spanish colonists. This was still true in the late twentieth century in many small villages of northern New Mexico and southern Colorado. The maker of religious art creates for a religious or spiritual purpose, not necessarily for an aesthetic purpose. The art piece communicates a religious and spiritual meaning. It provides a religious idea and tells about a happening in the life of Christ, a saint, or one of the apostles.

Colonial and modern religious arts and crafts can be seen at the International Folk Art Museum in Santa Fe, New Mexico; the Taylor Museum for Southwestern Studies of the Colorado Springs Fine Art Center; the Denver Art Museum; the Millicent Rogers Museum in Taos; the Amarillo Art Center in Amarillo, Texas; the Gene Autry Western Heritage Museum in Los Angeles; and the Smithsonian Institution in Washington, D.C. All of these institutions have fine collections.

Classification. Religious art in the American Southwest can be classified as SANTOS, *BULTOS*, *RETABLOS*, crosses, or *colchas* (embroidered bedspreads). Santos (saints) are images of Christ, saints, or angels carved in wood. The word "santo" is also a generic term for any painting or carving of a saint. *Bulto* is another term for a carved wooden santo, usually a larger size.

A retablo *shown with several* bultos. (Ruben G. Mendoza)

Retablos are usually flat or raised molded paintings used as *reredos*, altar pieces, or screens. Sometimes techniques are combined: The central image is carved, producing an inlay around the central figure or the protruding figures, and the background surroundings are suggested by paint. *Retablos* can be different sizes, from miniatures of a few inches to pieces more than a story high. Several *retablos* together can form a complete altar screen. The origins of wooden panels in gesso relief (gesso is a paste, often plaster of paris) can be traced to medieval Europe. In New Mexico, some *bultos* and *retablos* exist in which cloth, usually canvas molded with wet gesso, substitutes for part of the carving.

Production of Santos. There are three steps in making a santo. First, pieces of wood are carved and joined. Second pieces are sanded and gesso is applied. Finally, the santo is painted and decorated. Processes used in preparing the wood and selecting and mixing pigments traditionally have been considered family secrets passed down from generation to generation.

Other Art Forms. Maderos are large, simple crosses, carried by the Penitentes (Brotherhood of Our Lord) during Holy Week processions. *Antorchas de pro-*

cesión are processional templates made of tin containers. *Pantallas* (sconces), also made of tin plates, were designed to hold candles and to be hung on the walls of churches or home altars. *NACIMIENTOS* or *pesebres* (nativities) are nativity scenes. *Colchas* are bedspreads embroidered with religious motives used as wall hangings.

Cemetery Art. Most monuments used as ornamentation in cemeteries are niches, crosses, and iron or wooden bars. This type of art usually tends to be simple and rustic.

Descansos (resting places) are crosses erected on the roadside at the site where a person has died. *Nichos* (niches) are used in churches or private altars, and in cemeteries. *Santeros* (makers of santos and other religious art) began to make niches from tin when tin cans began to be used in New Mexico.

History. Hispanic religious art in the Southwest of the United States dates to the first Spanish explorers. The first group of colonists, who came to New Mexico with Juan de OÑATE in 1598, brought a santo, *La Conquistadora, Nuestra Señora del Rosario* (Our

Candles decorate the adobe shrine of El Tiridito in Tucson, Arizona. (Ruben G. Mendoza)

Lady of the Rosary). It was taken to El Paso after the Spaniards retreated as a result of POPÉ'S REVOLT, an Indian uprising in 1680. During the rebellion, churches and santos were destroyed by the Indians, leaving only a few mission churches, santos, bells, and fragments of wooden church adornments. *La Conquistadora* came back to New Mexico with Diego de VARGAS when he returned in 1693.

A unique indigenous religious art developed only in New Mexico. One factor that contributed to the emergence of religious art in New Mexico was the influence of the Franciscan friars, who seem to have had some training in art. They were responsible for the spiritual administration of the colonies in which they worked and used art as a tool to convert the Indians and maintain the faith of settlers.

During the colonial period, religious art was produced and available in every major city in Latin America. In South America, there were two well-known centers: the School of Cuzco in Perú and the School of Quito in Ecuador. The School of Querétano in Mexico was perhaps the most important center in New Spain, which included the areas that became Central America, Mexico, and American Southwest. Because of the relative isolation of New Mexico and southern Colorado from metropolitan colonial centers, these areas developed their own santero art to be used in churches and homes.

In 1767, believing that the churches were well established, the Spanish viceroy ordered that the remaining Franciscan missions ministering to the Spanish colonists be secularized and turned over to parish priests. After New Mexico ceased to be part of New Spain, and because of the instability in central Mexico and the relative lack of resources, the Mexican authorities had difficulty maintaining strong ties with the poor and isolated provinces of the north. The Mexican authorities placed the New Mexican churches under the jurisdiction of the Durango Diocese. Some of the remaining Spanish priests returned to Spain. During the period of Mexican control, New Mexico was practically abandoned. After New Mexico was taken over by the United States in 1848, Jean Baptiste Lamy was assigned as bishop to administer the province for the American church. He brought with him a number of French priests unfamiliar with Hispanic American practices and culture. Some Mexican priests returned to Mexico.

By 1850, there were only fourteen priests left in all of New Mexico. The new priests, accustomed to refined European art, saw New Mexican art as crude and ugly, inappropriate for religious purposes. The santos in many of the churches were given away and replaced with mass-produced religious art from the East. The people did not like the imported figures because they were foreign to them and did not serve their purposes. This was especially true for some groups, such as the Penitentes. They preferred the old figures, because those had arms and the legs that could be moved for transportation during Holy Week ceremonies. The Penitentes defied the bishop and continued making santos.

The figures of the Penitente artists were more theatrical and dramatic, showing an incredible amount of blood on the body. They often included a movable head or a beating heart. This dramatization was necessary for the ceremonies of the Penitentes.

Santeros After 1598. The first santos were brought to the Americas from Spain. The first religious art of the Southwest was made by settlers working under the guidance of the Franciscan friars. Many of the first painters, including the Franciscans, painted anonymously because of a Spanish belief that signing a religious work of art might be considered impious.

Few religious artists became known by name before the eighteenth century. Among the best-known eighteenth century artists is Fray Andrés García, to which *The Sepulchre* in Santa Cruz has been attributed. Far more artists are known from the nineteenth century. Antonio Molleno is called the chili painter because of the chili pepper designs on the corners of his RETABLOS. His *retablos* include *San Antonio de Padua* and *Nuestra Señora de la Purísima Concepcion.* José Rafael ARAGÓN was a *retablo* painter who worked for a number of churches. His figures feature elongated bodies and pure, bright colors.

Religious artists of the twentieth century include José Dolores LÓPEZ. He worked in unfinished wood, a style that became a tradition in the López family. He was proud that he only used his pocket knife for carving. Jimmy Trujillo was born in Abiquiú, New Mexico, in 1948 and later moved to Albuquerque. Introduced to carving by his grandfather, he became interested in the colonial style of making straw appliqué crosses, *retablos*, *nichos*, candle boxes, and small chests. He sculpted an intricate *matraca* (cog rattle) named *The Seven Pains of Our Lady of Sorrows*, with scenes symbolizing the life of Christ and related religious inferences. His works are primarily done in appliqué or inlay style with paja (straw), barley, corn, or cebada. Max Roybal, a legend as much as a *santero*, was born in Santa Fe, New Mexico, in 1912. He is a traditional *santero* who learned to carve from his grandfather at the

A knitted image of Our Lady of Guadalupe. (Ruben G. Mendoza)

age of seven. Many of his carvings are from scraps of wood. He carved a *retablo* for the San Felipe de Neri Church in Old Town Albuquerque for the bicentennial.

Santeras. Women have generally worked anonymously on santos, sanding or painting with no acknowledgment. They stitched torn garments or made new garments for the santos, working at home. They also made *colcha* (bedspread) embroideries to decorate churches. Benita Reino Lopez is considered to be the first documented *santera* in New Mexico.

Since 1970, some Hispanic women have decided to identify themselves as *santeras*. An exhibit at the Museum of International Folk Art in 1993 demonstrated women's role in traditional and contemporary Hispanic arts of New Mexico.

Among the better-known *santeras* is Marie Romero Cash. In 1982, she made an altar screen for the church at El Rito. As a member of a family of santeros, Gloria Lopez Cordova began carving at the age of eight. Frances Varos Graves began making *colcha* embroidery in 1930. Teresa Vigil Montoya was manager of Teresa's Art Gallery in Santa Cruz. She began making *retablos* in 1987 as a self-taught artist. Zoraida Ortega, a *santera* and weaver, has a *retablo* titled *The Four Apparitions of the Virgin of Guadalupe* hanging in La Madera church. Sabinita Lopez Ortiz has a santo titled *The Blessed Sacrament*, in which a figure holds the space shuttle *Challenger* aloft, at the Air and Space Museum of the Smithsonian Institution in Washington, D.C.   —*Sylvia P. Apodaca*

SUGGESTED READINGS:

- Boyd, Elizabeth. *Popular Arts of Spanish New Mexico*. Santa Fe: Museum of New Mexico Press, 1974. Describes art and crafts in colonial New Mexico.
- Espinosa, José Edmundo. *Saints in the Valleys: Christian Sacred Images in the History, Life, and Folk Art of Spanish New Mexico*. Rev. ed. Albuquerque: University of New Mexico Press, 1967. An analysis of Hispanic religious art by a scholar who lives and feels the meaning of art.
- Frank, Larry. *New Kingdom of the Saints*. Santa Fe, N.Mex.: Red Crane Books, 1992. A beautifully illustrated history of religious art in New Mexico.
- Kubler, George. *The Religious Architecture of New Mexico*. Colorado Springs, Colo.: Taylor Museum of the Colorado Springs Fine Arts Center, 1940. Documented study of religious art. Required reading for a scholar.
- Steele, Thomas J. *Santos and Saints*. Albuquerque, N.Mex.: Calvin Horn, 1974. Provides a historical and religious understanding of santo art.

- Wroth, William. *Christian Images in Hispanic New Mexico: The Taylor Museum Collection of Santos*. Colorado Springs, Colo.: Taylor Museum of the Colorado Springs Fine Arts Center, 1982. Study of the history of religious art from the 1700's to the mid-1800's.
- Wroth, William. *Images of Penance, Images of Mercy: Southwestern Santos in the Late Nineteenth Century*. Norman: University of Oklahoma Press, 1991. Continuation of Wroth's study of the religious art of New Mexico, covering 1860 to 1910.

Religious syncretism: Fusion of two or more systems of religious belief and practice. Religious syncretism is but one type of intercultural exchange or borrowing, in which subcultures come to influence one another. The model of religious syncretism is often used to explain the development of Afro-Latin religions.

Early Views of Syncretism. The earliest mention of syncretism appears in Plutarch (46-c. 120), as an act of blending, combining, and reconciling inharmonious elements for the purpose of forging unity in the face of danger. George Calixtus (1586-1656), a Lutheran professor at the University of Helmstedt in Germany, used the term in his effort to promote religious unity and acceptance of variations in Christianity. The concept appeared in the 1930's when Brazilian anthropologist Arturo Ramos used syncretism to describe the process of combining religious systems that seem incompatible. In the 1940's, Cuban anthropologist Fernando Ortiz applied the idea of syncretism beyond religion to processes of cultural change.

Melville J. Herskovits, a North American anthropologist writing in the late 1930's and 1940's about African cultural retentions in the New World, popularized the term syncretism among English speakers. His pioneering article on Haiti, Cuba, and Brazil developed the thesis that the fusion of African belief systems and Roman Catholicism was widespread. His work brought attention to Roman Catholic saints who were addressed by either their Spanish Catholic names or by the names of Yoruba gods from West Africa. For example, the Catholic female Santa Barbara becomes the *orisha* Changó, an ancestor deity of the Yorubaland people. These associations can vary from one geographic area to another. In parts of the states of Bahía and Río de Janeiro in Brazil, Herskovits identifies Changó with Saint Jerome. Some scholars suggested that religious syncretism was a case of the Africans' "confused imagery," which mingled native gods and goddesses with the saints of the Catholic church.

The Orishas and the Saints. As scholars learned more about Afro-Latin religions, they further developed the concept of religious syncretism. In the 1950's and 1960's, Roger Bastide offered a useful explanation by stressing the nature of the *orishas*, variable in form like the ancient Greek god Proteus.

A Yoruba god can be represented by as many forms as are available in nature. An *orisha* may be invoked in the form of a saint while worshiping, but this is only one of the potential forms of an *orisha* rather than the spirit itself. Thus, the Yoruba religion was inherently versatile and open to the kinds of cultural borrowing involved in syncretism. The fluid nature of the *orishas* can be seen in the example of Obatalá. This *orisha* is generally identified with Our Lady of Mercy (La Virgen de las Mercedes) because she is dressed in white and Obatalá represents all that is white. Obatalá, however, is a family of spirits, both male and female, who contain different characteristics (*caminos*). She represents intelligence, purity, and divine thought. She is the creator of Earth and sculptor of humanity, a symbol of passion and sensuality; she is blind but teaches reading. Although saints tend to be associated with a single set of characteristics, in an *orisha* these contrasting forces coexist simultaneously. Some other characteristics (*caminos*) of Obatalá are represented by Jesus of Nazareth, Saint Ann, Saint Joseph, and Saint Sebastian. The saints can therefore be seen as the outer shell of the *orishas* in Santería.

Ancestor worship among Afro-Latin Caribbean people has resurfaced in the United States in a new type of syncretism. Religions such as Puerto Rican Spiritism, Haitian vodun, Brazilian Candomblé, and the better-known Afro-Cuban Santería have all incorporated influences from the Yoruba *orishas*. In a multicultural society, syncretism is a natural and conscious process that embraces seemingly dissonant cultural items to create harmonious expressions not only in religion but also in folklore, dress, food, literature, music, and race mixing.   *—Andrés I. Pérez y Mena*

SUGGESTED READINGS: • Bastide, Roger. *The African Religions of Brazil: Toward a Sociology of the Interpenetration of Civilizations.* 1960. Translated by Helen Sebba. Baltimore, Md.: The Johns Hopkins University Press, 1978. • Bolívar Aróstegui, Natalia. *Las Orishas en Cuba.* Havana: Ediciones Unión de Escritores y Artistas de Cuba, 1990. • Canizares, Raul. *Walking with the Night: The Afro-Cuban World of Santería.* Rochester, Vt.: Destiny, 1993. • Gonzales-Wippler, Migene. *Santería: The Religion.* New York: Harmony, 1989. • Herskovits, Melville J. *The Myth of the Negro Past.* 1941. Boston: Beacon Press, 1958. • Murphy, Joseph M. *Santería: An African Religion in America.* Boston: Beacon Press, 1988. • Ortiz de Montellano, Bernard R. *Aztec Medicine, Health, and Nutrition.* New Brunswick, N.J.: Rutgers University Press, 1990. • Pérez y Mena, Andrés I. *Speaking with the Dead: The Development of Afro-Latin Religion Among Puerto Ricans in the United States.* New York: AMS Press, 1991. • Thompson, Robert Farris. *Flash of the Spirit.* New York: Vintage, 1984.

Remittance of earnings: Transfers in cash or kind sent home by people living abroad, usually close relatives and friends. Sending remittances is a common practice among Latinos and other immigrants in the United States and Canada.

Remittances express the continuing commitment of Latinos to their places of origin. Cash transfers are the most tangible sign of the immigrants' identification with their home societies. U.S. Latinos show a tenacious disposition to send money and gifts to support kin left behind in Mexico, Puerto Rico, Cuba, the Dominican Republic, and other countries. Many immigrants perceive such transfers as social obligations, especially when they hope to return to their home communities.

Latinos typically send cash to their dependents and immediate relatives, such as children, parents, and grandparents. Emigration is usually a family decision based on pooled resources, and emigrants are expected to contribute regularly to household subsistence in the home country. Remittances are used primarily to satisfy basic consumption needs (food, clothing, and shelter) and secondarily to educate the young, finance the passage of those wishing to emigrate, and, less frequently, for savings and investments. Some remittances are used to acquire or improve housing and to support businesses.

Remittances have a mixed effect on developing economies. On one hand, they raise local standards of living, increase holdings of foreign currency, facilitate the acquisition of consumer goods, and improve the country's balance of payments. Thousands of households in Latin America and the Caribbean literally depend on the money sent by relatives living abroad for their subsistence. Some Latin American and Caribbean countries such as the Dominican Republic and El Salvador derive more income from remittances than from major export crops. In this sense, remittances redistribute income from the advanced industrial nations to the developing economies of Latin America and the Caribbean.

Migrant workers often support families in their home countries and return home in the off season. (AP/Wide World Photos)

Business owners may send profits to relatives in other countries. (Hazel Hankin)

On the other hand, remittances tend to cause stagnation in local agriculture, raise unemployment, increase social inequality, and promote additional emigration. Migrant and nonmigrant households have different living standards based largely on access to remittances from relatives in the United States and other countries. In some cases, remittances create a greater demand for domestic servants to help care for those left behind. Furthermore, remittances reinforce the dependence of poorer countries on wealthier ones. The outward orientation of many Latin American and Caribbean countries depletes the necessary human resources to sustain social, economic, and political development. Finally, remittances may worsen inflation rates by increasing cash flow without corresponding increases in labor productivity.

From a sociological standpoint, remittances reflect the far-flung networks of cooperation and solidarity that Latinos and other immigrants maintain in two countries. Sending money home thus strengthens the ties that bind immigrants to their sending communities.

Receiving remittances draws households even further into the international movement of capital, goods, and people. Sending and receiving communities are linked through a dense network of social relationships across geopolitical frontiers. The continual exchange of money, gifts, and favors between immigrants and their home communities facilitates the immigrants' adaptation to the host society while maintaining close identification with their native cultures.

Renaldo, Duncan (Renault Renaldo Duncan; Apr. 23, 1904, Romania?—Sept. 3, 1980, Santa Barbara, Calif.): Actor. Renaldo was a foundling child, and his place of birth has never been firmly identified. He arrived in the United States in the early 1920's and began his career with such films as *Clothes Make the Woman* (1928) and *The Bridge of San Luis Rey* (1929). In 1931, he was arrested by immigration authorities and spent years embroiled in legal proceedings to remain in the United States. In 1936, Renaldo was unconditionally pardoned by President Franklin D. Roosevelt.

During the 1930's and 1940's, Renaldo appeared in a series of more than fifty short action films as one of the Three Mesquiteers. Between 1945 and 1950, he appeared in the title role of *The Cisco Kid* in twelve films and more than 150 television episodes, bringing a nonviolent affability to the character. In an effort to make the Cisco Kid more acceptable to Hispanic critics, Renaldo went to Mexico to meet with the Inter-American Relations Council. The costume he wore as the Cisco Kid, which he made himself, included accessories designed to represent all the nations of Latin America.

Renaldo's other credits include *Trapped in Tia Juana* (1932), *Rose of the Rio Grande* (1938), *Down Mexico Way* (1941), *For Whom the Bell Tolls* (1943), *The Daring Caballero* (1949), and the serials *The Lone Ranger Rides Again* in the late 1930's and *Zorro Rides Again* in 1937 and 1959.

Repartimiento system: A means of forcing Indians in colonial Mexico and Central America to labor on Spanish estates, especially in the silver mines. After the Spanish had plundered the treasures of Mexico during the era of conquest, the profitability of the colony came from the exploitation of indigenous labor. Spaniards who controlled Indians could put them to work on the farms and ranches, or in mines and textile sweatshops. For thirty years, the invaders exploited such labor by enslaving Indians or through the EN-COMIENDA SYSTEM. In the latter system, a Spaniard received a group of Indians in trust. He assumed responsibility for Christianizing them, but in turn he was entitled to receive tribute from them. Some collected such tribute in goods and money, but many demanded labor service. By 1549, however, the Spanish monarchy had outlawed almost all forms of Indian slavery and also prohibited holders of *encomiendas* from exacting labor.

Thus, Spaniards turned to the *repartimiento* system, another form of forced labor, to meet their need for workers. They based it on the preconquest *cuatequil*, by which Indian commoners provided rotating drafts of labor for state lands and public works such as roads, causeways, and temples. The Spanish system required each adult male Indian commoner between the ages of eighteen and sixty to provide about forty-five days of

Spaniards coerced Indians into laboring for low wages through the repartimiento *system.* (Ruben G. Mendoza)

repartimiento labor each year. In general they worked in one-week shifts, and only a few men were to be absent from a village at any given time. The Spaniards rationalized the justice and morality of *repartimiento* on two grounds: despite its coercive nature, the workers received a wage; and it prevented idleness and vagabondage among the Indians by forcing them to work for the common good, as the conquerors defined it.

Even so, the system inflicted abuse on the workers. It often took them out of their villages at crucial periods in the agricultural cycle, such as harvest time, to work the Spanish lands. Many workers never received their meager wages, and government officials failed to correct such mistreatment, sometimes because they were in league with the employers. There was little but their own consciences to prevent Spaniards from overworking the Indians.

Repartimiento flourished during the second half of the sixteenth century in the densely populated regions of central and southern Mexico. The tremendous decline in Indian population from epidemic disease intensified competition for the surviving workers. Soon after 1600, the government abolished *repartimiento* except for the mining industry. The great silver mines, such as Zacatecas and San Luis Potosí, however, lay chiefly in northern locales without large Indian populations. Unlike in central Mexico, *repartimiento* never took hold in those areas because of the scarcity of indigenous workers. Mine operators instead had to attract free laborers. Even in the Mexican heartland to the south, *repartimiento* died out by the mid-1600's, replaced by debt peonage and wage labor. In that, Mexico contrasted with Peru, where the *mita*, a system of forced labor similar to *repartimiento*, survived until the end of colonial rule.

Republic of the Rio Grande (1840): Self-declared state. After Texas declared its independence from Mexico in 1836, Mexican federalists in northeastern Mexico continued their struggle against Mexican centralism. In 1839, General Antonio Canales and other federalists raised the banner of federalism in the border state of Tamaulipas, sought the support of Texas, and raised a mixed Texan-Mexican force to fight the Mexican army. Despite some success in northern Mexico, Canales and his army were forced to retreat across the Rio Grande into Texas in early January, 1840. On January 18, Canales proclaimed the organization of a federalist Republic of the Rio Grande, with Jesus Cardenas as president and himself as commander in chief.

Canales proceeded to reinvade Mexico, only to be forced once again, a month later, to cross over into Texas to avoid a severe defeat. Although Canales and his forces won some significant battles, anticipated support from the Texas government never materialized. Efforts to create a federalist republic ultimately failed.

Republican National Hispanic Assembly of the United States (RNHA): Political organization. The RNHA was established in 1972 to address the needs of Hispanic members of the Republican Party. It sought to develop a strong, effective, and informed Republican Hispanic constituency. It also encouraged able and qualified Hispanic Americans to seek office at all levels of government.

The organization addressed national issues of concern to the Hispanic community and sought to have those concerns addressed at a federal policy level. The organization is the official Hispanic auxiliary of the National Republican Committee. Headquartered in Washington, D.C., the organization had chapters in seven states by the early 1990's.

Rescate, El (founded 1981): Nonprofit resource center. El Rescate (the rescue) is targeted at Central American REFUGEES and Latin American immigrants in Southern California. It was established by the Santana Chirino Amaya Central American Refugee Committee and the Southern California Ecumenical Council. It was originally funded to provide legal services to Salvadoran refugees who came to the Los Angeles area seeking political asylum. After the Salvadoran peace accord in 1992, El Rescate began to focus on the welfare of Latin American immigrants in the inner city.

El Rescate developed six departments to address the different needs of immigrants: legal services, social services, education, community economic development, youth employment and leadership, and human rights. The legal service department provided free legal representation on civil and immigration cases. It also monitored Immigration and Naturalization Service (INS) deportation practices and has pursued class action lawsuits against the INS. The department also has assisted immigrants in applying for citizenship and registering to vote.

The social service department has provided groceries, clothing, and disposable diapers to needy families and bus tokens to the homeless; run a housing shelter; and made referrals for medical services, employment,

El Rescate offers basic language classes. (David Bacon)

and education. The educational program has provided classes in English as a second language (ESL) and basic literacy, free of charge to the community. The economic development department established an association with the University of California, Los Angeles, extension program to provide business and management courses to community members. It also developed the Community Development Credit Union to facilitate granting of small personal and business loans.

The youth employment and leadership training department worked to keep youth out of poverty and away from violence. Young people were placed in government, labor, and community organizations to gain employment skills. Students gained leadership skills through organizing community forums and campaigns to improve conditions in the inner city.

El Rescate also monitored human rights violations during El Salvador's civil war. After the Salvadoran peace accord, it sent delegates to El Salvador to ensure equity in the reconstruction efforts. El Rescate receives funding from private foundations, churches, individual donations, and fund-raisers. It published *Index of Accountability*, a study of human rights violations during the Salvadoran civil war that was used by the United Nations.

Resident alien: Immigration status. A resident alien may also be referred to as a "lawful permanent resident" or a "documented noncitizen." These terms refer to a noncitizen who enters the United States with an immigrant visa or who has been lawfully granted the privilege of residing permanently in the United States in accordance with the immigration laws. Persons with this status are entitled to live and work in the United States and collect entitlement benefits, if categorically qualified. This status must be achieved by immigrants to the United States prior to completing the naturalization process.

Respeto: Consideration and deference for a person's elder. Regard for one's elders is particularly important in traditional Latino households, with their strict hierarchical distribution of power and weight of the extended family unit. Children are taught to respect elders in the community, as well as those in the immediate family. *Respeto* also refers to the ways in which deference is shown and proved. A lack of respect for one's elders is taken by many Latinos to be a telling sign of failed parenting.

Respiratory diseases: Diseases of the respiratory system, or pulmonary diseases, affect the lungs and bronchial tubes. They include cancer of the lung, pneumonia, and influenza.

Although mortality rates from cancer of the lung, pneumonia, and influenza are higher for non-Hispanic whites and blacks than for Latinos, they are high enough to place Latinos in an at-risk category. The lower rates for Latinos have been attributed to the fact that relatively few Latinas, as compared to non-Hispanic women, smoke tobacco.

Several factors place Latinos at risk for lung disease. Acquired immune deficiency syndrome (AIDS) affects the development of infectious and other lung diseases. The number of Latinos with AIDS increased by 11.5 percent from 1990 to 1991, an increase larger than for non-Hispanic blacks and whites. Alcohol and the use of illicit drugs also have adverse effects on the pulmonary system. The National Household Survey on Drug Use of 1988 found that the prevalence of

cocaine use was higher among Latinos (11 percent) than among non-Hispanic whites (10.8 percent) and non-Hispanic blacks (9.3 percent). The prevalence of alcoholism among Latino males was higher than for whites and blacks.

Certain socioeconomic factors place Latinos at particular risk for pulmonary disease. A large proportion of the Latino labor force works in production jobs for which occupational exposures pose a risk of respiratory disease. Some concern has been expressed for farmworkers, many of whom are Latinos. Their exposure to insecticides and fertilizers may put them at particular risk.

Tobacco use is the most preventable cause of respiratory disease, and lung cancer is one of the ten leading causes of death for African Americans and non-Hispanic whites. Data indicate that the use of tobacco by Latino males is comparable to that by white males, putting them at the same risk of cancer of the lung. Incidence of cancer of the lung in Latinos has been increasing.

Among Latinos, pneumonia and influenza represent the sixth leading cause of death. The incidence of tuberculosis is higher for Latinos than for non Hispanic whites. Although the rate was higher for other minority groups, Latinos experienced the highest annual increase from 1985 to 1990. The incidence of tuberculosis increased by 76 percent in the Latino population between the ages of twenty-five and forty-four. Among Latinos, Mexican Americans had the largest increase, followed by Puerto Ricans and Cuban Americans. Chronic bronchitis, though less common among Latinos, is another respiratory disease deserving study among Latino populations.

Respiratory disease affects black children more adversely than it does Latino children. The mortality rate for sudden infant death syndrome was 2.5 per 1,000 for Latinos, compared to 1.3 per 1,000 for non-Hispanic whites and 5.1 per 1,000 for African Americans. The registry of cystic fibrosis patients showed that 2.5 percent of the patients were Latino. For asthma, Puerto Rican children, however, had both the highest cumulative prevalence (children who ever had the disease), at 20.2 percent, and highest point prevalence rate (children who had the disease at the time), at 11.2 percent, of all ethnic groups.

Although Latino women have had a reduced risk for respiratory disease, there is some indication that rates are increasing, particularly for cancer of the lung. Researchers speculate that the increase of smoking among Latinas may be a contributing factor. It is not

Occupational factors put many Latinos at risk for respiratory diseases. (AP/Wide World Photos)

clear whether the reported increase in certain respiratory diseases among Latinos in general is a result of a tendency to move to urban environments, genetic predisposition, or diagnostic biases.

Retablo: Folk Mexican votive offering depicting miracles. *Retablos* are dedicated to a given saint. These offerings are commissioned from a painter of miracles by the person benefiting from the miracle. Painted on canvas or on tin or copper sheets, *retablos* portray the accident, misfortune, or illness affecting a person and the saint whose divine intervention was invoked. They are placed in churches alongside images of the saint who is said to have answered the prayers of the believer. The *retablo* form is one of the most important examples of Mexican folk painting.

A retablo *artist at work.* (Cheryl Richter)

As executive director of California Rural Legal Assistance, Cruz Reynosa struggled to obtain government financing.
(AP/Wide World Photos)

Revista: Theatrical performance including music and dance. Filled with satire and social commentaries, the *revista* is basically a musical review composed of a series of unconnected *cuadros* (scenes) presented in an arbitrary sequence. This arbitrariness and lack of a substantial libretto account for its low literary valuation. A parade of extravagant yet skimpy costumes, alternating with comic dialogue, musical numbers, and dances lacking dramatic purpose, the *revista* aims primarily at entertaining the audience, appealing visually and aurally rather than intellectually. It originated in the nineteenth century and still enjoys popularity in Latin American cities, where it appears in theaters and cabarets.

Reyes, Alfonso (May 17, 1889, Monterrey, Mexico—Dec. 12, 1959, Mexico City, Mexico): Poet, essayist, and educator. Reyes' father, General Bernardo Reyes, was governor of the state of Nuevo León. General Reyes, a man of letters as well as arms, awakened the literary vocation in his son.

In 1906, Reyes moved to Mexico City, where he was active with a group of young poets and scholars who, on the eve of the Mexican Revolution of 1910, initiated a cultural renewal and educational reform throughout the National Preparatory School and the National University. Reyes was responsible for establishing many cultural and educational institutions during his lifetime. He successfully combined two careers, one as a man of letters and the other as a diplomat.

Aside from his journalistic writing and numerous essay collections, his major works include *Visión de Anáhuac* (1917), which fuses poetry and history; *Ifigenia cruel* (1924), a dramatic poem; *Huellas, 1906-1919* (1922), a volume of verse; *Romances del Río de Enero* (1933), a cycle of poems; and *El plano oblicuo* (1920), a collection of short stories. Reyes stands out as one of Latin America's great prose stylists and cultural missionaries.

Reynosa, Cruz (b. May 2, 1931, Brea, Calif.): Government official. Born to farmworker parents, Reynosa received his undergraduate education at Pomona College. Following a two-year stint in the U.S. Army, he studied law at the University of California, Berkeley.

During the 1960's, Reynosa was an assistant chief of the Division of Fair Employment Practices in California. He served as the first deputy director, then as the director, of California Rural Legal Assistance. Reynosa was associate general counsel to the Equal Employment Opportunity Commission in 1967. He returned to teaching in 1972, at the University of New Mexico Law School, where he stayed for four years.

In 1976, Reynosa was appointed to the California Court of Appeals in Sacramento as an associate justice. In 1982, Governor Jerry Brown appointed him to the California Supreme Court, making Reynosa the first Latino to serve in that capacity. Reynosa was appointed to several presidential commissions, including the Select Commission on Immigration and Refugee Policy and the United Nations Commission on Human Rights.

Ribera Chevremont, Evaristo (1896, San Juan, Puerto Rico—1976): Writer. A self-educated high school dropout, Ribera Chevremont began working at a factory by the age of fifteen. He began his journalism career in 1918 as a reporter for *El Imparcial*, a news daily.

Although his early writing was in the modernist style, by 1927 he had become a leader of the postmodernist movement, creating a new school of literature he called *Girandulismo*. In 1930, he went to Madrid, where he studied under Jose Ortega y Gasset. He lectured often in the Madrid Atheneum. Upon his return to Puerto Rico, he contributed numerous articles and poems to various periodicals and wrote a column titled "Paginas de vanguardia" for the newspaper *La Democracia*. He consistently stressed the themes of political and economic liberation as a means of heightening Puerto Rican consciousness.

Ribera Chevremont's *La naturaleza en "Color"* (1943) expresses the critical and poetic ideas exposed in his original verse published in *Color* (1938). His major works of poetry are collected in the volumes *Antologia poetica, 1924-1950* (1957) and *Nueva antologia* (1966). Ribera Chevremont was influential in bringing Puerto Rican poetry into the contemporary currents of European, especially French, developments.

Richardson, William "Bill" (b. Nov. 15, 1947, Pasadena, Calif.): Legislator. Richardson's first love was baseball, but an elbow injury ended his professional prospects. Richardson attended Tufts University and completed a master's program at the Fletcher School of Law and Diplomacy. He first entered politics in 1978 as executive director of the New Mexico State Democratic Committee. Months later, he was planning a congressional campaign against Manuel Luján, a longtime incumbent. Despite his loss, Richardson's strong showing gained him respect and popularity in New Mexico.

Bill Richardson prepares to testify during hearings on corruption in professional boxing held by the House governmental affairs subcommittee. (AP/Wide World Photos)

Redistricting created a majority Hispanic seat in 1982, and Richardson, a Mexican American, was favored to win. He survived a bruising primary and won, thanks in large measure to his ability to forge a coalition among Latinos and Native Americans. A tireless campaigner, Richardson won the respect of his colleagues as a legislator. He served as chief deputy whip for the House Democratic leadership in the early 1990's and conducted diplomatic missions abroad for the Bill Clinton Administration.

Rio Arriba County, New Mexico: The county was one of the first of New Mexico and a core area of early Spanish settlement. It was one of the poorest counties in the United States in the late twentieth century.

Prior to formation of Rio Arriba County, the area called Rio Arriba covered the Arriba River drainage basin. The land has distinct geographical traits. The soil is poor and must be irrigated. It is good only for subsistence agriculture, not yielding enough for export. Spanish settlers found the summers hotter and the winters colder than those in Mexico City. The terrain is rough, and for many decades travel was possible only on trails and cart roads, hindering economic development.

A large population and commercial agriculture were not goals for this area held by Spain or, later, Mexico. Rio Arriba, and the rest of New Mexico, was to be a buffer for Mexico against the expanding American frontier. The main economic incentive for settlement was the availability of land. Many land-poor families left more established areas of Mexico to settle here. By 1700, there were few more than one thousand colonists in the territory. Only 176 land grants were made between 1695 and 1846, approximately one per year.

Farming and ranching were the two most common means of survival. The animal best adapted for this territory was the sheep. Sheep require less fodder in winter, are easier to herd than are cattle, and produce both meat and wool. By 1750, sheep production was the leading industry of the area.

Because of its lack of resources and trade, Rio Arriba emerged as one of the poorest counties in New Mexico, and later, in the nation. In the 1880's, less than 2 percent of New Mexico's mechanized equipment was in Rio Arriba County. The total amount of farmland was only 13 percent of the territory's total, and farms were small, frequently about ten acres in size.

During the early 1900's, Rio Arriba County finally found an exportable commodity. It became a major supplier of men for field labor and mining in other western states. This development dramatically altered the demography of the area. In the late 1920's, two-thirds of the male Hispanic American heads of households were working elsewhere at seasonal work. This left local work to the women and children. Most of these men returned to their homes during the Great Depression of the 1930's.

Four counties make up the territory once covered by Rio Arriba alone: Taos, Sandoval, Santa Fe, and Rio Arriba counties. Tourists consider the area to be scenic. The climate is dry and healthy. Quaint villages dot the landscape. Rio Arriba County continues to have a majority rural Hispanic American population. Poverty persists as a result of underemployment and unemployment. During the 1980's, 66 percent of the farmers worked at least part-time on land other than their own. Families stayed on their lands because of strong kinship ties. These characteristics give Rio Arriba County its distinct historical and cultural qualities.

Rio Grande Valley: Region on the U.S.-Mexico border. In the early 1700's, the Rio Grande Valley was the principal settlement area and economic base for the Spanish colonists. The region's early linkages and influence emanated from Mexico City. The story of the Rio Grande Valley in the twentieth century, on the whole, is one of dramatic economic success. The success is exemplified by huge cotton fields, orange groves, and vegetable farms as well as booming border industries. The attractiveness of the area is shown by the number of the retirement centers that have opened there.

The recent history of the Rio Grande revolves around the region's advantageous location relative to the shifting population and economic growth patterns of the United States and Mexico. Beginning in the 1950's, with the advent of technology that could better adapt the environment for human use, the center of gravity of the United States population began moving southwest. At the same time, the Mexican center of population moved north, with migrants sometimes moving out of the country and into the United States. In the path of this movement were major population and employment centers of the Rio Grande Valley such as El Paso, Brownsville, Del Rio, and Laredo in Texas and Ciudad Juárez, and Nuevo Laredo in Mexico. Cities on each side of the border were influenced by those on the other, with the region gradually acquiring a blend of Mexican and American culture (*see* BORDER REGION AND CULTURE).

The Rio Grande Valley, particularly the lower portion, gained from the booming vacation and retirement industries of the Sun Belt. This boom was an expres-

Women work with a primitive corn mill and cooking implements in Brownsville, Texas. (Library of Congress)

sion of rising standards of living in both the United States and Mexico. Agricultural output grew on both sides of the border, roughly balanced among three major crops: winter vegetables, citrus fruits, and field crops (mostly cotton and sorghum). Water is the single most important resource of the valley.

On the United States side, much of the population is of Mexican origin and speaks Spanish. Economic disparities between Anglo and Latino people were still pronounced in the late twentieth century, even after decades of mingling of the populations. Much of the region's business and industry, including agriculture, was controlled by the English-speaking Anglo minority.

On the Mexican side, the border states late in the twentieth century registered the country's highest levels of in-country migration, employment opportunity, and economic growth. Fueling prosperity were MAQUILADORAS, border industries established with ties to U.S. industries, sometimes with government assistance. These industries benefited from special rules on exports and imports. The growth of factory employment led to occasional labor shortages.

The Rio Grande Valley of the late twentieth century was in political ferment, and its transition to explosive population and economic growth was disquieting to many. The rising expectations of the Latino people of the Rio Grande Valley corresponded to changes in ethnic political representation and employment opportunity.

Ríos, Hermínio: Publisher and scholar. During the early 1970's, Ríos, a Mexican American, was active in getting microfilm copies made of Spanish-language newspapers as part of his work in what was then called La Raza Library at the University of California, Berkeley. He has also written on the history of the Spanish-language press. Ríos was also a co-owner, with Octavio ROMANO-V., of QUINTO SOL PUBLICATIONS.

Rivas, Marian Lucy (b. May 6, 1943, New York, N.Y.): Geneticist. Rivas is a specialist in medical genetics and computer science. She received her B.S. in biology from Marian College in 1964 and both a M.S. (1967) and Ph.D. (1969) in medical genetics from Indiana University. She has done research at The Johns Hopkins University, where she received the Johns Hopkins University Fellowship (1969-1971). From 1971 to 1975, she was associate professor of biology at Douglas College, Rutgers University, and associate professor at the Hemophilia Center of the Oregon Health Science University. She became a full professor at the Hemophilia Center in 1982. In addition, she has served as associate scientist at the Neurological Science Institute of Good Samaritan Hospital in Oregon. She has participated on genetics committees for the National Institutes of Health and has been engaged in genetics research in South America. Her areas of research include human gene mapping, genetic counseling, genetic aspects of epilepsy, and computer applications of clinical genetics.

Rivera, Chita (Dolores Conchita Figueroa del Rivero; b. Jan. 23, 1933, Washington, D.C.): Actress and dancer. An accomplished dancer, actress, and singer, Rivera began her dance training at the age of eleven and in 1950 entered the American School of Ballet. Rivera made her Broadway debut in 1952 in the chorus of *Call Me Madam*. She soon began appearing regularly on Broadway in such productions as *Can-Can* (1953), *Shoestring Revue* (1955), *Seventh Heaven* (1955), *Mr. Wonderful* (1956), and *West Side Story* (1957). Rivera married dancer and director Anthony Mordente, who also appeared in *West Side Story*. She received Tony Award nominations for her performances in *Bye Bye Birdie* in 1961, *Chicago* in 1976, *Bring Back Birdie* in 1981, and *Merlin* before winning the award for *The Rink* in 1984 and *Kiss of the Spider Woman* in 1993. She also appeared on stage in *Zenda*

(1963), *Threepenny Opera* (1966), *Born Yesterday* (1972), *Jacques Brel Is Alive and Well and Living in Paris* (1972), *Kiss Me, Kate* (1974), and *Sing Happy!* (1978).

Rivera, of Puerto Rican descent, played a major role in the film version of *Sweet Charity* (1969) and ap-

Chita Rivera starred in a Canadian theater production of Kiss of the Spider Woman. *(AP/Wide World Photos)*

Diego Rivera poses with his portrait of dancer Maudelle Bass. (AP/Wide World Photos)

peared in the film *Sergeant Pepper's Lonely Hearts Club Band* (1978). She has been seen on a variety of television programs and in 1985 was inducted into the Television Hall of Fame.

Rivera, Diego (Dec. 8, 1886, Guanajuato, Mexico—Nov. 25, 1957, Mexico City, Mexico): Painter. Rivera began studying art at the age of ten, working with several famous Mexican artists at the Mexico City Academy of San Carlos. He left the academy six years later because of artistic differences. A grant allowed him to study in Spain in 1907. He then traveled across Europe.

Rivera lived in the United States from 1930 to 1934. Rivera was married to Frida Kahlo, a well-known Mexican artist in her own right, as well as to Angelina Beloff and Guadalupe Marín.

Rivera, one of the best-known Mexican muralists, believed in the political inspiration possible through art and discussed such a purpose with David Alfaro Siqueiros, another member of the movement. In 1922, Rivera participated in his first mural, with Siqueiros, José Clemente Orozco, and twenty-two others at the Amphitheater Bolívar at the National Preparatory School in Mexico City. He painted the mural *Man at the Crossroads* (1933) at Rockefeller Center in New York City. It was never completed; in fact, it was destroyed because it included a portrait of Vladimir Ilich Lenin, leader of the Russian Revolution. Rivera reproduced the mural at the Palace of Fine Arts in Mexico City in 1934.

Between 1936 and 1940, Rivera painted only easel works, including landscapes, portraits, and a series of black dancers. He returned to wall painting in 1940, working throughout the United States and Mexico until his death.

Among other activities, Rivera became director of his old art school, the Academy of San Carlos, in 1929. He also designed the scenery and costumes for a ballet in Philadelphia, Pennsylvania, in 1932. His political activities were highlighted by membership in the Mexican Communist Party, several visits to the Soviet Union, and consultation with politicians including Leon Trotsky. Rivera was a cofounder of the Union of Revolutionary Painters, Sculptors, and Graphic Artists. He donated his house in Coyoacán (a suburb of Mexico City) to the Mexican people. It was later turned into the Frida Kahlo Museum.

Rivera and others who participated in the National Preparatory School mural initiated the Mexican political mural movement. Like those of Orozco, Rivera's ashes are in the Rotunda of Famous Men in the Civil Pantheon of Dolores.

Rivera, Edward (b. 1944, Orocovis, Puerto Rico): Autobiographer. Rivera grew up in New York City and attended parochial and public schools in Spanish Harlem, the Art Students' League during his senior year in high school, and the Pratt Institute for one semester. Following his high school graduation, he worked at various odd jobs in offices and factories, as well as in the New York Public Library. He enrolled in the City College of New York when he was nineteen, and two years later he was inducted into the Army.

Following his discharge, Rivera worked at a savings bank and resumed his studies at City College, from which he received an associate's degree. He was awarded a bachelor of arts degree in English in 1967 and holds a master of fine arts degree from Columbia University. He has taught at the City College of New York.

Rivera has published an autobiography titled *Family Installments* (1982). This work traces Rivera's roots and family life through his teenage years in New York City. Its impact lies in its inside view of a young Puerto Rican male's coming of age in Spanish Harlem during the 1940's and 1950's.

Rivera, Geraldo (b. July 4, 1943, New York, N.Y.): Investigative journalist and talk-show host. Rivera is of Puerto Rican background. He received a law degree from the University of Pennsylvania and a degree in journalism from Columbia University. He is a celebrated investigative television journalist, having written and produced various award-winning documentaries. He achieved wide recognition for his documentary *Willowbrook: The Last Disgrace*, exploring conditions at an institution for retarded children. As of 1994, he had won a Peabody Award and ten Emmy Awards.

Rivera built a reputation at *Eyewitness News* in New York City (1970-1974), then was a contributor to *Good Morning America* (1974-1978). He did specials called *Geraldo Rivera: Good Night, America* and was a senior correspondent with *20/20*.

Rivera's most publicized journalistic endeavor was *The Mystery of Al Capone's Vaults* (1986), which became the highest-rated syndicated show in television history. In 1987, he began hosting the successful talk show *Geraldo*. Shows often involved controversial issues. Rivera made news when a studio brawl broke out on the set between a black activist and neo-Nazis; his nose was broken by a chair used as a weapon by one of

Geraldo Rivera leaves the federal courthouse in Cleveland, Ohio, after defeating a libel lawsuit against him and the television show 20/20. (AP/Wide World Photos)

the brawlers. His autobiography, *Exposing Myself*, was published in 1991, the year he began hosting *Now It Can Be Told*, an investigative news magazine show. Rivera is one of the most visible Latinos in media and entertainment.

Rivera, Graciela (b. Puerto Rico): Opera singer. Rivera was a key figure in the development of opera in Puerto Rico in the 1950's. She was also a music educator in the New York City area from 1970 to 1987. As a singer, Rivera has the technical skill to sing the standard coloratura soprano literature (a voice capable of singing light and fast-running scales with ease) and a beautiful silky tone.

After one of her early recitals, a music critic from *The New York Times* described her as a charming and poised artist with a fresh and sweet soprano voice. Her interpretation of a demanding scene from *La Sonámbula* displayed a powerful coloratura voice that created

a sad, moving effect. Rivera's accuracy of intonation, clear enunciation, long sustained notes, and graceful phrasing made her one of the most accomplished singers on the American stage.

Rivera's debut with the New York City Opera was in 1951, and she later performed at the Metropolitan Opera House. Her performances include roles in *The Magic Flute* and the Puerto Rican opera *Nela*, in which she shared a New York City stage with José Ferrer in 1971.

Rivera, Henry Michael (b. Sept. 25, 1946, Albuquerque, N.Mex.): Government official. Rivera completed his undergraduate studies in economics at the University of New Mexico in 1968. He earned his law degree there in 1973 and completed an accounting degree at the University of Albuquerque in 1981.

Rivera, a Mexican American, was appointed to serve on the Federal Communications Commission by

President Ronald Reagan in 1981. He was the first Latino commissioner and served until 1985. Rivera has received numerous awards, including a Public Service Award for Outstanding Leadership in Government, conferred by the National Association of Black-Owned Broadcasters. He is a decorated Vietnam veteran, having earned the Bronze Star and the Army Commendation Medal.

Rivera, Tomás (Dec. 22, 1935, Crystal City, Tex.—May 16, 1984, Fontana, Calif.): Short-story writer and poet. Descending from a family of farmworkers, Rivera was able to experience at first hand the annual migration of laborers from Texas to a number of other states. He wrote about the people and environment with which he was familiar.

Rivera studied at Southwest Texas State University, from which he received a B.S. degree in education (1958) and a M.Ed. in educational administration (1964). He went on to the University of Oklahoma, from which he received a M.A. and a Ph.D. in Romance languages and literature. In 1979, he was appointed chancellor of the University of California at Riverside.

. . . y no se lo tragó la tierra (1971; *. . . and the Earth Did Not Part*, 1971), winner of the First Quinto Sol Literary Prize, is considered as a collection of fourteen short stories by some and as a novel by others. It proposes a reevaluation of Chicanos' socioeconomic condition. Although Rivera is best known for his short stories, he published poetry in a number of literary journals. Rivera's stories and poetry often reflect Chicano social reality; they also address the problem of alienated humanity.

Riverón, Enrique (b. Jan. 31, 1902, Cienfuegos, Las Villas, Cuba): Caricaturist. Riverón was admitted to art school at the age of fifteen. He also took some business classes, and at the age of eighteen he moved to Havana to take a job in a bank.

Riverón became interested in caricature on his own. His first publications were in newspapers and magazines in Havana. In 1921, he organized a society of caricaturists with whom he had his first exhibition. The city of Cienfuegos in 1924 awarded him a scholarship to study in Europe, and he attended the San Fernando Academy in Madrid, Spain. While in Spain, he designed stage sets and costumes for musicals at Teatro Eslava. He married Mexican actress and cabaret singer Adria Delhort, whom he met in Spain.

The couple moved from Madrid to Paris, where Riverón studied at the Grande Chaumiere. He contin-

ued to publish his work in magazines in Havana and Madrid. Riverón returned to Cuba in 1927 but settled in New York, New York, in 1928 after touring Latin America. He and Adria were divorced, and he married an American citizen.

Riverón published his work in such top U.S. magazines as *Life*, *The New Yorker*, and *Modern Screen*. He published frequently in *Cine Mundial* and gave up caricature and magazine illustration when that magazine ceased publication in 1950. He moved to Kansas and taught cartooning at the Wichita Art Association from 1949 to 1953 and painting at Wichita University in 1958 and 1959.

Roa Bastos, Augusto (b. June 13, 1917, Asunción, Paraguay): Writer. Roa Bastos was born in Asunción but was brought up in Iturbe, a provincial village where his father worked as a clerk on a sugar plantation. When he was eight years old, he was sent to Asunción to continue his studies at the Colegio de San José.

Roa Bastos volunteered to fight in the war against Bolivia, the Guerra del Chaco (1932-1935), when he was fourteen years old. He later took a low-level position at the Bank of London and South America, became a journalist in 1942, and eventually became editor of the Asunción newspaper *El Pais*. In the 1930's he wrote his first short story, published decades later as *Lucha hasta el alba* (1979). In 1937, he wrote a novel titled *Fulgencio miranda* that was never published. His first published book was a collection of poems, *El ruiseñor de la aurora* (1942). This was followed by a book of sonnets, *El naranjal ardiente: Nocturno paraguayo, 1947-1949* (1960). His collections of short stories include *El trueno entre las hojas* (1953) and *Madera quemada* (1967), and his novels include *Hijo de hombre* (1960; *Son of Man*, 1965) and *Yo, el Supremo* (1974; *I, the Supreme*, 1986). Roa Bastos has been called the most complex, brilliant, and densely textured writer in contemporary Latin America.

Roche Rabell, Arnaldo (b. 1955, Santurce, Puerto Rico): Artist. Roche Rabell, a gifted child, spent his childhood in Puerto Rico. The youngest of six children in his family, he painted as a way to show love and caring and make human contact after the tragic deaths of his older sister (accidentally shot) and his eldest brother. As a child, Roche Rabell built miniature cities, complete with Christmas lights. His formal art studies began in 1969, with Max Lopez at the Luchetti School.

Between 1974 and 1978, Roche Rabell studied architecture, design, and illustration at the University of

A rodeo participant practices roping. (Bob Daemmrich)

Puerto Rico. He quit those studies after being criticized for his painstaking attention to detail, then taught himself to paint. He literally dreamed of studying in Chicago, Illinois, and took those dreams as a premonition. He moved to Chicago to study at the School of Art Institute of Chicago, where he earned bachelor's and master's degrees in fine arts.

While at the School of Art Institute, Roche Rabell began to experiment with having his models participate in forming the artistic image. He placed a model under a canvas and applied paint with his hands, resulting in what he called "rubbings." In 1986, he began a series of self-portraits titled *Events, Miracles and Visions*. These works address his ethnicity as a Puerto Rican. *You Have to Dream in Blue* follows that lead, representing Roche Rabell with racial characteristics that are not his but are part of the Puerto Rican mix.

Roche Rabell tries to break down barriers between the artist and the work through visual, verbal, and physical contact, not to record or narrate but to "know" a subject in order to depict it. He attempts to evoke emotion and empathy from the viewer.

Rodeo: Sporting event derived from cattle ranch work. Rodeo grew out of cattle ranch work and consists of six standard events: saddle bronco riding, bareback riding, bull riding, calf roping, steer wrestling, and steer roping. Nonstandard events also include team roping of steers, horse races, and milking of wild cows. The Mexican version of rodeo, the *fiesta charra* or *jaripeo*, includes the felling of a steer by twisting its tail, the jumping from a tamed horse onto a bronco, and feats based on horseback bullfighting. In Chile, the rodeo is sometimes included as part of the festivities celebrating the harvest. Rodeo is also popular in Cuba.

Rodriguez, Abraham, Jr. (b. 1961, New York, N.Y.): Writer. Rodriguez's first book was *The Boy Without a Flag: Tales of the South Bronx* (1992). Several characters from "Birthday Boy," contained in that book of short stories, were further developed in *Spidertown: A Novel* (1993).

Rodriguez's writing focuses on the experience of being a Puerto Rican in New York. Much of his work describes the barrio and the life of the underprivileged; *Spidertown* concerns the world of drug dealers. Rodriguez also discusses the tensions of trying to assimilate while retaining the culture of Puerto Rico.

When he was ten years old, Rodriguez was given a typewriter by his father, a poet. At the age of sixteen, he dropped out of high school. After working at various jobs, he earned his high school equivalency diploma and attended City College of New York, where he wrote several prize-winning stories.

Rodríguez, Armando M. (b. Sept. 30, 1921, Gómez Palacios, Durango, Mexico): Educator and administrator. Rodríguez has been active as an administrator in the field of education, working at the federal, state, and local levels. He was an early advocate of bilingual and bicultural education, writing several important journal articles on the topic and making speeches in its support.

Rodríguez's family migrated to the United States when he was ten years old, settling in San Diego, California. He entered the U.S. Army in 1942 and served in the Signal Corps until the end of World War II. He attended San Diego State College on the G.I. Bill, earning his A.B. in 1949 and M.A. in 1953. He began teaching at Memorial Junior High School in San Diego while working on his master's degree. He did further graduate work at the University of California, Los Angeles.

In 1954, Rodríguez became a guidance consultant for the San Diego city schools. In 1958, he was named vice principal at Gompers Junior High School, advancing to principal of Wright Brothers High School in 1965. That year, he became the first Chicano consultant to the California State Department of Education. The following year, he headed the department's Bureau of Intergroup Relations. Rodríguez also worked for the United States Office of Education in Washington, D.C., as director of what became the Office for Spanish-Speaking American Affairs. In 1970, he was named Regents' Lecturer at the University of California, Riverside. He assumed duties as president of East Los Angeles College in 1973, leaving that position in 1978 to become a commissioner on the Equal Employment Opportunity Commission.

Rodríguez, Arsenio (Aug. 30, 1911, Güira de Macurije, Cuba—Dec. 31, 1970, New York, N.Y.): Percussionist and composer. Rodríguez, a blind Afro-Cuban, was important in the development of the CONJUNTO and the spread of SALSA music. The Cuban *conjunto* was a new type of band group composed of trumpets, voices, conga drums, bass, and piano, with a stronger and more percussive sound than that of the more delicate *charanga*. Its origin can be traced to the carnival parade and New Orleans jazz bands.

Rodríguez was a virtuoso percussionist and is credited with helping to bring the MAMBO into American dance halls. The mambo as a music form originated in Afro-Cuban religious music. Rodríguez also introduced the conga drums as a major and regular percussion instrument in the salsa rhythm section of the band.

Around 1948, Rodríguez moved to the United States. He made numerous recordings at Gabriel Oller's studio in midtown Manhattan, New York. He was also responsible for the revival of the *banda típica* in New York in the 1960's. His compositions are part of the repertory of nearly every SALSA band.

Rodríguez, Beatriz (b. Apr. 25, 1951, Ponce, Puerto Rico): Ballet dancer. Rodríguez grew up in Newark, New Jersey, where she began studying dance at the Newark Academy of Ballet at the age of nine. She attended an arts high school, where she became a member of a touring folk dance troupe. Rodríguez then joined the company of the New Jersey School of Ballet and, later, Richard England's Dance Repertory Company in New York City. After working with the Joffrey II dancers for two years, she was invited to join the Joffrey Ballet in 1972. She became a principal dancer with the company, becoming known for such roles as Profane Love in *Illuminations* (1980), the Chosen One in *Le Sacré du Printemps* (1987), and Chocolate from Spain in *The Nutcracker* (1993).

With her flair for combining dramatic emotional expression with technical precision, Rodríguez has been called the Joffrey Ballet's carnal temptress. She has numerous credits with that company. She has been honored by New York and Los Angeles Hispanic organizations, and in 1993 she received the *Dance Magazine* Award for lifetime achievement.

Rodríguez, Chepita (?—Nov. 13, 1863, San Patricio, Tex.): Rancher. Rodríguez and her father fled Mexico after General Antonio López de Santa Anna's rise to power in 1835. They arrived in Texas in 1836. After her father was killed in a skirmish shortly following their arrival, Chepita bore the son of a cowboy, who deserted her and took the child with him.

In August, 1863, two men arrived at Rodríguez's cabin, which was located near Goliad. One of them looked like the cowboy who had abandoned her years before. By the next morning, the young man had left, and so had the money that belonged to his partner, who lay dead, killed with Rodríguez's axe. To protect her supposed son, Rodríguez, with the assistance of a retarded man who lived nearby, carried the body to the Aransas River. The cadaver washed ashore shortly

thereafter. Because Rodríguez and her neighbor were the only people who lived upriver, suspicion fell upon them, and they were arrested.

In October, 1863, Rodríguez was tried and found guilty. Despite a recommendation for mercy by the jury because of her age and the circumstantial evidence against her, the judge ordered her hanged. Rodríguez was one of only three women in Texas to be given the death penalty by the early 1990's.

Rodríguez, Clara Elsie (b. Mar. 29, 1944, New York, N.Y.): Educator. Rodríguez is the author of *Puerto Ricans: Born in the U.S.A.* (1989) and coeditor of *The Puerto Rican Struggle: Essays on Survival in the U.S.* (1989) and *Hispanics in the Labor Force: Issues and Policies* (1991). Much of her work concerns immigration issues.

Rodríguez holds bachelor's degrees from the City College of New York (1965) and University of Michigan (1966). Her master's degree (1969) is from Cornell University, and her Ph.D. (1973) is from Washington University of St. Louis, Missouri. Rodríguez became an adjunct professor at Pace University in 1973 and was assistant professor and chair of the Puerto Rican studies department from 1974 to 1976. She was named dean of Fordham University in 1976 and held that position until 1981, when she was named as a professor at that university. Rodríguez has been honored as a visiting scholar at the Massachusetts Institute of Technology (1987-1988) and a visiting fellow at Yale University (1992).

Rodriguez, Juan "Chi Chi" (b. Oct. 23, 1935, Río Piedras, Puerto Rico): Golfer. Rodriguez became one of golf's most popular players as much for his flamboyance as for his skill. His love of the sport grew out of financial necessity. To add to his family's income, he began caddying at the age of six for a mere thirty-five cents per round. He soon began playing and found that he had a talent for the game.

After playing in the 1955 Puerto Rico Open, Rodriguez enlisted in the U.S. Army. He returned to his homeland in 1957 and became the caddie master at the local club.

Rodriguez joined the U.S. Professional Golfers' Association (PGA) Tour in 1960. He scored his first tournament win in 1963 at the Denver Open, and he went on to become one of the PGA's leading money winners for the rest of the decade. In twenty-five years on the tour, he won eight tournament titles and earned more than $1 million. His last PGA win came with a record

Chi Chi Rodriguez on his way to victory in the 1986 PGA Seniors Digital Classic. (AP/Wide World Photos)

Paul Rodríguez. (AP/Wide World Photos)

performance of nineteen under par at the 1979 Tallahassee Open.

Rodriguez joined the PGA's Senior Tour in 1985, and his career took off again. By 1987, he had won more titles on the Senior Tour than he had in twenty-five years on the PGA Tour. He continued to be a force on the Senior Tour into the 1990's.

Supported by his fans, called "Chi Chi's Banditos," Rodriguez became a consistent crowd-pleaser for his on-the-course antics. He also became a media favorite for his colorful and quotable observations on the sport. He was given the honorary title of Grand Marshal for the 1995 Tournament of Roses Parade.

Rodriguez, Patricia (b. Nov. 8, 1944, Marfa, Tex.): Artist. Rodriguez lived with her grandparents until she was seven years old and became interested in art several years later, finding support for her work in Baptist church programs for children. After she turned twelve, she joined her parents, Mexican Americans who traveled throughout the Southwest as migrant workers. The family soon settled in Oxnard, California.

Rodriguez finally had the chance to attend school full-time when she was thirteen years old, but she could neither read nor write, so she was kept busy with art projects. Teachers encouraged her artistic work, so she pursued that rather than vocational coursework. She received a bachelor of fine arts degree (1972) from the San Francisco Art Institute and a master's degree in painting (1975) from Sacramento State University. Later, she obtained credentials to teach at the community college level.

During five years of teaching at the University of California, Berkeley, Rodriguez developed the first course on Chicano art history. The course has been used as a model for others. Her artwork has been acquired by the Mexican Museum in San Francisco, California, and by the Arts Council of the Museum of Modern Art in New York, New York.

Rodríguez, Paul (b. Mazatlán, Mexico): Comedian and actor. The son of immigrant farmworkers, Rodríguez entered the U.S. Air Force in 1977. He studied at Long Beach City College and California State University at Long Beach before going into stand-up comedy. He achieved early success at the Comedy Store in Los Angeles and went on to play nightclubs and concert halls throughout the United States.

Rodríguez starred as Paul Rivera in the television situation comedy *AKA Pablo* in 1984. Produced by Norman Lear, the program contained pungent jokes

about the Hispanic experience, stirred criticism, and was canceled after six episodes. In 1988, he played Tony Rivera in *Trial and Error*, a short-lived series about a pair of mismatched Hispanic roommates. His other television credits include *The Newlywed Game with Paul Rodríguez*; *Paul Rodríguez Behind Bars*, produced for the Fox Network by his own company, Paul Rodríguez Productions; *El Show de Paul Rodríguez* on Univisión; and a highly rated cable television special, *I Need a Couch*. Rodríguez has also appeared in such films as *Quicksilver* (1985) and *Born in East L.A.* (1987). In 1986, he produced a comedy album titled *You're in America Now, Speak Spanish*.

Rodríguez, Peter (b. June 25, 1926, Stockton, Calif.): Artist. Rodríguez spent several years in Mexico beginning in 1968, and much of his work reflects that experience. His altars reveal his background growing up in northern California. He is also known for his abstract paintings, which often feature elements from nature including leaves, flower petals, and blades of grass.

In 1972, Rodríguez founded the MEXICAN MUSEUM in San Francisco, California. Through the museum and his other work, he has influenced development of Chicano art in the San Francisco Bay area.

Rodriguez, Richard (b. July 31, 1944, San Francisco, Calif.): Autobiographer and essayist. Rodriguez's parents, Leopoldo and Victoria Moran Rodriguez, were both Mexican immigrants. Rodriguez worked at a variety of jobs as a teenager and in his writing describes the physical pleasure of labor and social interaction with workers from Mexico. He notes that although, like them, he had dark skin, because of his education he was distinguished from them.

Educated in Catholic primary and secondary schools, Rodriguez received his B.A. from Stanford in 1967 and his M.S. from Columbia University in 1969. He did graduate work at the University of California, Berkeley, and received a Fulbright Fellowship (1972-1973) and a National Endowment for the Humanities Fellowship (1976-1977).

The work for which Rodriguez has received most attention is his autobiography *Hunger of Memory: The Education of Richard Rodriguez* (1981), which charts the fragmented course of Rodriguez's education. Reviewers have given Rodriguez more attention than most Mexican American authors receive. The book's notoriety can be attributed in part to the author's antagonism toward BILINGUAL EDUCATION and AFFIRMATIVE ACTION, even though he benefited from affirmative action. The book is also a universal and sensitive examination of the complexities of language.

Rodríguez de Tío, Lola (Sept. 14, 1843, San Germán, Puerto Rico—Nov. 10, 1924, Havana, Cuba): Writer. In 1865, Lola Rodríguez married Bonicio Tío Segarra, one of nineteenth century Puerto Rico's most impassioned journalists. Three years later, Rodríguez de Tió wrote a subversive verse to the music of *La Borinqueña*, a song that later served as Puerto Rico's national anthem. Her first book of poems, published in 1876, sold out immediately and earned her renown across the island.

Exiled in 1877, she and her husband lived in Venezuela for one year. Upon returning to the island, Rodríguez de Tío published several poems and became involved in politics. In 1887, Spanish authorities unleashed a systematic campaign of repression and torture against supporters of autonomy known as the *compontes*. Rodríguez de Tió labored to free sixteen political prisoners, the most famous of whom was autonomist spokesman Román Baldorioty de Castro.

Spanish colonial authorities again banished Ro-

Cookie Rojas played with the Philadelphia Phillies in 1963. (AP/Wide World Photos)

dríguez de Tió from Puerto Rico in 1889. After spending three years in Cuba, she was deported and moved to New York City. Rodríguez de Tió then helped José Martí create the Cuban Revolutionary Party, which had a goal of securing the independence of both Cuba and Puerto Rico. After traveling to Europe in 1924, Rodríguez de Tió returned to Havana and died shortly thereafter.

Rojas, Cookie (Octavio Victor Rojas y Rivas; b. Mar. 6, 1939, Havana, Cuba): Baseball player and manager. Rojas played in the major leagues from 1962 to 1977 with the Cincinnati Reds, Philadelphia Phillies, St. Louis Cardinals, and Kansas City Royals. Although he was primarily a second baseman, during his career Rojas played every position in the field and also served as a designated hitter.

A career .263 hitter with little power, Rojas was a fine fielder; in 1968, he led National League second basemen with a .987 fielding percentage. A five-time All-Star, Rojas retired after the 1977 season but returned to the sport in 1981 as a special assignment coach for the California Angels. In 1988, he was named the team's manager, but he was fired after compiling a 75-79 record.

Roland, Gilbert (Luis Antonio Dámaso de Alonso; b. Dec. 11, 1905, Juárez, Mexico): Actor. Roland's father was a bullfighter who moved his family to Texas when Mexican revolutionary Pancho Villa attacked Juárez. Roland began what was to be a long film career in 1923 and soon became known for his machismo, good looks, and roguish eyes. His many films include *The Plastic Age* (1925), *The Campus Flirt* (1926), *Camille* (1927), *The Dove* (1927), *Man of the North* (1930), and *She Done Him Wrong* (1933, with Mae West). With the advent of the talkies, Roland found his career limited by his strong accent. He did such Spanish-language films as *Yo, tu y ella* (1933) and *Julieta compra un hijo* (1935). With his dark looks, Roland played characters ranging from Latinos to Native Americans to Russians. In the 1940's, he appeared in six episodes of the Cisco Kid film series. His other films include *Pirates of Monterey* (1947), *We Were Strangers* (1949), *The Furies* (1950), *Crisis* (1950), *The Bullfighter and the Lady* (1951), *The Bad and the Beautiful* (1952), *The Treasure of Pancho Villa* (1955), *The Big Circus* (1959), *Cheyenne Autumn* (1964), *Islands in the Stream* (1977), and *Barbarosa* (1982). During the 1970's, he appeared in many French and Italian films.

Gilbert Roland. (AP/Wide World Photos)

Romance: Narrative ballad of Spanish origin. The *romance* shares with Spanish ballads a predominant triple meter, a minor mode, and sixteen-syllable lines rhymed or assonated. Many *romances* deal with the lives of famous people. *Romances* are found in Brazil, in the form of *romanceiro* or ballad repertory that originated in the Minho region of Portugal, in DÉCIMAS, in CORRIDOS, and in the Venezuelan *punto*. Unaccompanied *romances* have been found in the Andes; however, most *romances* show accompaniment, usually including a basic string ensemble called *murga*, featuring *requintos*, *tiples* (guitars with four courses of strings), and *bandolas* (instruments related to the mandolin, with four courses of three strings and two of two strings).

Romano-V., Octavio (Octavio Ignacio Romano-Vizcarra; b. 1923, Mexico City, Mexico): Essayist and publisher. Romano-V. was born in Mexico City and reared in National City, California. He dropped out of high school but received his B.A. and M.A. from the University of New Mexico and his Ph.D. in anthropology from the University of California, Berkeley (1962).

In 1967, while serving on both the California State Commission on Compensatory Education and the board of the Spanish Speaking People's Institute for Education, Romano-V. cofounded *El Grito*, a journal that was to have far-reaching consequences for Chicano studies and contemporary publishing ventures. It was founded with the mission of overcoming stereotypical representations of Chicanos. At the time, Romano-V. was an assistant professor of behavioral sciences at the University of California, Berkeley, School of Public Health. Besides being an author of numerous sociological and anthropological essays on the Chicano experience, Romano-V., as founder of QUINTO SOL PUBLICATIONS in 1967, was instrumental in creating cultural organisms through which Chicano thought and artistic discourse would take place within the international community.

Romero, César (Feb. 15, 1907, New York, N.Y.—Jan. 1, 1994, Hollywood, Calif.): Actor. A descendant of Cuban liberator and martyr José MARTÍ, Romero began his career as a dancer. He made his stage debut in 1927 and his screen debut in 1933. His early films include *The Devil Is a Woman* (1935), *Public Enemy's Wife* (1936), *Wee Willie Winkie* (1937), *Charlie Chan at Treasure Island* (1939), and *Captain from Castile* (1947), in which he played the explorer Hernán CORTÉS.

During the 1940's, Romero appeared as a slick dandy in six Cisco Kid adventure films. He also danced his way through a series of festive Latin-style musicals with Carmen MIRANDA, including *Weekend in Havana* (1941), *Springtime in the Rockies* (1942), and *Carnival in Costa Rica* (1947). In the 1960's, Romero achieved fame with the television generation as the clever Joker on the *Batman* series; he also appeared in such films as *Pepe* (1960), *Seven Women from Hell* (1961), *Two on a Guillotine* (1964), *Sergeant Deadhead* (1965), and *A Talent for Living* (1969). In the 1980's, Romero rode yet another wave of popularity, lending his smooth good looks and polish to the evening soap opera *Falcon Crest*.

Romero, Frank (b. 1941, East Los Angeles): Painter. Romero was a member of LOS FOUR, a collective artist group formed in Los Angeles, California, in 1974. Los Four also included Carlos Almaraz, Roberto de la Rocha, and Gilbert LUJÁN. The group had major exhibitions in the mid-1970's.

As a child, Romero was encouraged by his mother to be an artist. He pursued art whenever possible while in public schools and was given a scholarship to the Otis Art Institute in Los Angeles. He met Almaraz while he was a freshman at California State University, Los Angeles, and stayed with Almaraz in New York City in 1968 and 1969.

Romero's work often focuses on street scenes, making statements about barrio life in Los Angeles. Many of his works feature automobiles. The style of many of his paintings is somewhat expressionist. He worked on a major freeway mural for the 1984 Olympics held in Los Angeles.

Romero, José Rubén (Sept. 25, 1890, Cotija de la Paz, Michoacán, Mexico—July 4, 1952, Mexico City, Mexico): Writer. Romero was the son of Melesio Romero and Refugio González. He attended elementary school in his hometown. As an adolescent, he lived in Mexico City with his family for six years. He worked for the newspaper *El Universal* in Mexico City and in 1930 was appointed Mexican consul in Barcelona. Later, he became ambassador to Brazil (1937) and to Cuba (1939).

Apuntes de un lugareño (1932; *Notes of a Villager*, 1988) was his first novel. In it, he firmly established his style in describing rural and small-town environments, a mode of writing known as regionalism. *Desbandada* (1934) and *El pueblo inocente* (1934) both are typical regionalist novels.

César Romero with Alice Faye at a 1941 film industry banquet. (AP/Wide World Photos)

Romero is perhaps best known for *La vida inútil de Pito Pérez* (1938; *The Futile Life of Pito Pérez*, 1966), a novel in the picaresque tradition. Through the development of his picaresque antihero, and through the use of humor and cynicism, Romero offers insights into the Mexico of his time. Romero's main contributions to Mexican letters were using humor in the novel to criticize society and reviving the picaresque form.

Romo, Ricardo (b. June 23, 1943, San Antonio, Tex.): Educator. Romo has studied the development of barrios in Los Angeles, California, in the early twentieth century. He sees development of industrial and commercial zones near the barrios, along with the expansion of construction, transportation, and service industries, as having several effects: Development and expansion of industry created higher population densities in the barrios as people sought work nearby, expanded the geographic area of the barrios, and led to geographic dispersion of Latinos outside the barrios, especially into EAST LOS ANGELES. (*See* BARRIOS AND BARRIO LIFE.) He also observed that immigrants were attracted to the central city by the existing colony there. His studies of occupational mobility showed that immigrants from Mexico tended to remain in manual employment. Even Mexican Americans of the third generation had less chance for upward mobility than did their counterparts of European ancestry.

Romo began his teaching career in 1967 at Franklin High School in Los Angeles. He earned his B.A. in history that year, from the University of Texas at Austin. Romo was granted an M.A. in history in 1970 from Loyola University in Los Angeles. He left Franklin High School in 1970 to take a position as assistant professor at California State University, Northridge. He joined the faculty of the University of California, San Diego, in 1974. In 1975, he earned his Ph.D. in history from the University of California, Los Angeles. He became a professor of history at the University of Texas at Austin in 1980. In 1988, he became director of the Tomás Rivera Center at that university. Romo is the author of *East Los Angeles: History of a Barrio* (1983) and coeditor of *New Directions in Chicano Scholarship* (1978).

Rondon, Fernando E. (b. May 6, 1936, Los Angeles, Calif.): Diplomat. Rondon, a Mexican American, was graduated from the University of California, Berkeley. In 1976, he served with the U.S. State Department as deputy director for the eastern coast of South America. Rondon became the deputy chief of mission in the U.S. embassy in Tegucigalpa, Honduras, in 1978.

From 1980 to 1983, Rondon served as ambassador to Madagascar. In 1982 and 1983, Rondon served as ambassador to Comoros, following which he took on the responsibilities of the Andean director for the State Department. From 1983 to 1985, Rondon served as ambassador to Ecuador.

The mid-1980's were a tumultuous period in the history of U.S.-Latin American relations. Rondon held several sensitive posts in South America at a time when countries in Central America were undergoing internal strife as well as ever-changing diplomatic relations with the United States.

Ronstadt, Linda Marie (b. July 7, 1946, Tucson, Ariz.): Singer and composer. Ronstadt began singing and playing the guitar as a child with her Mexican grandfather and her father, sister, and brother. In 1964, she went to Los Angeles, California, where she formed the Stone Poneys, a trio, and began performing on the city's club circuit. Her first album for Capitol Records was *Stone Poneys* (1967). On her own, she later assembled a band and scored a number of hit singles. Her first best-selling album, *Heart Like a Wheel* (1974), contained two chart-topping singles: "You're No Good" and "When Will I Be Loved." Her 1975 album *Prisoner in Disguise* established her as one of the leading female rock singers of the mid-1970's.

Striving for new artistic horizons, Ronstadt recorded traditional Mexican songs on the album *Canciones de mi padre* (1987). Her powerful soprano voice was the perfect instrument for this flamboyant mariachi repertoire. During the 1980's, Ronstadt displayed impressive adaptability. She sang in the new wave rock style with the Cretones on the album *Mad Love* (1980), performed opera and operetta roles in *La Bohème* and *The Pirates of Penzance*, and accompanied Nelson Riddle and his band on tour.

Ros-Lehtinen, Ileana (b. July 15, 1952, Havana, Cuba): Legislator. During her political career, Ros-Lehtinen has broken down many barriers to women. In 1982, she became the first Latina elected to the Florida state legislature. In 1989, Ros-Lehtinen ascended to Congress following the death of the legendary Claude Pepper. Her historic election was a milestone for Hispanic constituents in her district, the heart of which is an inner-city neighborhood called LITTLE HAVANA. Ros-Lehtinen was the first Cuban American elected to Congress.

Ros-Lehtinen earned her undergraduate and graduate degrees from Florida International University. She

Linda Ronstadt was grand marshal of the 1991 Cinco de Mayo parade in San Francisco, California. (AP/Wide World Photos)

Ileana Ros-Lehtinen celebrates early favorable ballot counts in the 1989 election. (AP/Wide World Photos)

also did postgraduate work at the University of Miami. In addition to educational concerns, Ros-Lehtinen's service in the U.S. House of Representatives has focused on environmental concerns and U.S. policy toward Cuba. She once told an interviewer that her ethnicity affected every aspect of her life. Ros-Lehtinen has served on the House foreign affairs and government operations committees.

Rosario, Hector (b. Puerto Rico): Muralist. Rosario is a member of the Puerto Rican Art Association in Chicago, Illinois. He participated in the creation of *La Crucifixion de don Pedro Albizu Campos* (1971), which is in remembrance of the so-called "Tiger of Liberty" (ALBIZU CAMPOS) and four others who, in 1954, staged an attack on the U.S. House of Representatives. The mural measures 28 feet by 50 feet and was painted with Mario Galán and others. Rosario became prominent in the Puerto Rican art community in Chicago and became associated with political activism surrounding Puerto Rico's status as a commonwealth of the United States.

Roybal family: Edward Roybal was born on February 10, 1916, in Albuquerque, New Mexico. When he retired from Congress in 1992, his legacy was well documented: He was a "Cardinal" (a subcommittee chairman of the powerful House Appropriations Committee); he was the chairman of the Select Committee on Aging, an entity he founded and shaped to bring greater awareness to the elderly population; and, most important, he cut a wide swath for broader community and political involvement for Latinos by establishing the National Association of Latino Elected Officials (NALEO; later called the NATIONAL ASSOCIATION OF LATINO ELECTED AND APPOINTED OFFICIALS), the CONGRESSIONAL HISPANIC CAUCUS, and the Congressional Hispanic Caucus Institute, Inc.

Roybal's Depression-era work as a health-care educator was interrupted by his World War II military service. Following the war, a group of Mexican Americans in Los Angeles, California, saw the value of representation on the city council. As the group's candidate in a 1947 election, Roybal lost. For the next two years, Roybal, his family, and the group patiently registered Latinos to vote. Roybal's successful candidacy in 1949 put the first Mexican American on the Los Angeles City Council since 1881.

During Roybal's thirteen-year tenure on the council, his family and his home were important political resources for him. His daughter, Lucille Roybal-Allard, remembers campaigning early, licking stamps and registering voters. Her father's high profile affected Lucille in conflicting ways. Roybal's involvement in the city's political fortunes grounded his young daughter in the ethic of public service, but her father's rapid rise interfered with a child's need for personal identity and privacy.

Roybal was elected to Congress in 1962 and began important work on the national political stage. In a congressional career spanning three decades, he was a pioneer in social and economic reforms. In 1967, he introduced what became the first BILINGUAL EDUCATION act. Frustrated by congressional inattention to the U.S. Latino population, Roybal in 1976 organized the five Latino members of Congress into the Congressional Hispanic Caucus, ostensibly to promote legislative concerns of the Latino community. The caucus'

early years were spent teaching the U.S. political establishment about the community.

Lucille Roybal-Allard, born on June 12, 1941, in Los Angeles, California, began her career in community and advocacy work. While her father began the 1980's by opposing employer sanctions in what was eventually passed as the IMMIGRATION REFORM AND CONTROL ACT OF 1986, community activist Roybal-Allard found herself increasingly frustrated by obstacles created by policymakers. In 1987, Roybal-Allard reconsidered elected office. With grown children and with her husband living on the East Coast, she plunged into a successful race for the California state assembly. Her service there included time on the Rules Committee and the powerful Ways and Means Committee. In 1992, as Edward Roybal retired as a beloved elder statesman, Roybal-Allard was elected to Congress, establishing the first Latino national political family dynasty.

Rubalcaba, Gonzalo (Gonzalo Julio Gonzales Fonseca Rubalcaba; b. 1963, Cuba): Jazz pianist and composer. Rubalcaba is the product of several generations

Edward Roybal helped organize the Congressional Hispanic Caucus. (AP/Wide World Photos)

of popular and classical musicians. As a child prodigy, he participated in government-sponsored concerts. He received classical music training in piano and composition at the Amadeo Roldán Conservatory. He began to play jazz piano in jam sessions with the internationally famous Cuban group Irakere.

Rubalcaba made music history on May 14, 1993, with his triumphant American debut at New York City's Lincoln Center. Music critics compared Rubalcaba with jazz music's most revered pianists, including Oscar Peterson, Keith Jarret, Chick Corea, and even virtuoso Cecil Taylor. Rubalcaba has the technique and enough Latin passion to stir the spirit of his audience. He is an amazing improviser and an exquisite composer. His playing has been described as not only sophisticated but also full of depth.

Rubalcaba has recorded more than ten albums, among them *Discovery*, with Charlie Haden on the bass and Paul Motian on the drums; *The Blessing*; and *Suite 4 y 20*. Rubalcaba has performed SALSA music with his quartet but is also interested in Cuban music other than dance forms.

Ruíz, Caribe (d. 1988): Artist. Ruíz served as executive director of the Puerto Rican Congress in Chicago, Illinois. He encouraged collaborative murals beginning in 1972. Ruíz is especially associated with Mario Galán's 1974 work *Símbolos*, which features Taino (native Puerto Rican or Indian) designs. Ruíz served as an impetus to the Puerto Rico mural movement in Chicago.

Ruíz, Vicki L. (b. May 21, 1955, Atlanta, Ga.): Educator. Ruíz has written on women's history, Mexican American workers, and the Southwest. Her publications include *Cannery Women, Cannery Lives: Mexican Women, Unionization, and the California Food Processing Industry, 1930-1950* (1987). She also co-edited *Women on the U.S.-Mexico Border: Responses to Change* (1977), *Western Women: Their Land, Their Lives* (1988), and *Unequal Sisters: A Multicultural Reader in U.S. Women's History* (1990). In 1993, Ruíz edited the first volume on gender for the journal *Aztlán*.

Ruíz earned her B.S. from Florida State University in 1977, then her master's degree (1978) and Ph.D. (1982) from Stanford University. From 1982 to 1985, she was director of the Institute of Oral History at the University of Texas at El Paso, where she was also an assistant professor. She joined the faculty of the University of California, Davis, in 1985 and received tenure in 1987. Ruíz has served as vice chair of the Cali-

fornia Council for the Humanities. In 1991, the National Women's Political Caucus gave her a distinguished achievement award.

From 1988 to 1992, Ruíz was director of Mentorships for Undergraduate Researchers in Agriculture, Letters, and Science, a program that paired faculty and students of color on research projects. In 1992, she became the Andrew W. Mellon All-Claremont Professor in the Humanities at the Claremont Graduate School. She became chair of that school's history department in 1993.

Ruiz Belvis, Segundo (May 13, 1829, Hormigueros, Puerto Rico—Nov. 3, 1867, Valparaíso, Chile): Political reformer. Ruiz Belvis received his elementary education in Puerto Rico and attended college in Venezuela. He returned to Puerto Rico in 1860 after earning a law degree from the Universidad Central de Madrid. Ruiz Belvis then established himself as one of the island's leading abolitionists and openly expressed separatist sentiments.

In 1865, Spain invited representatives of Puerto Rico to propose reforms dealing with the composition and extent of local administration. Ruiz Belvis was elected as one of these emissaries and traveled to Spain. He helped draft the Bill for the Abolition of Slavery in Puerto Rico and contributed to a report advocating an autonomous form of government, as had been proposed in 1823.

Political turmoil in Spain, however, once again cast aside the question of reform. Ruiz Belvis publicly protested against this resolution, and Spanish authorities decided to exile him. Forewarned of this determination, he left Puerto Rico to gather the financial resources to launch a rebellion, as separatists were convinced that only an uprising would satisfy their demands. Ruiz Belvis went to New York, New York, to promote Puerto Rican independence. He then went to Chile, where he met a sudden death.

Ruiz-Conforto, Tracie (Tracie Lehuanani Ruiz; b. Feb. 4, 1963, Honolulu, Hawaii): Synchronized swimmer. Ruiz began her swimming career as a child at a public pool in Seattle, Washington. When she was eleven, the young swimmer paired with Candace Costie under the direction of coach Charlotte Davis. The two swimmers would spend the next ten years together as a duet team.

At the junior level, the pair swept the national championships. Moving to the senior level in 1981, they took the national title three straight years. At the 1982

World Championships, Ruiz won the solo competition with the highest score ever recorded in the sport. Ruiz and Costie also finished second in the duet competition.

At the 1984 Los Angeles Olympics, Ruiz took the gold medal in the solo competition, and she and Costie won the gold medal in the duet competition. In 1985, Ruiz married Mike Conforto, a Seattle health-club owner. In 1988, she won the silver medal in the solo event at the Seoul Olympics.

Ruiz de Burton, María Amparo (July 3, 1832, Loreto, Baja California—1895, Chicago, Ill.): Writer. María Amparo Ruiz was the granddaughter of José Manuel Ruiz, the governor of Baja California from 1822 to 1825. When U.S. forces took possession of Baja California in 1847, she met Captain Henry S. Burton, who was part of that expedition. She and her mother, along with almost five hundred other Baja Californians, left for Monterey as refugees. She stayed in the San Francisco area and in 1849 was married to Burton.

Burton fought for the Union in the Civil War and contracted malaria. He died in 1869. Ruiz de Burton's first novel, *Who Would Have Thought It?*, was published in 1872 under the names of H. S. Burton and Mrs. Henry S. Burton. Previously, she had written and produced a five-act comedy.

The Squatter and the Don was published in 1885 under the pseudonym C. Loyal, standing for *Ciudadano Leal*, or loyal citizen. This was a common closing for official government correspondence in Mexico. The pseudonym is ironic, as the romantic novel is critical of the American political structure. *The Squatter and the Don* was republished in 1993 by ARTE PÚBLICO Press as the first literary text in its "Recovering the U.S. Hispanic Literary Heritage" project.

In her later years, Ruiz de Burton attempted to gain recognition of her claim to land in Ensenada, Baja California, that had been granted to her grandfather, José Manuel Ruiz. Her efforts turned her mother and her brother against her and provoked her to write newspaper articles attacking colonization companies. She died in poverty, without having her claims recognized.

Rulfo, Juan (May 16, 1918, Apulco, Mexico—Jan. 7, 1986, Mexico City, Mexico): Writer. Rulfo was the son of Juan Nepomuceno Pérez Rulfo and María Vizcaíno Arias. He spent the first decade of his life at his grandparents' estate in San Gabriel, south of Guadalajara.

Juan Rulfo. (AP/Wide World Photos)

During the Mexican Revolution, his father, grandfather, and other relatives were killed.

Rulfo spent several years of his childhood in an orphanage run by the French Josephine nuns, and they taught him to read by the time he was eight years old. He went to high school and business school in Guadalajara and got a job in the migration archives upon arriving in Mexico City in 1935. He remained there for ten years.

He began writing while young but tossed his first novel into the wastebasket. In 1953, he published a collection of short stories under the title *El llano en llamas* (*The Burning Plain and Other Stories*, 1967). The novel *Pedro Páramo* followed in 1955 (English translation, 1959). Although Rulfo did not stop writing, he never published again, except for some screenplays. Rulfo's work was the first to speak simultaneously of the social and political realities of Mexico and the circumstances that created them—natural forces, the supernatural, and the values and consequences of the civilization that Mexico adopted.

Rumba: Afro-Cuban music and dance form from the 1930's. The music, in four-four time with accents on

Migrant farmworkers lived in this camp near Fresno, California, in the 1950's. (AP/Wide World Photos)

the first and third beats, is characterized by syncopation and offbeats. It relies on maracas, *palitos* (wooden sticks beaten on wood), claves, and bongos to accent the rhythm. It is sung by a soloist, who begins with the *llorao*, or introduction. A chorus joins in for refrains, and both engage in highly improvisational call-and-response exchanges. The rumba is danced in couples, in place, with relaxed knees. It follows a pattern of two quick steps and a slow step. It gave rise to the MAMBO and CHA-CHA.

Rumford Act (1963): Law regulating housing practices. This law was introduced in the California State Assembly by Byron Rumford. The act provided for fair and open housing practices by prohibiting discrimination against individuals who sought to purchase real estate in the state of California. Mexican American organizations were particularly vocal in their support for this law, but the act was revoked in 1964 as the result of voter approval of Proposition 14, an amendment to the state constitution. In 1967, the U.S. Supreme Court declared Proposition 14 unconstitutional and reinstated the provisions of the Rumford Act.

Rural settlements: Many Latinos, especially Mexican Americans, have settled in rural environments, creating vibrant new communities. Although the farm laborers they house are critical for contemporary agriculture, these rapidly growing settlements are not well known. The unique culture, contributions, and needs of most rural settlements are typically overlooked by researchers, policy makers, and the general public, all of whom tend to pay more attention to urban growth and issues of city life.

Latinos always have been an important part of the rural Southwest. When the region was governed by Spain and, later, Mexico, Mexican pioneers populated PUEBLOS (towns) and RANCHOS (farm communities) built around missions and presidios (forts). Demographic and architectural evidence of these early settlements still exists throughout the region. After the Southwest was annexed by the United States in 1848, a steady flow of immigrant workers from Asia and Mexico supplied the Southwest's expanding agriculture economy. Mexicans became the principal source of farm labor, especially after the BRACERO PROGRAM (a labor agreement between Mexico and the United States) was implemented in 1942. Few settled permanently near U.S. farms; instead, they migrated seasonally from their Mexican homes. Those who decided to settle in the United States usually abandoned agricultural employment and moved into urban-industrial centers such as Los Angeles. Small Mexican COLONIAS (quarters) emerged as segregated appendages to many rural communities.

In the mid-1970's, a larger flow of farmworkers began to settle permanently into the rural/agricultural landscape, using the *colonias* as a foothold. This was especially true in California, where farming was undergoing a significant transformation. Responding to surging worldwide demand for fresh produce, California farms concentrated on producing high-value specialty crops that required more labor and longer employment seasons. Improved farm jobs induced many migrant farmworkers to settle their families near employment locations, prompting sharp demographic changes. For example, Guadalupe, a rural California town, in 1960 was inhabited by 3,225 individuals, about 600 of whom were identified as Latinos by the Bureau of the Census. By 1990, Guadalupe's population had grown to 5,479, of whom 83 percent (4,547) were reported to be Latinos. More than 150 small rural communities throughout California have likewise been transformed into Mexican towns, and in 1990 their residents numbered more than 500,000, mostly immigrant farmworkers and their dependents.

Many Mexican rural settlements display distinct cultural elements derived from the shared Mexican home communities of the residents, especially those from the states of Jalisco, Guanajuato, Michoacán, and Zacatecas. They also suffer many difficulties as a result of sudden growth and the concentration of low-income residents. Severe housing shortages force families to crowd into substandard, aging structures. The overburdened community infrastructure, including schools, cannot meet the needs of a growing population, and an eroding tax base constrains local governments' ability to make improvements. Access to basic social and welfare services is difficult. The communities thus represent isolated pockets of concentrated and persistent poverty whose existence, although critical for agriculture, remains hidden from the public eye and whose needs remain unheeded by government agencies. Communities in Texas, for example, often were unlicensed and lacked sewage, water, and electricity systems.

The formation of new Mexican communities in the countryside also has been observed in other parts of the United States where agricultural intensification is taking place. These include the YAKIMA VALLEY (Washington), Caldwell (Idaho), Kennet Square (Pennsylvania), and many locations in the South and MIDWEST.

S

Sábato, Ernesto (b. June 24, 1911, Rojas, Argentina): Writer. Sábato spent his childhood in Rojas, a small provincial town, and in 1924 went to La Plata, capital of the province, to continue his education. A shy, quiet adolescent, Sábato was a brilliant student with influential opinions. In 1929, Sábato entered the School of Physical Sciences at the National University of La Plata. During his years there, Sábato wrote his first narratives and made sketches, watercolors, and oil paintings. He also read Marxist texts and joined the Communist Party. After completing his doctorate in the physical sciences, he taught at several institutions.

Sábato published his first novel, *El túnel* (*The Outsider*, 1950) in 1948. It became a best-seller and established his international reputation. His other novels include *Sobre héroes y tumbas* (1961; *On Heroes and Tombs*, 1981) and *Abaddón el exterminador* (1974). His major collections of essays include *Hombres y engranajes* (1951), *Heterodoxia* (1953), *El otro rostro del peronismo* (1956), *El escritor y sus fantasmas* (1963), *Tango: Discusión y clave* (1963), and *Tres aproximaciones a literatura de nuestro tiempo* (1968). Sábato's novels established him as a literary figure of international importance. Among his major themes are the essence and meaning of love, personal authenticity and existential conflict, and the generalized crisis of the modern world.

Saeta: Andalusian genre of religious songs. From the Spanish meaning "arrow," the *saeta* is a spontaneous outburst of devotion expressed through singing, generally in the FLAMENCO style. It fits under the category of *cante hondo* (deep song), as demonstrated by its vitality and reverence. It is connected with Holy Week processions and other religious events involving the Virgin Mary or Jesus. It is sung in *coplas* (stanzas) of four to six half lines of verse. During day-long religious processions, *saetas* alluding to such themes as passion and invoking the Virgin Mary are sung.

Saints: A saint is a deceased person who is decreed by the Roman CATHOLIC CHURCH to have performed extraordinary religious acts while alive—acts of healing, preaching, teaching, and dying to witness religious faith. At one time, the church declared there were some twenty thousand saints, but records have disappeared for most. Saints known to modern people have re-

placed many of the forgotten saints of the Middle Ages.

By the fourth century C.E., the practice of showing reverence to saints was widespread; during the early Middle Ages, however, the practice was sometimes discouraged because it was considered to be superstitious. The desperation caused by the Black Plague revived the custom of calling upon saints to help the sick and the dying. In the sixteenth century, the Church affirmed that calling upon saints for assistance was a good practice and would bring benefits to the faithful. Christian art represented saints in holy paintings and statues with emblems by which they could be known and halos around the heads. Every church and, indeed, every member of a trade or profession had particular saints who were called upon in time of need or for blessings.

Latino culture has retained its belief in the protection of saints. San Martín (Saint Martin) is known as the saint of healing. His story is well known among Latinos. He was born a black slave. When he was sold to a Christian family, they helped him to become a priest. One night, he was awakened by a voice that told him of a dying woman begging for confession. He rode forty miles to hear her confession. The woman did not die, and San Martín thus became the saint to call upon for healing powers. The *curanderos* (folk healers) of New Mexico ask for the assistance of San Martín while attempting to heal the sick (*see* CURANDERISMO).

Other *curanderos* have sometimes been called "saints" by the people they treated. One of these folk saints was Pedro JARAMILLO, who lived in Los Olmos, Texas. When he died, his grave was visited by the thousands of people who believed they had been helped by his healing powers.

Latino families often choose one saint as a protector to watch over the family. One popular patron saint is San Antonio (Saint Anthony); June 3 is *El día de San Antonio* (St. Anthony's Day) on the Catholic church calendar. Families attend Mass on their patron saint's day, pray together, and even hold a *velorio* (vigil) the night before. At midnight, food is served, and the atmosphere becomes more joyous.

Midnight is the customary hour when vigils (nighttime prayer observances) become less solemn, just as on *Nochebuena* (Christmas Eve) and *El día de los*

Processions honoring saints are an important part of the Latino religious heritage. (Ruben G. Mendoza)

reyes (Epiphany or Twelfth Night). *Luminarias* (small candles or bonfires) may be lit to show the way for the patron saint.

Salas, Floyd (b. Jan. 24, 1931, Walsenburg, Colo.): Writer. Salas' ancestors immigrated to Florida in the seventeenth century, then to Colorado over the Santa

Fe Trail in the mid-nineteenth century. The Salas family relocated frequently, and Salas attended six high schools in four years. He had a natural talent for fighting and was awarded a boxing scholarship at the University of California, Berkeley.

Salas taught creative writing at several Bay Area colleges in the 1970's and in 1975 was appointed assis-

Cuban American Alberto Salazar was a leading distance runner of the 1970's and 1980's. (AP/Wide World Photos)

tant boxing coach at the University of California, Berkeley. He was appointed as lecturer in creative writing at the University of California, Berkeley, in 1980.

Like the assertive protagonist of his first novel, *Tattoo the Wicked Cross* (1967), Salas' views have always challenged the status quo. His brief novel *What Now My Love* (1970) traces the dark side of the contemporary drug culture. Salas' third novel, *Lay My Body on the Line* (1978), examines the uprisings at San Francisco State University in the late 1960's. He discusses his life in *Buffalo Nickel: A Memoir* (1992). Salas' strength as a novelist lies in his ability to depict the ugly, marginal, criminal elements of society with brilliance and compassion.

Salazar, Alberto (b. Aug. 7, 1958, Havana, Cuba): Runner. Salazar came to the United States with his family in 1960 in the wake of the Cuban Revolution. He drew national attention as a high-school runner in New England, and he entered the University of Oregon, a perennial track power, in 1976. There he emerged as a star, winning the 1978 National Collegiate Athletic Association and 1979 Amateur Athletic Union cross-country titles. Prevented from competing in the 1980 Olympics by the U.S. boycott, he turned to marathon competition and soon became one of the world's best at the distance. He won his first marathon, the New York Marathon, in a record time in 1981, and he defended the title in each of the next two years. In 1982, he also captured the prestigious Boston Marathon title.

Salazar, Rubén (Mar. 3, 1928, Ciudad Juárez, Chihuahua, Mexico—Aug. 29, 1970, Los Angeles, Calif.): Journalist. Salazar came with his family to the United States from Mexico in 1929. He became a naturalized citizen in 1949. He received his B.A. from the University of Texas, El Paso. His journalism career began in 1952, when he became a staff member with the *El Paso Herald Post*; he held that position until 1954. He later held positions with the *Santa Rosa Press Democrat* and the *San Francisco News*.

Salazar joined the staff of the *Los Angeles Times* in 1959 and remained with the newspaper until his death in 1970, serving as a war correspondent from 1965 to 1966. After that, he was named bureau chief in Mexico City. He became a columnist for the newspaper in 1969. In addition to his newspaper work, Salazar served as news director of the Los Angeles television station KMEX until his death in 1970. He was hit in

Mexican American journalist Rubén Salazar was killed during a 1970 anti-Vietnam War riot. (AP/Wide World Photos)

the head by a tear gas canister fired through a window by a police officer during rioting surrounding the NATIONAL CHICANO MORATORIUM ON VIETNAM.

Salcedo, Manuel María de (Apr. 3, 1776, Malaga, Spain—Apr. 4, 1813, near San Antonio, Tex.): Soldier and administrator. Salcedo, born a Spanish nobleman, entered the army at an early age. Later, he served as an infantry captain under his father, then as governor of Louisiana. In 1800, when Spain agreed to cede Louisiana to France, young Salcedo was one of the boundary commissioners involved. At the age of thirty-one, he was appointed governor of Texas, taking office in 1808. Salcedo's initial rule was complicated by the need to devise procedures to handle runaway black slaves and American army deserters; he returned the slaves to their owners and allowed many deserters to settle in Texas.

Salcedo's attempts to govern Texas well met interference from the commandant general of the interior provinces, his uncle Nemesio de Salcedo, as well as other Spanish officials. In 1810, Miguel HIDALGO Y COSTILLA's Mexican revolution arose. Despite defeat of the rebels, unrest was rampant throughout NEW SPAIN. Salcedo attempted to retain order and to battle the revolutionary forces in Texas, but continued problems with higher-level Spanish administrators left the Texas government tottering by 1812. In early 1813, Salcedo surrendered Texas to the rebel forces, which declared Texas to be an independent republic. Salcedo was brutally assassinated by rebels at the age of thirty-seven.

Salinas, Baruj (b. July 6, 1935, Havana, Cuba): Artist. Salinas works in acrylics and other media. One of his more important works is a mural commissioned by the Sephardi School in Mexico's Federal District; Salinas himself is Jewish. His works are in collections of major museums in the United States, Spain, and Mexico.

Salinas migrated to the United States in the early 1950's and enrolled at Kent State University in Ohio. He earned a bachelor's degree in architecture in 1958. He became an American citizen in 1965.

Salinas has had solo shows in various Latin American countries, across the United States, and in Canada, Spain, France, and Switzerland. He was particularly interested in having a show in Israel and did so in 1976. He won a Cintas Foundation Fellowship in 1969 and has won various prizes for his works, particularly his watercolors. He often incorporates religious and ethnic traditions into his work.

Salinas, Porfirio, Jr. (1912, near Bastrop, Tex.—Apr. 18, 1973): Artist. Salinas was almost self-taught as a painter and had only three years of formal education. He was one of the first Mexican American artists to have work shown in the White House, and at one time, five of his works were displayed there. He was President Lyndon Johnson's favorite painter.

Salinas is known for Texas landscapes, particularly paintings of San Antonio and the bluebonnet flowers native to Texas. He also liked to paint bullfight scenes.

Salsa (food): Usually refers to a hot sauce or table sauce. Although the word "salsa" is simply Spanish for sauce, it is most commonly used to refer to certain Mexican sauces. One of these, *salsa picante*, is any of several commercially prepared hot sauces, made by infusing vinegar with crushed fresh CHILES. *Salsas picantes* vary in piquancy and taste, largely as a result of the types of chiles used in them. Most *salsas picantes* are red, though some are green and a few are yellow, all reflecting the component chiles. *Salsas picantes* are used for seasoning, both in the kitchen and at the table. The other common Mexican salsa is *salsa cruda*, a cold sauce made from chopped raw tomatoes,

chiles, and onions, sometimes with other seasonings, especially garlic and CILANTRO. The diner spoons *salsa cruda* onto various dishes such as *huevos revueltos* (scrambled eggs) and ANTOJITOS.

Salsa (music): Latin American dance music of Afro-Cuban origin. Salsa rhythms developed from Afro-Cuban dances such as the BOLERO, CHA-CHA, GUARACHA, and MAMBO. Salsa is characterized by three sections: a head (melody), a *montuno* (section improvised by the lead singer), and a mambo section. The *conjuntos de salsa* (bands) feature CONGA and BONGO drums, TIMBALES, and trumpets, with trombones, flutes, and clarinets sometimes added to the traditional instruments. Salsa originated in the 1940's, and already had been introduced into the United States by the 1950's. Merged with jazz traits, it became "Latin jazz." The 1960's and 1970's saw its return to more Cuban style. Salsa found its final urban form by the 1980's.

Salt War (1866-1877): Conflict over access to salt deposits. Early in the 1860's, prospectors found a huge deposit of salt about one hundred miles east of El Paso, Texas, close to the border with Mexico. Mexicans and Mexican Americans began using the salt because it was on open land and it was free. In 1866, however, Samuel Maverick, a local businessman, filed a claim to the area and began to collect fees, though many people continued to take the salt for free.

The next year, the dispute entered the political arena when local Republican Party officials bought part of Maverick's property and fenced it off. A fight over the sizable profits from the salt monopoly split the group. One faction, made up of Mexican Americans, led a call for free access to the salt deposits, but a larger group, the Salt Ring, continued to charge a fee. At one point, supporters of the Salt Ring attacked the office of the free salt leaders, killing one and injuring several others. No arrests took place, and the Salt Ring kept control of the deposits.

In the early 1870's, more complications developed when Charles Howard, a Civil War veteran from Missouri, bought control from the Salt Ring and cracked down on smuggling. In September, 1877, Howard had two Mexican Americans arrested for stealing salt. After a short trial and a conviction, a riot broke out in the Mexican area of El Paso. Rioting lasted for several days and caused much damage, although no deaths resulted. One group of rioters took Howard hostage and held him for several days until he agreed to stop making people pay for salt. After his release, Howard hunted down and killed Louis Cardis, a leader of the Mexican American community and of the free salt movement. The sheriff refused to arrest Howard.

In December, Howard closed all access to the salt deposits. A mob of five hundred angry Mexican Americans surrounded his home and set it on fire. Rioting ensued, and after four days two people lay dead. The mob took Howard prisoner, conducted a mock trial for the murder of Cardis, found Howard guilty, and shot him in front of a firing squad. Anglos in El Paso then attacked Mexicans in the streets, killing at least five, savagely beating dozens of others, and burning several homes and businesses. President Rutherford B. Hayes had to summon the United States Army to restore order.

The Salt War ended in racial violence as Texans turned on Mexicans and indiscriminately beat and killed them in the streets of El Paso. The murders and beatings went unpunished, as Anglo officials refused to bring charges against those responsible. The U.S. Army patrolled the streets of El Paso for several weeks in December and January before tempers cooled. Many Mexican Americans fled the city during the chaos and went to El Paso del Norte, on the Mexican side of the border. Only a few ever returned north of the Rio Grande.

Salvadoran Americans: Immigrants and refugees from El Salvador are one of the newest and least understood Latino subgroups. The vast majority of them have been in the United States only since the 1980's, when civil war in their small Central American homeland prompted them to flee. They have become the largest single Central American national group in the United States, with population estimates ranging from the 1990 census figure of 565,000 to press figures close to a million. Their presence has rapidly diversified the Latino community in cities such as Los Angeles. Up-to-date information about Salvadoran Americans is scarce, and non-Latinos often confuse them with the more numerous Mexican Americans. Salvadoran life in the United States is marked by the experience of civil war, refugee flight, and—in a large percentage of cases—undocumented legal status.

History. El Salvador is a country of 8,124 square miles wedged between Guatemala, Honduras, and the Pacific Ocean. The indigenous population of Pipil and other Indians declined dramatically after the Spanish Conquest in the mid-1500's. The area remained part of the Spanish district of Guatemala until independence from Spain in 1821. After a short-lived confederation

with four other Central American states (1823-1842), El Salvador began to attract British and American investment in its mines and coffee plantations. An oligarchy known as the Fourteen Families controlled virtually all the country's land and wealth by the early 1900's.

In 1932, Indians and peasants rebelled against the loss of jobs and wage cuts on the plantations. General Maximiliano Martínez's military government responded by executing thirty thousand people in the infamous *matanza* (massacre). A series of other dictatorships followed as the gulf between rich and poor widened.

In the late 1970's, popular discontent with a feudal way of life brought peasants as well as students, workers, and the clergy onto the streets in mass protests. The result was another military coup in 1979 and the launching of government-sponsored death squads that terrorized entire communities. Anyone suspected of criticizing the government, particularly young people, could be killed, tortured, or "disappeared." The Farabundo Martí National Liberation Front (FMLN) organized guerrilla resistance, and the country became embroiled in civil war.

An estimated seventy-five thousand Salvadorans were killed and hundreds of thousands were displaced during twelve years of civil war (1980-1992). For much of that time, the Salvadoran government enjoyed U.S. military and economic aid despite continuing human rights abuses, such as the rape and murder of four American nuns by the Salvadoran army in 1980. The assassination the same year of Archbishop Oscar Romero, an outspoken critic of the government, set off a wave of refugee flight. A major earthquake in 1986 vastly increased the homeless population. The violence escalated again in 1989 before a peace accord was finally reached in 1992. In 1994, the country was still struggling to rebuild its shattered economy.

Immigrants and Refugees. Salvadoran immigration to the United States was negligible until the 1970's, when thirty-four thousand immigrants arrived. This figure is a small fraction of the 214,000 Salvadorans admitted to the United States as legal immigrants in the 1980's or of the estimated 300,000 to 500,000 who crossed the border in the first three years of the civil war. Most who came were poor peasants who could not meet legal immigration requirements but were desperate enough to try the dangerous crossing illegally. The U.S. government refused to grant the Salvadorans refugee status, as was commonly done for other peoples fleeing from war, insisting that the Salvadorans

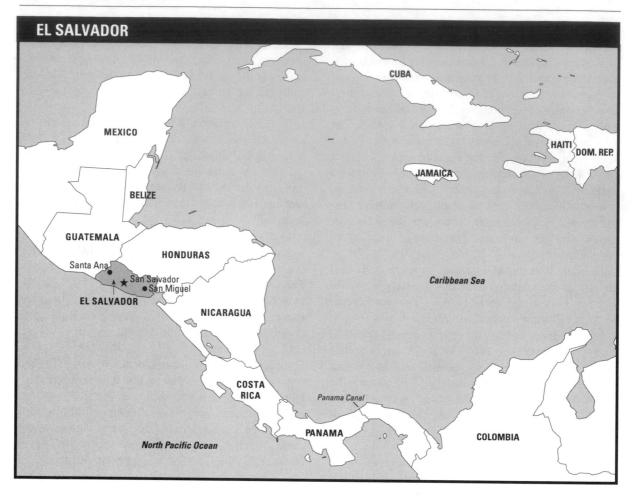

EL SALVADOR

were simply seeking better economic opportunities (*see* REFUGEES AND REFUGEE STATUS). This view was based on the American tradition of favoring those who were leaving Communist countries, such as Kampuchea (Cambodia), rather than U.S.-backed regimes.

Salvadorans came to the United States via Guatemala and Mexico with the help of COYOTES (smugglers), bribes, and counterfeit papers. Abuse and extortion were the rule. For example, in 1980, after paying a coyote $1,200 each, thirteen out of twenty-six Salvadorans died when they were abandoned with no provisions or directions in the middle of the Arizona desert.

In response to such abuses and to express their opposition to the U.S. role in El Salvador, Jim Corbett and other concerned Americans founded the SANCTUARY MOVEMENT in the early 1980's. The movement's network of safe houses for newly arrived refugees was loosely modeled on the Underground Railroad that helped escaped slaves in the mid-1800's. About three hundred religious congregations took part in the move-

ment, assisting at least 350 refugees and raising public awareness of their plight. Their efforts also spawned a network of private organizations devoted to helping refugees with emergency housing, social services, legal aid, English classes, and job training.

Once in the United States, Salvadorans were particularly vulnerable to immigration raids and deportations because many feared for their lives if they were to return to El Salvador. Their attempts to gain political asylum in the United States were unsuccessful, for both logistical and political reasons (*see* ASYLUM POLICIES). They found it hard to prove a "well-founded fear of persecution" because they had left in haste without documents and because the U.S. government was supporting the very government they feared. From 1984 to 1990, only eighteen hundred Salvadorans were granted political asylum, compared to sixteen thousand each of Nicaraguans and Iranians. At the end of 1990, more than twenty-nine thousand Salvadoran asylum cases were still pending with the IMMIGRATION AND NATURALIZATION SERVICE (INS).

By 1990, more than 100,000 undocumented Salvadorans had benefited from the amnesty provisions of the IMMIGRATION REFORM AND CONTROL ACT (IRCA) OF 1986 and had their status adjusted to that of legal immigrants. AMNESTY, however, applied only to those illegal immigrants who arrived before 1982, thus excluding large numbers of Salvadorans.

Economic and Community Life. The largest concentrations of Salvadoran Americans are in Los Angeles, Washington, D.C., and Houston. There are smaller communities in New York City, San Francisco, and Dallas. Like other Latino immigrants, Salvadorans often seek out barrios where they can be with others who share their language and culture, and where housing is relatively inexpensive. It is common for two or more families to share a small apartment or substandard housing such as garages and storage rooms; some boarding houses even rent out beds on a rotating basis to single male workers.

Salvadoran Americans are among the poorest Latino groups, with about one-fifth of all families living in POVERTY in 1989. This situation can be traced to their low socioeconomic status in El Salvador and their undocumented legal status in the United States. Most come from poor, rural backgrounds; only about one-third of those over the age of twenty-five had finished high school in 1990, and few had transferable urban industrial skills. The two largest categories of occupations among Salvadoran Americans of working age in 1990 were service (34 percent) and operators/laborers (26 percent), with only 6 percent in managerial and professional positions. They had a relatively high unemployment rate of 10 percent.

The employer sanctions imposed by the IRCA in 1986 made many U.S. employers wary of hiring Salvadorans and other undocumented workers. Consequently, Salvadorans tend to work in temporary, low-paying jobs, often for cash in the underground

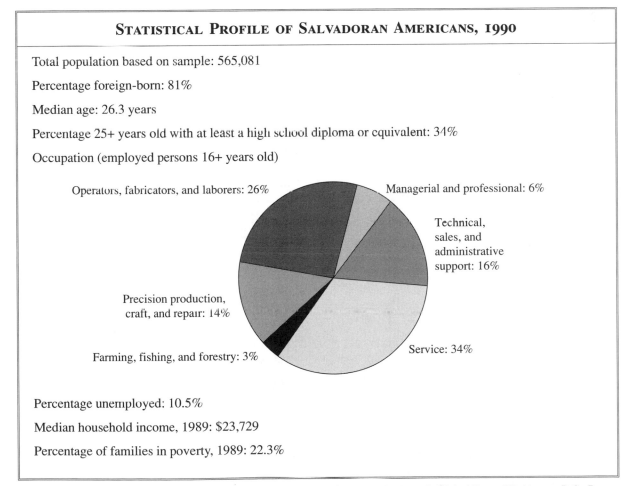

STATISTICAL PROFILE OF SALVADORAN AMERICANS, 1990

Total population based on sample: 565,081

Percentage foreign-born: 81%

Median age: 26.3 years

Percentage 25+ years old with at least a high school diploma or equivalent: 34%

Occupation (employed persons 16+ years old)

Operators, fabricators, and laborers: 26%

Managerial and professional: 6%

Technical, sales, and administrative support: 16%

Precision production, craft, and repair: 14%

Service: 34%

Farming, fishing, and forestry: 3%

Percentage unemployed: 10.5%

Median household income, 1989: $23,729

Percentage of families in poverty, 1989: 22.3%

Source: Data are from Bureau of the Census, *Census of 1990: Persons of Hispanic Origin in the United States* (Washington, D.C.: Bureau of the Census, 1993), Tables 1, 3, 4, and 5. Percentages are rounded to the nearest whole number.

SALVADORAN IMMIGRATION TO THE UNITED STATES, 1941-1990

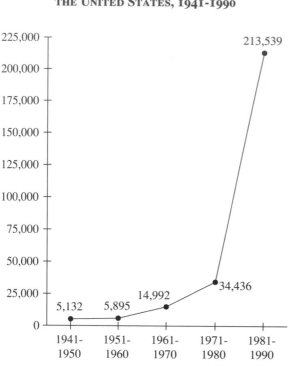

Source: Data are from Marlita A. Reddy, ed., *Statistical Record of Hispanic Americans* (Detroit: Gale Research, 1993), Tables 25 and 26.

economy. Common jobs are as domestics, gardeners, day laborers, factory hands, and garment workers. Exploitation of Salvadoran workers is rampant because employers can threaten them with deportation. Some Salvadorans have attempted to make a living independently as STREET VENDORS, much as they would in their homeland, but have often had to contend with police harassment.

Ironically, it became harder for Salvadorans to survive in the United States in the 1990's than it had been in the 1980's. Previously, public awareness of the civil war and sympathy for the refugees were high, church-sponsored aid programs proliferated, and jobs were plentiful. In the early 1990's, all workers were hurt by a recession, and the budgets of some social service programs shrank considerably. Nevertheless, a network of nonprofit organizations continued to serve Salvadorans' economic, legal, social, and cultural needs. In 1993, for example, the CENTRAL AMERICAN REFUGEE CENTER (CARECEN) in Los Angeles was fielding inquiries from three hundred people daily. Agen-

cies elsewhere included Clinica del Pueblo in Washington, D.C., the Central American Resource Center in Austin, Texas, and Casa El Salvador in Chicago.

Los Angeles, with a Salvadoran population of more than 350,000, has become the world's second largest Salvadoran city. Most Salvadoran Americans live in the Pico-Union district west of downtown, where restaurants, groceries, swap meets, and other small businesses are among the five hundred enterprises opened by Salvadorans in Southern California in the early 1980's. Thousands of Salvadorans turn out for the annual independence day parade in September, celebrated with food, music, and speeches at a local park. The El Salvador Soccer League has more than twenty teams, and even poor families indulge their teenage daughters in lavish QUINCEAÑERA celebrations. Although most Salvadoran Americans are Catholic, they are drawn in growing numbers to the many storefront Protestant Evangelical churches that dot the streets of the city.

Poor Salvadoran Americans live in the midst of a host of urban problems. Those trapped by circumstances in high-crime areas have expressed shock and dismay at the influence of gangs, drugs, and prostitution; some rarely leave their homes out of fear. In 1991, riots broke out in the heavily Salvadoran Adams-Morgan/Mount Pleasant district of Washington, D.C., after a police shooting (*see* MOUNT PLEASANT RIOTS). The incident confirmed the rise of black-Latino tensions in the city. The Pico-Union district was hard-hit by the LOS ANGELES RIOTS of 1992, which destroyed a number of Salvadoran homes and businesses. Gang members who have been deported home have begun terrorizing the city of San Salvador with Los Angeles-style gang graffiti and violence.

Most Salvadoran Americans immigrated to the United States for temporary refuge from violence. As stability gradually returns to El Salvador, some may consider returning to their country. The majority, especially the young, will probably build on the base they have already established, forging a unique Latino identity and community.   —*Susan Auerbach*

SUGGESTED READINGS: • Bachelis, Faren. *The Central Americans.* New York: Chelsea House, 1990. • Barry, Tom, and Deb Preusch. *Central America Fact Book.* New York: Grove Weidenfeld, 1986. • Haines, David W. *Refugees in the United States: A Reference Handbook.* Westport, Conn.: Greenwood Press, 1985. • Reimers, David M. *Still the Golden Door: The Third World Comes to America.* New York: Columbia University Press, 1985. • Siems, Larry, ed. and trans. *Be-*

tween the Lines: Letters Between Undocumented Mexican and Central American Immigrants and Their Families and Friends. Hopewell, N.J.: Ecco Press, 1992.

Samba: Afro-Brazilian music and dance form. The samba is played by an ensemble of drums (*bombos, cuicas,* and tambourines) and rattles (GÜIROS and *guaiás*) in four-four time, in an uneven rhythm. The simple texts are sung alternately by a vocalist and a chorus, in responsorial fashion. Derived from circle dances of Angola and the Congo, the choreography determined the early types; for example, the samba-de-roda is a round dance. An urban style of samba developed during the 1920's. This bouncy style with a rocking motion became a ballroom dance, supported by a large orchestra, in the 1930's.

Samora, Julian (b. Mar. 1, 1920, Pagosa Springs, Colo.): Sociologist. Among Samora's most important publications are *La Raza: Forgotten Americans* (1966), *Los Mojados: The Wetback Story* (1971), *A History of the Mexican-American People* (1977), and *Gunpowder Justice: A Reassessment of the Texas Rangers* (1979). His expertise led to appointments to and work with many prestigious commissions and research organizations, including the U.S. Commission on Civil Rights, the National Institute on Mental Health, and the President's Commission on Rural Poverty. He has also served as editor of the journals *Nuestro* and *International Migration Review*, among others. He directed the Mexican Border Studies Project at the University of Notre Dame. Among his many honors is the 1979 La Raza Award from the NATIONAL COUNCIL OF LA RAZA.

The Brazilian band Corpo Santo performing at a carnaval. (Lou DeMatteis)

After earning his B.A. from Colorado's Adams State College in 1942, Samora taught for a year in a Walsenburg, Colorado, high school. Several scholarships enabled him to continue his education. He received his M.S. in sociology in 1947 from Colorado State University at Fort Collins and his Ph.D. in sociology and anthropology in 1953 from Washington University in St. Louis, Missouri. He taught at Adams State College while pursuing his education and became an assistant professor at the University of Colorado Medical School in 1955. In 1957, he joined the faculty of Michigan State University. He moved to the University of Notre Dame in 1959 as a full professor, serving there until 1985, when he was named professor emeritus.

San Angelo, Texas: County seat of Town Green County in the Texas Plains. According to the 1990 census, San Angelo had a population of 98,458, of whom 25,501 were Latinos. Mexican Americans constituted 92 percent of the Latino community.

The town was named in the 1880's for Angela de la Garza, the wife of Bart DeWitt, who founded the town around Fort Concho in the 1870's. Hispanic heritage in this region dates back to at least the Jumano Indian Mission, established in the 1630's. Because the Plains Indians, Apaches, and Comanches were able to dominate the area with horses and arms introduced by the Spaniards, no permanent civilian settlements were possible until the 1800's. The COMANCHEROS traded with the Indians but did not colonize the region.

As early as the seventeenth century, Spanish explorers traded with the Indians in the region for freshwater pearls known as Concho pearls. These expensive treasures are sold in local jewelry shops. They are found only in the Concho River and its tributaries in this region. The pearls are produced by river mussels, which also served as a main part of the diet of local Indians and early settlers.

The first civilian settlers in San Angelo were Spanish and Mexican sheep and goat ranchers, the *pastores*, from New Mexico. San Angelo remained a major settlement for sheepherders and a center for the production of wool and mohair (*see* SHEEPHERDING). In 1962, San Angelo became the headquarters of the Texas Sheep and Goat Raisers Association in recognition of its role as a primary market for sheep and wool.

In the late nineteenth century, the primary Mexican American neighborhood was established as the Santa Fe barrio, north of the tracks of the Santa Fe Railroad. Mexican Americans arriving in 1910 and subsequently, during the MEXICAN REVOLUTION, made the Oriente

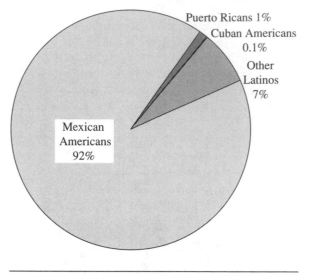

LATINO POPULATION OF SAN ANGELO, TEXAS, 1990

Total number of Latinos = 25,501; 26% of population

Puerto Ricans 1%
Cuban Americans 0.1%
Other Latinos 7%
Mexican Americans 92%

Source: Data are from Marlita A. Reddy, ed., *Statistical Record of Hispanic Americans* (Detroit: Gale Research, 1993), Table 111.
Note: Figures represent the population of the Metropolitan Statistical Area as delineated by the U.S. Bureau of the Census. Percentages are rounded to the nearest whole number except for Cuban Americans, for whom rounding is to the nearest 0.1%.

barrio, west of Fort Concho, the largest center of Latinos in San Angelo. The increase in size of the Latino population in this area dates to the coming of the railroad in the 1880's. After the Mexican Revolution, increases in the number of Latinos in San Angelo were linked primarily to the development of large-scale farming and ranching. Most Latinos that immigrated to the area in the late twentieth century found employment in agribusiness.

San Angelo's Fiesta del Concho is a special one-week event in June featuring a parade, arts and crafts, and food vendors. Fiestas Patrias in mid-September have been celebrated by Latinos since the late 1800's. The events of these fiestas relate directly to Mexican American culture. Beginning in 1984, they were celebrated at Fort Concho. Tourism is drawing an increasing number of visitors to San Angelo's historic sites such as Fort Concho, the Jumano Indian Mission, and Iglesia Santa María.

San Antonio, Texas: This was the first Spanish city in TEXAS. According to the 1990 census, its 620,290 Latino residents, 48 percent of the city's population, constituted the state's second largest Latino community.

The area near the source of the San Antonio River, occupied by the Payaya Indians, was named San Antonio de Padua by the Spanish governor, Domingo Terán de los Ríos, in 1691. The mission San Antonio de Valero (later known as the Alamo) was established in San Pedro Creek by Fray Antonio Olivares in 1718, with authorization from the Spanish viceroy, the Marques de Valero. In 1731, the first civilian colonists in Texas arrived in San Antonio from the Canary Islands and Cuba. These immigrants formed the settlement of Villa de San Fernando, later renamed San Antonio de Béxar in honor of the viceroy's brother, the Duke of Béxar. This villa became the city of San Antonio, which had the first organized civil government in Texas.

After Mexico gained its independence from Spain in 1821, San Antonio remained the chief city in Texas. Most of the ALAMO was destroyed in the famous battle of 1836 for Texas independence. Anglo immigrants added their cultural influence to San Antonio's original character of Indian, Spanish, and Mexican heritage.

San Antonio shows the dominant influence of Spanish and Mexican cultures in its language, architecture, place names, ranching practices, food, and entertainment. The history of most Latinos in San Antonio, however, has been one of a long struggle for socioeconomic parity with Anglos.

Mexican Americans from San Antonio have played leading roles in Texas, achieving widespread influence in the cultural and political life of the state. In 1994, of the five Latino members of the U.S. Congress elected in Texas, three were from San Antonio: Henry Barbosa GONZÁLEZ, Henry Bonilla, and Frank Tejeda. Another major political figure from San Antonio is Henry Gabriel CISNEROS. He began his political career as a city council member in 1975 and served as mayor from 1981 to 1988. In 1984, Cisneros was the first Latino to be considered seriously for the vice presidential slot on the Democratic ticket. He was appointed to several presidential commissions in 1986 and 1987 and was named U.S. secretary of housing and urban development in 1993.

San Antonio Independent School District v. Rodríguez (Mar. 21, 1973): Case involving funding of education. This case, cited as 411 U.S. 1, was filed by Demetrio Rodríguez and other parents in the Edgewood school district on behalf of pupils from Texas school districts with low tax bases. It challenged Texas' system of school financing, which relied heavily on local property taxes. The Supreme Court held that although Texas school districts varied widely in their spending per pupil, the pupils in the poorer districts nevertheless were not experiencing violation of their constitutional rights.

Texas' schools were financed primarily in two ways. The state appropriated an amount for each district to provide a basic education. Additionally, each school district also chose to levy property taxes to supplement the meager state appropriation. *San Antonio Independent School District v. Rodríguez* originated in the claim by families living in poorer districts that Texas' system of school financing infringed upon their children's right to an equal education. The U.S. district court agreed, saying that education was a fundamental right of citizens and that wealth was a "suspect" classification, calling for close judicial scrutiny. The district court also held that the Texas school districts had failed to demonstrate any reasonable or rational basis for their system of school funding.

The Supreme Court, however, reversed the district court decision. Although the Court agreed that "suspect classifications" called for close judicial scrutiny, it denied that persons living in a district poorer than other districts formed any kind of suspect class, on the

LATINO POPULATION OF SAN ANTONIO, TEXAS, 1990

Total number of Latinos = 620,290; 48% of population

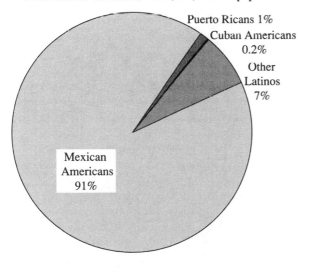

Source: Data are from Marlita A. Reddy, ed., *Statistical Record of Hispanic Americans* (Detroit: Gale Research, 1993), Table 111.

Note: Figures represent the population of the Metropolitan Statistical Area as delineated by the U.S. Bureau of the Census. Percentages are rounded to the nearest whole number except for Cuban Americans, for whom rounding is to the nearest 0.1%.

grounds that many individual residents of poorer districts were wealthy. Although "the poor" might form a suspect class, the Supreme Court held that the families that brought the case had not proved discrimination against the poor. The Court also denied that education was a fundamental constitutional right and added that even if education were essential to other constitutional rights (such as the right to vote), it had not been proved that the children from the poorer districts were not receiving an education.

Finally, the Court turned to the most important issue raised by the families of the students. The families held that Texas' system violated the FOURTEENTH AMENDMENT's promise of equal protection under the laws. Once again, the Court pointed out that all children in the state did receive a basic education. The justices argued that although the state's financing system was "concededly imperfect," it was designed for a legitimate purpose: to give local school districts a large degree of autonomy.

The Court's decision was controversial and resulted in four different opinions being written. The overall vote on this case was 5-4. In his dissent, Justice Thurgood Marshall argued that education was such an important interest that the Court should subject Texas' law to strict judicial scrutiny.

The effect of the case was to allow states to maintain a school system that spent relatively little money on students in poorer districts as compared to those in wealthier areas. In many cases, the districts with poorer funding were inhabited largely by Latinos and members of other minority groups. In 1989, the Texas Supreme Court ruled in *Edgewood v. Kirby* that the state's system of financing schools was not efficient and ordered redesign of the financing system so that districts would have relatively equal access to funds (*see* SCHOOL FINANCE).

San Diego, California: The near perfect Southern California port of San Diego was discovered by Spanish explorer Juan Rodríguez CABRILLO in 1542. Surprisingly, there were no efforts to settle the area until 1769, when a group of Catholic priests established a mission close to the Pacific Ocean in the area now known as Mission Valley. A presidio, or military post, was built nearby on higher land. There was no further substantial settlement of the San Diego area during the Spanish colonial period, which ended in 1821 when Mexico became independent.

The Mexican period, although brief (1821-1848), saw active development of San Diego under several

important governors. The oldest surviving section of town was built beneath the presidio. It includes several stately adobe houses such as Casa Estudillo and Bandini House, which have been refurbished and now form the nucleus of Old Town State Park.

Among the many land grants made during the Mexican period were prosperous ranchos bearing historic Spanish names that still dominate the landscape of greater San Diego County. The most famous of these is the Los Penasquitos (little cliffs) Rancho, eight thousand acres slightly north of San Diego. It was granted in 1823 to Captain Francisco Ruiz, commander of the San Diego presidio. The property passed to another Mexican notable, Don Francisco Alvarado, who was a San Diego councilman (*regidor*) and treasurer. It remained in his family through the first period of U.S. statehood after 1848 and was eventually sold by other owners for prime suburban real estate development in the 1960's.

Another historic rancho that would lend its name to contemporary San Diego County was originally granted as Rancho Santa Margarita y las Flores to Pío Pico, the last Mexican governor, and his brother Andrés (*see* PICO FAMILY). It eventually became the U.S. Marine base of Camp Pendleton.

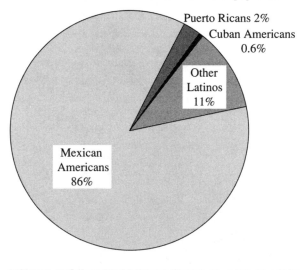

LATINO POPULATION OF SAN DIEGO, CALIFORNIA, 1990

Total number of Latinos = 510,781; 20% of population

Source: Data are from Marlita A. Reddy, ed., *Statistical Record of Hispanic Americans* (Detroit: Gale Research, 1993), Table 111.

Note: Figures represent the population of the Metropolitan Statistical Area as delineated by the U.S. Bureau of the Census. Percentages are rounded to the nearest whole number except for Cuban Americans, for whom rounding is to the nearest 0.1%.

The traditional settlement patterns laid out during the Spanish and Mexican periods were altered during the first fifty years of California statehood. The city's growth as the first West Coast port to receive Atlantic Coast goods by sea caused New Town to emerge around Horton's Plaza. Stately "Yankee" mansions were built on the hills overlooking the new town center.

Political and economic Americanization of San Diego in the nineteenth and twentieth centuries did not remove the Hispanic flavor of many of the city's subcommunities and suburbs. As the California city closest to the Mexican border, San Diego would always have a strong Mexican American component. This is most visible in the city's southernmost extension, San Ysidro, the economic existence of which rests on border transactions, primarily immigration and tourism.

By the late twentieth century, both long-settled Chicanos and newly arrived Mexican immigrants played major roles in San Diego's cultural and political life. Latinos constituted 20 percent of the city's population in 1990, and Mexican Americans were the overwhelming majority within that group.

San Jacinto, Battle of (Apr. 21, 1836): Military encounter that won Texas' independence from Mexico. By the spring of 1836, the situation looked critical for Texans fighting for their independence. On March 6, Antonio López de Santa Anna had overrun Texas fighters at the ALAMO; three weeks later, Mexican troops had captured and executed some 340 Texans at Goliad. Outrage and panic spread. By early April, many Texas settlements were in a state of hysteria, fueled by rumors of Mexican troop movements and atrocities.

The remaining troops of the Texas Army under the command of Sam Houston had been reduced by massive desertions in the wake of the panic. As more men left to take their families to safety, Houston's army quickly dwindled to between seven hundred and eight hundred men. The Texans were plagued by lack of equipment and unrelenting rains, and they were pursued by an advancing Mexican army that greatly outnumbered them. Houston began retreating north and east before the advancing Mexican army led by Santa Anna.

The retreat continued throughout the first weeks of April, 1836, with both armies covering many miles each day despite rains that turned the Texas plains into quagmires. Santa Anna, instead of continuing on the heels of Houston's forces, led a large detachment first to Harrisburg, then to New Washington, in an attempt to capture Texas president David G. Burnet and the interim Texas government. This proved to be a costly mistake: The government officials escaped to safety minutes ahead of Santa Anna, and Houston, seeing his chance, halted his retreat and headed after Santa Anna's detachment. It seemed clear that the decisive battle was imminent, and both armies raced for strategic Lynch's Ferry, the last retreat over the San Jacinto River.

Houston beat Santa Anna to the plain in front of the river by three hours on April 20, 1836. When Santa Anna's troops arrived, the two armies engaged in light skirmishes, but with little effect. The next morning, Santa Anna's forces were joined by General Cós and another five hundred troops, giving the Mexicans an almost two-to-one advantage over the Texans. Houston, to keep up morale, withheld news of the new troops from his men. Meanwhile, Santa Anna, apparently convinced by the odds and by his prior successes that defeat of the Texans was certain, set his soldiers to performing routine camp duties.

At 4 P.M., Houston led his men in a surprise attack on the Mexican forces. Santa Anna was so overconfident that he apparently had not even posted sentries. He and his troops were caught completely off guard. Houston's troops won the battle in less than twenty minutes and with very light losses. For hours after the battle was won, Houston's men, now out of control, carried on a merciless slaughter of the Mexicans they had come to hate and fear. They killed more than six hundred, including many soldiers trying to surrender, and took more than seven hundred prisoners. The next day, a disguised Santa Anna was captured several miles away, attempting to escape. The captive dictator agreed to order all Mexican troops to withdraw across the Rio Grande, thus ending Mexico's attempts to control Texas.

San Jose, California: The fourth-largest city and the oldest civic settlement in California, San Jose is located in Santa Clara County in Northern California. Latinos constituted 26.6 percent of its 822,000 city residents according to the 1990 census. Most of the area's Latinos are of Mexican descent, although there are increasing numbers of Latinos from Puerto Rico, Cuba, and other Latin American nations.

Spaniards and Mexicans have figured prominently in San Jose's history. On November 29, 1777, Lieutenant José Joaquín Moraga founded El Pueblo San José de Guadalupe on the Guadalupe River. Earlier that year, Captain Juan Bautista de Anza had established the nearby Santa Clara mission. He had selected the site on the main camping and fishing grounds of the Costanoan Indians, who called the area Só-co-ís-tá-ká (at the laurel).

San Jose was born out of necessity: The Spanish government had been experiencing difficulty in supplying its military and religious settlements in California. The Spanish viceroy in Mexico directed Felipe de Neve, the governor of ALTA CALIFORNIA, to develop an agricultural center. De Neve ordered Moraga to establish San Jose. San Jose was thus the area's first civic town, or pueblo. LOS ANGELES was another such civic pueblo.

The first group of pioneers under Moraga included nine soldiers skilled in agriculture, two settlers, and three laborers. From that humble beginning, the Santa Clara Valley became a fertile region famous for its plums, at one time producing one-third of the world's prunes. It has been home to major fruit orchards, vineyards, vegetable farms, and livestock and poultry raising.

San Jose remained a small, quiet pueblo, but it was the major community north of Monterey until the mid-1800's. In 1848, Mexico ceded California to the United States by the TREATY OF GUADALUPE HIDALGO. The American acquisition and the GOLD RUSH brought legions of newcomers to California. In San Jose, the new arrivals began to outnumber the early Spanish settlers, increasing the population from about seven hundred to about three thousand in less than one year.

The city developed economically as a supply base for prospectors during the gold rush. After completion of a railroad link to San Francisco in 1864, San Jose flourished as a point of distribution for the growing agricultural wealth of the Santa Clara Valley. It eventually became an important packing and shipping center. Such food-related industries as processing, packing, freezing, canning, and drying flourished.

New industries came to the area after World War II, and San Jose became a center for agricultural and food machinery manufacture, chemical production, computer manufacture, and aerospace and atomic-power equipment production. Nearby New Almaden became one of the most productive mercury mines in the world. It ended operations in 1975.

After the territory came under the U.S. flag in 1849, San Jose became the first capital of CALIFORNIA. The percentage of Latinos steadily declined until the MEXICAN REVOLUTION combined with World War I to begin a long process of mass immigration to the United States. As in other American cities, Latinos in San Jose experienced discrimination in housing, education, and employment. The vast majority were concentrated in the poorest sections of town and worked in the lowest-paid jobs. Political representation for the Latino population proved elusive.

In the 1970's and 1980's, increasing political participation and coalitions brought some improvements. A number of public agencies adopted AFFIRMATIVE ACTION plans to increase hiring of Latinos, public schools implemented BILINGUAL EDUCATION programs, and some Latinos were elected to public office.

The city has several Spanish-language newspapers and radio and television stations. Citywide celebrations occur on September 16 (celebrating Mexican independence from Spain), May 5 (CINCO DE MAYO), and December 12 (honoring Our Lady of GUADALUPE, the patron saint of Mexico).

San Juan, Olga (b. Mar. 16, 1927, Brooklyn, N.Y.): Actress. Born to a Puerto Rican family, San Juan was trained as a singer, dancer, actress, and comedian. She established herself as an energetic New York nightclub entertainer and radio personality, sometimes billed as "The Puerto Rican Pepper Pot." San Juan made her film debut in 1944 in *Rainbow Island* and went on to act in numerous film musicals of the 1940's. Her other film credits include *Duffy's Tavern* (1945), *Out of This World* (1945), *Blue Skies* (1946), *Variety Girl* (1947), *One Touch of Venus* (1948), *Are You with It?* (1948), *The Beautiful Blonde from Bashful Bend* (1949), *The Countess of Monte Cristo* (1949), and *The Third Voice* (1960). She also appeared on Broadway in the stage musical *Paint Your Wagon*. San Juan married actor Edmund O'Brien, and their daughter, Maria O'Brien, also became an actress.

San Pascual, Battle of (Dec. 6, 1846): The Battle of San Pascual, the bloodiest battle of the California campaign in the MEXICAN AMERICAN WAR, pitted Stephen Kearny's Army of the West against Andrés Pico's troops in Kearny's first battle of the war (*see* PICO FAMILY). Although Kearny claimed victory, the outcome is debatable.

When war with Mexico was declared, Kearny, a veteran of U.S. Army frontier service, was ordered to take his First Dragoons of Fort Leavenworth to help subdue dissidents in New Mexico and California. Meeting no resistance in New Mexico, Kearny left one-third of his troops to occupy Santa Fe and set out for California with his Army of the West. He was joined by Kit Carson, who brought him dispatches from

1940's film star Olga San Juan. (AP/Wide World Photos)

Commodore Robert Stockton and Colonel John C. Frémont assuring him that California was safely under control of U.S. forces. Hearing this, Kearny sent more of his troops back to Santa Fe.

Stockton's and Frémont's optimism was premature. The CALIFORNIOS, stinging from arrogant treatment by U.S. officers, rebelled at the first opportunity. By the time Kearny arrived in California, the situation was serious.

Meanwhile, Kearny's troops were in terrible shape. They had crossed more than one thousand miles of rough terrain, including the brutal Colorado Desert. Many of their horses and mules had died en route, and those left were near collapse. The troops, low on water and provisions for many weeks, were in desperate need of food and rest. In this condition, on December 5, 1846, they were met by Captain Archibald H. Gillespie and a small detachment sent by Stockton from San Diego.

Gillespie reported that Andrés Pico and a large number of troops were camped only a few miles ahead at the Indian village of San Pascual. That night, Kearny sent Lieutenant Thomas C. Hammond, several dragoons, and Rafael Machado, Gillespie's guide and a Pico deserter, to reconnoiter the village. Machado stole into San Pascual to gather information from its Indian inhabitants. Growing impatient, the dragoons rode down the steep hill toward the village. Their clinking sabers alerted the Californios, and the patrol narrowly escaped capture.

Kearny had lost his greatest strategic asset, surprise, and his men and mules were exhausted; nevertheless, upon hearing Hammond's report, he immediately ordered his troops awakened to prepare for a predawn attack. The wisdom and rationale of that decision are still debated. The fact that Kearny and his men had marched more than one thousand miles without a fight possibly influenced his decision; Kearny's low opinion of Mexicans' courage and the opportunity to capture fresh horses perhaps also swayed his thinking.

The battle began in confusion. Some of Kearny's troops mistakenly charged too soon, and few carbines would fire because rain had dampened the gunpowder. Pico's troops, splendid horsemen, fought the battle mounted on fine horses and equipped with lances. In the fierce encounter, Pico's soldiers killed twenty-one Americans and wounded many others, including Kearny. Few Californios were killed or injured. Still, Pico eventually retreated, and Kearny claimed victory. After tending their wounded and burying their dead, Kearny and his men limped on to San Diego to join with other U.S. troops engaged in the California phase of the Mexican American War.

San Xavier del Bac mission (founded in 1700): Near Tucson, Arizona. This was one of several missions established in northern Mexico during the late seventeenth and early eighteenth centuries.

The MISSION SYSTEM was initiated by Spain while it was colonizing the area. The missions were run by Jesuits, whose task was to convert the native peoples living in the region to Christianity and make them loyal subjects to the Spanish crown. San Xavier del Bac was the farthest north that the Spaniards came. History has conflicting versions of how the native Americans received Father Eusebio Francisco KINO and other Jesuits.

Father Kino established the mission at San Xavier as a *visita*, a place he visited occasionally to say mass and perform baptisms. He also taught the native Americans agricultural and livestock-raising methods. Father Kino died in 1711 and was followed by a succession of other Jesuits who rarely visited the mission and made little impact. In 1732, funds arrived from Spain to help continue the work of the missions. By 1744, Joseph de Torres Perea, another Jesuit, described the mission as having four hundred families, most of whom were Christian in name only. Baptismal records showed more than two thousand baptisms, but virtually none of the couples were married in the church. Residents of the mission maintained the traditions they had prior to the missionaries' arrival.

The Jesuits were expelled from the Santa Cruz Valley, where San Xavier was established, in 1767 and were replaced by the Franciscans. Father Francisco Tomás GARCÉS arrived at San Xavier in 1768 and continued the work of the mission. San Xavier was abandoned during Mexico's War of Independence from Spain. It deteriorated, and its buildings were used for barracks, stables, and barns.

San Xavier served as the center of religious life for Tucson and the surrounding areas during the 1850's and 1860's. In 1874, President Ulysses S. Grant allowed 71,000 acres of the land around San Xavier to be used exclusively by the Tohono O'dham (then called Papago) Indians. All Anglo and Hispanic residents were forced out in 1881. Most of those evicted were Mexicans who lost their land, homes, and fields. Only descendants of José María Martínez were allowed to stay on the land they claimed through a small land grant in 1851, before San Xavier became part of the United States. In 1913, the Franciscans again took

The mission of San Xavier del Bac. (Alan Benoit)

over the neglected mission and began ministering to the Indians living on the reservation. The mission was restored by Eleazar Herreras during the 1930's.

Today the San Xavier del Bac mission operates as a church and school for the Tohono O'dham Indians. Each Easter season it runs the San Xavier Pageant and Fiesta, which celebrates the founding of the mission. The mission building is much different from the temporary structure that Father Kino used. The church is an ornate building of Spanish-style Baroque architecture.

Sánchez, George Isidore (Oct. 4, 1906, Barela, N.Mex.—Apr. 5, 1972, Austin, Tex.): Educator. Sánchez was among the most distinguished Mexican American scholars of his time, focusing on the educational and social needs of Spanish-speaking groups in the United States. His philosophy and methods formed the core of most early bicultural and BILINGUAL EDUCATION programs. Sánchez is noted for promoting curriculum enrichment for Spanish-speaking children as a means of overcoming their environmental, social, and economic deficiencies. He saw Anglo culture in the early part of the twentieth century as being unwilling to accept Mexican Americans as equals, with cultural conflicts exacerbated by the flood of immigration following the Mexican Revolution.

Sánchez grew up in the mining town of Jerome, Arizona. When the mining boom collapsed following World War I, he helped to support his family by playing the coronet at social gatherings. He also had a short boxing career, fighting as a teenager under the name Kid Féliz. He taught school during the early 1920's, then served as a principal and supervisor of the Bernalillo County, New Mexico, schools during the second half of the decade. He earned a B.A. in Spanish and education from the University of New Mexico, then a master's degree (1931) in educational psychology and Spanish from the University of Texas at Austin. In 1934, he was awarded a doctorate in educational administration from the University of California, Berkeley. Sánchez surveyed schools and education while working for the New Mexico State Department of Education (1930-1935) and for Venezuela's Ministry of Education. He also served as president of the LEAGUE OF UNITED LATIN AMERICAN CITIZENS (1941-1942).

Most of Sánchez's teaching career, beginning in 1940, was spent at the University of Texas at Austin, where he taught Latin American education. His most important book is probably *The Forgotten People: A Study of New Mexicans* (1940), which describes Mexican Americans in that state as victims of Anglo imperialism. He wrote many other books on various topics, with a focus on education both in the United States and in Spanish-speaking countries.

Sanchez, Ildefonso "Poncho" (b. Oct. 30, 1951, Laredo, Tex.): Conga jazz drummer and bandleader. Sanchez, the youngest of eleven children in his family, grew up in Laredo and soon manifested his love for dance and music. As a child he was fascinated with the music at family gatherings, where his father and uncles played the bass, violin, and mandolin. As a seventh grader, he began to sing with the school band. In 1972, he started to play jazz with vibraphonist Cal TJADER. By 1979, he had formed his own band, which played jazz and Latino music, including salsa and romantic boleros. He became one of the most popular Mexican percussionists in the United States and traveled with his musical group, the Poncho Sanchez Latin Jazz Band, formed in 1980.

After recording a series of albums for the Concord Jazz label, he drew national and international attention. His album *La Onda Va Bien* won him his first Grammy, in 1980. He tried not to limit his band to jazz or Latin music, offering elements of Latin jazz, salsa, rhythm and blues, and pop as well. For his humanitarian efforts, Sanchez was honored with the Goodwill Ambassador Award in 1987.

Sánchez, Luis Rafael (b. Nov. 17, 1936, Humacao, Puerto Rico): Writer. Sánchez was born in a small coastal town to a working-class family. After receiving elementary and high school education in his native town, he attended the University of Puerto Rico, where he majored in theater arts.

Sánchez spent a year, on a fellowship, at Columbia University, where he studied theater and creative writing. After graduation from the University of Puerto Rico, he taught theater arts at the university's experimental high school. Later, he studied Spanish literature at New York University, from which he obtained an M.A. in 1963. He received his Ph.D. from the University of Madrid in 1973.

Sánchez began his writing career as a playwright. His first play was *La espera* (pr. 1959). His major plays include *O casi el alma* (pr. 1964, pb. 1965) and *La pasión según Antígona Pérez* (pr., pb. 1968). His collection of short stories titled *En cuerpo de camisa* appeared in 1966, and a novel, *La guaracha del Macho Camacho* was published in 1976, with the English translation *Macho Camacho's Beat* published four years later.

Sánchez is one of Puerto Rico's most important literary figures, notable for his creation of a neobaroque Latin American literature. His influence can be detected in the works of younger Puerto Rican writers.

Sánchez, Phillip Victor (b. July 29, 1929, Pinedale, Calif.): Diplomat and publisher. Sánchez, a Mexican American, attended California State University, earning his undergraduate degree in 1953 and his master's degree in 1972. During the administration of President Richard M. Nixon, he worked in the U.S. Office of Economic Opportunity, as assistant director in 1971 and as director in 1972. He served as ambassador to Honduras from 1973 to 1976, then went on to serve as ambassador to Colombia until 1977.

After serving as vice president of the Pan American Bank from 1978 to 1982, Sanchez joined Woodside Industries as president. He became publisher of *Noticias del Mundo* and the *New York City Tribune* in 1987. Three years later, Sánchez became vice president of New World Communications.

Sánchez, Ricardo (b. Mar. 29, 1941, El Paso, Tex.): Poet. Sánchez was the thirteenth child of New Mexican-born parents. By the age of eleven, he had taught himself to read. He began writing poetry at an early age. When his aspirations of becoming a poet were scorned by his teachers, Sánchez dropped out of school and joined the Army, eventually earning a General Equivalency Diploma. Although he served several prison terms for criminal activity, Sánchez subsequently earned a Ph.D. in 1974.

After obtaining a fellowship in journalism in Richmond, Virginia, Sánchez worked at the University of Massachusetts, Amherst, as a writer and instructor. He later directed the Itinerant Migrant Health Project in Denver, Colorado. Having continued to write in the Army and while in prison, by 1971 Sánchez had published a volume of poetry, *Obras*, and founded a Chicano publishing house. His major volumes of poetry are *Canto y grito mi liberación* (1971; expanded bilingual edition, 1973), *Hechizopspells* (1976), *Milhuas Blues and gritos norteños* (1978), *Brown Bear Honey Madness: Alaskan Cruising Poems* (1981), *Amsterdam Cantos y Poemas Pistos* (1983), and *Eagle-Visioned/*

Phillip Sánchez is sworn in as head of the Office of Economic Opportunity. (AP/Wide World Photos)

Feathered Adobes (1990). Considered one of the outstanding poets of the CHICANO MOVEMENT, Sánchez has indicted U.S. society with his depictions of rootlessness, anguish, cultural violation, and racial oppression.

Sánchez, Robert Fortune (b. Mar. 20, 1934, Socorro, N.Mex.): Catholic archbishop and educator. Growing up as one of three sons of Julio Sánchez, a Mexican American lawyer, Sánchez finished his high school education at St. Mary's Boys High School in Phoenix, Arizona, before attending seminary school in Santa Fe, New Mexico. Sánchez later traveled to Rome to study at the North American College. He was ordained to the priesthood in 1959 and received his degree from the Gregorian University in Rome in 1960.

After returning to New Mexico, Sánchez taught high school in Albuquerque and served as a pastor of two parishes. His interest in education led him to earn a certificate in counseling from the University of New Mexico. He also completed a year's study of canon law at Catholic University in Washington, D.C. Sánchez was elected president of the archdiocesan Priests' Senate in 1973. Pope Paul VI appointed Sánchez in 1974 to serve as the archbishop of the Santa Fe archdiocese. With his consecration as the first Mexican American archbishop, Sánchez became the highest-ranking American-born Latino to serve in the Catholic church. Aware of the importance of his achievement in serving as an inspiration to other Latinos, Sánchez requested that his consecration ceremony be held at the University of New Mexico's athletic arena so that the maximum number of his parishioners might attend. Sensitive to the needs of his diverse flock, Sánchez later celebrated the first Mass to be delivered in three languages—English, Spanish, and Tewa.

Sánchez, Rosaura (b. Dec. 6, 1941, San Angelo, Tex.): Educator. Sánchez has served as chair of the National Council on Chicano Sociolinguistic Research. She has written in both Spanish and English, on topics including CODE SWITCHING and BILINGUALISM in higher education. Among her publications is *Chicano Discourse: Socio-Historic Perspectives* (1983).

Sánchez holds a B.A. and M.A. in Spanish literature from the University of Texas at Austin. Her Ph.D. in romance linguistics was granted by the same institution in 1974. She began her teaching career as an assistant professor at the University of California, San Diego, in 1972, and rose to the rank of associate professor in 1979.

Sánchez Korrol, Virginia (b. New York, N.Y.): Historian. Sánchez Korrol has written or edited several books about Puerto Ricans living on the U.S. mainland, including *The Puerto Rican Struggle: Essays on Survival in the U.S.* (1980) and *From Colonia to Community: The History of Puerto Ricans in New York City, 1917-1948* (1983).

Sánchez Korrol holds a B.A. from Brooklyn College of the City University of New York (1960) and M.A. (1972) and Ph.D. (1981) degrees from the State University of New York at Stony Brook. She is married to physician Charles Korrol. She has worked as a high school English teacher in the public schools of Chicago, Illinois, and as an associate professor of Puerto Rican studies at Brooklyn College, where she has chaired her department and shared directorship of the Center for Latino Studies. Sánchez Korrol has also worked as a consultant to the New York State Department of Education.

Sánchez Vilella, Roberto (b. Feb. 19, 1913, Mayagüez, Puerto Rico): Government official. Sánchez Vilella was graduated from Ohio State University in 1934 with a degree in civil engineering. He returned to Puerto Rico upon his graduation to provide professional engineering services to the Economic Reconstruction Plan established by President Franklin D. Roosevelt.

Sánchez Vilella became involved in a reform movement and helped to found the Popular Democratic Party (PARTIDO POPULAR DEMOCRÁTICO). The party emphasized economic equality, political freedom, and social justice. In the 1940's, Sánchez Vilella served in a variety of governmental administrative posts, including administrator of the Transportation Authority. During the following decade, he was the executive secretary of Puerto Rico. In 1960, Sánchez Vilella was elected by the Popular Democratic Party to make recommendations to a board examining Puerto Rico's electoral structure. He also made recommendations to improve diplomatic relations with the United States. Sánchez Vilella was elected governor in 1964 and served one term.

Sancocho: Soup of meat and starchy vegetables. *Sancocho* is a loose term describing a broad range of Puerto Rican soups, all containing meat and some combination of starchy root vegetables, plantains, squashes, and other vegetables. Chunks of these ingredients are cooked in broth, which usually is thickened only by the starch that escapes when cooking the roots or plantains. *Sancocho* usually is served with bread as a one-dish meal. *Sancocho* is an occasional part of cuisine along the Atlantic coast of Central America as far south as Colombia. The name of the dish comes from the word *sancochar*, which means "to boil gently."

Sanctuary movement: Offering of shelter from immigration authorities to REFUGEES. The sanctuary movement in the United States was both a protest movement and a response to an international refugee crisis in Central America caused by civil war. The controversy surrounding the sanctuary movement was fueled by the heavy involvement of churches and synagogues throughout the United States, all organized around the publicly proclaimed intention to violate United States immigration laws by granting ASYLUM to refugees from Central America, primarily El Salvador. Those organizing these efforts clearly associated their humanitarian actions with criticism of American foreign policies in relation to Central American countries, specifically El Salvador.

In the early 1980's, nearly two million people were displaced within Central America as a result of political unrest. Although thousands remained in refugee camps in Central America, thousands more streamed

into Mexico, and from there made their way into the United States. Salvadorans fled their country because of United States policies in El Salvador. Because the United States officially supported the Salvadoran government, it was the policy of the Ronald Reagan Administration (1981 to 1989) to deny admission to most Salvadoran refugees, rejecting the pleas that they faced political repression or personal danger. These numerous refugees brought highly publicized testimony of the repressive and unpopular regime in El Salvador, leading large numbers of Americans to openly question the wisdom of U.S. support for the José Napoleón Duarte government in El Salvador.

As large numbers of Salvadoran refugees entered the United States with horrific stories of conditions in their homelands, clergy in Arizona and New Mexico became involved. At first, these clergy provided housing and other assistance as they were able. They offered sanctuary in part because they believed that application for asylum was more effective when made from within the United States than from outside.

The Reverend Jim Fife, a Presbyterian minister who was one of the early clergy involved, brought an activist background to his concerns about the refugee popu-

Monks at a Vermont priory pose with masked Guatemalan refugees to whom they have offered sanctuary. (AP/Wide World Photos)

El Rescate offered assistance to refugees, particularly those from El Salvador. (AP/Wide World Photos)

lation. The theoretical leader of the movement, however, was a Quaker rancher and former teacher, Jim Corbett. Corbett drew parallels between the need for organized aid for the Salvadoran refugees and the largely Quaker involvement in the abolition movement against slavery in the nineteenth century, particularly the establishment of a linked chain of safe houses known as the Underground Railway. The abolition "railway" guided escaped slaves to the free northern states, and the sanctuary movement's leaders saw their cause as a means of guiding Salvadoran refugees safely away from the civil strife in their homeland. Corbett's ideas led to a nationally organized campaign of churches and synagogues providing sanctuary to arriving refugees.

The growing media attention to the organized campaign of civil disobedience was perceived by members of the IMMIGRATION AND NATURALIZATION SERVICE (INS) as a politically calculated attempt to embarrass the Reagan Administration, and in 1983, the INS launched an investigation in the southwestern states. By November, 1984, "Operation Sojourner," an under-

cover infiltration of the sanctuary movement, led to the arrest and trial of several of the leaders of the movement, including Fife and Corbett.

The trial produced a national response. In January, 1985, SANTA FE, NEW MEXICO, declared itself a sanctuary city, and the governor of New Mexico declared his support for the sanctuary movement. National politicians openly questioned the Justice Department's case, accusing the INS of political motivations in prosecuting the movement's leaders. The trial resulted in a number of convictions of sanctuary leaders, including Fife. Among those acquitted was Corbett, the main theorist of the movement. On July 1, 1986, the presiding judge, Earl Carroll, sentenced five defendants to probation, suspending the sentences of the other defendants.

Although the concerns that propelled the sanctuary movement to national and international attention continued beyond 1986, the political situation in El Salvador slowly brought changes in the movement. By 1987, refugees were no longer "going public," and although illegal immigration continued to be a controversial problem in American public opinion, it was no longer the center of a nationally recognized sanctuary movement.

Sangría: Punch of red wine, fruit juice, sugar, and water. Sangría was invented in Spain, where it typically contains red wine, orange juice, orange wedges, a little sugar, and sparkling water. In Mexico, the amount of sugar is increased, and limes and lime juice usually replace the oranges and orange juice. The Spanish version mixes everything together and lets it steep. Mexican sangría, as served in restaurants and bars, more often is made to order, often with the wine floated over a denser layer of syrup made from limes, lime juice, and sugar. Sangría usually is served over ice in tall glasses, either with a meal or alone. Puerto Rican sangría often includes rum.

Sanromá, Jesús María (Nov. 7, 1902, Carolina, Puerto Rico—Oct. 12, 1984, Guaynabo, Puerto Rico): Classical pianist. At the age of fourteen, Sanromá received a scholarship from the Puerto Rican government to continue his piano studies at the New England Conservatory in Boston. In 1920, he won first prize in the Mason & Hamlin piano competition. Part of the prize was a grand piano that he kept all of his life.

Sanromá was the first official pianist of the Boston Symphony Orchestra (1926-1944). There he established associations with some of the most celebrated musicians of the world, among them violinist Jascha Heifetz; conductors Serge Koussevitzky, Leonard Bernstein, and Arthur Fiedler; and composers Igor Stravinsky, Paul Hindemith, George Gershwin, and Heitor Villa-Lobos. Sanromá's interpretations, particularly of contemporary music, won praises from music critics. Among his numerous recordings are his excellent renditions of hundreds of Puerto Rican *DANZAS*.

Santa Barbara, California: City in southwestern California on the Santa Barbara Channel of the Pacific Ocean. Santa Barbara, about ninety-five miles northwest of Los Angeles, is the seat of Santa Barbara County. Latinos (mainly of Mexican descent) represented 15.2 percent of the city's population of 85,571 according to the 1990 census. Latinos, as shown in the accompanying chart, are an even larger proportion of the population of the surrounding area.

The Santa Barbara area was first sighted by Europeans in 1542, when Juan Rodríguez CABRILLO, a Portuguese navigator in the Spanish service, claimed it for Spain. On December 4, 1602, Sebastian Vizcaino, a Basque navigator also in the Spanish service, anchored

offshore. The ship's priest named the channel and shoreline after the saint whose feast day it was—the Roman virgin who was beheaded by her pagan father when she became a Christian. The Indians who lived in the area were Chumash.

In 1782, the Spanish viceroy of Mexico ordered the founding of a presidio (a townlike fortress settlement) to secure Spanish control of its empire in the New World against other European nations. Under the oversight of Governor Felipe de Neve, Lieutenant José Francisco Ortega established what would be the last military and administrative outposts built by Spain in America.

In 1786, Father Fermín Francisco de LASUÉN founded the Santa Barbara mission. The present mission building was constructed in 1815 to replace one destroyed by an 1812 earthquake. The building is renowned for its architectural beauty (which shows Moorish and Spanish influences) and is one of the area's principal tourist attractions.

In the eighteenth and early nineteenth centuries, the area was home to many leading families of Spanish and Mexican descent, including the Guerra, Carrillo, and Ortega families. Drawn by the 1848 GOLD RUSH

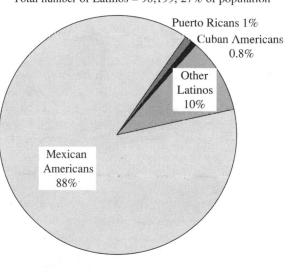

LATINO POPULATION OF SANTA BARBARA, CALIFORNIA, 1990

Total number of Latinos = 98,199; 27% of population

Puerto Ricans 1%
Cuban Americans 0.8%
Other Latinos 10%
Mexican Americans 88%

Source: Data are from Marlita A. Reddy, ed., *Statistical Record of Hispanic Americans* (Detroit: Gale Research, 1993), Table 111.

Note: Figures represent the population of the Santa Barbara-Santa Maria-Lompoc, California, Metropolitan Statistical Area as delineated by the U.S. Bureau of the Census. Percentages are rounded to the nearest whole number except for Cuban Americans, for whom rounding is to the nearest 0.1%.

and a strong potential for agricultural development, newcomers from the United States and abroad soon outnumbered the original settlers and their descendants.

The oil industry brought further economic growth, and the city and immediate area also gained importance as an agricultural and livestock center. Modern Santa Barbara's economy is based on tourism, mineral production—including the production of oil and natural gas from offshore wells—and electronics and aerospace manufacturing. In addition, fishing and farming contribute to the region's economy.

Many Latinos, principally from Mexico, came to Santa Barbara attracted by the work opportunities, particularly during the period of the Mexican Revolution (1910-1921) and after World War I. For the most part, they have remained segregated and have had access only to low-paying jobs. Since the 1960's, antidiscrimination laws, affirmative action, increased political participation, and heightened pride in ethnic identity have effected some improvements in the employment picture. A small percentage of Latinos are now employed at managerial and professional levels in both the public and private sectors.

The legacy of Spain and Mexico is found in Santa Barbara's architecture, in the names of its streets and places, and in Spanish-language newspapers and television and radio stations. Civil events such as a midsummer fiesta celebrating Old Spanish Days and other festivities such as the horseback expeditions of the Rancheros Visitadores also help to keep alive the area's Spanish and Mexican heritage.

Santa Cruz Valley: Extends from Nogales, Sonora, Mexico, into Tucson, Arizona. During the reign of New Spain, the Santa Cruz Valley was occupied in the north predominantly by the Pima and Tohono O'dham Indians (previously referred to as Papagos) and in the south by Hispanics engaged in mining for Spain.

Colonial Spain counted on missions as frontier institutions. The Society of Jesus, or Jesuits, first entered the northern Piman territory in 1572. Priests were sent to bring Native Americans to the missions, convert them to Christianity, and have them declare allegiance to Spain. The work of the missionaries was to pacify the Indians, allowing Hispanics to move farther north to Pimería Alta (northern Sonora, Mexico, and southern Arizona).

In the early 1600's, the Jesuits advanced northward into Yaqui and Opata territory. In 1687, Father Eusebio Francisco KINO entered the Santa Cruz Valley. In 1691, he advanced into Arizona, later beginning missions at SAN XAVIER DEL BAC in 1700 and in Tumacacori in 1702. The latter was completed in 1706 with the establishment of a presidio (military post) in Tubac. The Guevavi mission, founded by Father Kino, was also located in the Santa Cruz Valley.

By the 1730's, Hispanic settlers were mining silver at Arizonac, slightly south of what is now the United States-Mexico border. Hispanics built more presidios, occupied by Mexicans, to fend off the Pima and the Apache Indians. In this manner, they were able to advance their population even farther north. Missions and presidios aided further northward movement during the eighteenth century.

In November, 1751, the Pima Indians revolted against the white settlers and attempted to expel them from their territory. Initially the revolt went well for the Pimans. All non-Indians were eliminated, and some were killed, including missionaries Tomás Tello at Caborca and Henry Ruhen at Sonoita. Lieutenant Colonel Diego Ortiz Parrilla, the governor of Sonora, was able to negotiate a peace settlement. Northern Pimans began returning to their villages in the spring of 1752. After the revolt, the native people tended to concentrate in Tucson rather than spreading themselves along the river valley as they had done before.

The Bourbons of France, concerned that the Jesuits had gained too much influence, expelled them from the Spanish empire in 1767. The MISSION SYSTEM dwindled following the expulsion, although the Franciscans replaced the Jesuits. Hispanics began participating in more agricultural activity as the mission farms began to be used for the raising of animals. Hispanic populations began to thrive as this agricultural activity increased.

During the final decade of the eighteenth century and the beginning of the nineteenth century, the Apache threat to Hispanics decreased as a result of successful military expeditions and negotiations. When Mexico won its independence from Spain in 1821, however, Spain stopped its aid to the Hispanic settlements. The Apache once again took over the northern part of the Sonoran Desert.

Today Hispanics comprise the largest minority in the Santa Cruz Valley. The mission at Tumacacori has been made into a national monument. The mission at San Xavier del Bac is open to visitors and houses a school for the Tohono O'dham. Tubac has an active artist community.

Santa Fe, New Mexico: Capital of New Mexico. Founded as the capital of the Spanish province of New

Mexico in 1610, this city has been a governmental seat longer than any other in the United States.

In 1610, Pedro de Peralta, the governor of the Spanish province of New Mexico, founded Santa Fe. Its full name was Villa Real de la Santa Fe de San Francisco de Asis (royal city of the holy faith of Saint Francis of Assisi). The new city was the capital of the province. It was laid out according to Spanish law, with a central plaza. The corners of the plaza pointed to the cardinal directions. At least one hundred families were awarded *encomiendas* by 1680.

As were many other villages, towns, and cities, Santa Fe was abandoned during the Pueblo Revolt (POPÉ's REVOLT) of 1680. As were the other towns, it was repopulated by the Spanish after the revolt. The leader of this effort, as in many other cases, was Diego de VARGAS. In 1695, forty-six families, with a total of 146 people, resettled. Some were families that had previously lived in Santa Fe, but most were new fam-

LATINO POPULATION OF SANTA FE, NEW MEXICO, 1990

Total number of Latinos = 50,947; 44% of population

Puerto Ricans 0.3% Cuban Americans 0.2%

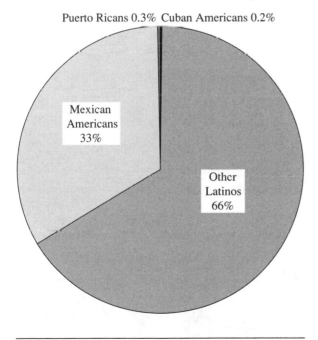

Source: Data are from Marlita A. Reddy, ed., *Statistical Record of Hispanic Americans* (Detroit: Gale Research, 1993), Table 111.
Note: Figures represent the population of the Metropolitan Statistical Area as delineated by the U.S. Bureau of the Census. Percentages are rounded to the nearest whole number except for Cuban Americans and Puerto Ricans, for whom rounding is to the nearest 0.1%.

ilies recruited from the Zacatecas-Sombrerete area. These families were both Spanish and mestizo.

Santa Fe quickly became a principal location for military troops, exploratory expeditions, and mission work. The town was supplied by the Catholic mission supply trains. The Catholic mission of San Miguel, built in about 1610, is one of the oldest missions in the United States.

The year 1821 marked the opening of the historic SANTA FE TRAIL. This trail was the longest commercial road in the United States at the time. It covered 780 miles from Independence, Missouri, to Santa Fe, New Mexico. Thousands of wagonloads of goods and settlers traveled the trail between 1822 and 1880, when a railroad line to Santa Fe was completed. The trail fell into disuse, but Santa Fe remained an important city in the Southwest.

After the MEXICAN AMERICAN WAR, in 1848, the territory of New Mexico was ceded to the United States. Santa Fe remained the capital of the Territory of New Mexico. When New Mexico became a state in 1912, it retained its traditional capital of Santa Fe.

Santa Fe remained primarily a trading center for ranchers, farmers, and the local Native American population. In the early 1940's, construction of the Los Alamos Scientific Laboratory changed the face of the city. This center for atomic research brought more Anglos into the area and restructured the economy.

Concern with the environment and ambience of the area caused the local government to zone the city so as to protect its traditional Spanish-Pueblo Indian type of architecture. This helped to maintain the Southwest flavor of the area. Significant buildings such as the Palace of the Governors and the Chapel of San Miguel are protected as historical sites.

Tourism became an important industry in Santa Fe. The dry climate makes the area attractive as a summer vacation spot, and winter skiing is available in the nearby mountains.

Santa Fe Expedition (1841): The Santa Fe Expedition of 1841 was, on its face, a failed attempt to establish a trade route from Austin to Santa Fe. Although the venture was touted as an economic one, some observers perceived a covert mission of peacefully bringing New Mexico under Texas' jurisdiction.

The Santa Fe Expedition was commissioned by Republic of Texas president Mirabeau B. Lamar. Lamar dreamed of adding territory as far west as Santa Fe or beyond to the Texas Republic. Partly to further this end, he outfitted a wagon train that left Austin on June 21,

1841. The 321 men (270 soldiers, plus merchants and reporters) set out under the command of Colonel Hugh McLeod, their covered wagons loaded with $200,000 worth of merchandise.

The publicized goal of the expedition was to facilitate the opening of a trade route from Austin to Santa Fe. The Republic of Texas was in dire financial straits; this expedition, Lamar hoped, would siphon off some of the rich Santa Fe trade currently going north to Missouri.

The military troops also carried instructions to encourage the *nuevomexicanos* to peacefully join the Republic of Texas. There was a widespread belief among Texans that the residents of New Mexico would welcome joining Texas. If so, the sight of Texas soldiers marching through their lands and giving them encouragement might trigger a popular movement for annexation.

The expedition was ill-fated from the start. Much of its thirteen hundred-mile route went through desertlike plains, and the men suffered from the scorching heat and lack of water. To make matters worse, the wagon train took many wrong turns and went miles astray. When food ran low, the men began killing and eating the horses. Less than one hundred miles from Santa Fe, they were captured by Mexican troops. Weakened by the harsh environment, dwindling supplies, and skirmishes with the Kiowa, McLeod's men were unfit to defend themselves when they were intercepted by troops sent by Governor Manuel ARMIJO, who had been monitoring their progress.

Armijo chose to interpret the expedition as a military invasion. He had a number of the Texans shot on the spot; survivors were bound and sent on a brutal forced march, first to Santa Fe, then on to Mexico City, where they were imprisoned and put to hard labor. It was many months before diplomatic negotiations effected their freedom.

The Santa Fe Expedition was a fiasco on all fronts. Its failure was an embarrassment to Lamar and almost forced his resignation. No economic ties with Santa Fe resulted, and the expedition did nothing to help Texas gain jurisdiction over New Mexico. Instead, anti-Texas sentiment among the *nuevomexicanos* increased.

Santa Fe Trail: Trade route. The Santa Fe Trail opened to travel between Missouri and Santa Fe in 1821. This trade route facilitated the shipping of

A wagon train on the Santa Fe Trail in the 1830's. (Museum of New Mexico)

American guns and munitions to Taos, Santa Fe, El Paso, and remote locations in the northern provinces of Mexico. From these areas of commerce, weapons could be traded to the Apache, Comanche, and other tribes in Arizona, western Texas, and Chihuahua. This arms trade adversely affected the security of settlers in New Mexico. As early as 1823, New Mexicans learned that Americans had furnished guns and ammunition to Navajos, and by the late 1820's New Mexicans recognized that American armaments had shifted the balance of power to the Indians.

Santamaría, Ramón "Mongo" (b. Apr. 7, 1922, Havana, Cuba): Percussionist, bandleader, and composer. Santamaría was born in the Jesús María district of Havana, to parents of African descent. His mother wanted him to study the violin as a child, but he soon became fascinated by the drums. He dropped out of school to play professionally.

By 1950, he was in New York City with his cousin Armando Peraza and was playing with the *orquestas* of Gilberto Valdés, Pérez PRADO, and Tito PUENTE. His involvement with the *charanga* orchestra (composed of flute, violins, percussion, and voices) was influential in shaping American pop music. His bands came to include other instruments such as the trumpet, saxophone, bass, shakers, and jazz drums. Santamaría considered the 1955 recording *Changó* as his best album. He became a celebrity among Latinos and jazz musicians.

In California, Santamaría met Latin-jazz vibraphonist Cal TJADER. They made numerous recordings, including *Más Ritmo Caliente* (1957), *Yambú* (1958), *Mongo* (1959), and *Demasiado Caliente* (1960). Santamaría's musical association with other popular artists, such as Joe LOCO, La Lupe, Charlie PALMIERI, Chick Corea, João Donato, and Dizzy Gillespie, is documented in his impressive discography. By 1995 Santamaría had won two Grammy Awards, and his recordings from the late 1950's were reissued on compact disc.

Santana, Carlos (b. July 20, 1947, Autlán de Novarra, Mexico): Guitarist and bandleader. Santana decided to learn to play the guitar when he was fourteen years old. At the legendary Woodstock Festival of 1969, his group, Santana, played "Soul Sacrifice," mesmerizing the multitudes assembled there. His group's first

Innovative guitarist Carlos Santana. (AP/Wide World Photos)

album, *Santana* (1969), immediately followed. It reached the number one position on the record charts and by 1991 had sold four million copies.

Santana is credited with being instrumental in the creation of LATIN ROCK. He is a tremendous performer and a sensitive virtuoso guitarist. His interest in combining elements of jazz, rock, Latin, and many other musical styles made him popular in the 1970's. Santana's influence in American music is permanent.

The Santana album *Abraxas* (1970) includes "Samba pa tí," "Oye como va" by Tito PUENTE, and "Black Magic Woman" by Peter Green. These are still among the most popular songs his group has performed. Music by his group is characterized by long instrumental improvisations and a distinctive vocal blend. Santana has also recorded outside his band, doing jazz-fusion albums with various star performers including Airto MOREIRA, Stanley Clarke, Ian McLaughlin, Herbie Hancock, and Wayne Shorter.

Santería: Santería is a complex religion found mainly in Cuba. It is a combination of Catholicism and West African religions. Santería has spread throughout the United States, particularly in areas with high concentrations of Cuban Americans and Puerto Ricans, such as New York City, Washington, D.C., and Miami, Florida. The growth of Santería in the United States can be traced to the migration of Cubans to the United States following the success of Fidel CASTRO's revolution in 1959.

History. Santería is a Caribbean religion found primarily in Cuba. African slaves incorporated the worship of their spirit ancestors into the Catholic religious practices taught to them by the Spanish. Santería is deeply rooted in West African religions, especially that of the Yorubas of Nigeria. The original Yoruba practices underwent numerous changes and adaptations in the Americas. The Yorubas in Latin America were influenced by the Catholic saints, which they linked to their gods and goddesses. This combination gave rise to Santería, a Spanish word for worshiping of the saints.

An example of this is Changó, the god of thunder and lightning, whose corresponding Catholic god is Saint Barbara, virgin martyr of the Middle Ages. These entities are not the same thing; each is an aspect of or path to the same thing and they are worshiped separately. Santería became a strong influence in Latin America and the Caribbean region; it moved from Cuba to Puerto Rico, Panama, Venezuela, and the Dominican Republic. From these countries it moved with the migration of Latinos to the United States.

One of the primary characteristics of Santería is ancestor worship. The deceased in one's family must be fed symbolically and periodically by placing items such as water, food, flowers, and candles at specific places in the house. According to Santería priests, called *santeros*, ancestors come before the saints during ceremonies. Santería is both a religious system that honors ancestors and a contact point between humankind and the forces of nature, which are viewed as manifestations of God.

Links to Catholicism. A strong link between the Roman Catholic church and Santería is Mass (*see* CATHOLIC CHURCH AND CATHOLICISM). Followers of Santería are strongly encouraged by *santeros* to attend Mass. Santería masses are always said in honor of the Santería gods, known as *orishas*, particularly on days devoted to them.

Catholicism is important to Santería practitioners, who consider themselves to be good Catholics as well as good worshipers of Santería. The Catholic influence on Santería is demonstrated by the prayers, which are printed in collections referring to Santería gods as Catholic saints. Holy water is also a shared characteristic of Catholicism and Santería. For example, the cleansing baths in Santería rituals have holy water as the purification substance, and all Santería initiates need to be baptized as Catholics. The ceremony of baptism uses holy water to reject the devil. All things sprinkled with holy water are considered to be baptized, and evil spirits are thought to be frightened away by contact with holy water.

The Catholic church has tolerated Santería and Santería practitioners. Historically, this was not the case, but after the Second Vatican Ecumenical Council (VATICAN II, 1962-1965), the Catholic church generally became more tolerant. For example, Latin was no longer required for Mass, and the church altar was positioned so that the priest faced the congregation. Acceptance of Santería by the Catholic church has been crucial to the thousands of Latinos who practice the two religions.

Curative Aspects. Santería has been important to its practitioners in the Latino community because their mental and spiritual health were deeply connected with their beliefs. Many Latinos relied on the healing aspects of Santería as much as they did on standard medical practitioners. A *santero*, for example, might be consulted for a medical problem and often would refer the patient to an accredited medical doctor if root remedies and herbs were ineffective. There have been doctors in urban areas of the United States who were

A santero *dispenses advice with the aid of a tarot deck.* (Impact Visuals, Allan Clear)

accredited medical doctors as well as practitioners of Santería methods of healing. They used their spiritual powers for diagnostics, then determined the proper prescription to cure the ailment.

Santería has manifested miracle cures among its believers. There have been numerous stories of someone going to a regular doctor without being cured, then getting results from a *santero*. Most often, cures happened after application of some herbal remedy.

Latino reliance on Santería for healing, spiritual, and mental health purposes has not been lost on the community of social and psychological workers who serve the Latino community. Many of these individuals see the *santero* as an important figure in the community and seek a *santero*'s advice on certain problems affecting Latinos. For example, when an individual seeks assistance with psychological problems, the psychologist might ask if the patient would prefer referral to a *santero* for help. Often, this cooperation between social service agencies and the acknowledged spiritual leader results in the individual's successful return to a healthy life in his or her community.

Many non-Hispanics in the United States and Canada find it difficult to understand the role of Santería in society. Santería practices have, however, played important religious and healing roles in the lives of many Latinos. —*Gregory Freeland*

SUGGESTED READINGS: • Brandon, George. *Santería from Africa to the New World*. Bloomington: Indiana University Press, 1993. • Gleason, Judith. *Santería, Bronx*. New York: Atheneum, 1975. • Gonzalez Wippler, Migene. *Santería: The Religion*. New York: Harmony Books, 1989. • Morales Dorta, Jose. *Puerto Rican Espiritismo: Religion and Psychotherapy*. New York: Vantage Press, 1976. • Murphy, Joseph. *Santería: An African Religion in America*. Boston: Beacon Press, 1988. • Ruiz, Pedro. "Santeros, Botanicas, and Mental Health: An Urban View." *Transcultural Psychiatric Research Review* 9 (1972): 176-177.

Santiago, Benito (Benito Santiago y Rivera; b. Mar. 9, 1965, Ponce, Puerto Rico): Baseball player. Santiago made his major league debut with the San Diego Padres in 1986. A six-foot, one-inch catcher with a pow-

Baseball star Benito Santiago after hitting a home run. (AP/Wide World Photos)

erful throwing arm, Santiago won the 1987 National League Rookie of the Year Award with a .300 average, 18 home runs, 79 runs batted in, and 21 stolen bases; he also set a major league rookie record with a 34-game hitting streak. In 1988, he won the first of three consecutive Gold Glove Awards. In 1989, he was selected to the National League All-Star Team for the first of four consecutive seasons. He signed as a free agent with the Florida Marlins for the 1993 season.

Santiago, Isaura (b. Jan. 19, 1946, Brooklyn, N.Y.): Educator and administrator. Santiago in 1986 became president of Hostos Community College, part of the City University of New York system. The college, formed in 1968, primarily serves the Latino population of the South Bronx and offers bilingual programs.

Santiago, of Puerto Rican background, entered Brooklyn College in 1963 and soon found that her education had left her ill-prepared. She switched from the science curriculum, which she found sexist and discriminatory, to liberal arts, graduating in 1967. She worked her way through school as a temporary office worker, with one assignment at a legal services firm. She considered becoming a lawyer but decided that she preferred teaching. After encountering discrimination against Spanish-speaking children on her first teaching assignment, Santiago went to work for ASPIRA, which promotes higher education. She eventually rose to the position of executive deputy director before leaving in the late 1960's to teach at Hunter College.

Santiago earned her master's degree in education in 1969 from Brooklyn College. She began teaching elementary education at the City University of New York in 1972 and developed a graduate bilingual education program. She earned her doctorate in 1977 while involved in the legal case of *Aspira of New York v. Board of Education of the City of New York*, which concerned rights of non-English-speaking children within the city's school system. Her dissertation documented the case, and her research was published in 1977 as *Aspira Versus Board of Education of the City of New York: A History*. In 1979, Santiago joined the faculty of Columbia University, where she served until being named as president of Hostos Community College.

Santiesteban, Humberto "Tati" (b. Nov. 3, 1943, El Paso, Tex.): Public official. Santiesteban was born at a time when Mexican Americans had little role to play in the established Anglo government in Texas. He sought to change that condition.

Santiesteban was graduated from the New Mexico Military Institute in 1956. After his graduation, he served in the U.S military as a first lieutenant from 1956-1959, during the time that President Dwight D. Eisenhower was sending the initial U.S. advisers to Vietnam. He was awarded his LL.B. from the University of Texas Law School in 1962. He served in the Texas House of Representatives from 1967 to 1972 and began serving in the Texas State Senate in 1973.

Santo Domingo emigration: Massive emigration from the DOMINICAN REPUBLIC to the United States that began during the 1960's. Hundreds of exiles fled Rafael Leónidas Trujillo's dictatorship (1930-1961) in the Dominican Republic, mostly to Puerto Rico, Venezuela, and Spain. Trujillo's policies, however, restricted the mobility of workers both on and off the island. Before 1961, only 16,674 Dominicans had immigrated to the United States. After Trujillo's assassination in 1961, however, thousands left the country. Between 1961 and 1991, the United States admitted 534,884 Dominicans.

The earliest wave (1961-1963) had well-defined political characteristics. Many migrants were linked with the slain dictator, including government officials, military personnel, political leaders, and members of the elite. In 1963, the overthrow of President Juan Bosch initiated a new wave of immigrants, mostly composed of liberal and left-wing exiles. The civil war and U.S. military occupation of the Dominican Republic in 1965 closed a cycle of political violence, but international migration increased as a result of continuing economic hardship and political instability.

During the 1960's, middle-class Dominican professionals and entrepreneurs moved abroad in search of a better life. Since the 1970's, the lower-middle classes have predominated in the diaspora. In the 1980's, the Dominican exodus intensified, with more than 250,000 Dominicans gaining legal entry into the United States. Thousands more came illegally, usually crossing the Mona Channel to Puerto Rico in makeshift boats called *yolas*.

Economic as well as political factors motivated the Dominican exodus. Most Dominicans moved abroad seeking higher wages and better jobs. Living conditions have worsened and poverty has increased since the 1970's. The decline in the international price of export commodities such as sugar seriously hurt the Dominican economy. The scarcity of arable land led thousands of peasants to migrate to the capital and abroad. Urban unemployment and underemployment soared as public services degenerated.

Dominican immigrants celebrate at New York's Dominican Day parade. (Richard B. Levine)

Dominican governments, especially under Joaquín Balaguer's presidencies (1966-1974 and 1986-1994), have adopted a development strategy based on export industrialization and public sector expansion financed by external loans. Under pressure from the International Monetary Fund, the Dominican government has taken draconian fiscal measures to reduce the public debt, such as devaluing the Dominican peso, raising the price of basic foodstuffs, and freezing salaries. The crisis of the Dominican economy is also a political crisis insofar as the state's development model displaced vast numbers of workers.

Most Dominican migrants are of urban origin, principally from large cities such as Santo Domingo and San Francisco de Macorís. Most urban dwellers, however, were born in rural areas, particularly the Cibao region. Many Dominicans first migrate to the main cities of their country and then move on to the United States, Puerto Rico, Venezuela, Spain, and elsewhere. Those leaving the country are primarily in mid-range occupations, such as elementary school teachers, office personnel, and craft workers. Owners of small and medium-sized plots of land are overrepresented in the outflow; landless peasants and unemployed workers are underrepresented. In general, the migrants are more skilled, educated, and urban than is the population of the DOMINICAN REPUBLIC as a whole.

Santos and santo art: Religious images of Jesus Christ and the Catholic saints in the form of carved or sculpted figures and paintings or carvings on wood, as well as works in canvas, paper, hide, or textiles.

History and Style. Although "santos" is a general term used to signify representations of saints, it has a more specific meaning in the Southwest, especially in New Mexico and southern Colorado. In those areas, santos are a type of folk art with a unique style and function. They were created by people who wanted to have likenesses of the saints they venerated, in the belief that the saints would intercede for them in avoiding or recovering from a misfortune, in helping them obtain a favor, or in becoming worthy of God's grace.

The Spanish missionaries and colonists in North America enjoyed displaying images of the saints in their churches, missions, and homes. A small number of santos were imported during the colonial period from Mexico and used in California and Texas. These imports, however, were the exception in New Mexico. The New Mexico province was so isolated and difficult to reach that the Spanish and Mexican govern-

ments generally tended to ignore it, with the result that lay settlers there began to produce their own santos in the late eighteenth century.

The most common types of santos are wood carvings in the round (*BULTOS*) or paintings in tempera on wood panels with carved elements (*RETABLOS*). The size of carved santo figures ranges from a few inches to larger than life size. Likewise, santo panels may be quite small or large, multipaneled works that cover a substantial portion of a wall, usually behind the altar of a church or on a side of the nave. Santos are distinguished by their vivid colors and their dramatic stylized depiction of the saints.

Most of the santos from the colonial period were unsigned pieces made for use as religious objects, not as works of art. In the latter half of the nineteenth century, the santos tradition began to decline because of changes in church patronage and the increasing popularity of imported plaster saints. A revival of santos making was sparked in the 1920's by the interest of Anglo artists in Santa Fe and Taos in the region's traditional crafts and Spanish colonial style. Families of *santeros* (santos makers) passed on their skills, and tourists and collectors began to buy santos at fairs, exhibitions, and shops in Santa Fe. In these new markets, santos were mainly valued for their aesthetic qualities rather than their religious function. Hispanos, however, continued to use santos in their home shrines. By the late twentieth century, a small number of traditional *santeros* were inspiring a new generation of New Mexican artists, who saw santos as an important symbol of their heritage.

The Saints and Their Meaning. The most popular subjects for santos were the Crucifixion, the Virgin Mary as Nuestra Señora de Guadalupe or Nuestra Señora de Dolores (Our Lady of Sorrows), San Antonio de Padua, San José, San Miguel Arcangel, and San Rafael. The popularity of these figures arises from their association with the survival of the original settlers and later migrants in the arid and harsh environment of New Mexico.

Believers pray to santos of the Crucifixion asking for help in fighting against shame and sinfulness and in being able to tolerate frustration and find acceptance. Nuestra Señora de Guadalupe is typically shown standing on a half moon, clothed in a blue mantle emblazoned with stars. She has a crown on her head and is surrounded by the rays of the sun. She is usually asked to make the petitioner strong in the face of the unknown. The Virgin as Nuestra Señora de Dolores is presented wearing a red tunic and blue mantle, with

Bultos *and* retablos *are the most common forms of santo art*. (Security Pacific Bank Collection, Los Angeles Public Library)

her heart pierced by at least one sword. Sometimes she is shown with seven swords, representing the seven sorrows of her life in respect to Christ. Women appeal to her for help in childbirth and in dealing with the effects of a death in the family.

The saints take various forms as santos. San Antonio de Padua, with thick, slightly tonsured hair and a belted blue robe, holds a rosy-cheeked infant Jesus in his left hand. He is asked to ensure the well-being of animals and crops as well as the fertility of a married woman. Crowned and bearded San José holds a flowering staff in one hand and the baby Jesus in the other. He is believed to help men fulfill their duties as fathers and heads of families. San Miguel Arcangel is depicted carrying a sword, a symbol of his conquest over Satan, and scales that are used to weigh the virtue of souls on judgment day. San Rafael Arcangel is usually shown carrying a fish and a pilgrim's staff in memory of his curing blindness. He is asked to intercede for the cure of blindness and against the influence of the devil.

—*Francisco A. Apodaca*

SUGGESTED READINGS:

• Boyd, Elizabeth *The New Mexico Santero*. Santa Fe: Museum of New Mexico Press, 1969. • Boyd, Elizabeth. *Popular Arts of Spanish New Mexico*. Santa Fe: Museum of New Mexico Press, 1974. • Espinosa, José Edmundo. *Saints in the Valleys: Christian Sacred Images in the History, Life and Folk Art of Spanish New Mexico*. Rev. ed. Albuquerque: University of New Mexico Press, 1967. • Frank, Larry. *New Kingdom of the Saints*. Santa Fe: Red Crane Books, 1992. • Martinez, Eluid Levi. *What Is a New Mexico Santo?* Santa Fe, N.Mex.: Sunstone Press, 1978. • Mather, Christine. *Baroque to Folk/De lo Barroco a lo popular*. Santa Fe, N.Mex.: Museum of International Folk Art Foundation, 1980. • Steele, Thomas J. *Santos and Saints*. Albuquerque, N.Mex.: Calvin Horn, 1974. • Weigle, Marta, et al., eds. *Hispanic Arts and Ethnohistory in the Southwest*. Santa Fe, N.Mex.: Ancient City Press, 1983.

Sarape (serape): Traditional poncho. The *sarape* is a blanket made of wool or coarse cotton and worn as a cape by men in Mexico and Guatemala. *Sarapes* are woven in braid lacing of vivid colors and often have a slit in the middle for the head. The choicest come from Saltillo, Mexico. The *sarape de saltillo* is made with different colored weft threads resembling a rainbow.

Two young girls wear sarapes *for a parade.* (Impact Visuals, Kirk Condyles)

No fixative is added to the yarn, so that after the first wash, colors bleed into one another, enhancing the rainbow effect. This technique was developed by indigenous families resettled in Saltillo by the Spanish government at the end of the sixteenth century.

Sardiñas, Eligio "Kid Chocolate" (Oct. 28, 1910, Havana, Cuba—Aug. 8, 1988, Miami, Fla.): Boxer. A leading boxer during the early 1930's, Sardiñas won his first title in the junior lightweight class in July of 1931 by defeating Benny Bass. He then moved into the featherweight class with a title knockout win over Lew Feldman in October of 1932. Sardiñas lost the junior lightweight title in December of 1933 and relinquished his featherweight title two months later. He retired in 1938 with a 132-10-6 record and 50 knockouts. "Kid Chocolate" was elected to the Boxing Hall of Fame in 1959.

Sarduy, Severo (Feb. 25, 1937, Camagüey, Cuba—August, 1993, France): Novelist. Born to a working-class family (his father was a railway worker), Sarduy left for Havana in 1956 to study medicine. In Havana, he began working part-time in an advertising agency and publishing poetry, short stories, and art criticism.

By the end of 1959, Sarduy had gone to Paris with a scholarship from the Cuban government to study art history. He later became a citizen of France. Throughout his life, he participated actively in French cultural life. His first novel, *Gestos* (1963), written in an "objectivist" style reminiscent of the French *nouveau roman*, evokes the events of the anti-Batista struggle in the late 1950's. His novel *De donde son los cantantes* (1967; "From Cuba with a Song," in *Triple Cross*, 1972) is a dazzling attempt to answer the question "What is Cuba?" It marked Sarduy's debut as a major Latin American author. His later novels include *Cobra* (1972; English translation, 1975), *Maitreya* (1978; English translation, 1987), and *Colibrí* (1984). He also wrote several books of essays and poetry. Sarduy, often considered one of the most experimental and theoretically sophisticated of Latin American novelists, created fiction that is revolutionary in both style and content. Its major preoccupations are painting, language, national identity, and destiny.

Sassen, Saskia (b. Jan. 5, 1945, The Hague, The Netherlands): Educator. Sassen has studied various topics concerning investment and labor, with publications including *Exporting Capital and Importing Labor: The Role of Caribbean Immigration to New York City* (1981), *The Mobility of Labor and Capital: A Study in International Investment and Labor Flow* (1988), and *The Global City* (1991), which concerns the financial services industry. She has worked as a consultant on several projects sponsored by the United Nations, was a member of the Ford Foundation Hispanic Research Task Force (1983-1985), and was part of the Stanford University Project on U.S.-Mexico Relations (1984-1986).

Sassen studied in Argentina and Italy, earning first-year certificates, before being granted her M.A. in sociology from the University of Notre Dame in 1971. Her Ph.D. in economics and sociology was granted in 1973 by the same institution. She studied at the Université de Poitiers in France in 1973 and 1974, earning the Maîtrise de Philosophie. In 1974 and 1975, she was a postdoctoral fellow at the Harvard University Center for International Affairs.

Sassen began her teaching career in 1976 at the City University of New York. In 1985, she taught at Queens College and Graduate School as a professor. That same year, she became a professor at the Columbia University Graduate School of Architecture. She was the school's director of urban planning (1987-1990), chair of the division of urban planning (1988-1990), and director of Ph.D. program beginning in 1989.

Saturday Spanish schools: Form of alternative education. They are voluntary, are tutorial, and usually emphasize Hispanic values and culture.

Saturday Spanish schools have been modeled on "separatist" forms of educational philosophy, as opposed to assimilationist forms. They emphasize three main areas—language, culture, and the teacher. One type, the *escuelita*, or "little school," emphasizes Spanish-language instruction in reading, writing, and language for the purpose of increasing fluency. It emphasizes Hispanic, as opposed to Anglo-American, culture. Other subjects studied include science and math.

All types of Saturday Spanish schools are supported by volunteers from the Hispanic community. The schools have fund-raising events to finance their activities. Teaching methods are primarily tutorial, and instruction may be on Saturdays or after school. Some universities have Hispanic students who volunteer their time to teach in these schools.

These schools' main purposes have been to reduce the high dropout rate among Hispanic students and to affirm students' cultural heritage (*see* DROPOUTS AND DROPOUT RATES). They have supplemented and ex-

Saturday Spanish schools emphasize instruction in reading and writing. (Impact Visuals, Loren Santow)

tended BILINGUAL EDUCATION but not limited themselves to language classes. Community groups have the advantage of drawing from the diverse talents of the community and offering pertinent role models to youngsters.

Dropout rates in some communities approach 50 percent. Community leaders perceive a need to develop self-esteem and the desire to succeed in students. The special programs of Saturday Spanish schools work because they offer teachers to whom students can relate and with whom they have a one-on-one relationship. The voluntary nature of attendance provides a sense of empowerment.

As one example, Project ONDA (Opportunities for Networking and Developing Aspirations) works with thirty at-risk high-school students at a time. They attend ten Saturday classes. The objectives are to raise self-esteem, provide role models, and implement support groups. Volunteers and parents counsel participants about goal-setting, being responsible, and prioritizing demands.

A program for female Hispanics is the Pasadera (or Stepping Stone) Program in San Antonio, Texas. Its students are high-risk girls in middle school. The goal is to train them in assertiveness, physical wellness, and substance abuse issues.

Hispanics, particularly Mexican Americans in communities where their traditions have been preserved, have a strong value system that affects views on schooling. Their identification with family, commu-

Puerto Rican émigré Arthur Schomburg was a pioneer in the field of black studies. (AP/Wide World Photos)

nity, and ethnic group is embodied in the spirit of La RAZA, the belief that all Hispanics have a common spiritual bond. The community efforts of voluntary classes relate to this spirit. Hispanics generally believe in the personalization of human relationships, as accomplished in the *escuelita* movement with its basis of one-on-one tutoring. The attitude of respect for elders is extended in the Saturday Spanish schools through family involvement.

Schomburg, Arthur Alfonso (Jan. 24, 1874, San Juan, Puerto Rico—June 10, 1938, New York, N.Y.): Collector. Schomburg, who chose to identify himself as a Puerto Rican of African descent, is celebrated for his collection of items related to what was then called Negro history. His collection formed the basis for the Schomburg Center for Research in Black Culture, a branch of the New York Public Library. The Carnegie Foundation purchased Schomburg's collection in 1926 and donated it to the library system, which built a branch in Harlem to house the items.

Schomburg received his early education in Puerto Rico and St. Thomas, Virgin Islands. He emigrated to New York, New York, in 1891, ending his formal education. He worked as a secretary for Las Dos Antillas, a revolutionary party seeking independence for Cuba and Puerto Rico. From 1906 to 1929, he worked for Bankers Trust Company. On the strength of his language skills, he rose from messenger to chief of the foreign mailing section.

In 1911, Schomburg and John Edward Bruce founded the Negro Society for Historical Research. In 1922, Schomburg was elected president of the American Negro Academy, a research society. After selling his collection to the Carnegie Foundation, he became the first curator of the Negro Collection at Fisk University. He left that position in 1931 to be the curator of the Schomburg collection.

School closures: This term refers to a variety of issues relevant to Latinos, including the closing of neighborhood schools as part of consolidation plans and the closing of schools by districts in cost-cutting moves. The focus of this discussion is state-ordered school closings in response to *BROWN V. BOARD OF EDUCATION* (1954), as an act of defiance against the desegregation order (*see* SEGREGATION, DESEGREGATION, AND INTEGRATION).

In the wake of *Brown v. Board of Education* (1954), state and local governments formally closed public schools in acts of defiance against the desegregation

order. In several highly populated areas in Virginia and in Little Rock, Arkansas, state governments chose to end public education instead of complying with court-ordered desegregation. In Virginia, this resistance put more than ten thousand students out of schools.

Private academies were formed in some areas, serving white children and hiring the white teachers who had formerly worked in public schools. Students whose parents could not afford private education were denied public education while these challenges to *Brown v. Board of Education* were fought in the press, the courts, and political arenas. By 1959, challenges in the courts and rulings supporting the state's responsibility to provide public education led to Virginia school closures being overturned. Public schools reopened in the affected areas. Schools in Little Rock, Arkansas, were also reopened amid massive press coverage and police protection. In the Deep South, other states contemplated ways of fighting desegregation, but Virginia's experience led most to avoid school closures as a means of blocking court-ordered desegregation.

The school closures that occurred in the wake of *Brown v. Board of Education* were not used to avoid integration of Latinos; that case did not specifically affect students of Latino descent. Several court cases that followed *Brown v. Board of Education* used that case in support of desegregation of Latino students, among them *CISNEROS V. CORPUS CHRISTI INDEPENDENT SCHOOL DISTRICT* (1972) and *Keyes v. Denver School District Number One* (1973). In both these cases, Latinos sought to be identified as a specific minority group so that *Brown v. Board of Education* would apply to them; the alternative was that they be categorized as "other white."

In the case of Latinos, race was not usually given as the reason for segregation. Public officials were able to maintain segregation by separating students on the basis of such criteria as English language skill. School officials assured anyone who questioned segregation that it was not an application of "separate but equal" but instead separate schooling based on differences in the ways students needed to be taught.

Thus, school closures were not used as a method to avoid desegregation in terms of Latinos, but failure of school closures to maintain segregation prompted school officials to look for other ways of segregating, when it was desired. Some of these methods of segregation have been applied to Latino students. In one specific incident, the "Mexican school" in Sequin, Texas, failed to open in September, 1932. In that particular case, the League of United Latin American Citizens (LULAC) formed a committee to investigate the closure; it was told that Mexican parents did not send their children to school until the end of the cotton-picking season. LULAC assured school officials that students would come if the school were opened. Within several days, approximately twenty Mexican American students enrolled at the school.

School finance: Procedures used to raise money to fund education. U.S. schools spend more than $100 billion annually to educate the nation's children. School finance involves the important issues of how much education should cost, how the burden of paying for public education should be distributed, and how society should allocate money to bring about educational objectives.

American public education historically has been financed largely through local property taxes. Use of property taxes as a source of school funding leads to disparities in school quality because schools in low-income areas have lower tax bases and thus fewer funds. This difference in available funds perpetuates educational, and therefore income, disparities. Another disparity caused by using local property taxes as a funding source is that school districts with low property tax bases may have to charge a higher assessment per dollar of property value in order to generate enough funding. In this case, property owners in low-valued areas, many of whom have low incomes, are forced to pay higher rates of property taxes.

State aid provides additional funds for such things as transportation and special services needed by school systems. Formulas for state aid are varied and complicated. Most are based on the average daily attendance and number of students in a school, adjusted by such things as the number of students with handicapping conditions or other special needs. State aid may be adjusted to account for variations in the property tax base, giving more funds to less wealthy districts than to wealthy districts. State aid is apportioned by state legislatures, thus making it a political issue subject to lobbying and other influences.

Federal aid, usually targeted to help specific populations, is another factor in the complete school funding package. Among federal aid programs that have impli-

Latino students protest tuition hikes at the City University of New York. (Hazel Hankin)

cations for educational equity are Title I aid, bilingual education aid, school lunch funding, Head Start programs, and education block grants.

Specific issues relevant to the Latino population include equity problems caused by using local property taxes as a major fund-raiser for schools, variation among states in the apportionment of state aid, and variations in federal aid depending on the whim of the current administration. Group action can help to change some of these inequities.

In 1968, Demetrio Rodríguez and six other Texas parents sued the San Antonio Independent School District, charging that the district violated the U.S. constitution through its system of financing education largely through property taxes. The district court found that the system violated the equal protection clause, but the U.S. Supreme Court, in SAN ANTONIO INDE-PENDENT SCHOOL DISTRICT V. RODRÍGUEZ (1973), overturned that ruling. In 1989, however, the Texas Supreme Court ruled that the state's system of public finance for schools was unconstitutional and mandated legislatures to prepare a new funding plan by the early 1990's.

Traditional approaches to school finance tend to give the least to those who already have the least. Political activism to change these approaches and creativity in finding new sources of funding will likely form important parts of the Latino educational agenda.

School voucher proposals: A form of educational finance reform. The government would give education aid (vouchers) directly to families to spend at the school, whether public or private, the children of the household attend.

Voucher plans can be implemented in a variety of ways. Each child could receive a voucher worth a specified amount, to spend wherever his/her family decided. In other scenarios, only low-income families would get vouchers. In other plans, students with handicapping conditions or in other situations that would raise the cost of their education would receive "supplemental" vouchers. The range of voucher proposals leaves many questions unanswered; among them the source of funding, whether federal, state, or local. Unless proposals involve funds other than from local sources, voucher proposals will not correct inequities between schools in rich and poor neighborhoods; local funding based on property values perpetuates those inequities.

Financing experts generally agree that any voucher proposal would probably have to be phased in, because school finance reform tends to be gradual. Several phase-in possibilities include the distribution of any new state aid to families in the form of vouchers. Public schools would be required to educate all students residing in their district as they currently do, but the vouchers would allow families to send students to out-of-district schools or private schools. This plan seems to benefit higher-income families, because the value of a voucher would probably be insufficient to pay an out-of-district student's tuition. Thus, the only families who would benefit from the vouchers would be those with sufficient discretionary money to supplement them. To counteract this possibility, another option would be to fund only families below a certain income limit. Another proposal suggests giving vouchers to all families, with or without children, and providing the legal option of selling vouchers.

Implications of voucher plans include the potential to provide greater individual control over educational policy and practice. This is a result of increased school responsiveness, in that schools would have to listen to the needs and desires of parents and students in order to keep up their enrollments, as competition might occur among sites at which students "spend" their vouchers. Many individuals would find this refreshing, especially Latino and African American parents who perceive a lack of influence under the traditional system.

Another implication might be increased financial assistance to parochial schools. Many parents may choose, given the option, to spend vouchers on parochial schools instead of public schools. In areas with large Catholic populations, vouchers could help financially struggling parochial schools.

Another part of the scenario involving voucher programs is that schools would differ widely in terms of teacher salaries, staffing ratios, curricula, and per-pupil expenditures. For this reason, some analysts worry that instead of improving conditions for the poor and underrepresented, vouchers could contribute to elitism and social division. Different economic classes and cultural and religious groups could segregate themselves based on their differing abilities to pay and/or their beliefs.

Science and magic: The relationship between "science" and "magic" can be examined as one of basic opposition or as part of a continuum connecting protoscience, pseudoscience, and science. In discussing these terms in a Latino context, it is important to consider the differences between science, magic, and ethnoscience (native science).

A curandero *may foretell the future and offer a variety of cures for illnesses.* (City Lore, Martha Cooper)

The relationships between science and magic can be looked at using the methods of the history of science and modern anthropology, which provides ways of looking at the development and construction of knowledge within a given culture or society. Modern Western science is most often considered to include use of the scientific or experimental method, which posits a systematic procedure for scientific investigation involving the observation of phenomena, the formation of hypotheses concerning the phenomena, experimentation to test the hypotheses, and a conclusion that validates or modifies the hypotheses.

Magic refers to the body of knowledge involving the supernatural and the forecasting of events. It also is associated with the specific practices of using charms, spells, rituals, and divination to produce supernatural effects. Magic is often related to religion and medicine, in that it uses supernatural or magical methodology in healing or in explaining natural phenomena.

Science and magic are at times seen to be in opposition with respect to medical practices. This is especially true in Latino communities in conflicts between the scientific medical establishment and folk healing practices of *curanderos*, particularly when they use supernatural and magico-religious cures (*see CURAN-DERISMO*). Modern anthropologists have used the concept of ethnoscience to explain the relationship of magic to science in Latino communities.

Ethnoscience is an anthropological method that examines the boundaries of categories in systems of classification and analyzes native observations and definitions of physical phenomena. It can also be defined as the system of knowledge and cognition typical of a given culture, which can be examined from an etic (outside) or emic (native) perspective. An example of this would be the contrast between magical and empirical or natural etiologies (modern Western) with respect to illness and the treatment of illness. Ethnoscience, with its native concepts such as those of folk medicine, posits that the personal relationship of groups or individuals with spirit forces is an important part of achieving desired results. From this perspective, ceremony and ritual take the place of experiment.

Magic was a precursor to science, in that it was an early attempt to understand nature and the working of the human body. *Curanderos* and *BRUJOS* in Latino communities are empirical healers who employ physio-therapeutic methods often combining magic and science, retaining elements of magic that have proved to be successful. *Curanderos* and *brujos* also use homeopathic magic, based on similitudes; contagious magic, based on the destruction or removal of an evil force; and direct magic, which requires special rituals to prevent disease or cure an illness.

Science and medicine: This area of inquiry examines the connections and correlations between science and medicine. One interesting issue in the history of science and medicine is the role of science, especially modern science, in medicine. Science in this context refers to advances in laboratory sciences in medicine, particularly the display of clinical applications of the basic sciences.

In the field of Latino and Chicano studies, Bernard Ortiz de Montellano's work on the empirical value of Aztec medicine offers a good example of how to look at the role of increased scientific knowledge in medicine. Scholars in this field of study investigate such

Antonia Novello takes the oath of office as surgeon general of the United States. (AP/Wide World Photos)

issues as the nature of scientific medicine and how medicine becomes scientific. Also important is the issue of the primacy of modern Western medicine in the study of native and traditional systems of medicine. Such topics as the value and functions of CURANDE-RISMO, or Mexican and Mexican American folk medicine, also receive attention.

Those who study these themes come from the disciplines of history of science, history of medicine, medical anthropology, and ethnomedicine. Historians who have studied Aztec and pre-Columbian medicine have used the historical approach in looking at works important to that area of study, such as the centuries-old studies by Fray Bernardo de Sahagún and Francisco Hernández. Others have emphasized the importance of studying native cultural contexts, especially the connections between Aztec religion, worldview, and medicine.

Bernard Ortiz de Montellano, a chemist and anthropologist, has examined the empirical basis of Aztec medicine, especially medicinal plants and herbs (*see* AZTEC CIVILIZATION). He has reconstructed the Aztec worldview and culture, bringing the assumptions of modern science to the study of Aztec ethnobotany. He has studied the degree to which Aztec medicine was scientific. Much of his work has focused on studies of the chemically active ingredients of commonly used Aztec medicinal plants and the efficacy and therapeutic value of Aztec medicine. Among the plants he studied are *maguey* (agave), used for wounds; *matlaxihuitl* (*Commenlina pallida*), used as a hemostat; *cihuapatli* ("women's medicine," *Montanoa tomentosa*), used to hasten childbirth; *tlalquequetzal* (*Achillea millefolium*), used for coughs; *tlapatl* (*Datura stramonium*), a powerful hallucinogen used for fevers and chest pains; and *cacamotic* (*Ipomoea purga*), a purgative.

Aztec medicine, even when judged by standards of effectiveness and in comparison with modern Western medicine, was surprisingly advanced. Modern scientists have recognized many of the discoveries of the Aztecs and continue to use traditional folk knowledge of herbal cures in their search for new drugs and treatments.

Science and technology, Latino achievements in: Latinos have made many contributions in the areas of science, medicine, technology, and engineering. Some of these contributions are relatively unknown, for a variety of reasons.

Introduction and Approaches. Elias Trabulse has referred to the history of science in Mexico as a "secret

history." He argued that Mexican science and scientific achievements have not been studied or written about in appropriate ways. The same could be said about the contributions to science and technology of all Latinos. Dissemination of information concerning the contributions of Latinos and Latin Americans is hampered by the fact that this body of knowledge is for the most part in Spanish; little has been translated into English.

Various factors have slowed dissemination of information concerning Latinos' scientific achievements. Among them is the fact that studies of Latino contributions to science have not been cultivated as part of the scholarship of science. The few studies that exist are incomplete or lack rigor. Latino contributions must also be contextualized and connected to economic history as well as to the histories of agriculture, mining, engineering, and other applied fields; the history of Latino contributions in science and technology is one strand in a larger tapestry of historical contributions. Many Latinos are in the process of reclaiming and documenting this scientific and cultural legacy.

Issues of what have been called cultural colonization and MESTIZAJE (the mixing of cultural traditions) must be considered in a discussion of approaches to the study of Latino contributions to science. For example, lands occupied by Native Americans were colonized by Europeans beginning in the fifteenth century. As this colonization proceeded, the technology of Europe supplemented or replaced indigenous tools and methods. Historically, the Latin American scientific legacy was overshadowed by the supposedly superior Western tradition. This has led some to believe that scientific activity is foreign to Latinos rather than recognizing that the scientific traditions are simply different.

The contributions of Latinos in the area of science and technology can be explored from four vantage points: contributions of Native Americans and what have been called the areas of ethnoscience, such as ethnobotany, ethnoastronomy, and ethnomathematics; the role of Spanish science, especially the impact that it had on indigenous American societies; the history of Latin American science; and the history of science in the United States. The history of the contributions of U.S. Latinos merges elements from all these traditions and cultural contexts.

Native American Contributions. Native Americans made significant contributions in the area of science and technology, especially in the areas of agriculture, medicine, ethnobotany, mathematics, and astronomy. The term "ethnoscience" was coined to refer to such

The pre-Columbian peoples of Latin America had elaborate systems of medical practice, as depicted in this Mayan bas-relief. (Ruben G. Mendoza)

contributions. Some scholars reject the term "cthno-science" because they want to stress that non-Western contributions deserve to be called "science" as much as do Western contributions. Modern science is multicultural in the sense that it incorporates elements of scientific information and mathematical knowledge from many sources, such as the Mayan concept of zero and Aztec medical practices. Frequently, the scientific and technological traditions that were incorporated into modern science are not acknowledged; all the information and tools in use are assumed to come from the mainstream tradition.

The MESTIZAJE or mixing of different cultural and ethnic traditions must be acknowledged; if not, there can be no comprehensive understanding of the history of science. Part of this understanding involves considering the extent to which modern science has its origins in non-European cultures. With respect to Latinos, this means studying the contributions of pre-Columbian cultures as well as those that arose from cultural interaction following the colonization of the Americas by the Spanish.

Pre-Columbian Contributions. Pre-Columbian peoples such as the Aztecs, Maya, and Incas, as well as other indigenous peoples of North and South America, made significant contributions in the area of health and medical practices. They had highly developed systems of health practices and knowledge of medicinal plants and herbs. The Aztecs possessed a well-developed botanical and anatomical nomenclature and a sophisticated body of knowledge of the surgical treatment of wounds. Medical botany was especially advanced among the Aztecs, the Maya, and the indigenous people of what is now the southwestern United States. (*See* AZTEC CIVILIZATION; MAYAN CIVILIZATION.)

Some of the most important Native American contributions are in the area of agricultural technology. Among these are the *milpa* and *chinampas* farming systems. Developments in agriculture brought about significant contributions in domestication of crops. Through careful observation and prediction, Native American peoples learned to domesticate such crops as potatoes, MAIZE, peanuts, peppers, and tomatoes.

Associated with crop technology is knowledge of medicinal plants and herbs. Among indigenous contributions are such plant products as quinine, used for malaria; ipecac, used as an emetic; sarsaparilla, used as a tonic; curare; and coca. The idea of scientific collections of plants may well have been suggested to Europeans by the gardens that so astonished explorers of Aztec Mexico. Early Mexicans had a number of botanical and zoological gardens, many of which surpassed those of Europe in their extent and arrangement. There is some debate as to whether they were botanical gardens in a modern sense.

One of the most important gardens was constructed in 1467 by Moctezuma, in Huastepec, in what is now the state of Morelos. The garden had plants and trees from all over Mexico, including cacao trees and the aromatic vanillas from Veracruz. Plants were collected for their beauty, aroma, or medicinal use; in addition, some were believed to be sacred, with important religious significance for the Aztecs.

Archaeoastronomy, Ethnoastronomy, and Mathematics. Studies of archaeoastronomy and ethnoastronomy indicate that native people of the New World were careful observers of the natural world and the skies. Archaeoastronomy deals with ancient findings in the field of astronomy, and ethnoastronomy studies the cultural premises behind those findings. Mesoamerican peoples had substantial knowledge concerning the movements of the stars, the sun, and the moon.

Mayan and Aztec astronomical observation was based on religious beliefs and was not observation for its own sake. As was the case with medicine, beliefs concerning ASTRONOMY and astrology were closely connected to pre-Columbian religious and cultural worldviews.

Along with their advances in astronomical observation, the Maya and Aztecs developed mathematics, systems of numeration, and a highly advanced calendar. Studies of hieroglyphic records from Mayan documentation have revealed the sophistication of Mayan mathematics and calendar systems. Mayan mathematics is significant for its use and development of the concept of zero.

Early Spanish Scientific Activity. Scientific investigation began and spread in the New World from the cities that are now Mexico City, Mexico, and Lima, Peru. From the sixteenth to the nineteenth centuries, the Spanish empire in the New World needed an applied system of science and technology to aid in maintaining its dominance. Central scientific concerns were navigation, mining, and metallurgy.

Much valuable scientific information is found in the chronicles of the Spanish explorers and colonizers. In a sense, the first important scientific contributions by Spanish-speaking peoples of the New World are the documents left behind by the early European explorers of the regions where many Latinos live today. These documents often contain historical and scientific information on the discovery of exotic flora and fauna. Such documents include travel literature, letters, and diaries written by explorers, colonists, and missionaries.

Sixteenth century ethnographers and natural historians contributed much to the knowledge of the New World with their encyclopedic descriptions and their works of natural history. These scholars for the most part imposed Western forms of encyclopedic classification and structure on material from the New World.

Peter Martyr (1459-1535) was an Italian humanist who lived and wrote in Spain about the New World; he never traveled to the Americas. His most significant work is *Decades de Orbe Novo* (1511-1526). This work, based on conversations with Spanish explorers and letters from those who were living or had lived in the New World, contains valuable information on plants and animals from the New World.

Gonzalo Fernández de Oviedo (1479-1557) was a soldier-historian who made many trips to the New World. Among his main works are the *Historia Natural* (1535) and the *Sumario* (1526). These works contain diffuse accounts of ethnographic and topographic information on New World flora and fauna.

The writings of explorer Alvar Núñez CABEZA DE VACA are some of the first natural histories done by Spanish-speaking people in the area that is now the United States. His main work, *Los Naufragios* (the shipwrecks), contains ethnographic material, geography, and natural history. Cabeza de Vaca left Spain with an ill-fated expedition led by Pánfilo de NARVÁEZ. His writings record his travels through what is now the southwestern United States.

Significant scientific work during the early years of colonization involved Spanish study of Aztec contributions to ethnobotany and medicine. From this work came the publishing of the Codex Badianus-Cruz, an illustrated Aztec text discussing herbal medicines. Bernardino de Sahagún (c. 1490-1590), a Spaniard, wrote works that came to be known as the Florentine Codex and the *Historia General*. These also contained information on Aztec health practices, especially herbal medicine. Sahagún was a Franciscan historian, philologist, and ethnographer who went to New Spain, learned the Nahuatl (Aztec) language, and used systematic questionnaires given to native informants in his investigations of the native cultures of New Spain. His chief work is the *Historia de las cosas de Nueva España*, which was not published until 1829.

Spanish Influences in the New World. Spain's King Philip II was interested in science and stimulated scientific inquiry in New Spain (Mexico). He brought about important reforms in public health and organized important scientific and research projects. Of special significance is the expedition of Spanish physician Francisco Hernández (c. 1517-1587). Hernández was commissioned by Philip II to do a study of Mexican medical history in 1570. The expedition was to study Mexican medicinal plants and herbs and to investigate native health practices. Hernández traveled throughout Mexico collecting information on medicinal plants, herbs, animals, and rocks. He also experimented on the therapeutic effects of local drugs. In addition, he studied Mexican archaeology and practiced medicine.

Medicine and health care in New Spain underwent enormous changes within the context of conquest and colonization by Spain. The Spanish brought European medical institutions, personnel, and knowledge to Mexico. The Spanish generally found the magico-religious and empirical procedures of Nahuatl medicine to be unacceptable. The philosophical and religious character of Nahuatl medicine and health care differed from the distinct philosophical base of European and Spanish medicine and care.

The founding of the University of Mexico was important for the beginnings of science in Mexico. On September 21, 1551, Prince Philip (later to be King Philip II) issued a royal proclamation that laid the basis for the founding of the Royal and Pontifical University of Mexico. The royal proclamation stipulated that in the City of Mexico a university be founded with all the faculties (disciplines). Native Americans and the sons of Spaniards would be instructed in the tenets of the Catholic faith. The medical curriculum at the University of Mexico was based on that of the University of Salamanca.

José de Acosta (1539-1600), a Jesuit, wrote the *Historia Natural y Moral de las Indias* (1590), considered by many to be the most original and influential of all the works of this type. This work contains important facts concerning history, geography, plants, and animals from the New World, especially from Mexico and Peru. It was translated into English in 1604.

Two other Jesuits made significant scientific contributions in New Spain during the seventeenth century.

Fray Eusebio Francisco KINO (1645-1711) was a missionary who was an expert in the areas of mathematics, astronomy, geography, and natural history. He focused his work in the desert regions of what are now the U.S. state of Arizona and the Mexican state of Sonora. Fray Juan de Steinffer (1664-1716) also worked in Sonora and is remembered for his work on Mexican medicinal plants and herbs.

Seventeenth Century Advances. One of the most significant areas of scientific contributions concerns mining and metallurgy. The most important work in this area is perhaps that of Alvaro Alonso Barba y Toscano (1559-1662). He was a priest and mining expert who worked in Bolivia. His most significant contribution is *Arte de Metales*, first published in 1640. It is considered the most important text on mining and metallurgy of the seventeenth century. It contains significant contributions in the process of amalgamation. With respect to astrological and astronomical studies in seventeenth century Mexico, significant works include those of Diego Rodriguez (1596-1668), such as his *Observation of the New Comet* (1652), and the writings of Carlos Sigüenza de Góngora (1545-1600).

Geography and Botany in the Eighteenth Century. Jorge Juan Ulloa (1713-1773) and Antonio de Ulloa (1716-95) made valuable geodesic measurements during the eighteenth century. In addition, the Spanish Crown sponsored important scientific botanical expeditions. José Pavón (1742-1816) and José Celestino Mutis y Bossío (1732-1808) in 1783 explored what is now Colombia, and the famous Expedition to New Spain (1787) was directed by Martin de Sessé (1751-1808) and José de Mociño (1757-1819). These scientific expeditions continued the work of Francisco Hernández. The expeditions led to establishment of modern botanical studies in Mexico City with the founding of the chair of botany at the University of Mexico and the creation of the Mexican Botanical Garden by Spanish pharmacist and botanist Vicente Cervantes (1755-1829). Cervantes did substantive research in the area of New World flora, especially Mexican plants.

Another important figure in eighteenth century science was the Jesuit Francisco Xavier Clavijero (1731-1787), known for his botanical and natural history writing, especially the *Historia Antigua de México*. A contemporary of Clavijero was José Antonio de Alzate y Ramirez (1737-1799), who studied theology as well as mathematics, medicine, and natural history. His principal contributions to Mexican science relate to scientific journalism and the diffusion of important scientific works and ideas.

The eighteenth century closed with the important geographic work of expeditions by Gaspar de POR-TOLÁ (c. 1723-1784) and Alejandro Malespina (1754-1810). Portolá conducted and documented expeditions along the West Coast from San Diego to Monterey. Malespina made important geographic studies of Central and South America. He is also remembered for his journey to Alaska in 1791. Spanish physician Francisco Javier de Balmis (1753-1819) made an expedition to conduct studies of vaccination against smallpox in the Caribbean, Venezuela, and Mexico.

Nineteenth Century Science. The nineteenth century saw the establishment of important scientific institutions in Latin America, such as the Observatorio of Bogotá and the Real Seminario de Mineria of Mexico. Antonio del Río (1765-1849) and brothers Fausto (1754-1833) and Juan Jose Elhuyar (1754-1796) were important figures in the development of mining and metallurgy in Mexico. Del Río discovered tungsten and vanadium and was instrumental in the introduction of modern chemistry into Mexico. The nineteenth century also witnessed acceptance of the doctrines of Positivism and Darwinism in Latin America. In the area of medicine, Cuban physician Carlos J. Finlay (1833-1915) made pioneering contributions to research on malaria and the transmission of this illness by mosquitoes.

Mexicans made important contributions in the area of mining. They are credited with the discovery of the most important quicksilver (mercury) mines in the Americas, at New Almaden. Mexicans helped to develop this mine and others in California and elsewhere in the Southwest through their knowledge and manual labor. They used Spanish methods of mining that had been developed in Mexico, such as the so-called patio process of separating silver from ore with the use of quicksilver. This technique was invented around 1557 by Bartolomé de Medina. Mexicans developed quartz mining in the gold regions of California in the nineteenth century and introduced the arrastra method of separating gold from ore.

Twentieth Century Science. During the twentieth century, Argentina and Mexico most closely followed the patterns of European science. Argentina was especially noteworthy because of the influence of German scientists. This can be seen in the area of physics at the University of La Plata. Significant scientific developments took place in Mexico, such as the expansion of the National Observatory and the foundations of schools of chemistry, geographic studies, and biological studies. The Spanish Civil War provoked Spanish Republican scientists to go into exile. Many went to Latin America, where they stimulated Latin American science.

During the twentieth century, several Latin Americans have won the Nobel Prize in acknowledgment of their scientific contributions. Among those who have received this award are Agentinean Bernardo Houssay for medicine in 1947, Venezuelan Baruj Benacerraf for medicine in 1980, and Argentinean Luis F. Leloir for chemistry in 1970.

Latino Scientists and Their Contributions. There have been many contributions in the area of science by Latinos, both those born in North America and those who emigrated there. Latinos, however, had relatively little representation in the fields of science, mathematics, and technology.

Some important work has been done in the area of Latinos and mathematics. Luis Ortiz Franco has pointed out that mathematics has been an important part of Latino cultural and scientific activity. Ortiz Franco trained at Stanford University (Ph.D., 1977) in mathematics education. He has worked for the National Institute of Education and the U.S. Department of Education, where he advocated increasing funds to promote research on the teaching and learning of mathematics among Latinos.

Latinos have made important contributions in the areas of physics and chemistry. Luis Walter ALVAREZ completed most of his life's work at the University of California, Berkeley. In 1960, Alvarez announced his discovery in bubble chambers of very short-lived subatomic particles called resonances. In 1968, he was awarded the Nobel Prize in Physics for this discovery. In 1980, he was part of a team of scientists, including his son Walter, that postulated that the extinction of the dinosaurs was caused by a large body, such as an asteroid or comet, crashing into the earth. Alvarez is considered one of the most distinguished and respected physicists of his time.

Another important Latino physicist is Alberto Vinicio BÁEZ, born in Puebla, Mexico. He has taught physics and mathematics and done research at Cornell University and Stanford University, among other institutions. His main area of research is the use of X rays for various purposes including optics, holography, and instrumentation for astronomy.

Guatemalan Victor PÉREZ-MÉNDEZ is a noted expert in the area of experimental heavy ion physics. He began work in 1951 as a research scientist at the Law-

Luis Alvarez, winner of the 1968 Nobel Prize in Physics. (AP/Wide World Photos)

Science students present Secretary of Education Lauro Cavazos with a shirt from their club. (AP/Wide World Photos)

rence Berkeley Laboratory. His areas of research are nuclear and high energy physics, radiation detectors, and medical imaging.

George CASTRO, born in Los Angeles, California, is a physical chemist and an expert in research management. He has worked in the area of organic photoconductors and the electronic properties of organic solids at the IBM Almaden Research Center in San Jose, California.

Latinos have also made important contributions in the area of engineering. Margarita H. Colmenares was born in Sacramento, California, to a family that came from Mexico. She has worked for the Chevron Corporation and has served as a White House Fellow (1991-1992). In the latter capacity, she served as special assistant to Deputy Secretary of Education David T.

Kearns. In 1989, Colmenares became president of the Society of Hispanic Engineers. She has worked at encouraging Latinos to pursue careers in engineering.

Biomedical Sciences. Lauro F. CAVAZOS is known for his contributions in both science and government. He received a bachelor's degree in zoology and a doctorate in physiology. Following several years of teaching, he became dean of Tufts University in 1964, then president of the health sciences center at Texas Technological University. Cavazos' area of research is the physiology of the reproductive system; he has written several important guides to human dissection. In 1988, Cavazos was named U.S. secretary of education by President Ronald Reagan, making him the first Latino to be appointed to a cabinet-level position. Cavazos resigned this position in 1990.

Antonia Coello NOVELLO became the U.S. surgeon general on March 9, 1990. She was the first woman, first Latina, and first Puerto Rican to fill that post.

Faustina Solis is known for her valuable contributions in the area of health education and social services. She worked at improving health conditions in poor Latino communities in California and along the U.S.-Mexico border. Solis was born in Mexico and moved to California with her family in the years after the Mexican Revolution. She became a full professor in the school of medicine at the University of California, San Diego, a significant accomplishment given that she had neither a medical degree nor a doctorate. Solis was brought to that university to work in the department of community and family medicine and to serve in the rural health program. She aided in setting up comprehensive health programs along the Mexican border.

Marian Lucy RIVAS is a specialist in medical genetics and computer science. Her areas of research are human gene mapping, genetic counseling, genetic aspects of epilepsy, and computer applications of clinical genetics.

Astronomy and Space Sciences. Several Latinos have contributed to space exploration and space science. Among these are astronaut Ellen OCHOA, who began working for the National Aeronautics and Space Administration (NASA) in the mid-1980's. While at NASA she worked as a researcher and chief of the intelligent systems technology branch at NASA's Ames Research Center in Mountain View, California. She was graduated in the astronaut class of 1990, becoming the first Latina astronaut. Ochoa also holds three patents in optical processing.

Another Latino astronaut is Franklin Ramón CHANG-DÍAZ, born in Costa Rica. Chang moved to the United States, to study science, when he was eighteen years old. He became a naturalized U.S. citizen. He was selected as a mission specialist candidate in 1980 and had participated in four NASA space shuttle missions by the early 1990's.

Astronaut Sidney GUTIERREZ was born in Albuquerque, New Mexico. He became an astronaut for NASA in 1985 and has participated in several space missions. He has served as commander for the Shuttle

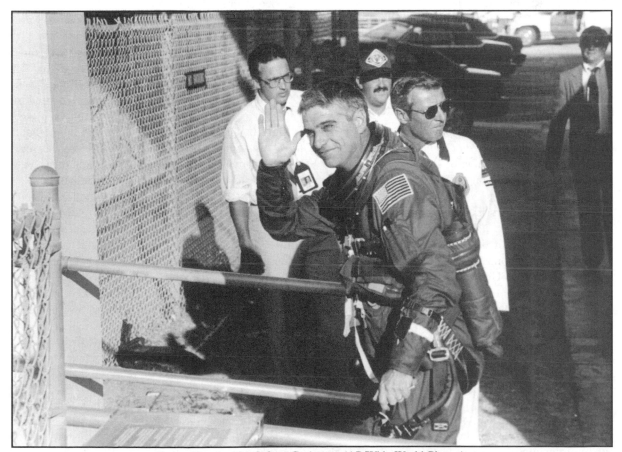

Space Shuttle pilot Sidney Gutierrez. (AP/Wide World Photos)

Avionics Integration Laboratory and as a pilot on the crew of the STS-40 Spacelab Life Sciences (SLS-1) craft on a nine-day mission launched on June 5, 1991. Gutierrez also served as commander of the STS-59 Space Radar Laboratory (SL-1) in April, 1994.

Adriana C. Ocampo worked as a planetary geologist on NASA's mission projects to Jupiter and Mars. She was born in Baranquilla, Colombia, and grew up in Argentina. After settling with her family in California, she studied aerospace engineering and geology. She eventually went to work for the Jet Propulsion Laboratory.

Scientific and Technological Organizations. Latinos in the areas of science, technology, and medicine are often involved in professional organizations concerned with scientific advancement and development. They belong to inclusive organizations as well as those that specifically target participation of Latinos in the sciences. Two important Latino organizations are the SOCIETY OF HISPANIC PROFESSIONAL ENGINEERS and the Society for the Advancement of Chicanos and Native Americans.   —*Rafael Chabrán*

SUGGESTED READINGS:

• Cohen, I. Bernard. "The New World as Source of Science for Europe." In *Actes du IXe Congrés International d'Histoire des Sciences.* Madrid: Asociacion Para la Historia de la Ciencia Española, 1960. One of the first and most important articles on the subject. An excellent introduction to the topic of science in the New World.

• Engstrand, Iris H. W. *Spanish Scientists in the New World: The Eighteenth Century Expeditions.* Seattle: University of Washington Press, 1981. A study of the Malaspina expedition (1789-1794) and the Royal Scientific Expedition to New Spain (1785-1803).

• Glick, Thomas F. "Science in Latin America." In *The Cambridge Encyclopedia of Latin America and the Caribbean*, edited by Simon Collier, Harold Blakemore, and Thomas E. Skidmore. Cambridge, England: Cambridge University Press, 1985. A brief panoramic survey of science in Latin America. The best overview in English, by one of the few U.S. historians of Spanish and Latin American science.

• Kanellos, N. "Science." In *The Hispanic-American Almanac*, edited by Nicolás Kanellos. Detroit: Gale Research, 1993. This article contains a short essay on the contributions of Latinos, with selected biographies.

• Kidwell, Clara Sue. "Native Knowledge in the Americas." *Osiris* 1 (1985): 209-228. An excellent study of the contributions of Native Americans to the
areas of archaeoastronomy, ethnobotany, agriculture, and technology. Discusses the problems and issues in this type of research.

• Stresser-Péan, G. "Science in Pre-Columbian America." In *Ancient and Medieval Science.* Vol. 1 in *History of Science*, edited by Rene Taton. Translated by A. J. Pomerans. London: Basic Books, 1963. A general outline of science in the Americas before the coming of the Spanish.

• Trabulse, Elias. *Historia de la Ciencia en Mexico.* 5 vols. Mexico: Conacyt, Fondo de la Cultura Economica, 1983-1989. The best overall treatment of the history of science in Mexico. It is both a study and an anthology, with valuable bibliographic information and excellent illustrations.

Sculpture and sculptors: Ancient American artists used stone and clay to produce architectural, figural, and functional sculpture. Painted wood sculpture of the colonial period was largely religious in nature and dependent upon Spanish models. Twentieth century Latino sculptors developed individual styles that often alluded to earlier forms and themes.

Pre-Hispanic Sculpture. Carved and modeled works from ancient cultures, ranging from the early Olmec to the later Aztec, are among the world's great sculptures, technically adept and formally expressive. In both Mesoamerica (Mexico and Central America) and the Andean region of South America, stone was used for figurative and decorative architectural reliefs, as well as for human and animal images carved in the round. Clay was employed for vessels, figurines, and some kinds of architectural decoration. Jade and other semiprecious stones were also used for sculptures.

Tools were simple, of stone or bone, with metal tools appearing very late in this period. Many diverse artistic forms and styles can be found in ancient sculptures, most of which combined functional purpose with religious significance. Although the degree of realism varied by culture and epoch, almost all sculpture showed awareness of the natural world. That knowledge was often blended with tendencies toward abstraction to create works at once recognizable and symbolic. Artists, who were respected members of their cultures, used traditional forms and styles; the notion of individual artistic expression had no place in ancient American art. Communication among pre-Hispanic cultures created a network of stylistic and technical influences traceable in surviving works.

Possibly the earliest known sculpture is a bone carved into an animal head, circa 10,000 B.C.E., found

Giant ancient sculptures near Tula, Mexico. (Diane C. Lyell)

near Mexico City. Between about 1200 and 400 B.C.E., Olmec sculptors made a series of giant heads, recognizably human and yet clearly abstracted, as well as highly realistic figures of athletes and stylized jade reliefs. The south pyramid at TEOTIHUACÁN, the great ceremonial and urban center north of Mexico City, built before 300 C.E., features elaborate friezes, with protruding heads of feather-serpents alternating with stylized representations of Tlaloc, the rain god. Also from Teotihuacán are a colossal basalt figure of a deity, stone vessels in the form of jaguars, stone and clay funerary masks, and columns covered with relief carvings.

The line between sculpture and other media is often unclear. Craft objects can be considered sculpture, and much painted pottery takes the form of sculpture. Small clay pieces in the forms of animals, birds, and people were made throughout Mesoamerica from earliest times to the Spanish Conquest. The most impressive were in western Mexico, first at Chupícuaro, then in cultures of Colima, Guerrero, Jalisco, and Nayarit. The Zapotec center of Monte Albán, near Oaxaca, has yielded large urns decorated with rolled clay images of deities. There is some evidence that late versions of these were mass-produced.

The Maya produced sophisticated sculpture, stone stelae, ruler portraits with glyphs giving names and dates, and possibly the first *chac mool* figures, which may represent sacrificial victims and have influenced modern artists. Elaborate ceremonial ball-game markers, *hachas*, *palmas*, and yokes, have been found at Mayan and Veracruz sites.

Aztec sculpture is rich in images from nature and in representations of deities. Many important pieces survive, including the great stone statue of the goddess Coatlicue found in the main plaza of Mexico City, the calendar stone found near the main temple enclosure at TENOCHTITLÁN in 1502, and highly realistic representations of snakes, squash, and shells.

In the Andes, the Moche created ceramic vessels that also functioned as portrait sculpture. Nasca artisans made pottery, ranging from abstract to figural, and animal masks of supernatural beings. Incan sculpture is largely confined to the portable arts, using precious and semiprecious metals in simple, yet elegant, designs.

Ancient American sculpture can be found in most major museums of the world. The most comprehensive collection is that of the National Museum of Anthropology in Mexico City. Modern and contemporary artists in different media and cultures have been inspired by the power and mastery of pre-Hispanic sculpture. British sculptor Henry Moore did a series influenced by the *chac mool*, and Coatlicue appears as a kind of machine in Diego RIVERA's frescoes in Detroit, Michigan.

Colonial Sculpture. After the Spanish conquests of the early sixteenth century, sculpture remained a key medium for artists, particularly those working for the Roman Catholic church. Churches commissioned crucifixes; sculptures of saints, angels, and other religious figures; and decorative carvings. Religious sculpture tended to be realistic in appearance, with generalized, idealized features. Sculptures designed for interiors were of painted wood, often elaborately decorated and gilded with a technique known as *estofado*. *Estofadores* worked with sculptors called *santeros* or *bulteros*.

Processional sculptures and those designed for altars were often worked very simply, with only heads and hands carved, and bodies dressed in clothing. Sculpture for church façades was usually of stone. In some parts of Latin America, figures, such as that of the crucified Christ, were made of *caña de maíz*, a corn paste. These sculptures were painted, resulting in a light and inexpensive, yet highly realistic, image. Sculptors joined forces with painters to produce enormous altarpieces, known as RETABLOS.

Sculptures imported from Spain, especially from Andalusia, served early native carvers as models, as did European prints. In some cases, Spanish sculptors came to the Americas to work and to train others. Many native artisans, already expert in carving, were retrained to create statues of Christian saints and martyrs. Stone atrial crosses bearing the face of Christ, dating from about the time of the Conquest, show both indigenous and Spanish stylistic and technical traits.

Most colonial sculpture followed European styles, from Renaissance to Baroque, rococo, and neoclassical. Works are often dramatic and expressive by European standards. Technical achievements varied according to place and artists' training. Artists in larger cities tended to conform to European standards more than did artists in the provinces.

A small number of colonial sculptors are known by name, but most were anonymous. Paralleling conditions in Europe, most Latin American artists in the colonial era worked on commission; that is, works were made to order for specific patrons, either religious or secular. By the eighteenth century, artists began to rely more upon a free market. Between the sixteenth and nineteenth centuries, the era from the

A sculptor at work. (Smithsonian Institution)

Spanish Conquest to Latin American independence movements, sculpture shifted gradually from reliance on European forms and styles to the assertion of indigenous and individual styles, often in intriguing combinations. The far reaches of the Spanish Empire, such as Guatemala or what is now the southwestern United States, developed regional, local, and individual styles that can be used to identify provenance. In some cases, local imagery is used as subject matter. José Rafael ARAGÓN, a nineteenth century New Mexican *santero*, was responsible for a large number of highly individualized works and for the training of at least one follower, known as the Santo Niño Santero. Sometimes technical variations characterize the art of a region. Guatemalan sculptors, for example, employed silver leaf, rather than gold, under paint.

Modern and Contemporary Sculpture. The modern and contemporary periods are best known for painting, but sculpture continued to be a major force throughout Latin America. Many sculptors studied in Europe and produced work linked stylistically to the major movements of European modernism. National art traditions from the ancient and colonial past inspired many; often indigenous imagery and modernist forms are combined.

Maria Martins (1900-1973), a Brazilian, was associated with the international surrealist movement. The socialist-realist sculpture of Octavio Medellín (b. 1907), who left Mexico for Texas in 1920, relied on ancient American art and Mexican history for its style and subjects. Sculptors such as Alicia Peñalba (b. 1918), an Argentinean living in Paris, and Edgar Negret (b. 1920) and Eduardo Ramírez Villamizar (b. 1923), both Colombians, produced work reflecting awareness of avant-garde European movements such as constructivism and geometric abstraction. Venezuelan Jesús Rafael Soto (b. 1923) was a kinetic sculptor. Raul Valdivieso (b. 1931), from Chile, worked in London, Paris, and the United States before settling in Spain. His large cast bronzes were abstractions of natural forms.

Internationally, the best-known Latino sculptures were the balloon-like creatures of Colombian Fernando BOTERO (b. 1932), exhibited on the Champs-Elysées in Paris in 1993 and on New York's Park Avenue the following year, and the enigmatic figural constructions of Venezuelan Marisol Escobar (b. 1930), known by her first name alone. Both Botero and Marisol evoked the forms of pre-Hispanic art in contemporary fashion.

In the United States, sculptors of Latino origin worked in a variety of styles. Some, like Luis TAPIA (b. 1950), from Santa Fe, New Mexico, combined woodcarving with painting to produce RETABLO-like constructions reflecting a Spanish colonial artistic heritage. Félix A. López (b. 1942) carved modern BULTOS that placed him in the tradition of the colonial *santeros*. Pedro PEREZ (b. 1951), a Cuban who moved to New York, employed a modern vocabulary and materials to create glittering sculptures that evoked colonial gilded sculpture.

Los Angeles artist Gilbert LUJÁN (b. 1940), known as "Magu," made small, humorous constructions on Latino themes. Luis Alfonso JIMÉNEZ, Jr., (b. 1940) employed a realistic style and machine-age technology (fiberglass and epoxy) to make larger-than-life-sized sculptures critiquing racial stereotypes in general and the Chicano experience along the Mexican-United States border in particular. Robert Graham (b. 1938) was born in Mexico City and moved to Los Angeles. His life-sized, classical nude figures of men and women, often designed for public places, are well known and are often perceived as deriving in part from the public art tradition of modern Mexico. He was the official sculptor for the Los Angeles Olympics in 1984. Californian Manuel Neri (b. 1930) made plaster casts of human torsos, which he then painted and altered to create universal statements about human emotions and histories.

Pure abstraction was the rule in the granite monoliths of Texan Jesús Bautista MOROLES (b. 1950), at once ancient and modern in their power, simplicity, and materials, and reminiscent of pre-Hispanic ensembles.

Some sculptors blurred the boundary between art and craft, as pre-Hispanic and colonial artists did; others employed age-old techniques in their work, either to reproduce earlier forms or to comment upon them. Felipe Archuleta (b. 1910), a self-taught artist from Tesuque, New Mexico, used traditional methods of the *santeros* to produce a new kind of sculpture, large animals made of wood and other materials. His works combined colonial carving with the ancient American reverence for nature. Carmen LOMAS GARZA (b. 1948), from Texas, created sculptural installations in the form of folk-style altars, or *ofrendas*, reminiscent of Hispanic traditions for Day of the Dead (DÍA DE LOS MUERTOS), also including images that go back to ancient times. —*Susan Benforado Bakewell*

SUGGESTED READINGS:

• Beardsley, John, and Jane Livingston, with essay by Octavio Paz. *Hispanic Art in the United States: Thirty Contemporary Painters and Sculptors.* New

Modern sculptors employ traditional themes and images, using both established and innovative materials and methods. (Ruben G. Mendoza)

York: Abbeville Press, 1987. Museum exhibition catalog surveying Latino art in the United States since about 1950. Profusely illustrated. Good general bibliography, as well as bibliographies and biographies for individual artists.

• Cancel, Luis, et al. *The Latin-American Spirit: Art and Artists in the United States, 1920-1970.* New York: Harry N. Abrams, 1988. Museum exhibition catalog consisting of seven well-illustrated essays on aspects of Latin-American art in the United States, biographies of artists, notes, and an excellent bibliography.

• Castedo, Leopoldo. *A History of Latin American Art and Architecture from Pre-Columbian Times to the Present.* New York: Praeger, 1969. Introductory survey of Latin American art in all media, from earliest times to the mid-twentieth century. Illustrated with black-and-white photographs. Good general bibliography.

• Findlay, James A. *Modern Latin American Art: A Bibliography.* Westport, Conn.: Greenwood Press, 1983. A comprehensive, general bibliography covering late nineteenth and twentieth century art, arranged by country and then by medium. Sources on individual artists are not included.

• Kubler, George. *The Art and Architecture of Ancient America: The Mexican, Maya, and Andean Peoples.* Harmondsworth, Middlesex, England: Penguin Books, 1990. Development of ancient American art in Mexico and Central and South America, from earliest times through the Aztecs. Well illustrated; has maps, charts, notes, and bibliography.

• *Mexico: Splendors of Thirty Centuries.* New York: Bulfinch Press, 1990. Exhibition catalog documenting Mexican art from the sixth century B.C.E. to the twentieth century. Essays by experts, bibliography, and many color illustrations.

• Pierce, Donna, and Gabrielle Palmer. *Cambios: The Spirit of Transformation in Spanish Colonial Art.* Santa Barbara: University of New Mexico Press, 1992. Introduction to Spanish colonial sculpture throughout Latin America and the southwestern United States. Discusses development of new, regional traditions. Maps, bibliography, and many color illustrations.

Secada, Jon (Juan Secada; b. 1964, Cuba): Singer and composer. Secada's debut album *Secada* won the Grammy Award for best Latin pop album in February, 1993. The recording, which had sold more than six million copies worldwide by 1994, contains the popular song "Otro Día Mas Sin Verte" (also recorded in English as "Another Day Without You").

Secada grew up in Cuba but at the age of eight immigrated to Miami, Florida, leaving his parents and friends behind. He moved to the Spanish-speaking community of Hialeah and lived with some distant relatives. He was graduated from the University of Miami and became a music teacher before joining the chorus of Gloria ESTEFAN's famous group MIAMI SOUND MACHINE.

Secada's successful collaboration with Estefan generated the tunes "Coming Out of the Dark" and "Can't Forget You." With his interpretation of "Siempre hay algo," Secada attracted attention. He is known as a crooner with the ability to belt out songs like a soul singer and a Latin American respect for traditional long-lined melody.

Segovia, Josefa (?—July 5, 1851, Downieville, Calif.): Historical figure. Of Mexican origin, Josefa Segovia lived in Downieville with a man named José and possibly worked in a local saloon. Contemporaries described her as an attractive woman, and she probably had to resist frequent unwelcome advances. No evidence suggests that she was a prostitute.

On the night of July 4, 1851, a drunk miner named Fred Cannon either fell against or kicked the door of Segovia's cabin. Testimony varies as to whether Cannon then broke in on her or left immediately. José approached Cannon requesting payment for the broken door early the next morning. Cannon refused, and an argument ensued. Segovia joined the debate, and her initial exchanges with Cannon were good natured. When Cannon called her a whore, Segovia became enraged and stabbed the miner through the heart. Cannon died instantly.

Segovia was brought to trial immediately. The jury, perhaps influenced by the crowd outside the courthouse, which grew in size and became increasingly vociferous as the day wore on, condemned her to death by hanging. Segovia's story illustrates the low regard and prejudice that Americans in California held toward dark-skinned, Spanish-speaking women.

Segregation, desegregation, and integration: Mexican Americans and other Latinos in the United States have faced DISCRIMINATION in schooling, housing, and the use of public facilities, particularly in the border states in which they have tended to concentrate. Unlike the discrimination experienced by African Americans in the South before the Civil Rights movement, segregation of Latinos was often enforced by custom rather than law. Some social scientists in the late twentieth century have argued that discrimination against Latinos has not been so severe as to require their protection under AFFIRMATIVE ACTION laws.

Educational Segregation in the Southwest. Neither Mexican American nor Puerto Rican children were deliberately segregated by public authorities in the schools of the Midwest and Northeast. In Texas, Arizona, and Southern California, however, Mexican American children were segregated from the 1920's to the 1950's. Their segregation from English-speaking non-Hispanic white schoolchildren was enforced not through state law but through the decisions of local school boards dominated by non-Hispanics. Segregation of black children from white children in the public schools, by contrast, was the law throughout Texas until the Supreme Court's 1954 decision in *BROWN V. BOARD OF EDUCATION.* Mexican American children attending the same schools as non-Hispanic children often were assigned to a separate Mexican room; because of language difficulties, they might be held back several grades or even classified as retarded. Those relatively few Mexican American children who got to high school were often pressured into choosing a vocational rather than a college preparatory curriculum. Separate meant inferior: School facilities for Mexican American children were often of lower quality than those for whites, and teachers were often less experienced.

Local public school authorities pointed to the use of the Spanish language by Mexican American schoolchildren as a reason for separating them from non-Hispanic children, but Mexican American children who could speak English were also segregated. Many Mexican American children came from migrant farmworker families, and it was argued that they needed segregated schooling to catch up with white children academically. Another reason for segregation, not often voiced publicly by administrators, was the widespread prejudice among non-Hispanic parents against Mexicans.

The Struggle Against School Segregation. Lawyers representing the LEAGUE OF UNITED LATIN AMERICAN CITIZENS (LULAC), founded in Texas in 1929, argued that Mexican American schoolchildren were white and that segregating them violated both Texas and federal law. In the case of *Salvatierra v. Independent School District* (1930), the appeals court disapproved of the segregation of Mexican children in general terms but permitted the school in question (in Del Rio, Texas) to continue segregating them. In *DELGADO V. BASTROP INDEPENDENT SCHOOL DISTRICT* (1948), the segregation of Mexican schoolchildren in Texas was outlawed; local school authorities, however, dragged their feet in enforcing the court order. In *Hernandez v. Driscoll* (1957), the ban on segregation of Mexican schoolchildren in Texas was reaffirmed.

Integrated schools were a rarity in much of the United States before the Supreme Court's landmark Brown v. Board of Education *ruling.* (James Shaffer)

In Lemon Grove, California, Mexican immigrant parents, aided by the Mexican consulate, hired non-Hispanic lawyers to fight against school segregation. Although the Lemon Grove parents won a favorable ruling in 1931, segregation continued in other school districts in Southern California. In *MÉNDEZ V. WESTMINSTER SCHOOL DISTRICT*, Gonzalo Méndez and other Mexican American parents sued the Westminster school district, in Orange County, California. A federal court decision condemning segregation in 1946 was upheld in 1947.

The court-ordered end of de jure school segregation did not always end de facto school segregation. In 1955, the ALIANZA HISPANO-AMERICANA, a fraternal insurance association, had to sue the school board of El Centro, California, to force it to desegregate. In 1965, Mexican American activists joined forces with black leaders to compel BUSING to accomplish integration in Riverside, California. In El Paso, Texas, busing that began in the 1970's helped integrate Mexican American and white schoolchildren. In the 1980's, however, political scientist Gary Orfield found that Mexican American pupils in San Antonio were still heavily concentrated in predominantly Mexican American schools; he also discerned a trend toward increased segregation of both Mexican American and Puerto Rican pupils from non-Hispanic white pupils throughout the United States. By 1990, a renewed immigrant influx had made the goal of school integration harder to achieve.

In the late 1960's, the school authorities of Houston, Texas, faced with the Supreme Court mandate to end racial segregation in schools, decided to comply by mixing Mexican American and African American schoolchildren, in schools separate from non-Hispanic white schoolchildren. The authorities argued that Mexicans were white, so black-white integration had been accomplished. THE MEXICAN AMERICAN LEGAL DEFENSE AND EDUCATION FUND (MALDEF), created in 1968, fought against such subterfuges. Partly as a result of MALDEF efforts, Houston's integration plan, endorsed by a 1970 appellate court decision (*Ross v. Eckels*), was struck down by the Supreme Court in *Keyes v. Denver School District Number One* (1973). The Supreme Court explicitly labeled Mexican Americans as victims of past discrimination whose children should be integrated with those of non-Hispanic whites. After the mid-1970's, however, MALDEF shifted from fighting for integration to campaigning for BILINGUAL EDUCATION and equalization of school funding.

Residential Segregation. By 1990, there were Hispanic neighborhoods (barrios) in most large American cities: Mexican American in southwestern cities, Puerto Rican in New York City, and both Puerto Rican and Mexican in Chicago. Questions arose whether such neighborhoods were voluntary and temporary communities, like the "Little Italy" neighborhoods of an earlier era, or products of involuntary segregation, like the African American urban ghettos.

For years, small towns in southern and western Texas had distinct white and Mexican sections, with the Mexican section much less well provided with sewer systems and other services. Throughout the first half of the twentieth century, non-Hispanic white homeowners, landlords, and real estate agents often refused to sell or rent to Mexican Americans. In some neighborhoods of Los Angeles, California, and San Antonio, Texas, restrictive covenants, which were not outlawed by the Supreme Court until 1948, legally barred homeowners from selling to Mexican Americans. In 1949, Ignacio LÓPEZ, editor of the San Gabriel Valley newspaper *El Espectador*, denounced white real estate developers in Upland, California, for refusing to sell a home in the Campus Garden Tract to a Mexican American World War II veteran. The developers responded by opening an adjacent tract to Mexican Americans. As late as 1955, a real estate board in Los Angeles County expelled members for selling to Mexican Americans. In the 1920's, Mexican immigrants also faced discrimination in housing in midwestern industrial cities, as did Puerto Ricans arriving in the Chicago and New York City areas in the 1940's and 1950's.

Despite such discriminatory practices, the walls of the barrio were easier to scale than were those of the black ghetto. In the 1960's, sociologists William Kornblum and Gerald Suttles found that Chicago whites were more accepting of Mexican Americans as neighbors than of African Americans. A study by social scientists Joan Moore and Frank Mittelbach, based on data from the 1960 census, showed that Mexican Americans in thirty-five southwestern cities, although highly concentrated, were less residentially segregated from whites than were blacks. Douglas Massey and Nancy Denton, looking at census data for cities across the United States in the 1970's and 1980's, found the same patterns. Puerto Ricans on the mainland had levels of segregation that were closer to those of African Americans. This was attributed to the greater degree of African ancestry among Puerto Ricans. Unlike African Americans, Massey and Denton argued, Mexican Americans could move into white neighborhoods and

Discriminatory practices have often relegated Latinos to neighborhoods with substandard housing and services. (David Bacon)

blend into them as their education and income levels increased.

Housing discrimination against Mexican Americans lessened over time, although at varying rates in different parts of the country. A Mexican American could often escape discrimination by claiming to be Italian, Spanish, or Native American. This ploy was also used by some Puerto Ricans. The wealthier, the lighter-complexioned, and the more fluent in English an individual Latino renter or home buyer was, the easier it became to "pass" as non-Hispanic, especially in large cities. Furthermore, adaptation to American ways could make second- and third-generation Latinos seem less like members of a racial minority and more like part of the mainstream culture.

Segregation in Public Accommodations. Latinos have encountered discrimination in admission to restaurants, theaters, swimming pools, and other facilities, similar to the discrimination that African Americans have faced. In some cases, Latinos were excluded entirely; in other cases their participation was restricted, such as being allowed to use public swimming pools only at certain hours or being allowed to sit only

in a certain part of a motion picture theater. Such discrimination was commonplace in South Texas and Southern California, and it cropped up occasionally in the 1920's in some midwestern cities.

From the 1890's until the 1960's, segregation of blacks from whites in public accommodations in the South was often a matter of both law and custom; discrimination against Mexican Americans in public accommodations was solely a matter of custom. Historian David Montejano showed that in South Texas, the severity of such discrimination varied from one county to the next. It was most rigorous in counties where non-Hispanic truck farmers employed Mexican Americans as seasonal farm laborers; it was least strict in such border cities as Laredo, where a Mexican American upper class existed.

In the late 1930's and the 1940's, Ignacio LÓPEZ used his newspaper, *El Espectador*, to denounce public swimming pools and motion picture theaters that excluded Mexicans in Southern California. Although the boycotting and public pressure urged by López sometimes won changes, a lawsuit was necessary in one case. By the mid-1960's, discrimination against Mexican Americans at public accommodations was a thing of the past in the Los Angeles area. In Arizona, in the early 1950's, the ALIANZA HISPANO-AMERICANA campaigned against public swimming pools that barred Mexicans; such pressure brought about change. In Texas, the AMERICAN G.I. FORUM and LULAC led the fight in the late 1940's. As late as 1970, however, the bowling alley in Ozona, Texas, still excluded Mexican Americans. By the mid-1980's, with the growth of Mexican American political power in Texas, such discrimination had faded away.

Segregation: A Useful Concept? The term "segregation" was used in the 1980's to describe the Mexican American experience by Mexican American historians and by representatives of some Mexican American advocacy organizations. In doing so, they implicitly compared Mexican Americans to African Americans. Many who questioned the application of the term to Mexican Americans emphasized the greater urgency of African American ghetto problems. Doubts remained as to whether Hispanics should be a protected class under AFFIRMATIVE ACTION. Latinos were perceived as having more in common with European immigrants than with African Americans. The truth probably lies in the middle: Mexican Americans and other non-black Hispanics historically have faced more segregation than have European immigrants but less than black people.   —*Paul D. Mageli*

SUGGESTED READINGS:

• Garcia, Mario D. *Mexican Americans: Leadership, Ideology, and Identity, 1930-1960.* New Haven, Conn.: Yale University Press, 1989. Highly informative on the struggles against segregation waged by newspaper editor Ignacio López and by LULAC. Because of the focus on generational change, Garcia does not cover the late 1960's and 1970's. Photographs, endnotes, and index.

• Glick, Lawrence B. "The Right to Equal Opportunity." In *La Raza: Forgotten Americans*, edited by Julian Samora. Notre Dame, Ind.: University of Notre Dame Press, 1966. One of the few easily accessible sources on housing discrimination against Mexican Americans in southwestern cities (the Midwest is ignored). Stresses the effect of color differences within the group on Anglo realtors' willingness to discriminate.

•Gonzalez, Gilbert G. "The Rise and Fall of De Jure Segregation in the Southwest." In *Chicano Education in the Era of Segregation*. Philadelphia: Balch Institute Press, 1990. Offers the most complete account of the *Méndez v. Westminster School District* case, emphasiz-

ing the role played by parents. Well written and informative.

• Massey, Douglas, and Nancy Denton. *American Apartheid: Segregation and the Making of the Underclass.* Cambridge, Mass.: Harvard University Press, 1993. The authors, who focus on African Americans, argue that Mexican Americans are less segregated from non-Hispanic whites than are black people, but that Puerto Ricans are more segregated from non-Hispanic whites than are Mexican Americans. A quantitative sociological snapshot, with little historical background on Hispanic groups.

• Montejano, David. *Anglos and Mexicans in the Making of Texas, 1836-1986.* Austin: University of Texas Press, 1987. Montejano finds economic reasons for both the rise of segregation and its decline. The struggle against segregation is not treated in depth. Especially informative on concepts of race as applied by Anglos to Mexicans. A pioneering work of scholarship.

•San Miguel, Guadalupe, Jr. *"Let All of Them Take Heed": Mexican Americans and the Campaign for Educational Equality in Texas, 1910-1981.* Austin: University of Texas Press, 1987. The most complete history of the struggle against school segregation in Texas. Shows how the activists' goal shifted in the 1970's from integration to bilingual education. Long on facts; short on analysis.

• Skerry, Peter. *Mexican Americans: The Ambivalent Minority.* New York: Free Press, 1993. Skerry, an expert on ethnic politics, denies the relevance of the racial minority model. Based on secondary sources and on field research (including interviews with those who remember the discrimination of the 1940's) in San Antonio and Los Angeles. The endnotes are a mine of sources for further reading.

Segura, Francisco "Pancho" (b. June 20, 1921, Guayaquil, Ecuador): Tennis player. Born into a poor family of nine children, Segura learned to play tennis after his father became caretaker of a local club. Only five feet, six inches tall and left bowlegged from a serious case of rickets, Segura developed a powerful two-handed stroke to make up for his small size. After accepting a scholarship to the University of Miami, he won three consecutive National Collegiate Athletic Association singles titles from 1943 to 1945.

In 1946, Segura turned professional, soon becoming a fixture on the circuit, winning national professional singles titles in 1950, 1951, and 1952 and doubles titles in 1948, 1954, 1955, and 1958. Segura later

Pancho Segura, a leading tennis star of the 1940's and 1950's. (AP/Wide World Photos)

served as the resident professional at the Beverly Hills Tennis Club and as the tennis director at the LaCosta Resort in Carlsbad, California. In 1984, he was inducted into the International Tennis Hall of Fame.

Seis: Folk music and dance indigenous to Puerto Rico. The *seis* is highly syncopated. Six couples facing each other perform *zapateado* steps, creating intricate figures and exchanging lines and partners. The *seis* originated from ancient rituals of the Catholic church during the Feast of Corpus Christi. A secular version developed in the early 1900's. It was faster and livelier, and it became known as *sangre vida* (lively blood). Different forms developed in many regions. The *seis* is performed in different moods, such as the *seis enojao* (angry seis) and *seis enamorao* (seis in love). The *seis chorreao* is in a faster tempo and is danced until the dancers are exhausted.

Select Commission on Immigration and Refugee Policy (1977): Congressional commission. After receiving a report from President Jimmy Carter on the recommendations of his White House Conference on Hispanic Affairs, Congress created a select commission to study the status of "illegal aliens" in the United States. In the commissioner's final report, issued in July of 1981, the investigators said that "immigration policy was out of control." It was estimated that more than twelve million people were in the country illegally. The commission called for a new program that would allow for fifty-thousand temporary workers per year to be admitted into the country. These workers would be allowed to work for anyone but would not be allowed to bring their families with them. They would also be ineligible for most social welfare programs, even though their employers would be required to pay Social Security and payroll taxes. These latter provisions would reduce the economic incentive for businesses to hire foreign workers. The new program was never put into effect. The problem of UNAUTHORIZED WORKERS and migrants was not dealt with to any large degree by Congress until passage of the IMMIGRATION REFORM AND CONTROL ACT OF 1986.

Selective Service Act of 1917: Military draft legislation. This act contained a provision to make Mexican citizens who lived in the United States register with local draft boards during World War I, even though they were not eligible to be drafted. Because most Mexican-born individuals residing in the United States were afraid that they might be drafted anyway, many chose not to register. Although it was not intended to be overtly discriminatory, the legislation seemed to violate the rights of Mexican nationals in the United States. Mexicans had been encouraged to seek U.S. agricultural jobs vacated in the wake of limits placed on the entry of Chinese laborers by restrictive U.S. immigration laws.

Selena (Selena Quintanilla Perez; Apr. 16, 1971, Lake Jackson, Tex.—Mar. 31, 1995, Corpus Christi, Tex.): Singer. At the time of her murder, Selena was considered by many to be the outstanding performer of Tejano music. Police arrested Yolanda Saldivar, a former president of Selena's fan club, for the shooting murder. Saldivar surrendered to police after spending eight hours barricaded in her truck, holding a gun to her head, at the motel where the shooting occurred. She recently had worked at the Quintanilla family's clothing boutique in Corpus Christi. The family had intended to confront Saldivar about discrepancies in accounting at the boutique, and this confrontation was believed to have motivated the murder.

Selena began her music career singing with her father's band. She won a 1994 Grammy for *Selena Live* in the category of best Mexican American album, and at the TEJANO MUSIC AWARDS she claimed honors for female entertainer of the year, female vocalist of the year, best record of the year, and best album. She had planned soon to release her first English-language album. Her single "Amor Prohibido" ("Forbidden Love") had sold 400,000 copies in the United States.

Selena was known as "the Mexican Madonna" because of her suggestive clothing and stage presence. Unlike Madonna, however, Selena promoted family values. She was married to a musician in her band, Selena y los Dinos.

Sephardim (Spanish Jews): Religious group. The Spanish Inquisition began in 1480 and included a campaign to eradicate the Jewish faith from Spain. In 1492, members of the Jewish faith were forced to convert to Catholicism or else be expelled from Spain. The community of Jewish people who were expelled was called Sephardim. Its members first took refuge in Portugal, then in Morocco and Italy, then later in the Balkans.

The name Sephardim has also been applied to the descendants of the Spanish Jews expelled from Spain in 1492. The name is also used to distinguish this group from Ashkenazim, Jews who settled in northern Europe. The Sephardic heritage was derived from the Babylonian diaspora; the Ashkenazic heritage was derived from Palestinian antecedents. The name Sephardim probably refers to Sardis, the capital of Lydia, an island in Asia Minor that probably had a Jewish colony.

After being exiled from Spain, the Sephardim people settled in various places but always preserved their own language, LADINO, a combination of Spanish and Hebrew. The Sephardic cultural heritage is highly prized by the group and includes rituals, customs, and literature.

The city of Salonika in Macedonia was an important center of Sephardic culture up to World War II, when German forces destroyed the city. The Netherlands was another Sephardic cultural center.

Early Jewish immigrants to the United States were predominantly Sephardic. About 20 percent of all Jewish people in the world were Sephardic in the 1990's. Chief among the institutions in the United States that promote and preserve the Sephardic heritage is the Sephardic Jewish Brotherhood of America in New York, New York.

Serna v. Portales (decided July 17, 1974): Litigation concerning BILINGUAL EDUCATION. In this case, cited as 499 F. 2d 1147, a federal appeals court ruled that a New Mexico school system that provided no bilingual education for its sizable Latino population was in violation of the CIVIL RIGHTS ACT OF 1964.

Serna v. Portales was a class action suit brought by the parents of Spanish-surnamed students in a New Mexico school system. These families pointed out that 34 percent of elementary school students in the Portales municipal school system had Spanish surnames; at one of the four elementary schools, the proportion was 86 percent. Despite the large numbers of Latino students, the plaintiffs alleged that the Portales school system made no effort to help these students with their special needs.

The New Mexico state constitution stipulated that public schools must teach in English. The Portales school administration, however, made no effort to help Latino students reach a level of English proficiency that would allow them to succeed in the classroom. Plaintiffs also complained of other actions and inactions of the Portales school system, including the failure to hire Spanish-surnamed teachers, administrators, or secretaries; and failure to include in the curriculum the contributions of persons of Spanish descent to the history of New Mexico and the United States.

In arguments before a U.S. district court, the Latino families argued that the Portales school system was in violation of the Civil Rights Act of 1964, which forbids discrimination based on national origin by any program receiving federal funds. The families also argued that the school system was violating their rights under the FOURTEENTH AMENDMENT, which promises equal protection under the law for all citizens. The Latino families won their case in the lower federal court, with the judge agreeing that the school system was violating both the Civil Rights Act of 1964 and the Fourteenth Amendment.

The court devised a plan that would allow the Portales municipal school system to come into compliance with federal law. Meanwhile, the school district carried an appeal to the Tenth Circuit Court of Appeals.

The appeals court agreed with the lower court, upholding both its decision and its specific plan for remedying the problems in Portales. On one question, the Circuit Court of Appeals retreated slightly from the district court decision. The appeals court based its decision solely on the Civil Rights Act of 1964 and did not consider constitutional grounds in ruling against the Portales school district. The judges noted that the U.S. Supreme Court had recently ruled in favor of Chinese immigrant children in California, in the 1974 case of *LAU V. NICHOLS* (414 U.S. 563). The *Lau* case was essentially similar to *Serna*, and the U.S. Supreme Court had based its decision solely on the Civil Rights Act.

The school system of Portales was forced to carry out the court's plan, which included curricular changes and the hiring of bilingual teachers. Together with the *Lau* decision, the *Serna* case put all school districts on notice that they must consider the needs of non-English-speaking communities. One limitation in the *Serna* decision was the court's insistence that the decision applied only to districts with "a substantial group" of non-English-speaking students.

Serra, Junípero (Nov. 24, 1713, Petra, Majorca, Spain—Aug. 28, 1784, Carmel, Calif.): Missionary. Serra, baptized as Miguel José, entered the Franciscan order when he was sixteen years old. He was ordained in 1738 and taught at Lullian University in Majorca for twelve years. In 1749, he left for the New World, to join the San Fernando missionary college in Mexico. Serra became famous as a missionary to Mexican Indians, making long trips through the wilderness despite being lame. Until 1758, Serra served in the Sierra Gorda missions. From 1758 to 1767, his efforts shifted to southern Mexico.

Father Junípero Serra. (Library of Congress)

In 1767, Serra became the superior of Lower California's Franciscan missions. In 1769, he and Gaspar de PORTOLÁ founded Mission San Diego, the first mission in ALTA CALIFORNIA. Serra founded eight more missions over the next three years, strengthening Spanish control of this portion of Mexico. The missions were located in Carmel, San Antonio, San Buenaventura, San Francisco, San Juan Capistrano, San Gabriel, San Luis Obispo, and Santa Clara. Serra's proponents view him as a great benefactor of the Indians who introduced them to Mexican agricultural practices. In 1988, Serra was beatified for his work. Some Indian tribes of California claim that he actually enslaved their ancestors.

Serra, Richard (b. Nov. 2, 1939, San Francisco, Calif.): Sculptor. Serra studied at the University of California at Berkeley and at Santa Barbara. He earned an M.F.A. at Yale University.

Serra works with various "unorthodox" materials, as in his 1967 work with vulcanized rubber. He has stacked, leaned, and propped heavy steel and lead sheets against walls or on top of one another, focusing on balance as an artistic goal. Others of his works include a row of burning candles in a wooden rack and tangles of fabric strips hanging from a wall. In 1968, Serra worked with molten lead. He has constructed landscape-scale works such as steel sheets set in earth. He has also made films investigating questions of process and perception in art. Serra is best known for innovations in materials and scale, with an "industrial" aspect.

Although most of Serra's works are too large for indoor display, he has had New York City gallery exhibitions in addition to exhibitions in Bern, Switzerland; Amsterdam, The Netherlands; Rome, Italy; and Cologne, Germany. In 1969, he exhibited at the Whitney Museum in New York City and displayed giant sawed logs at the Pasadena Art Museum in California. In 1971, he submitted to the Whitney Competition a steel ring, 26 feet in diameter, set in pavement in the Bronx, New York.

Serrano, Andrés (b. Aug. 15, 1950, New York, N.Y.): Conceptual artist and photographer. Serrano's 1987 work *Crucifix Submerged in a Jar of Urine* was one of the first to use bodily fluids in abstract work. Serrano, an artist of Cuban heritage, had eighteen solo shows between 1990 and 1993, featuring such works as his 1992 corpse photos with cause of death titles such as *Hacked to Death*, *Death by Fire*, and *Infectious Pneu-*

monia. He works in a still-life mode but employs theatricality to catch popular attention. Serrano is a renegade in the contemporary world, converting the ugly, repugnant, and unusual into works of art.

Serrano v. Priest (1971): Case involving funding of education. In this case, cited as 5 Cal. 3d 584, the California Supreme Court ruled as unconstitutional the state's system of funding public education (*see* SCHOOL FINANCE). Like most states, California had relied upon a system of local property taxes to support local schools; the result was inferior schools in less wealthy school districts. The *Serrano* case offered promise to schools in poorer districts, but the case's importance was largely ended by the U.S. Supreme Court ruling in SAN ANTONIO INDEPENDENT SCHOOL DISTRICT V. RODRÍGUEZ (1973).

In a lower California Court, plaintiffs were led by John Serrano, Jr., the father of a boy enrolled in an EAST LOS ANGELES public school. The plaintiffs argued that California's method of financing elementary and secondary education was contrary to both the state and national constitutions. This system relied heavily on local property taxes to fund local schools. The plaintiffs pointed out that children in poorer districts received an education inferior to that of children in wealthier areas. The lower court held, however, that the plaintiffs had no sound basis for challenging the constitutionality of California's system. On appeal, the California Supreme Court reversed the lower court's ruling and remanded the case for retrial.

The state supreme court ruled 6-1 that the state system of financing public education was indeed contrary to the California and United States constitutions. The court held that the California school funding law must be subjected to strict scrutiny because public education was a fundamental interest of the state and because wealth was a "suspect classification" calling for strict judicial scrutiny. Subjecting the California law to this strict scrutiny, the court ruled that the law failed because it violated the FOURTEENTH AMENDMENT's promise of equal protection under the law for all citizens.

Both locally and in the nation as a whole, advocates for the poor believed they had won an important victory, one that might erase the worst examples of inequality in public education. Because the California Supreme Court made no final judgment in the *Serrano* case, only sending it back to the lower court for retrial, the decision could not be appealed to the U.S. Supreme Court.

Two years after the *Serrano* decision in California, the U.S. Supreme Court ruled in the opposite direction in the similar case of SAN ANTONIO INDEPENDENT SCHOOL DISTRICT V. RODRÍGUEZ. The Court declared that education was not a fundamental constitutional right and that states could have a legitimate reason for funding local schools through local property taxes. Since the *Rodríguez* decision, the *Serrano* case has had little legal importance.

The *Serrano* case encouraged California and certain other states to reexamine their methods of funding public schools. The result has been an easing of some of the worst examples of educational inequality, examples that were based not only on wealth but also on ethnic identity, which correlates strongly with wealth in the United States.

Seven Cities of Cíbola. *See* **Cíbola**

Sheen family: The Sheen family name has been associated with the stage and the motion picture business since the 1950's, when Martin Sheen joined the Off-Off Broadway Living Theater in New York, New York. Martin Sheen's birth name is Ramón Estevez. He was born on August 3, 1940, in Dayton, Ohio. His stage debut was in the role of Ernie in *The Connection* in 1959. He has appeared in numerous major roles. Among the most notable were the lead in Shakespeare's *Hamlet* and *Romeo and Juliet* with the New York Shakespeare Festival (1967 and 1968) and an appearance in *Death of a Salesman* at Circle in the Square in 1975.

Sheen's film debut was in *The Incident* in 1967. His television debut came in the soap opera *As the World Turns* (1967-1968). He has been described by critics as an intense and serious actor and has been compared with screen idol James Dean for his portrayal of an unhappy and restless man rebelling against society in the film *Badlands* (1973). Among Sheen's other films are *Catch-22* (1970), *Apocalypse Now* (1979), *Gandhi* (1982), and the science-fiction thriller *Firestarter* (1984). Sheen also appeared in the television miniseries *Blind Ambition* (1979) and *Kennedy* (1983) and as guest artist in numerous series. He is also a director, producer, and playwright. He won an Emmy for *Babies Having Babies* (1986) and was nominated for Emmy Awards for *The Execution of Private Slovak* (1974) and *The Atlanta Child Murders* (1985).

Sheen is the son of Francisco Estevez and Mary Ann Phelan. In 1961, he married Janet Sheen. The couple had three sons: Emilio, Ramón, and Carlos. Emilio

Estevez, the son of Martin and Janet Sheen, was born on May 12, 1962, in New York, New York. By his mid-twenties, he was one of the film industry's most productive actors. He began acting as a child, in neighborhood and school plays. When he was in second grade, he sent a science-fiction story to the producers of the *Night Gallery* television series. The story was rejected, but he was not discouraged. He wrote and starred in *Echoes of an Era*, a high school play about the Vietnam War. Among his screenplays are *That Was Then . . . This Is Now* (1985), *Wisdom* (1986), and *Clear Intent* (1986).

Estevez made his motion picture debut in *Tex* (1982) and got his first starring role in the film *Repo Man* (1984). To prepare for the character of a young punk in Los Angeles who takes a job repossessing cars, he studied punk rock music and visited clubs as well as going on the job with a real-life repo man. He also starred in *Young Guns* (1988), *The Breakfast Club* (1984), and *St. Elmo's Fire* (1985). Like his father, he has been compared to James Dean. He directed the films *Wisdom* and *Men at Work* (1990), starring in the latter with his brother Charlie Sheen.

Charlie Sheen (born Carlos Estevez, on September 3, 1965, in New York) is the youngest of the Sheen family. He attended the University of Kansas. He is also an actor as well as producer and director of short films. At the age of nine, he made his television debut as an extra with his father in *The Execution of Private Slovak*.

Following his film debut in *Grizzly II* in 1984, he appeared in such films as *Red Dawn* (1984), *Ferris Bueller's Day Off* (1986), *Lucas* (1986), and *Platoon* (1986). In 1987, he had a starring role in *Wall Street*, in which Martin Sheen played his father in a supporting role. He was given the Discovery of the Year Award in 1987 by the Hollywood Women's Press Club. He is the author of *A Peace of My Mind* (1988), a poetry collection.

Sheepherding: The natives of the New World saw their first sheep when the ovines were unloaded from the ships of Christopher Columbus onto the shores of Santo Domingo, Hispaniola, in 1493. Shortly after that, sheep were introduced into Mexico following the Spanish Conquest of 1521. In 1598, Basque explorer Juan de OÑATE introduced the first sheep flocks to the northernmost frontiers of New Spain, the area that later became New Mexico. As Spanish ranches and villages appeared along the Rio Grande, native Indians acquired flocks of sheep, mainly through raids but also

A Mexican American family herding sheep. (AP/Wide World Photos)

through trade. Herding quickly became a major economic asset for southwestern Indians, particularly the Navajo. Blanket weaving became a staple of the society. By 1789, sheepherding was of such importance that the Spanish government controlled the export of ewes from New Mexico to maintain the quality of breeding stock.

In the 1850's, thousands of sheep were herded to California from New Mexico to satisfy the meat-supply demands of the GOLD RUSH. Immigrant Basque shepherds were recruited to work on the burgeoning sheep ranches of California. There they worked as itinerant herders; however, a number of them purchased ranch properties and became successful producers.

In the late 1860's and early 1870's, when gold was discovered in the interior Western states, sheep pro-duction shifted from California to the Great Basin to satisfy demands for meat. Sheep herds of a vast scale were raised in Nevada, Idaho, Oregon, Utah, Colorado, Wyoming, and Montana. In all these states, Basque shepherds participated in the development of sheep enterprises.

Sheepherding in southern South America started shortly after 1547, when Miguel de Urruita, a Basque, introduced sheep into the Argentine *pampas*. The tough native grasses were more suitable for cattle than for sheep; thus, initially, a vigorous cattle industry developed. By the first quarter of the nineteenth century, however, some of the large *estancias* (ranches) were overgrazed, and annual ground covers took root. Sheep grazing could not be practiced, and by the 1830's, in spite of the poor quality of Argentine sheep, 7 percent of Argentina's exports were products from the sheep industry. Initially, Irish immigrant herders dominated all aspects of sheep raising north of Buenos Aires, but by 1840, Basque immigrant shepherds controlled most areas south of Buenos Aires.

Sheep raising in early nineteenth century Argentina was risky. The value of one animal barely equaled that of an egg; it was said that sheep were bought so that their carcasses could be used for furnace fuel. Starting in the 1850's, conditions improved with an unprecedented economic boom that influenced the economic welfare of Argentina well into the twentieth century.

Sheila E. (Sheila Escovedo; b. Dec. 12, 1959, Oakland, Calif.): Drummer and singer. Sheila E. is the daughter of Juanita Escovedo and drummer Peter Escovedo, the son of Mexican immigrants. During the 1960's, her father became famous for his conga drumming with the band Santana. As a toddler, Sheila E. would sit, captivated, listening to her father practice the conga drums. Amazed at what she saw her father doing, she would attempt to duplicate his drumming rhythm.

With the encouragement of her father, Sheila E. began taking violin lessons when she was ten years old. As a teenager, she became proficient at playing keyboards and guitar. In addition to her musical talent, she was also an excellent athlete. She remained committed to playing the drums and as a teenager began playing professionally. In the early 1970's, her father allowed her to join the band in which he played, Azteca. She toured Europe and Asia with the band. In addition to working with Azteca, Sheila E. worked as a studio musician for Herbie Hancock, Lionel Richie, Diana Ross, Marvin Gaye, and others. In 1984, Sheila E. began working for Prince. With Prince's encouragement, she decided to become a solo performer. She released her first solo album, *The Glamorous Life*, in 1984. Sheila E. remained an active performer, releasing the albums *Romance 1600* (1985) and *Sheila E.* (1987).

Sierra, Paul Alberto (b. July 30, 1944, Havana, Cuba): Artist. The son of a lawyer, Sierra attended private school. He planned to be a physician, but he filled his notebooks with drawings. In high school, he studied film and painting. Although his father collected painting books, Sierra received little encouragement or training in the art field.

In 1961, the family immigrated to the United States, living in Miami, Florida, before moving to Chicago, Illinois. Beginning in 1963, Sierra spent three years at the School of Art Institute of Chicago, where Rufino Silva was one of his teachers. Sierra dropped out but kept in contact with Silva. He married a writer, with whom he had a daughter. The couple divorced in 1970. In 1975, he married a writer and management consultant.

Sierra by necessity learned to create his paintings mostly at night. He earned his living in commercial art, working as an advertising layout artist and creative director of a small agency. He spent the first five years of his artistic career in photography and filmmaking, painting little. His second honeymoon, in Puerto Rico, inspired him to use tropical imagery and exotic coloring in his paintings, as in *Cuatro Santos* (1985), an oil on canvas, and *Three Days and Three Nights*. He has painted Latin American countries other than Puerto Rico, but he knows them only through research, not through visits. Sierra has said that he has been inspired by Francis Bacon, Francisco de Goya, Jackson Pollock, and Willem de Kooning.

Sierra, Rubén (b. Dec. 6, 1946, San Antonio, Tex.): Director, playwright, and actor. Sierra attended St. Mary's University in San Antonio and earned a master's degree in directing from the University of Washington. His earliest play was *La Raza Pura: Or, Racial, Racial* (1968), a multimedia satire on racism that was later produced for public television. From 1972 to 1977, Sierra worked with the Teatro de Piojo (Theater of the Louse), a group of students and artists that produced political drama. He also directed, acted, and created traditional *actos* and wrote *Manolo* (1976), one of the first full-length Chicano dramas.

From 1978 through 1992, Sierra served as artistic director of the Seattle Group Theater. His other works include *The Millionaire y el Pobrecito* (1980), a play for young audiences; *Articus and the Angel* (1981), a musical; and *I Am Celso*, a one-man show. In 1989, Sierra moved to Los Angeles, where he taught at the California Institute for the Arts and the University of Southern California. He became a full professor at California State University in 1993. That year, he helped to found the East L.A. Classical Theater Company.

Sierra, Ruben Angel (b. Oct. 6, 1965, Rio Piedras, Puerto Rico): Baseball player. Sierra, a switch-hitting outfielder, made his major league debut with the Texas Rangers in 1986 at the age of twenty. A year later, he became the youngest player since 1965 to hit thirty home runs in a season and tied for the American

League lead in outfield assists. In 1989, Sierra led the American League with 119 runs batted in and 14 triples; he also hit 29 home runs, batted .306, and finished second in the voting for the American League Most Valuable Player Award. A three-time All-Star with the Rangers, Sierra was traded to the Oakland Athletics in 1992. While with Oakland, he won All-Star honors in 1994.

Silex, Humberto: Labor leader. Silex entered the United States from Mexico in 1921 and served in the United States Army. He took a job at the American Smelting and Refining Company in El Paso, Texas, where many Mexican Americans worked. He organized the workers into Local 509 and became president of that union. By the 1930's, he was a well-known and outspoken union leader. His persistent demands angered industrial and government leaders, leading to his arrest and a questioning of his loyalty to the United States. In a dramatic court case, he successfully fought efforts to have him deported as an undesirable alien, and he was allowed to stay in the United States. He continued to work for the rights of workers, but out of the public eye.

Simpson-Mazzoli bill. *See* **Immigration Reform and Control Act of 1986**

Sinarquista movement: Mexican fascist movement. The Sinarquistas were sympathetic to the Francisco Franco regime in Spain. The movement began in the late 1930's, with wealthy landlords and businesspeople as its main supporters and members. The Sinarquistas deplored the MEXICAN REVOLUTION (1910-1921) and what they called the excesses of it. They advocated an authoritarian regime and were spiritually and politically guided by the local Catholic hierarchy.

Under religious pretensions, the movement urged Mexicans to strengthen their ties with Spain and opposed communism and the United States. Any force interpreted as distancing Mexicans from their Catholic and Spanish roots was opposed by the movement. German agents used the movement for their political and intelligence objectives during World War II.

There was a local base to the movement, composed of Mexicans from small towns who opposed both administrative misrule and government bureaucrats. It also included peasants whose lot was not improved by the revolution. The movement reached a peak in the early 1940's, when it claimed to have more than one million adherents. The movement spread to the U.S. Southwest but probably did not attract more than a few thousand members.

Siqueiros, David Alfaro (Dec. 29, 1896, Santa Rosalía de Camargo, Chihuahua, Mexico—Jan. 6, 1974, Cuernavaca, Mexico): Muralist. Many of Siqueiros' ideas concerning social reform came from his grandfather, a poet and politician. He attended prep schools in Mexico City and took art classes at San Carlos Academy, with emphasis on indigenist painting, and at the "Open-Air School" at Santa Anita. By 1913, he had taken part in a Mexican national conspiracy; the next year, he served in the revolutionary troops.

From then on, Siqueiros interspersed his political and artistic activities. In 1922, he joined more than twenty other artists working on the Mexican National Preparatory School wall murals. During 1924, Siqueiros painted murals at the University of Guadalajara. From 1930 to 1934, he painted murals in the United States at the Chouinard School of Art, the Plaza Art Center, the Stock Exchange Club, the California School of Fine Arts, San Francisco Junior College, the Detroit Institute of Fine Arts, and Radio City in New York, New York. Siqueiros also painted outdoor three-dimensional murals at Mexico's National University (1957) and the Hotel de Mexico (1965) (*see* MURAL ART).

Siqueiros' first show was in Mexico City in 1932. Other major exhibitions included one in New York City in 1934, the Twenty-fifth Biennale in Venice, Italy, in 1950, and the first Inter-American Biennale in Mexico in 1958. He founded the Siqueiros Experimental Workshop in New York in 1935, the Centro Realista de Arte Moderno in Mexico in 1944, and the Mexican Art Academy in 1968. He lectured throughout the world and published a book on how to paint murals.

Siqueiros became a member of the Mexican Communist Party executive committee in 1922 and was executive secretary of the Mexican Communist Party in 1959. In 1924, he and other muralists formed the executive committee of *El Machete*, the official paper of trade unions and the Communist Party. Siqueiros did no painting between 1925 and 1930 because of his union work. In 1930 and between 1960 and 1964, he was imprisoned in Mexico for political activities. As an antifascist, in 1937 he played a major role in the Spanish Republican Army during the Civil War. He spent political exile in numerous countries throughout his life.

A founding member of the Mexican muralist movement, Siqueiros is known for his experiments in por-

Renowned muralist David Siqueiros. (AP/Wide World Photos)

traying the influence of modern progress on society, using ancient techniques as well as modern materials and methods. He was awarded the Mexican national art prize in 1966 and the Lenin Peace Prize by the Soviet Union in 1968.

Sixty-fifth Infantry Regiment: U.S. Army unit. Latinos in the U.S. military typically shouldered a heavy burden, holding a disproportionate share of lower-level positions involving greater danger (*see* MILITARY PARTICIPATION). According to the 1940 Census, the United States had a Hispanic population of approximately 1.3 million. An estimated 333,000 Hispanics served in World War II, a larger share of the population than for any other ethnic group.

More than sixty-five thousand Puerto Ricans served in the armed forces during World War II. The 295th and 296th Infantry regiments of the Puerto Rican National Guard participated in the Asian and Pacific campaigns against the Japanese. Many of the National Guards went to Europe as replacements for the Sixty-fifth Regiment, a regular U.S. Army unit composed entirely of Puerto Ricans. During operations in Europe, this regiment suffered large casualties, and twenty members were killed in action.

Skin color: During and following the period of conquest by light-skinned Europeans, dark skin color became associated with people of lower status. These included members of indigenous Indian tribes and slaves later imported from Africa as well as children born to mixed-race couples.

Although SLAVERY ended in the Americas more than a century ago, a specter of slavery still plagues many Latin American countries. Its most brutal lasting effect concerns attitudes about skin color. Because dark-skinned individuals, as a legacy of slavery, have long been perceived and treated as inferior, they have not been granted the same opportunities and thus have become inferior in status according to some measures. This attribution of inferiority not only has influenced the self-esteem of dark-skinned individuals but also has shaped their daily interactions with others in Latin America and in Latino society.

Legacy of Inferiority. Since Christopher Columbus' arrival in the Americas in 1492, issues of skin color have affected many Latin Americans. In his writings, Columbus described the brown-skinned natives as inferior to whites because of both their dark physical appearance and their naïve acceptance of strangers on their land. This naïveté was interpreted as a sign of

mental inferiority that, in turn, was seen by the Spaniards as giving them the right to exploit the indigenous people and take their best land. The Spanish colonists' denial of basic rights to native peoples tied skin color to the political structure from the outset of colonial adventures.

The vicious cycle of DISCRIMINATION in the Americas that began with the first European contact expanded with the institution of black slavery. Africans were brought to South America and the Caribbean expressly to serve the needs of European colonists and their descendants, who were the undisputed masters. European theories of white racial superiority reinforced the belief that enslavement of black people was justified.

As a rule, light-skinned Latin Americans, including the ruling elite, have treated dark-skinned individuals as inferior. There were varying degrees of racial mixing throughout Latin America, but dark-skinned people often sought to deny their Indian or African roots in hopes of assimilating into the dominant society. Discrimination against dark-skinned individuals has persisted as a remnant of conquest and slavery in many Latin American countries and among the Latino populations of the United States and Canada. These remnants are in part responsible for the disadvantaged socioeconomic and political circumstances of many dark-skinned Latinos.

Although blatant, overt, individual and institutional prejudice against dark-skinned individuals has declined in the late twentieth century, discrimination and inequality based on skin color persist. For example, Puerto Ricans who have dark skin are discriminated against in Puerto Rico, but seldom overtly. If they travel to the mainland United States, they face more overt double discrimination both as Puerto Ricans and as dark-skinned individuals.

Puerto Ricans, as of the early 1990's, had the highest rate of poverty of any Latino subgroup. Cuban Americans were relatively prosperous, but immigrants who arrived during the MARIEL BOAT LIFT of 1980 did not fare as well. Many of those *marielitos* were Afro-Cubans with dark skin. Their relative lack of success, in large part a result of their socioeconomic and educational background in Cuba, reinforced negative stereotypes about dark-skinned Latinos. Darker-skinned Mexican Americans have reported more employment discrimination and government harassment than lighter-skinned compatriots, and those with darker skin are more often suspected of being in the United States without documentation.

Psychological Impact. Throughout their lives, dark-skinned Latinos are taught that being treated as inferior is normal. Stereotypes cast them as mentally inferior, dirty, sexually promiscuous, athletic, and aggressive. Judgments such as these and the social reactions that accompany them represent a potent kind of cultural definition. Many girls from Mexican and Mexican American families, for example, are warned against staying out in the sun because having darker skin will make them less attractive as marriage partners. Although leaders of the CHICANO MOVEMENT have celebrated their people's heritage of *mestizaje* (racial mix-

ing), such stereotypes and actions based on them persist (*see* STEREOTYPES OF LATINOS).

Negative stereotypes can damage an individual's perception of self, inducing shame and confusion. Individuals are generalized to have the supposed traits of their group. Such generalizations do not take into account factors that affect individuals. If, for example, dark-skinned individuals are overrepresented in professional sports, that may be a result more of motivational and environmental factors than of innate abilities and skills. Dark-skinned individuals may see sports as an escape from the lower socioeconomic

Dark-skinned Latinos such as these Cuban refugees are often the victims of dual prejudice. (Impact Visuals, Arvind Garg)

status that might otherwise be imposed on them, and they may have a greater desire to succeed knowing what faces them if they do not.

When society stigmatizes certain aspects of physical appearance or behavior, individuals with those traits or behaviors are made to feel inferior. Comparative studies on perception of skin color have shown that systematic devaluation of dark skin in American society has made it more difficult for many dark-skinned individuals to maintain a favorable self-concept.

The desire to meet artificial standards of appearance or behavior can implant feelings of self-hatred, psychological despair, and rage. This may govern how dark-skinned individuals act and present themselves in society.

Myths, stereotypes, and labels related to dark skin color remained in place in the late twentieth century, even though concerted efforts had been made to eradicate them. Although many changes have occurred in the five centuries since Columbus' arrival in the Americas, the devaluation of dark skin has not disappeared from many Latin American societies or from the United States. *—Jose Alfredo Nunez*

SUGGESTED READINGS: • Feagin, Joe R. *Racial and Ethnic Relations.* 3d ed. Englewood Cliffs, N.J.: Prentice Hall, 1989. • Fine, Michelle, and Cheryl Bowers. "Racial Self-Identification: The Effects of Social History and Gender." *Journal of Applied Social Psychology* 14 (March-June, 1984): 136-146. • Goffman, Erving. *Stigma: Notes on the Management of Spoiled Identity.* Englewood Cliffs, N.J.: Prentice-Hall, 1963. • Karenga, Maulana. *Introduction to Black Studies.* Los Angeles, Calif.: University of Sankore Press, 1989. • Katz, Phyllis A., and Sue R. Zalk. "Doll Preferences: An Index of Racial Attitudes?" *Journal of Educational Psychology* 66 (October, 1974): 663-668. • Shelibow, Barbara. "An Investigation into the Relationship Between Self Esteem and Skin Color Among Hispanic Children." *Graduate Research in Education and Related Disciplines* 7 (Fall, 1973): 64-82. • Williams, Eric. *From Columbus to Castro: The History of the Caribbean, 1492-1969.* New York: Vintage Books, 1984.

Slavery: Slavery was one of the major forces that shaped Latin American societies from the late fifteenth century to relatively recent times. Its influence can be traced in the social, racial, religious, and artistic structures of the Spanish-speaking New World and in the culture and traditions of many Latinos in the United States and Canada.

History. Slavery already existed in pre-Columbian times in the Americas, among the Aztecs, Maya, and Incas, but it experienced a tremendous growth during the COLONIAL PERIOD. Spain and Portugal, the first European nations to establish control over large portions of the Americas, had had long exposure to the slave trade, both from experience with antiquity and the Middle Ages and from Atlantic explorations in the fifteenth century. Beginning in the middle decades of the fifteenth century, the Portuguese and, later, the Spaniards began to use African slaves in the sugar plantations of the Canary Islands, the Azores, Cape Verde, and Madeira.

The decisive moment for the trans-Atlantic slave trade came in 1504, when Spanish trade officials first allowed the importation of black Africans into the newly discovered Caribbean colonies of Hispaniola, Cuba, and Puerto Rico in response to the high mortality rates among the natives of those islands. As the original inhabitants disappeared, the Caribbean became a kind of second Africa, a place where black slaves and persons of mixed or pure African descent became the majority of the population (80 percent or more by some calculations) and would later have a major cultural impact. Slaves were also the backbone of Caribbean economies from the sixteenth to the late nineteenth century. They worked primarily on plantations in the large-scale production of sugar, tobacco, cacao, coffee, and other tropical products exported to European and world markets.

The pattern established in the Caribbean held true for the rest of Latin America. Slavery flourished in coastal areas where the native Indian population had become depleted or was insufficient to run a plantation economy. Unlike Africans, Indians were by law free subjects of the Spanish Crown, could not be enslaved outright, and had a variety of legal rights and a status that black persons did not enjoy.

The case of NEW SPAIN (modern-day Mexico) is in many ways typical. By the late sixteenth century, the Indian population of Mexico had been decimated, and wholesale importation of slaves began in earnest. Between 1570 to 1650, it has been estimated, one out of every two black slaves sent to the Americas went to Mexico and was put to work in sugar mills or silver mines. Slaves worked long hours—sometimes as much as twenty hours per day—and their living conditions were often much worse than those of Indian laborers, partly because slave owners were not subject to the supervision of church or secular officials (unlike those who held Indians). This situation provoked major slave conspiracies in 1608 and 1611. These were harshly put down by authorities. Outside the big plantations, there developed a slave elite, often urban, of highly skilled craftsmen, private servants, and concubines owned by the upper classes of New Spain. Because Spanish traditional law regarded the freeing of slaves as a worthy goal, the major Mexican cities soon could count a large number of black and mulatto freedmen.

In New Spain, black slavery reached its zenith in the early seventeenth century and thereafter began to decline as the Indian population recovered and grew. In other areas of Hispanic America, however, the institution continued to flourish. In Peru's coastal plains and in the Portuguese colony of Brazil, slavery became the backbone of the economy. Brazil became the world's largest producer of sugar in the late sixteenth century, largely as a result of slave labor. By the eighteenth century, slavery had become an important issue in the struggle for supremacy among European nations. Included in the concessions Spain made to Great Britain

by the Treaty of Utrecht in 1713 was the *asiento*, or exclusive right to supply Hispanic America with African slaves.

Humanitarian pressure and the onset of the Industrial Revolution prompted Great Britain to abolish the trade and free its Caribbean slaves in the early decades of the nineteenth century. British pressure forced other European powers, including Spain, to follow suit. Fewer slaves reached the New World from Africa in the nineteenth century, but slavery was remarkably resilient in Hispanic America, especially in countries with plantation economies such as Cuba and Puerto Rico. Although its final abolition was not the subject of a major armed conflict as in the United States, slavery did not end in Cuba until 1886 and in Brazil until 1888.

Importance. The importance of African slavery in the history of Latin America is crucial. Without African slaves, the Iberian powers would have found it impossible to develop and populate Latin America. In addition, the cultural and ethnic presence of Africa is

Slavery helped support the Caribbean economies during the sixteenth through eighteenth centuries. (Library of Congress)

Cuban slaves prepare for punishment. (Library of Congress)

one of the major components of modern Latin American culture. African influence shows itself especially in Brazil and the Caribbean Basin, in the sounds of Afro-Cuban and SALSA music, in the religious practices of SANTERÍA and Candomblé, and in the ethnic heritage of a large segment of the Latino population in the United States.   —*Fernando González de León*

SUGGESTED READINGS: • Bowser, Frederick. *The African Slave in Colonial Peru, 1524-1650* Stanford, Calif.: Stanford University Press, 1974. • Curtin, Philip. *The Atlantic Slave Trade: A Census*. Madison: University of Wisconsin Press, 1969. • Mellafe, Rolando. *Negro Slavery in Latin America*. Translated by J.W. S. Judge. Berkeley: University of California Press, 1975. • Palmer, Colin. *Slaves of the White God: Blacks in Mexico, 1570-1650*. Cambridge, Mass.: Harvard University Press, 1976. • Toplin, Robert Brent, ed. *Slavery and Race Relations in Latin America*. Westport, Conn.: Greenwood Press, 1974.

Sleepy Lagoon case (1942-1943): Murder case and aftermath. From August 2, 1942, through the spring of

1943, a series of incidents beginning with the death of José Díaz and followed by the zoot-suit riots focused national attention on the Mexican American community's struggle for civil rights in Los Angeles, California.

On the evening of August 1, 1942, two groups of Chicano boys fought over a pretty girl. The fight occurred in a gravel pit known as Sleepy Lagoon, on the outskirts of Los Angeles. On the morning of August 2, 1942, José Díaz lay mortally injured, the victim of a severe beating. He died without recovering consciousness.

An autopsy revealed that Díaz's death was the result of a severe fracture of the base of the skull. No weapon was found, and no proof of murder was established. The incident quickly captured the imagination of the press.

Twenty-three Chicano youths and one Anglo were arrested and charged with murder. Two of the indicted youths asked for separate trials and were subsequently released. The remaining twenty-two were tried together on a total of sixty-six charges. In January, 1943,

Servicemen board a streetcar looking for Latino zoot suiters. (AP/Wide World Photos)

the jury returned first-degree murder convictions for three of the youths. Nine youths were found guilty of second-degree murder, and five were found guilty of assault. The five remaining defendants were found not guilty.

The jury verdicts in this case led to the creation of the Sleepy Lagoon Defense Committee, headed by Carey McWilliams. In October, 1944, the California District Court of Appeals reversed the trial court's verdict and freed all the youths for lack of evidence.

In 1943, the legal case became a focal point for extreme and widespread anti-Mexican feelings, fueled by sensationalized press accounts of a "Mexican Ameri-

can crime wave." Press accounts fueled the public's pressure on the police to deal with this purported crime problem. The result was a series of systematic round-ups of Mexican American youth by police.

In response to pressure from the federal government, which was concerned that the press's use of the label "Mexican" in crime stories was inflammatory, the press adopted the negative epithets of PACHUCO and zoot suit in crime-related stories. The subsequent police crackdown on "zoot suit hoodlums" and "pachuco gangsters" led to Los Angeles police raids on the barrios. In a two-day sweep, six hundred Chicanos were arrested. The Los Angeles Sheriff's Bureau of

Foreign Relations also targeted Chicanos, who were characterized as having an "inborn characteristic desire to kill, or at least to let blood."

During the first days of June, 1943, roaming gangs of U.S. Navy and Army military personnel attacked people of Mexican appearance, particularly those who dressed in zoot suits. The peak of this street war was reached on June 7, 1943, when fleets of taxis filled with sailors and soldiers cruised the streets looking for victims. Rather than protecting the victims, the local police and military law enforcement personnel on duty followed the attackers and arrested the victims of these brutal attacks. The attacks became known as the zoot-suit riots.

The Sleepy Lagoon case led to open grand jury hearings on the problems of Mexican Americans. The zoot-suit riots raised the moral consciousness of concerned Anglos regarding the violations of Mexican Americans' civil rights.

Smits, Jimmy (b. July 9, 1955, New York, N.Y.): Actor. Smits was born to working-class parents. His father came to the United States from Surinam, a Dutch colony in South America; his mother emigrated from Puerto Rico. As a youngster, he lived in Puerto Rico for two years with his mother and two sisters, and he attended school there. When he was fifteen years old, Smits was living with his family in Brooklyn, New York. After finishing high school, he earned his bachelor's degree from Brooklyn College and went on to earn his M.F.A. from Cornell University.

Smits began his acting career in Off-Broadway productions. He also worked as a community organizer before acting with the New York Shakespeare Festival, sponsored by the Public Theater. His film debut as a bad guy in the Gregory Hines-Billy Crystal buddy picture *Running Scared* (1986) brought him to the attention of casting directors. He auditioned and won the role of Victor Sifuentes on the television series *L.A. Law*, which debuted in 1986. Smits's character was a savvy former public defender who became the first Latino attorney at a private law firm. Smits worked hard to establish Sifuentes as a fine courtroom lawyer and not just a token minority member of the firm. His efforts were rewarded with four Emmy nominations as best supporting actor in a dramatic series, and he ultimately won the Emmy in that category in 1990.

Smits appeared as the romantic lead in Jane Fonda's film production *Old Gringo* (1989) before leaving *L.A. Law* in 1991. He later appeared in the Blake Edwards film comedy *Switch* (1991) opposite Ellen Barkin and

in the television film of Stephen King's novel *The Tommyknockers* (1993). Smits returned to series television in 1994, when he was cast in the role of Brooklyn-born detective Bobby Simone on the critically acclaimed *NYPD Blue*, a show produced by *L.A. Law* executive producer Stephen Bochco.

Smuggling: Illegal transportation of goods across a border. Smuggling has long occurred from Latin American countries to the United States and Canada. The first major wave of smuggling was the importation of alcoholic beverages from the Caribbean area and Mexico during Prohibition (1919-1933). Later, the smuggling problem concerned illegal drugs, particularly marijuana and cocaine.

In 1919, the United States embarked on the Prohibition campaign, an attempt to outlaw the sale of alcoholic beverages. Most historians agree that the attempt failed. One of the reasons Prohibition did not work was the relative ease of smuggling huge quantities of alcohol into the United States from countries where it was still legal. This process was referred to as "bootlegging," from the habit of hiding bottles of liquor in boots, either to smuggle it or to have it available outside the home.

The Caribbean region is known for production of rum. Fortunes were made by liquor dealers in South and Central America who ran rum up the East Coast of North America to sell it at inflated prices. From Mexico, tequila and other alcoholic beverages were smuggled in by land.

Prohibition was repealed in 1933, but a new type of prohibition became prevalent in later decades. A number of "recreational" drugs, among them marijuana and cocaine, are illegal to produce or sell in the United States and Canada. Much of the world's marijuana and cocaine production occurs in Latin America.

Reliable data on smuggling of marijuana into the United States are difficult to compile, but judging by the number of arrests made (a very small percentage of marijuana smugglers are caught and arrested), much of the drug comes from Mexico. Between 1975 and 1979, the Mexican government used the defoliant paraquat on marijuana crops, and the greatest profits shifted to Colombia. This defoliant, however, posed a serious health hazard for American smokers of marijuana, and when the United States withdrew its support from the paraquat program, it was discontinued.

As of the 1980's and early 1990's, Colombia produced about 80 percent of the world's cocaine. Much of the crop is exported to the United States. The coca

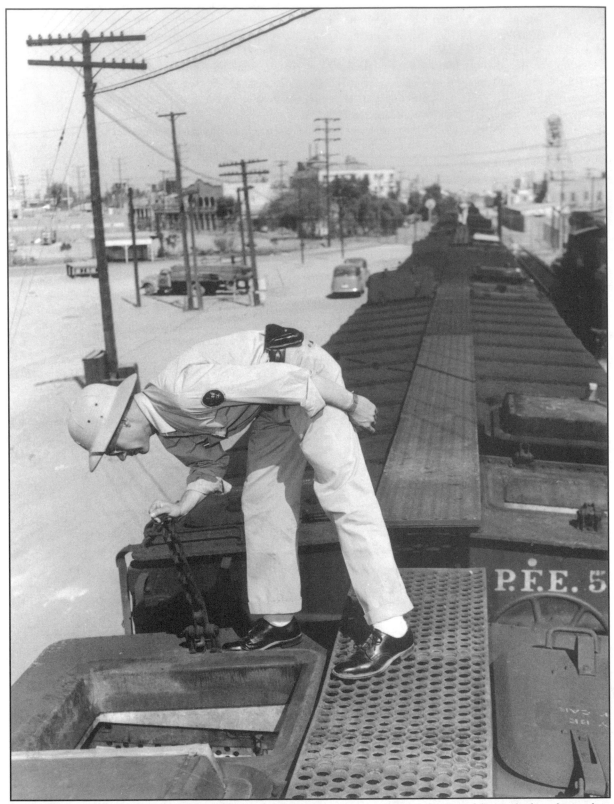

A Border Patrol agent inspects a refrigeration compartment on a train crossing into the United States, looking for workers being smuggled into the country. (AP/Wide World Photos)

leaf, the source of cocaine, is legally grown in Peru and Bolivia, then processed in Colombia.

A series of agreements have been reached between the United States and its southern neighbors, but these agreements have had little effect on the smuggling of drugs. Outside the three-mile limit of ocean territory that belongs by international law to the United States, the Coast Guard is powerless to stop smugglers. Not every ship and plane entering the U. S. territory can be searched. Furthermore, the Colombian government has shown little cooperation in controlling the DRUG TRADE, which provides billions of dollars of revenue for Latin America. With these obstacles to law enforcement in place, smuggling remained likely to continue.

Sobadores: Massage therapists. *Sobadores* (literally, "kneaders" or "rubbers") are massage specialists who practice therapeutic and healing massage according to traditional Indo-Hispanic methods. *Sobador*, as the massage is called, is an important tradition in New Mexico that has been practiced for hundreds of years. It incorporates vigorous massage and some traditional spiritual methods. It is utilized by both Latinos and non-Latinos. Within the United States, *sobadores* are most common in the Southwest.

Soccer: The world's most popular sport, soccer has more than 150 million registered participants worldwide. Several Latin American countries rank among the world's traditional soccer powers, and Latinos constitute a large portion of the more than 16 million registered players in the United States, where soccer is the second most popular participatory sport, behind only basketball.

Rules and History. Soccer is a relatively simple team sport. The object of the game is to maneuver a round ball with the feet, head, or body—but not the hands—into a goal past a defender known as the goalie. Goalies are the only players allowed to touch the ball with their hands. In modern organized soccer,

Schoolchildren play an informal soccer game. (James Shaffer)

teams consist of eleven players per side; the teams compete on a field of slightly more than 110 yards in length and 70 yards in width and attempt to score into a goal 8 yards wide and 8 feet high. Casual and recreational games are often played with different numbers of players, however, and fields of widely differing sizes are commonly used.

Soccer's simplicity and the fact that little equipment is needed to play have contributed to the game's enduring worldwide popularity. References to soccerlike games appear in ancient Chinese and Roman texts, and related sports achieved wide popularity in medieval Europe, where nearby towns would sometimes engage in games involving hundreds of players over long distances. In pre-Columbian America, the Maya played a game in which players had to propel a ball through a stone hoop using only their hips; other Indian groups, such as the Tarahumaras of northern Mexico, participated in marathon soccerlike games that involved kicking a ball from the high mountains to the valleys.

The game took on its modern form in nineteenth century England, where the first organized league was begun in 1863. By the turn of the century, the English version had spread around the world; the 1904 formation of the Fédération Internationale de Football Association (FIFA) gave the growing sport an international governing body. Professional leagues soon flourished in dozens of countries, notably in Europe and South America.

In 1930, the first FIFA world championship, known as the World Cup, was held in Uruguay, and the host country captured the title. Other major competitions include the Olympic Games, where soccer has been played since 1900; the European Cup, a contest begun in 1955 among the champions of Europe's professional leagues; and the Copa de Libertadores, a South American equivalent of the European Cup, begun in 1960. A match between the winners of the European and South American competitions for an unofficial professional world championship has been held on a

Organized soccer leagues proliferate in cities with significant Latino populations. (David Bacon)

more or less regular basis since 1960. World Cup championships, which are held every four years, are the world's most widely followed sporting events. An estimated two billion people watched television broadcasts of the final game of the 1994 competition, hosted by the United States. The U.S. team managed to reach the second round of competition.

Latinos and Soccer. Soccer has been played in the United States since the nineteenth century, but the sport long faced an uphill struggle for attention with such native sports as baseball, basketball, and American football. When emigration from Latin America to the United States increased after World War II, however, the sport grew in popularity in the Latino communities of every major U.S. city. Professional soccer has not flourished in the United States, but many U.S. Latinos retain a strong rooting interest in teams and players from their countries of origin.

On the recreational level, soccer, or *fútbol*, ranks among the most popular participatory sports in Latino communities. Organized games and *cascaritas* (pick-up games) abound. Adults and children play in weekend leagues, and a league game often becomes a family affair, with families of the team members getting together for a postgame picnic. Because soccer is a year-round sport, there are winter, spring, and summer leagues.

Although U.S. soccer has struggled to earn international respect, the strong bond between the sport and Latino culture has produced some of the country's best players. The U.S. national team that achieved unprecedented success by advancing to the second round of the 1994 World Cup finals featured five Latino players—Marcelo Balboa, Fernando Clavijo, Hugo Perez, Tab Ramos, and Claudio Reyna. Moreover, Arturo Angeles, a Mexican American, was one of the handful of world-class referees chosen to officiate at the tournament. —*Horacio R. Fonseca*

SUGGESTED READINGS:

• Brown, Michael. *Soccer Rules in Pictures.* New York: Perigee Books, 1990. A simplified version of the rules of the game, with pictures that provide examples of the offside rule, the difference between direct and indirect kicks, and other fine points.

• Gardner, Paul. *The Simplest Game.* 2d ed. New York: Collier Books, 1994. A narrative of the sport's development in the United States. Focuses on historical aspects of the game.

• Hollander, Zander. *The American Encyclopedia of Soccer.* New York: Everest House, 1980. An overview of soccer in the United States. Especially useful for

information on college soccer and the early U.S. professional leagues.

• Morrison, Ian. *The World Cup: A Complete Record.* London: Breeder Book Sport, 1990. Excellent text and pictures on the history of the FIFA World Cup. Covers the tournaments since 1930 and includes statistical data on each of the games played, together with names of the team members of the participating nations.

Social bandits: Mexican outlaws of the nineteenth and twentieth centuries as well as Mexican American social bandits in the American Southwest. British historian Eric J. Hobsbawm first articulated the concept of social bandits, concluding that they reflect the disruption of an entire society and the rise of new classes and social structures. Another distinguished scholar, Eric Wolf, argues that the bandit is a popular hero as well as a primitive revolutionary who articulates peasant emotions. These scholars provide the framework for understanding the social bandits of Mexico and the southwestern United States.

The problem of brigandage did not develop in Mexico until after independence in 1821. The Spanish viceroyalty represented a strong central authority that would deal with unrest effectively by means of its Acordada, a special police force. Fiscal and economic decline during the republic's early years resulted in no less than eight hundred revolts between 1821 and 1875. Bandits therefore took the initiative in controlling small regions. As the Indian communities and church lost their lands to liberal governments, unrest mounted.

In the mid-nineteenth century, Benito Juárez began the process by which bandits became more prominent. He enlisted bandits to fight against his conservative opponents and then against Mexican emperor Ferdinand Maximilian and his French protectors. Juárez assumed that he would be able to crush subsequent bandits once he regained the capital, but a divisive policy of anticlericalism as well as continued economic stagnation served to encourage further bandit activity, often with the backing of local villages.

In the United States, the new Mexican American society often showed resistance to its reduced standard of living in the form of social bandits. In California, Tiburcio Vásquez nurtured a burning hatred of Anglo-American hegemony. In 1852, a fight broke out at a dance VÁSQUEZ was attending in Monterey. The death of an Anglo constable in that fight resulted in vigilantes pursuing Vásquez, who easily eluded them. Vásquez

Benito Juárez organized bandits in his campaign to gain control of Mexico. (Institute of Texan Cultures)

became a bandit, robbing coaches but distributing the fruits of his raids among poor Mexicans of the Salinas Valley. He was imprisoned several times and died by hanging as punishment for a murder conviction.

Joaquín MURIETA left Sonora to prospect for gold in California following the GOLD RUSH of 1848. Being driven from one place to another by brutal Anglo-American ruffians engendered a thirst for revenge. An excellent shot, outstanding horseman, and dignified rebel to the end, Murieta became a symbol of the decline of CALIFORNIOS.

The most influential social bandit was Juan CORTINA of Texas. A descendant of the original Hispanic settlers of the lower Rio Grande valley, Cortina resented the Anglo-American injustices committed against local Mexicans. When, in 1859, a Brownsville marshal pistol-whipped a ranchero friend of his, Cortina shot the marshal and seized control of the town. During his brief occupation of Brownsville, Cortina paid for the arms and munitions that he obtained and called upon the population to overthrow their oppressors.

The MEXICAN REVOLUTION of 1910-1921 produced Mexico's most famous bandit, Francisco "Pancho" VILLA. Born in the state of Durango in 1878, Villa grew up on a large hacienda. Villa killed a Spanish foreman who raped his sister. Villa became a bandit who lived by rustling cattle and acquired fame for his courage. Villa was a natural guerrilla who gained the support of

Pancho Villa rose to fame during the Mexican Revolution. (Institute of Texan Cultures)

Artist Isaias Mata with 500 Axos de Résistencia, a mural in San Francisco, California, illustrating the struggle to achieve social objectives. (Robert Fried)

countless cowboys and landless people. His Division of the North became the largest military unit during the Mexican Revolution. Villa's concern for children and education endeared him to many, but after Venustiano Carranza articulated a nationalist ideology, Villa's influence declined. His March, 1916, invasion of New Mexico temporarily revived his power. He was assassinated in 1923 by order of the Mexican government.

Socialism: The ideology of socialism is based on the principle of common ownership of the means of production, with a goal of equality in the political, economic, and social spheres of life. Socialists believe that true freedom and equality cannot be achieved until productive property is collectivized, the social structure of capitalism eliminated, and political institutions brought under the control of the working class. Socialism aims to replace the capitalist system of free enterprise, private property, and production for profit with an economic system based on state or community ownership of the means of production and an equitable distribution of goods and services.

Socialism takes various forms. Democratic socialism is often combined with liberal, humanist, or religious values and goals. It typically seeks to retain the system of political democracy while establishing equality of opportunity, implementing a full program of social welfare, and collectivizing the means of production. Radical, Marxist, and Leninist schools of socialism favor a completely egalitarian, classless, and stateless society. They usually call for revolution to change control of the state; once in power, they would engage in the rapid collectivization of property, suppress counterrevolutionary groups, and establish a single-party dictatorship.

Radical Latino political activists and scholars have adapted socialist ideology to the conditions of U.S. minority groups. They provide a fundamental critique of U.S. capitalism and insist that the problems faced by Latinos, such as POVERTY, political powerlessness, RACISM, and cultural intolerance, are unlikely to be resolved within the existing social structure. Socialists argue that Latinos must defy capitalism in order to challenge the political and economic domination of non-Latino elites.

Despite high rates of poverty among Latinos, socialism has not had broad appeal in the Latino community. The high point of Latino radicalism was during the CHICANO MOVEMENT in the 1960's. Chicano college students were exposed to socialism through the Civil Rights movement, the farmworkers' struggles for union-

ization, and the antiwar movement. They were also strongly influenced by the Black Power movement, which stressed pride in black culture and black control of community institutions. Similarly, Puerto Rican independence movements attracted some activists with socialist beliefs. Cuban Americans are perhaps the least likely to advocate socialism, because most deliberately fled from Fidel CASTRO's socialist state.

Although both the Chicano movement and the Puerto Rican independence movement attracted socialists, both essentially were led by nationalists. Nationalists focused on the preservation of Latino cultural identity. They rejected assimilation and efforts to form coalitions with non-Latinos, limiting the size of their movements. Variants of socialism, however, continue to provide Latino activists with powerful tools to critique contemporary U.S. society and its treatment of minority groups.

Sociedad Progresista Mexicana: Mutual aid society. The society, originally part of the mutual aid society Sociedad Zaragoza, formed in 1929 in California. Many of its founding members were Mexicans who immigrated to the United States around the time of the Mexican Revolution (1910-1921). It served as a mutual aid group for the Mexican community, providing affordable insurance and a cultural base for its members. In the 1930's, the society worked with other mutual aid societies on community aid and improvement projects (*see* MUTUALISTAS). Over the years, it has also provided money for Mexican American students attending college. The society is located in the Los Angeles area.

Society of Hispanic Professional Engineers (SHPE): Professional organization. The SHPE was founded in Los Angeles, California, in 1974 by Rodrigo Garcia, George Esquer, Fernando Nuñez, Richard Carrisoza, Alex Nidaurrazaga, and Bill Nuñez. The founders wanted to provide role models for the Hispanic community. The organization formed professional and student chapters throughout the nation. The SHPE provides scholarships to students, organizes programs to prepare students for technical careers, develops retention programs for students in postsecondary education, organizes forums on technical information, and organizes conferences and workshops on career enhancement.

Sofrito: Lightly sautéed mixture of puréed aromatic herbs and oil, used as a seasoning. *Sofrito* (or *soffrito*) long has been a stock sauce in Greece, Spain, and Italy, where it usually is made with olive oil, garlic, parsley, and sometimes other ingredients. It was carried to the Americas by the Spanish, and it took root especially in Puerto Rico and Cuba. *Sofrito* is made by grinding or pureeing garlic, onions, green pepper, CHILES, CILANTRO, ham, and lard or vegetable oil. Other ingredients, particularly tomatoes, parsley, or other herbs, may be added. *Sofrito* is sautéed briefly to blend the flavors. It is used to flavor stews, soups, and many other dishes.

Soldaderas, Las: Women who participated in wars and revolutions throughout the history of Mexico, particularly during the MEXICAN REVOLUTION. The participation of women in Mexican military life had pre-Columbian origins. The cosmic role that motherhood played in Mesoamerican life manifested itself into deification of an Earth Mother/war goddess in tribal life. Cihuacóatl and Coyolxauhqui were war goddesses who could rouse warriors into combat. Women fought in defense of their families, kinship groups, and property in the intertribal warfare common until the Aztec hegemony. The Aztecs eliminated warrior goddesses and discouraged women from bearing arms in conquest. Instead, women were encouraged to provide personal comfort and sexual services to warriors.

The SPANISH CONQUEST further defined the word *soldadera*. *Soldadera* specifically referred to a servant who took the soldier's pay and bought him food and supplies. A small number of Spanish and African women participated in the conquest of Latin America. The most famous *soldadera*, however, was Malinalli Tenepal, an Indian of noble background from Coatzacoalcos province. She is often referred to by her Spanish name, Doña Marina. Able to learn Spanish, Marina, who became known as La MALINCHE, became the head interpreter for Hernán CORTÉS and bore him a son. As part of Spain's consolidation of the conquest, women served in armed groups as foragers, cooks, tailors, and nurses. Female soldiers participated in the armies of both sides during the Mexican struggle for independence from Spain.

Throughout the nineteenth century, women attempted to incorporate themselves into the Mexican army, with varying success. Officers often discharged *soldaderas* because they slowed down the movement of troops. *Soldaderas* also served U.S. and French armies. These women sometimes sought spouses among the soldiers; others were looking only for gainful employment. Some were heroic, others parasitical camp followers.

Soldaderas acquired their greatest fame during the Mexican Revolution (1910-1921). Women by the thousands served the various factions. Many were abducted by force; others simply followed their husbands to combat zones. Some fought for ideological or economic reasons. Although officers often considered *soldaderas* to be disruptive, enlisted men glorified them

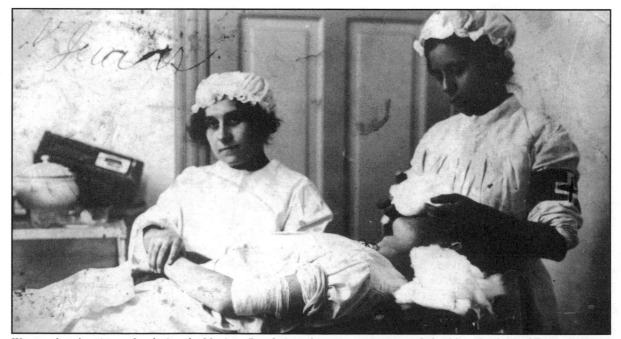

Women played various roles during the Mexican Revolution; these two treat a wounded soldier. (Institute of Texan Cultures)

as warriors, sexual companions, and domestic servants. Many *soldaderas* became enshrined in folklore.

The *soldaderas* seem to have favored Venustiano Carranza's faction more than the others. Carranza had promoted many women's causes and even established a pension fund for his soldiers' widows. More important, many female Carrancistas were actual fighters. Francisco "Pancho" VILLA, on the other hand, constantly tried to limit the role of women in his army and attempted to relieve the *soldaderas* of their function as camp followers. On one occasion, he ordered the execution of ninety women.

After the revolution, *soldaderas* were banished from federal service. Few ever received pensions or honors, but many learned confidence from their experiences, demonstrated leadership, and participated in political movements. As years went by, *soldaderas* appeared increasingly in literature, *CORRIDOS*, art works, and films. *Soldaderas* later became a symbol of militancy during the CHICANO MOVEMENT of the 1960's.

Solís, Gloria: Muralist. Solís worked on the mile-long mural story on the walls on West Hubbard Street in Chicago, Illinois. She painted with José G. González, José Maldonado, Nancy Marrero, Sergio ZAMBRANO, and seven assistants on the first eight panels of the thirty-two-panel work *La Raza de Oro*, which honor pre-Columbian cultures.

Solis, Hilda L.: Public official. Solis was reared in the San Gabriel Valley in California. She earned her bachelor's degree at California State Polytechnic University in Pomona and completed a master's program at the University of Southern California. Solis then went to work for the federal government in Washington, D.C., as a management analyst in the Office of Management and Budget.

After her service in the nation's capital, Solis served as director of the California Student Opportunity and Access Program in a local high school district. She was also elected to the Rio Hondo Community College Board, serving as vice president and president. In 1992, she was elected to the state assembly from the newly reapportioned Fifty-seventh Assembly District of California. In the assembly, Solis focused her legislative energies around the issues of education, labor, commerce, and the environment.

Son: Cuban song and dance form of the nineteenth century. The *son* is in moderate tempo and in duple meter with syncopation. It shows Hispanic and African influence, as seen in its call-and-response patterns. Singers are accompanied by guitars, *tres* (three-course guitars), maracas, bongos, and claves. Later ensembles added to or restructured the original instrumentation. The *son* is danced by couples doing the *zapateado* (foot stamping) without touching. Types of *sones* are the MARIACHI, accompanied by violins, a *vihuela* (five-course guitar), and a harp; and the Mexican *chilena*, from the Pacific Coast of Mexico, characterized by violin, *jarana* (five-course guitar), and harp.

Sonora: Mexican state bordering the United States. Sonora is characterized by booming agriculture and warm winter weather that attracts tourists. The interior features high mountains, mesas, and plateaus, interspersed with flat valleys.

Retaining the patina of Mexico's rich colonial history, much of the Sonora region has escaped complete modernization. By 1791, the Sonora area was one of the largest producers of silver in the world. The rugged Sonoran mountains served as a refuge for Apaches fighting the United States in Arizona in the nineteenth century. Before that, Sonoran Indians fought the Spanish.

In a major revolt in 1680, the peaceful Pueblos, with the help of Apaches and Navajos, drove all Spanish from the region for a period of about twelve years (*see* POPÉ'S REVOLT). Despite periodic droughts and extremes of heat and cold in the desert, and also despite political intrigues and uprisings that destabilized life, Mexican Indians steadfastly remained in Sonora.

Historically, the Sonoran MESTIZOS on both sides of the Rio Grande were bound by language, religion, and a proud social heritage. The Sonoran mestizos continue to have greater cohesion as a group than either Indians or Anglos. The history of border development, however, has formed a wedge between Hispanic people in Sonora and those of the American Southwest. This wedge separates the old, deeply rooted agricultural and pastoral society still characteristic in much of Sonoran from American Latino society, composed in significant part of recent immigrants from Mexico. Fragments of older societies are often at the mercy of an Anglo-dominated border economy.

The unique agrarian and Indian culture of the Sonoran people nevertheless continues. Since the mid-1950's, arid northwestern Mexico has become the agricultural growth center of the country. During the latter half of the twentieth century, it was one of the most rapidly developing farming areas in the world. About two million acres were under irrigated cultiva-

The Pecos Pueblo was destroyed during the Pueblo Revolt of 1680. (Ruben G. Mendoza)

tion in the early 1990's. The area became known as the granary of Mexico. Advances in crop production served to tie this part of Mexico even closer to the United States.

The colorful Sonoran Mayos and Yaqui Indians retain much of their societal structure and traditional attachment to the land. The communal land-use philosophy of Sonoran Indians, however, came into conflict with established mestizo-owned farms and ranches. Protesting Indians still found themselves, late in the twentieth century, being removed by the Mexican army from land parcels taken over by powerful ranchers. Sonoran Indians became more open and vociferous in their support of the indigenous people of Chiapas in their quest for land reform.

In addition to being one of Mexico's most important farming areas, Sonora is also noted for its mineral wealth, deserts, and cattle ranches. The region grew as tourists flocked to see and experience its scenic attractions, beaches, and fishing resorts. Two of Sonora's major nonagricultural growth centers were Guaymas, on the Gulf of California, and the picturesque mountain villages of the Sierra Madre.

Sonoratown: Barrio in Los Angeles, California. Most Mexican residents of Los Angeles lived in Sonoratown in the second half of the nineteenth century. Located adjacent to the original Los Angeles plaza, the Mexican barrio received its name from Anglo Angelenos who perceived the community as an area where Mexican culture continued to persist in the post-Conquest period. The barrio was the poorest section of Los Angeles. Extreme racial violence directed against Mexicans by Anglos, declining land values, and spacial segregation forced Mexican people into exclusively Mexican enclaves. Although it lacked the public services other Angelenos enjoyed, the barrio created a feeling of identity among Mexican Angelenos and provided the means for cultural survival.

Sonorense system: Cultural system that evolved in colonial Mexico, especially SONORA. Because of its remote location, colonization of Sonora did not begin until the early seventeenth century. Settlement was spearheaded by the military and the Jesuit missionaries, and later by miners. Because of the continued threat of Indian depredations and periodic uprisings,

Sonora never developed beyond frontier status during the early Spanish colonial era. After Sonora was separated from Nueva Vizcaya and eighty years before the end of the colonial period, there was considerable growth and development in the region. New communities of Spaniards and mestizos grew up next to missions, presidios, and *reales de minas* (MINING districts).

In the 1780's the *villa* (town) of Pitic (now Hermosillo) was founded with the extensive planning that characterized the Spanish founding of civil settlements in the Americas. It illustrated the Spanish policy of combining military and civilian settlements in the northern frontier, as evidenced in SANTA FE, NEW MEXICO, and in San Antonio de Béxar, in Texas. Under this policy, both civil and criminal jurisdiction would be in the hands of the captain of the presidio. A governor would be appointed to administer and develop the new settlement by distributing lands and building lots, determining water rights, and following royal instructions. The *villa* would be given four leagues of land to distribute among the settlers, along with common lands (*ajido*) for pasture, wood, and water. Settling families had to occupy and improve the land for four years, after which they were given ownership. The Plan of Pitic also accommodated a pueblo of Seri Indians within its jurisdiction, subject to the villa's laws and sharing privileges but having the right to elect its own representatives to the town council.

Settlement in Sonora reflected generous royal policy toward civilian settlers on the northern frontier. The government provided settlers with livestock, seeds, and tools, as well as tents for use en route to the settlement, per diem payments while on the trail, and a year's salary after they had arrived.

Society in Sonora was not homogeneous. There were basically three classifications of people in Sonoran society. One was the Spaniards or GENTE DE RAZÓN (civilized people), a group that often included people of mixed blood and other Europeans, because only the governor, officers of the presidio, and a few merchants of the *reales* could trace their origins to pure Spanish blood. A second was the Christianized, settled Indians who were organized into pueblos and curacies. Finally, there were the missionary Indians governed by the Jesuits.

The Sonorense system provided governmental administration and encouraged settlement. (Security Pacific Bank Collection, Los Angeles Public Library)

Sonoran settlers, or *POBLADORES*, came to the frontier by right of occupation, not by discovery and exploration alone. Their adobe building practices, foods, and reliance on government support of new settlements shaped Spanish society on the frontier as it pushed northward, establishing characteristics that could still be observed in the Southwest of the twentieth century.

Sons of America: Patriotic organization. This fraternal order of American-born Hispanic men "who place fealty to country above every other consideration" is known formally as the Order of the Sons of America. It was founded in 1921 in San Antonio, Texas, and in 1929 associated with the newly founded LEAGUE OF UNITED LATIN AMERICAN CITIZENS. The group's objectives include enhancing appreciation of the American heritage of freedom and promoting a feeling of devotion to the country, its institutions, and the Constitution. The organization also places emphasis on respect to the flag, support and defense of public schools, and opposition to foreign interference in state and federal affairs. Above all, the organization seeks to defend the United States from subversive ideas in opposition to constitutional government.

This organization actively opposes what it views as overly liberal immigration policies and believes that immigration should be restricted. It advocates for a strong national defense and a strong military establishment.

Four parallel institutions work together under the umbrella of the Sons of America: the Valley Forge Sons of America Headquarters, a national research center, a patriotic education center, and a service center of the order. These bodies cosponsor a council of honor that grants award certificates, medals of honor, scholarships, and other awards for people or organizations that promote the order's agenda.

Local groups present flags to schools and churches as well as marking historical places. The order has helped to preserve many historical landmarks throughout the continental United States.

Sopa: Soup. *Sopa* ranges from light broths to thick stews, and it is important in Latin American cuisines. Fancy meals are begun with soups, and poor people may have to be content with soup alone. Mexico had a rich pre-Columbian culinary tradition of soups, and distinctive Spanish styles complemented the native ones. Brazil adopted thick vegetable soups from both American Indian and African slave cuisines, and the Portuguese tradition contributed its fine fish soups.

Locros, starch-thickened vegetable soups, are common from Ecuador to Argentina, and Puerto Rican soups often feature *fideos*, or thin pasta. In Mexican usage, *sopa aguada* refers to a liquid soup and *sopa seca* refers to various dry dishes, especially rice and pasta.

Sopaipillas: Puffy, fried dessert made from wheat tortilla dough. *Sopaipillas* are legitimate New Mexican food, found only rarely in Mexico and then only across the border in Chihuahua. They are made by rolling out dough for wheat tortillas, cutting it into triangles, and frying it in deep fat. If the consistency and thickness of the dough are correct and the temperature of the oil is right, the triangles will puff into diaper-shaped pillows. These can be dusted with confectioner's sugar and cinnamon. More commonly, they are broken open, and honey is drizzled into their hollow interiors. They usually are eaten as dessert.

Sori, Susana (b. 1949, Camagüey, Cuba): Artist. Sori arrived in Chicago, Illinois, with her family in 1961. She earned a B.A. at Michigan State University in 1972.

Sori had early exposure to philosophy and metaphysics. By the time she attended college, she knew that she wanted to be an artist. She has said that she had put religion behind her by that time but began having experiences that she called perceiving a different reality. She wanted to communicate her perceptions and gave up painting for four years. She did not paint again until she visited India. After her return to Chicago, she attended the Art Institute of Chicago in 1977. Studying the works of Rafael Soriano gave her hope that art could show things beyond the barriers of the mind. Other Cuban artists helped her to realize that she had to recapture for herself the Cuban culture that she had rejected.

In 1981, Sori was awarded a Cintas Foundation Fellowship. In 1987, her work appeared in a group show, "Latin American Drawing at the Art Institute of Chicago," and at the First Biennial at the Museum of Contemporary Hispanic Art in New York, New York. Her work has been held in the collections of the Art Institute of Chicago, the Brooklyn Museum, the Cuban Museum of Art and Culture in Miami, Florida, and other major museums.

Sosa, Dan, Jr. (b. Nov. 12, 1923, Las Cruces, N.Mex.): Judge. Sosa was graduated from New Mexico State University with a Bachelor of Science degree. In 1951, he earned a law degree at the University of New Mexico. He began his career as an assistant district attorney for the state of New Mexico. He was elected as a city judge in Las Cruces in 1952.

From 1956 to 1964, Sosa served as district attorney for the Third Judicial District in the state of New Mexico. He began service as chief justice of the New Mexico Supreme Court in 1973. A large part of his legacy is his role as a founder of the MEXICAN AMERICAN LEGAL DEFENSE AND EDUCATION FUND. He is also a member of the Hispanic Bar Association and has chaired the Freedom Foundation National Jury Awards Committee.

Sosa-Riddell, Adaljiza (b. Dec. 12, 1937, Colton, Calif.): Educator. Sosa-Riddell is active in the CHICANO MOVEMENT and has expressed her opinion that true empowerment will come only with establishment of an independent nation-state. Her opinions are based in part on her childhood experience of poverty and work as a migrant crop picker. Her father was arrested several times for radical socialist activities.

Sosa-Riddell earned her bachelor's (1961) and master's (1964) degrees in political science at the University of California, Berkeley. Her master's thesis was on Mexican nationalism. While working on her master's degree, she married William Riddell, another student. They moved to Colton following graduation, and there Sosa-Riddell taught elementary school for seven years. Sosa-Riddell earned her Ph.D. in political science from the University of California, Riverside, in 1974, with her dissertation on the topic of local governing elites in Mexico. She began lecturing in the department of political science at the University of California, Davis, in 1971 and was later named director of the CHICANO STUDIES PROGRAM. She was a founding member of the National Association for Chicano Studies in 1971, and from 1972 to 1974 she chaired the Committee on Status of Chicanos of the Western Political Science Association. She also helped found MUJERES ACTIVAS EN LETRAS Y CAMBIO SOCIAL in 1981 and has remained dedicated to that group's goal of fostering the development of Latina scholarship.

Soto, Gary (b. Apr. 12, 1952, Fresno, Calif.): Poet. Soto grew up in and around the fields of the San Joaquin Valley. These early years in an agricultural milieu, as well as his later years as a factory worker, are reflected in his poetry.

Soto attended local schools and in 1974 was graduated magna cum laude from the California State University, Fresno. He then studied at the University of

California at Irvine, receiving a master of fine arts degree in creative writing in 1976. After spending a year as visiting writer at San Diego State University, he moved to the University of California, Berkeley, in 1977. He became a lecturer in the Chicano studies department.

Some of Soto's major volumes of poetry are *The Elements of San Joaquin* (1977), *The Tale of Sunlight* (1978), *Father Is a Pillow Tied to a Broom* (1980), *Where Sparrows Work Hard* (1981), and *Neighborhood Odes* (1992). No other Chicano poet writing in the early 1990's had received as much recognition from the mainstream American poetry establishment as Soto. One of the first Chicanos to be nominated for the Pulitzer Prize (1978), Soto was also nominated for the National Book Award in 1978 and has been the recipient of many literary prizes and honors.

Soto, Jorge (b. 1947, New York, N.Y.): Artist. Soto is a self-taught artist whose works show elaborate linear patterns. Through his work, he attempts to recover African and Taino Indian aesthetics.

Soto became identified with the Taller Boricua (Puerto Rican Workshop) of New York City and participated in its formative years in the early 1970's. The Taller Boricua began in 1969 in East Harlem's Museo del Barrio, located across the street from the political militants of the YOUNG LORDS Party. During its early years, the Taller Boricua participated in the political movement, making political posters and exhibiting in the community. It offered young artists an environment in which they could develop a sense of identity while they sharpened their professional skills. Other artists associated with the Taller Boricua are Carlos OSORIO, Ralph ORTIZ MONTAÑEZ (Ralph Ortiz), Rafael Colón Morales, Marcos Dimas, and Nitza Tufiño.

Soto, Pedro Juan (b. July 11, 1928, Cataño, Puerto Rico): Writer. Soto is the eldest of six children of Alfonso Soto, a barber and sometime seller of coffins, and Elena Suárez. His childhood household commonly indulged in spiritualist practices. Soto has stated that being surrounded by voices of spirits in his childhood awakened his imagination.

After completing his elementary and secondary education in Cataño and Bayamón, Soto moved to New York when he was eighteen years old. He entered Long Island University in 1946, earned a bachelor's degree, and joined the Army. He later used his veteran's benefits to study for a master's degree in education at Columbia University. After earning a doctorate in Latin American studies from the University of Toulouse in France, he became a faculty member of the University of Puerto Rico.

Soto's novels place him within a generation of writers who moved from writing about the problems of the rural migration of Puerto Ricans to the United States to the urban experience of rootlessness and alienation in a foreign culture. They include *Los perros anónimos* (unpublished, written in 1950), *Usmaíl* (1959), *Ardiente suelo, fría estación* (1961; *Hot Land, Cold Season*, 1973), *El francotirador* (1969), *Temporada de duendes* (1970), and *Un oscuro pueblo sonriente* (1982).

Soto Vélez, Clemente (b. 1905, Lares, Puerto Rico): Writer and political activist. Soto Vélez's work embodies the spirit of his birthplace, known for the famous GRITO DE LARES, the 1868 rebellion against Spanish colonial power. Although he received a minimal formal education, at the age of twenty-two he moved to the capital, where he worked as a journalist and editor at the newspaper *El Tiempo*. In 1928, he cofounded a literary group, El Hospital de los Sensitivos. He published poems under his name and that of the group until he formed another group in 1929.

Soto Vélez became increasingly radicalized. In 1936 he and other Nationalist Party leaders were found guilty of conspiring to overthrow the United States government. He spent seven years in federal prison. Soto Vélez was not permitted to return to Puerto Rico and moved in 1937 to New York, where he became active in uniting the political, creative, and economic resources of the Puerto Rican community. In 1954, he published his first book of poetry, *Abrazo interno*. He later published *Arboles* (1955), *Caballo de Palo* (1959), and *La tierra prometida* (1979). Both his poetry and his activism have influenced the cause of freedom for Puerto Rico.

South American immigrants and immigration: South Americans constitute a small but significant part of the Latino population of the United States. Unlike Mexicans and Puerto Ricans, the two most populous Hispanic groups in the United States, South American immigrants are generally from the middle or upper economic classes of their native countries and are often highly educated.

Historical Background. Before the late twentieth century, South Americans rarely traveled to the United States and even more rarely became U.S. citizens. The trip by boat is long, difficult, and expensive. After airplane travel became more affordable, immigration

increased, but it still accounted for a small proportion of the total influx of Spanish-speaking people.

The IMMIGRATION AND NATIONALITY ACT OF 1952 (McCarran-Walter Act), which set quotas for immigrants of particular nationalities, was replaced in 1965 by a new immigration act. The new act abolished quotas but instead gave preference to prospective immigrants with high levels of education and those who showed evidence that they could support themselves financially.

The result was a huge increase in the number of Latino immigrants in general, and South Americans were favored. They were usually not living in poverty in their homelands but instead were looking for even better opportunities. In this sense, they were far more similar to the earlier immigrants from Europe than to those from other Latin American countries in the twentieth century.

Accurate figures on net South American immigration are difficult to gather because the IMMIGRATION AND NATURALIZATION SERVICE (INS) does not provide statistics on the numbers of people who return to their place of birth. The INS has estimated that nearly one million South Americans moved to the United States between 1961 and 1990, roughly one-fourth of them from Colombia. More than 40 percent of those arrived between 1980 and 1990.

Demographics. By far the largest group of South American immigrants in the United States, estimated in 1980 at more than 150,000, is from Colombia. In 1980, about 90,000 people of Ecuadoran background lived in the United States. Guyanans emigrated in large numbers in the 1980's, with approximately 80,000 entering the United States. Peruvians were the third-largest South American immigrant group in the 1980's, behind Colombians and Guyanans and slightly ahead of Ecuadorans.

The largest concentration of South Americans in the United States is in and around NEW YORK CITY, especially the JACKSON HEIGHTS section of Queens, where about fifty thousand Colombian immigrants live. To a certain extent, other South American groups blend into this community, but it is separate from the Puerto Rican and Dominican communities that make up the majority of New York's Hispanic population. Smaller South American communities exist in FLORIDA, CALIFORNIA, and WASHINGTON, D.C.

Although there are undocumented aliens from South America in the United States, the number is small. South Americans cannot travel to the United States by land without traveling long distances through

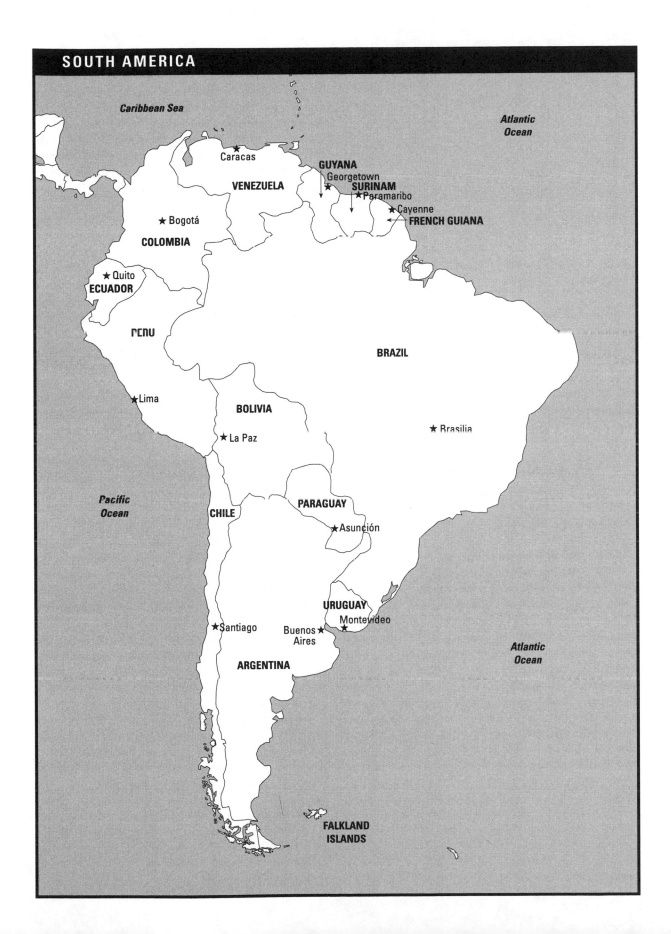

SOUTH AMERICA

Caribbean Sea

Atlantic Ocean

★ Caracas

VENEZUELA

GUYANA
Georgetown
★

SURINAM
★ Paramaribo

★ Cayenne
FRENCH GUIANA

★ Bogotá
COLOMBIA

★ Quito
ECUADOR

PERU

BRAZIL

★ Lima

BOLIVIA

★ La Paz

★ Brasilia

Pacific Ocean

PARAGUAY

CHILE

★ Asunción

URUGUAY
★ Montevideo

★ Santiago

Buenos
Aires ★

Atlantic Ocean

ARGENTINA

FALKLAND ISLANDS

IMMIGRANTS FROM SOUTH AMERICA BY COUNTRY OF BIRTH, 1961-1990				
	1961-1970	1971-1980	1981-1989	1990
All of South America	228,300	284,400	370,400	85,800
Argentina	42,100	25,100	20,300	5,400
Brazil	20,500	13,700	19,500	4,200
Chile	11,500	17,600	19,400	4,000
Colombia	70,300	77,600	100,200	24,200
Ecuador	37,000	50,200	43,500	12,500
Guyana	7,100	47,500	84,000	11,400
Peru	18,600	29,100	48,700	15,700
Venezuela	8,500	7,100	14,800	3,100

Source: Data are from *Statistical Abstract of the United States* (Washington, D.C.: U.S. Bureau of the Census, 1991), p. 11.

Note: The numbers for All of South America include immigrants from countries not listed separately.

Central America and Mexico, crossing a number of heavily guarded borders. By and large, the South American population of the United States has entered the country legally and gained citizenship through normal channels.

Social and Economic Conditions. The South American community in the United States is very different from most U.S. Hispanic cultures. In particular, South American immigrants have little in common with the Mexican and Puerto Rican immigrants who make up the vast majority of U.S. Latinos.

South American immigrants tend to be well educated and to come from the upper and middle classes of South American society. South Americans typically come to the United States either to flee from political turmoil and repressive governments or to better their economic situation. Many South American immigrants return to their countries of origin, and many travel to and from South America on a regular basis. Many are businesspeople and professionals of various sorts. On the whole, South American immigrants tend to have smaller families than Mexican Americans or mainland Puerto Ricans. Few South American immigrants are migrant laborers or live on public assistance. Many Colombians in New York and Miami are members of the middle and upper classes. For these and other reasons, there is little identification between South Americans and other Latinos in U.S. society.

—Marc Goldstein

SUGGESTED READINGS: • Gann, L. H., and Peter J. Duignan. *The Hispanics in the United States: A History.* Boulder, Colo.: Westview Press, 1986. • Portes, Alejandro, and Ruben G. Rubaut. *Immigrant America: A Portrait.* Berkeley: University of California Press, 1990. • Reimers, David M. *Still the Golden Door: The Third World Comes to America.* New York: Columbia University Press, 1985. • Shorris, Earl. *Latinos: A Biography of the People.* New York: W. W. Norton, 1992. • Weyr, Thomas. *Hispanic U.S.A.: Breaking the Melting Pot.* New York: Harper & Row, 1988.

South American native communities: The continent of South America includes some of the most diverse physical environments in the world, from the high Andes to the tropical rainforests of the Amazon River basin. Scholars estimate the population of South American Indians at the time of first European contact at between 7 and 39 million, compared with recent population estimates of 7 to 15 million.

More than 90 percent of the Indian population of modern South America is concentrated in Ecuador, Colombia, Peru, and Bolivia. Peru has the largest Indian population, estimated at 4.8 million in 1990.

Throughout the diverse regions of South America, people have established unique and specialized indigenous cultures, the numerical majority of which have long since passed into extinction. A brief summary of South American indigenous populations requires some framework for classification of cultural types and regions.

Julian Steward divided South American Indian cultures into four large groups defined by a variety of commonly held traits and linguistic affiliations. Steward's system is essentially evolutionary, assuming a development through the various stages.

The first group is the marginal, hunter-gatherer peoples of the southern tip of the continent as well as sections of the interior of South America. These peoples share a number of strikingly similar cultural traits with the marginal hunter-gatherer and seminomadic tribes of the North American plains and Canadian plains areas.

The second type, circum-Caribbean cultures, are represented in South America along the northern coastal regions of the Gulf of Mexico and into Central America. The third type, diminished circum-Caribbean (tropical) tribal groupings, occupy rain forest and wooded environments. They are associated with the Amazon region. Diminished circum-Caribbean groups share significant traits with the eastern woodland tribes of North America. The fourth category, the high cultures of the Andean territories, are found primarily in Peru and Bolivia.

Different Classification Systems. Classification systems of this type are always controversial. George Peter Murdock has suggested that Steward's system is not nearly detailed enough to do justice to the diversity of cultures. Murdock suggested a number of culture categories that divided the South American continent into twenty-four cultural regions. Many of these regions more or less followed geographical divisions between modern states. In the tropical regions, however, the cultural divisions become smaller and more complex, reflecting a greater variety in the tropical forest tribes.

John Howland Rowe's work on the problems of linguistic classification estimates that there may be more than 250 different language systems in South America. Of these, he estimated that only about one hundred are documented in any form.

A primary criticism of classification systems in general, whether linguistic or other types, can be summarized as a lack of information. Much fieldwork and linguistic study needs to be done before a scientifically serious anthropological overview of the cultures of South America can be made and widely accepted. Given these problems, Steward's categories serve as well as other systems to briefly introduce the largest divisions of South American culture.

The Marginal Cultures. It is frequently assumed that the cultural complexion of the peoples who occupy the extreme, or marginal, geographical regions of the North American and South American plains manifests cultural traits once common throughout North and South America. It is also frequently assumed that the other three cultural groups developed from these simple, widespread forms.

Steward, however, notes that there is not enough similarity among peoples of the extreme North and South to justify this assumption. These various groups share only the most generalized traits, such as small seminomadic groups, simple dwelling construction, and the lack of a priest-temple-religion complex or a war complex that included captive-taking. These hunter-gatherer groups did not have agricultural practices and did not use animals, with the rare exception of dogs. The introduction of the horse allowed for larger complexes of society to develop, such as in the North American Plains tribes as well as the tribes of the Chaco.

The Circum-Caribbean Cultures. Steward assumes that the high cultures of the Andes, of which the Incas

A folkloric band plays music of the Andes on traditional instruments. (Don Franklin)

are the primary people, would not have developed much later than those of the northern mesoamerican Maya and later Aztec because the potato, so central to these civilizations, was originally a South American plant. The Andean high cultures shared with the circum-Caribbean cultures certain important traits such as intensive farming, large population centers, and stable settlements. There also developed strong class differentiation and governmental structures as opposed to rule by family elders. There were religious buildings associated with a well-developed local architecture and art tradition. Among the artistic skills shared by both the high cultures and the circum-Caribbean cultures are the use of pottery, feathers, and cotton garments.

Unique to the circum-Caribbean societies were activities related to coastal experience, as one would expect, including use of seafaring boats and intensive fishing. A stratified society developed on three levels: aristocracy and priesthood, commoners, and prisoners of war who were used as slaves. Steward suggests that military service was an important way in which commoners could achieve higher social status—through the capture of many slaves and display of human trophies of war. Elements of circum-Caribbean groups have been noted in southern United States groups such as the Natchez and Chickasaw tribes. Certain religious features are shared among these peoples as well, such as the existence of a priestly class.

The circum-Caribbean cultural complex was severely affected by the arrival of the Spanish and European conquerors. Only remnants of these cultures survive, in northern Colombia and mixed with such tribal groups as the Mosquito Indians of Nicaragua. The once numerous populations of the Caribbean islands are extinct, replaced by the Afro-Caribbean/Spanish cultures that dominate in Cuba, Haiti, Jamaica, and the other Caribbean islands.

Diminished Circum-Caribbean Cultures. Unique to the South American environment are the tropical forest contexts, within which a unique configuration of tribal traits developed from circum-Caribbean roots. These tribes developed farming, using manioc, arrowroot, and yams. They use pole-and-thatch houses, dugout canoes, domesticated cotton, the loom, tobacco, blowguns, bark cloth, hammocks, and hollow-log drums.

The tropical forest tribes are much less stratified than are the circum-Caribbean tribes, and they are more egalitarian, similar to marginal tribes. Tropical tribal lineage is predominantly patrilineal. The war complex is developed among tropical tribal groups, as

is the use of shamans who practice healing and magical curative arts. As one moves from the tropical centers to the outer areas of the Amazon and Orinoco rivers, similarities to the circum-Caribbean tribes begin to diminish.

The High Cultures. Andean culture, most preeminently and successfully represented in Inca culture, developed its complex societal forms on the basis of intensive farming using terracing and irrigation. As a result, large population centers gave rise to highly differentiated cultures of stratified societies. According to Steward, Peru became so intensely populated that it could no longer sustain large numbers of captives as slaves. This inspired territorial conquest, with central empires collecting tribute to support themselves.

Religious culture probably developed from localized tribal/familial worship of gods. A full priesthood developed, with a state cult and a dominant priest class. The priests over the state cult had dominance over the local shamans, who continued to practice local religious practices apart from the rites of the central shrines.

In an interesting summary of the development of the Andean, AZTEC, and MAYAN CIVILIZATIONS (the three main high cultures of Mesoamerica and South America), Steward noted that the Mayan centers were not so much population centers as ritual centers that could sustain a population that was widely spread in the surrounding area. In contrast, the Andean and Aztec cultures could not afford the vulnerability of widespread settlements and therefore developed highly populated centers that could sustain long periods of warfare.

Theories of Development. The relationship of these four cultural categories is controversial. Rather than a simple development from the "simple" to the more "complex" cultures, some anthropologists have suggested that traits developed as a result of numerous migrations and contacts.

In a classic essay, Robert Carneiro wrote in 1961 that a close relationship exists between the form of agriculture and the resulting development of civilization. Carneiro suggests that availability of land will result in less intensive agriculture and more movement among smaller groups of people. Carneiro proved that the movement of "slash-and-burn" cultures in the tropical forests was not based on exhaustion of the land after cultivation but rather on the relative ease of finding new lands that required less labor than would fertilizing and weeding older farm areas. If new land is

The ruins of Machu Picchu in Peru. (Envision, Jack Stein Grove)

available, it will be used for greater convenience. If, however, arable land is limited, then more intensive farming techniques will be developed, often requiring more intensive systems of generating human labor.

As one moves from "marginal" to "tropical" to "high" cultural areas in South America, one also moves from greater to lesser accessibility to arable land, from lesser to greater levels of intensive farming, and from lesser to greater areas of population concentration. This compelling theory of the relationship of cultural development and environment presents an interesting theoretical relationship between cultural development and practical needs of everyday subsistence.

—*Daniel Smith-Christopher*

SUGGESTED READINGS:

• Lyon, Patricia J., ed. *Native South Americans: Ethnology of the Least Known Continent.* Boston: Little, Brown, 1974. Numerous helpful articles include Julian Steward's "American Culture History in the Light of South America," George Peter Murdock's "South American Culture Areas," John Howland Rowe's "Linguistic Classification Problems in South America," and the classic essay by Robert Carneiro, "Slash-and-Burn Cultivation Among the Kuikuru and Its Implications for Cultural Development in the Amazon Basin."

• Olson, James. *The Indians of Central and South America: An Ethnohistorical Dictionary.* New York: Greenwood Press, 1991. The most important bibliographical source for further reading.

• Salzano, Francisco, and Sidia M. Callegari-Jacques. *South American Indians: A Case Study in Evolution.* Oxford, England: Clarendon Press, 1988. Includes important statistical information as well as helpful geographical surveys.

• Skar, Harald O., and Frank Salomon, eds. *Natives and Neighbors in South America: Anthropological Essays.* Göteborg, Sweden: Göteborgs Etnografiska Museum, 1987. An important survey of contemporary issues. Discusses modern liberation/political movements among natives of Central and South America.

• Steward, Julian. *Handbook of South American Indians.* 7 vols. Washington, D.C.: Government Printing Office, 1946-1959. A standard reference work, still widely used.

• Taylor, Robert B. *Indians of Middle America.* Manhattan, Kans.: Lifeway Books, 1989. Particularly good on circum-Caribbean tribal traditions.

South Texas: South Texas is the area south of a line drawn northwest from Victoria to SAN ANTONIO, then southwest to Laredo, according to the South Texas Historical Association. It has the largest proportion of Latinos of any region in Texas, with 50 percent Latinos in its northernmost county (Béxar) and 82 percent in its southernmost county (Cameron), according to the 1990 census.

This is a region with a rich Hispanic heritage. The first Spanish expedition to land in Texas, in 1519, explored the region that was inhabited by Indians later called Coahuiltecans. Using horses and guns that were introduced by the Spaniards, the Apaches and Comanches occupied the region in the late eighteenth century. Following the beginning of immigration into the region from the United States, all major Indian tribes were expelled in the nineteenth century.

The Spanish missions in South Texas commemorate the effort to convert Texas Indians to Catholicism. Five missions were established along the San Antonio River in the area that later became part of the city of San Antonio. San Antonio was the primary Spanish city in Texas and the major stop on EL CAMINO REAL to Goliad. The missions became well-established cattle ranches by the mid-eighteenth century, and they supplied the colonial settlers. Canary Islanders began settling near the mission ranches, some of them taking over the ranches by the end of the eighteenth century. It was on South Texas brush country that ranches developed into the gigantic enterprises that are characteristic of Texas heritage. Many of the descendants of Spanish *vaqueros* still owned parts of the original ranches near the end of the twentieth century.

During the nineteenth century, following Mexico's achievement of independence from Spain in 1821, Mexicans took control of Texas briefly. This period was characterized by political unrest and increasing immigration from the United States that culminated in Texas' declaration of independence from Mexico. San Antonio and Goliad were key sites in Texas' war of independence. This period began the long struggle of Texans of Mexican origin for socioeconomic equality in South Texas.

The region of South Texas is the home of several million Mexican Americans, a large proportion of whom live in poverty. The most dramatic examples are the COLONIAS, villages in the Rio Grande Valley that lack adequate water supply, sewage disposal, and health care. In 1994, however, incomes in South Texas were still three times as high as those in the adjacent Mexican territory. This contrast led many Mexicans to cross the border to work in South Texas. The valley area is home to more than 100,000 migrant farmwork-

A turn-of-the-century South Texas family. (Library of Congress)

ers between October and April. These workers were mainly Mexicans until the late 1970's, when a strong flow of immigration began from Central America. Most Central Americans, however, did not want to settle in South Texas and quickly moved to Latino communities in Houston and outside Texas.

By the early 1990's, Mexican Americans in South Texas had taken a leadership role in Texas political and cultural life. Their influence was widespread in government, economic development, and education of Hispanic Texans.

Southwest: American region that has become the center of emerging Latino political and economic power as well as a center for leisure pursuits and border industries. By the year 1500, a remarkable urban culture, that of the pueblo-dwelling Indians, had reached and passed its zenith in the American Southwest. This occurred before the extensive colonization by Spanish-speaking people moving northward out of Mexico. By 1600, the Spanish Empire of the Southwest had established presidios, or military bases, at Sante Fe and San Antonio; missions or religious gathering points at Taos

Mexicans gather near the U.S.-Mexico border, waiting until nightfall when it will be easier to cross undetected. (AP/Wide World Photos)

and Nogales; and pueblos or trading points along the Colorado and Gila rivers.

The early nineteenth century brought a flood of Anglo settlers into the region by way of historic trails that linked the east with Santa Fe and with Spanish settlements along the Gila River and in California. The last tide of immigration came from the south. It was larger than earlier flows, although its exact dimensions are difficult to discover. This immigration consisted of Spanish-speaking people from the border states of Mexico.

Over the centuries, the Southwest culture of Indian and Spanish origins remained mostly unblended with the Anglo-American culture predominating in much of the United States. The Southwest by the end of the twentieth century contained by far the largest land area of Indian reservations in the United States and the highest percentage of the population identifying itself as Hispanic. The Southwest was the only large area of the United States in which a large proportion of people bought groceries and conducted other everyday transactions in a language other than English.

The Southwest of the late twentieth century emerged as particularly critical to the changing patterns of American society. Mexico lost half of its territory in the TREATY OF GUADALUPE HIDALGO (1848) with the United States. More than a century later, Latinos began to regain some of their power in the region. By the end of the twentieth century, the majority of elected local and state officials in the Southwest had Spanish surnames. In the United States as a whole, Latinos were second to Anglos as a whole in household purchasing power; in the Southwest, the purchasing power of the two groups was almost equal.

The U.S.-Mexico border became a frontier between prosperity and poverty. Its entire length evidenced abrupt points of cultural contact. In few other places were there such obvious social and economic disparities across an international border. Because these contrasts were visible to all, strong incentives existed for Mexicans to cross the line, if only temporarily, to a land of plenty.

Cultural diversity is still readily visible in the Southwest, and the social and political significance of Latinos and Native Americans is much greater now than even decades earlier. From California to Texas, various Latino interest groups seek solutions to the chronic discrepancy in power between Anglos and Latinos. By the end of the twentieth century, that power was beginning to fall into balance as Latinos exercised the political power inherent in their large numbers.

Southwest Voter Registration Education Project (SVREP): The SVREP is a nonpartisan, nonprofit civic organization founded in 1974 to increase the political participation of Mexican Americans, African Americans, and Native Americans in the Southwest through voter registration campaigns, nonpartisan voter education, voting rights litigation, and research on voter participation. In the early 1990's, the SVREP had offices in San Antonio, Texas, and Los Angeles, California, with a combined staff of fifteen people.

The Southwest Voter Registration Education Project encourages Latinos to participate in the democratic process. (Bob Daemmrich)

The SVREP was established through the efforts of William VELÁSQUEZ, a Chicano activist in San Antonio, Texas. It was modeled on the Voter Education Project developed in the South by African Americans during the Civil Rights movement of the 1960's.

From its inception, the SVREP has been a grassroots organization with a focus on the training and development of community volunteers. Its voter registration drives typically include local volunteer recruitment, training sessions on voter mobilization, coalition building, and leadership networking. In large urban areas, the SVREP has won pledges from organizations, social service agencies, and businesses to register their members, clients, and patrons. Its New Citizen Program encourages noncitizens to become citizens and thus become eligible to vote, and its Media Program develops bilingual public service announcements encouraging people to vote.

By the early 1990's, the SVREP had conducted more than seventeen hundred voter registration drives in two hundred communities in fourteen western states. By its own account, it had registered two million voters and trained twelve thousand community leaders. It had also established seventeen regional planning committees in Texas, California, and Arizona to facilitate the formation of political networks and minority public policy in the Southwest.

In addition to voter registration campaigns, the SVREP has participated in the successful litigation of more than eighty voting rights lawsuits. In the 1990's, it was particularly involved in cases concerning voter redistricting plans and at-large election systems. The organization established Fair Redistricting Committees in Arizona, California, Colorado, and Texas.

In 1986, the SVREP founded the Southwest Voter Research Institute, which became a separate nonprofit organization. The institute monitors the voting patterns and political opinions of Latinos and their community leaders, provides expert testimony in vote dilution lawsuits, and studies the impact of public policies on minority communities, sharing this information with elected officials.

Spain: Third-largest and fourth-most-populous European country. Spain was an early world power; a revitalized modern Spain is seeking full participation in European affairs and is striving to regain its influence in Latin America.

Geography. Spain, with an area of about 195,000 square miles, covers 85 percent of the Iberian Peninsula. The country has a Mediterranean coastline about 1,030 miles long and an Atlantic coastline about 440 miles long. Spain's land borders are with Portugal, to the west of the scarped edge of the tablelands, and with France, which shares the Pyrenees.

Spain consists of vast central tablelands surrounded by distinct regions. The tablelands include the Meseta Central and the Ebro basin. They are desolate, monotonous, and flat, except for a few east-west trending sierras and for *cuestas* (gradual slopes). The mountain ranges are relatively easily crossed through their many passes. The *cuestas* are low rises that lead up to *páramos* (bleak plateaus). The arid, rocky surfaces of the *páramos* are a result of deforestation, particularly of the holm oak, and overgrazing.

In the north, Galicia, Asturias, and the Basque provinces extend from Portugal to the Pyrenees. Galicia has an undulate and rounded terrain, a mild maritime climate, and few mineral resources. Galicia's many rivers drain into fjordlike rias, which have facilitated the fishing industry. Asturias and Cantabria are scenic, with the Cantabrian Mountains and valleys exhibiting the effects of glaciation. The Basque provinces (Alava, Guipúzcoa, and Vizcaya) occupy a transitional zone between the Cantabrians and the Pyrenees and between the humid coast and the semiarid Meseta Central, a plateau region covering almost half of Spain, with Madrid near its center. These provinces are a major industrial region because of their good harbors, mineral deposits, hydroelectricity, and proximity to West European markets.

The Pyrenees mountain range extends about 260 miles along the French-Spanish border. The highest crests rise to more than eleven thousand feet in elevation. Although the Spanish side has a more gradual descent, steep foothills and ridges and narrow gorges limit transportation. The small mountain nation of Andorra has survived on the southern slope of the eastern Pyrenees because of its isolation. Most cross-border traffic uses the *autopistas* (freeways) along narrow coastal plains at either end of the Pyrenees.

In the east, narrow coastal plains extend from the French-Spanish border south through the city of Murcia. In Catalonia (a region of northeastern Spain including the provinces of Gerona, Barcelona, Lérida, and Tarragona), the coastal plain has a mild climate and moderate precipitation that foster tourism along the Costa Brava ("rugged coast") to the north of the city of Barcelona and along the Costa Dorada ("golden coast") to the south. The city of Barcelona ranks second in population to Madrid (1.6 million versus 2.9 million, estimated in 1991) and is a leading industrial

Windmills and an ancient castle loom above the vast plains of central Spain. (Michele L. McGrath)

center. South of Catalonia, coastal plains stretch discontinuously through the Levant (provinces of Castellón de la Plana, Valencia, Alicante, and Murcia). The climate changes from mild in the north to hot and semiarid in the south. The port of Valencia is Spain's third-largest city and services a rich agricultural area where oranges and other cash crops are grown. Spain as a whole had an estimated population of thirty-nine million in 1991.

Andalusia extends from southern Portugal east to the Mediterranean and north to the Sierra Morena. The heart of Andalusia is the Guadalquivir basin, where gently rolling, semiarid land is farmed intensively anywhere irrigation is feasible. The risk of crop failure from drought has sustained the division of the land into *latifundia* (large estates typically devoted to commercial production). Although more than two dozen districts in Spain produce wines, none is more renowned than Jerez, at the southern end of the basin, where sherry, a fortified white wine, is produced. Inland along the Guadalquivir River lies Seville, Spain's fourth-largest city, one of its most beautiful and historic. The Costa del Sol ("sun coast") lies between

Estepona and Motril and has become a mecca for pleasure seekers.

Metropolitan Spain also includes the Balearic Islands (Majorca, Minorca, Ibiza, and thirteen smaller islands) in the western Mediterranean Sea and the Canary Islands. The Canaries rise from the Atlantic Ocean off the northwestern coast of Africa. Formerly layover points for mariners sailing to the New World, the Canaries are a popular non-summer destination for northern European tourists.

Although Spain reduced its presence in Africa during the twentieth century, it retained five places of sovereignty in North Africa: Ceuta, Melilla, Chafarinas Islands, Alhucemas Islands, and Peñón de Vélez de la Gomera. The last three lie off the northern coast of Morocco. Ceuta, a Spanish military station and seaport, occupies a promontory across the strait from Gibraltar, a promontory claimed by Spain but a British colony since 1713. Ceuta and Gibraltar, the Pillars of Hercules, are militarily strategic because they flank the western end of the Mediterranean. Melilla is a Spanish presidio and commercial port on Morocco's northern coast.

History. The earliest records of settlement in Spain are from Paleolithic times, when cave dwellers from the province of Santander to the western Pyrenees left ceiling drawings and paintings. The Iberians, a Neolithic people probably from northern Africa, inhabited the peninsula by 3000 B.C.E. They produced an artistic culture near the Ebro River and along the Valencian coast. By the twelfth century B.C.E., the Phoenicians traded with peoples of southern Spain, establishing trading posts at the present-day sites of Cádiz and Málaga. Twice, around 900 B.C.E. and 600 B.C.E., the Celts moved south into northern Spain. Celts and Iberians advancing onto the Meseta Central mixed to form the Celtiberians. About 600 B.C.E., Greeks reached Spain and established colonies along the Mediterranean coast and perhaps beyond. They refined the relatively primitive art styles of Iberia. In the third century B.C.E., Carthage, a powerful city on the North African coast, invaded southern and eastern Spain to gain advantage in its war with Rome. The Carthaginians

Spanish conquistadores *were among the first Europeans to explore the Americas.* (Institute of Texan Cultures)

founded Carthago Nova (present-day Cartagena) in 227 B.C.E., but they failed to win allies and drove more Iberians onto the Meseta Central.

The Romans landed in Spain in 218 B.C.E., defeated the Carthaginians, and drove them off the peninsula by 205 B.C.E. Spain, known as Hispania to the Romans, was at the western end of their empire. Hispania soon became the granary and the wealthiest province of Rome, although the Romans needed nearly two centuries to subdue all local resistance. Rome built roads, bridges, aqueducts, and other works to resettle the indigenous people in hundreds of cities. Henceforth, Spanish civilization would be urban. By 1990, about 91 percent of Spain's population resided in urban areas.

Roman Spain prospered until early in the fifth century, when three Germanic tribes—the Suevi, the Vandals, and the Alans—poured in at the invitation of a Roman general. Because these tribes ravaged the country, the Romans signed a pact in 418 C.E. with the Visigoths, a Romanized Germanic tribe, granting them Aquitania (a Roman division of southwestern Gaul) in exchange for restoring Spain to Rome. The Visigoths drove the Suevi into far Galicia, defeated the Alans, and forced the Vandals out of Andalusia and into North Africa. Contrary to their agreement, the Visigoths assumed control of Spain and established a capital at Toledo. Rome left a threefold legacy: Vulgar Latin that evolved into Spanish, Roman law, and Catholic Christianity.

Arab armies invaded in 711 and had conquered most of the peninsula by 718. They were soon joined by other Muslims, including Berbers, Copts, and Syrians. By the tenth century, Spain had a Muslim majority. After the fall of the Caliphate of Córdoba in 1037, al-Andalus (Muslim Spain) splintered into twenty-six city-states.

Although a skirmish at Covadonga in the eighth century began the Reconquest of Spain, the first major blow the Christian Spaniards dealt to the Muslims was in 1086, when Toledo surrendered. The Muslim Spaniards regrouped by twice inviting other Muslims—the Almoravides and then the Almohades—into al-Andalus. Seville fell to the Christians under Ferdinand III in 1248. After the fall of Seville, all that remained of al-Andalus was the kingdom of Granada, which surrendered on January 3, 1492.

Modern Spain begins with the reign of Isabella and Ferdinand, *los reyes católicos* (the Catholic Monarchs). Married in 1469, they united her Castile and his Aragon in 1474. They accomplished much, including beginning the Spanish colonial empire, but the Catho-

---

FACTS AT A GLANCE

Capital: Madrid

Area: 194,885 square miles

Population (estimated, 1994): 39,770,000

Percentage living in urban areas: 91

Estimated 1991 Gross National Product (GNP): $486.614 billion

Type of government: parliamentary monarchy

---

lic Monarchs also initiated harsh treatment of Muslims and Jews. The choices given to those people were conversion to Catholicism or exile. Most Jews left Spain by the early 1500's. Although most Muslims initially remained in Spain as converts to Christianity (*moriscos*), many were killed or exiled between 1609 and 1611.

The sixteenth century is often called Spain's golden century because the reigns of Charles V (1516-1556) and Philip II (1556-1598) fashioned Spain's ascendancy to a world power. While soldiers, missionaries, adventurers, and others sailed to the New World, however, much of Spain lay neglected and in disrepair. The wealth of the New World was squandered in various European wars, especially that against the Protestants of the Spanish Netherlands. Poverty and dissatisfaction were widespread in Spain. Philip responded by suppressing dissent, especially against Catholicism, and by relocating the capital to the more centrally located Madrid.

The beginning of the Bourbon dynasty in 1700 signaled Spain's attempt to catch up with the rest of Europe. The Treaty of Utrecht, which ended the War of the Spanish Succession (1701-1714), stripped Spain of its European possessions, ceded Minorca and Gibraltar to the British, and demanded the Spanish Crown's renunciation of any claims to the French throne. Spain was left free to concentrate on itself and its overseas possessions. The Bourbon monarchs responded by instituting many reforms, only to be resisted by the Spanish masses. They succeeded in completing long-needed public works projects and in initiating many economic reforms. An argument over succession to the crown in the early 1800's emboldened Napoleon Bonaparte to place his brother Joseph on the Spanish throne. Enraged Spaniards, with British assistance,

Spanish schoolchildren in traditional costume perform a folk dance on the streets of Segovia. (Michele L. McGrath)

fought the War of Independence (1808-1814), after which the crown was given to Ferdinand VII, an ineffectual absolutist. Spanish colonies in the Americas had taken over their own governance during the war. Except for Cuba and Puerto Rico, all had declared their independence by 1821.

In the nineteenth century, liberal forces in favor of a constitutional monarchy and individual rights gathered strength. The First Spanish Republic (1873-1874) ended abruptly because of regional independence movements. Liberal principles triumphed in Spain, but at a tremendous cost. The Second Republic was established in 1931 with broad public support, but extreme forces vied for control of the government. In 1936, the Popular Front, a coalition of republicans, socialists, syndicalists, anarchists, and communists, won election. The army, under General Francisco Franco, soon revolted. Madrid surrendered unconditionally to the Nationalist army forces on March 29, 1939, ending the civil war. The human toll was astounding: about one million dead, more than 400,000 refugees in France alone, and about two million persons passing through prisons and concentration camps in Spain by 1942.

After World War II, Franco's dictatorship was isolated internationally until the Pact of Madrid (1953), in which the United States promised Spain economic aid in exchange for American defense bases on Spanish soil. The infusion of aid allowed Franco to rebuild the country and prepare it for economic growth. Two days after Franco's death on November 20, 1975, Juan Carlos was proclaimed king. Juan Carlos adroitly guided Spain to establish it as a stable democracy. The country passed a liberal constitution in 1978, was admitted to the North Atlantic Treaty Organization (NATO) in 1982, and entered into the European Community (EC) in 1986.

People. The Spanish nation is an amalgam of the many people who have conquered and occupied Spain or settled there. The modern Spaniard may have the physical characteristics of the people of the Mediterranean region, northern Europe, or sub-Saharan Africa. The Basques and the Catalonians, historically and linguistically linked to the Provence region of southeastern France, have maintained strong separate identities and have won limited regional autonomy. The gypsies have never been assimilated. They preserve the flamenco songs and dances of Andalusia.

Immigration to North America. Spaniards or their descendants have resided in the American Southwest since the sixteenth century (*see* SPANISH AMERICANS). They established and operated missions and trading posts in the Taos-Santa Fe area of New Mexico, the Los Angeles and San Francisco areas, and parts of western Texas.

The number of Spaniards immigrating annually to North America in the twentieth century has been small, but it has increased over time except when reduced by changes in immigration policies. Spanish immigration to the United States peaked around 1921, before the first restrictive quotas. In that year, 23,813 Spaniards immigrated to the United States. During the 1920's, only 28,958 Spaniards immigrated to the United States, and a larger number—38,960—emigrated back to Spain. The U.S. Immigration and Nationality Act of 1965 overturned the national origins system, but during the 1960's only about 44,700 Spaniards immigrated to the United States, representing 1.3 percent of U.S. immigration. Canada received even fewer Spaniards, and they made up a smaller proportion of Canada's immigrants. The numbers of Spaniards immigrating to Canada and the United States declined after 1970. Improved political and socioeconomic conditions in Spain encouraged residents to stay, and emigrants chose other destinations, particularly France and Germany.

Spanish immigrants to North America in the late twentieth century were likely to be family members of citizens or permanent resident aliens. Many were professionals, scientists, or nonperformance artists, or worked in occupations with labor shortages.

Relations with the United States. Spain's relations with the United States were often strained before 1900 because the two countries competed for control in the New World. Spain was unable to keep the Americans out of its Louisiana Territories and East and West Florida. The competition for land was resolved with the ADAMS-ONÍS TREATY (1819), by which the United States acquired the Floridas and the Spanish claims to the Pacific Northwest, renounced claims to Texas, and assumed the claims of its own citizens, up to $5 million, against Spain. The treaty did not end the rivalry.

The United States angered Spain in 1822 by being the first nation to recognize the newly independent countries of mainland Latin America. President James Monroe then proclaimed in 1823 that the United States would consider any European move to recolonize the Americas as "dangerous to our peace and safety." Hoping to regain legal control of its former colonies, Spain condemned the MONROE DOCTRINE as the "doctrine of false international law." Although the Monroe Doctrine accepted existing colonies in the Americas, even in 1823 some Americans discussed the advantages of taking Cuba from Spain. As the naval power and maritime commerce of the United States expanded, suggestions to seize Cuba became more frequent. By the 1880's, military strategists wanted bases in the Caribbean and the Pacific. When the SPANISH-AMERICAN WAR erupted in 1898, American military forces were prepared to deal Spain a swift and humiliating defeat. Spain lost CUBA, PUERTO RICO, the Philippines, and Guam, almost all of its colonies outside Africa.

After 1898, bilateral relations warmed because neither country felt threatened by the other. Trade increased but was disrupted by political unrest between 1927 and 1939. During the Spanish Civil War (1936-1939), the U.S. government repeatedly refused the pleas of the Loyalist government in Madrid for war supplies. U.S. caution stemmed from concerns with the Leftist leanings of the government and from fears of being drawn into a larger European war. Although the U.S. government intended to press for an end to Franco's rule, the emergence of the Cold War with the Soviet Union in 1945 forced American acceptance of Spain's dictator so that Mediterranean sea lanes would be kept open.

As Spain has democratized and modernized and the United States has become more familiar with Hispanic culture, the two countries have come to understand and appreciate each other more. Their people will continue to interact as Spain seeks to become an intermediary between Europe and Latin America and as the United States pursues greater trade with its southern neighbors. —*Steven L. Driever*

SUGGESTED READINGS:

• Busselle, Michael, and Nicholas Luard. *Landscape in Spain*. London: Pavilion, 1988. With a commentary by Nicholas Luard, Busselle's stunning photography of nontourist Spain offers glimpses of beautiful landscapes that have barely changed in centuries.

• Cortada, James W. *Two Nations over Time: Spain and the United States, 1776-1977*. Westport, Conn.: Greenwood Press, 1978. A chronological summary of the basic tenets suggesting the directions of Spanish-U.S. relations.

• Crow, John A. *Spain: The Root and the Flower*. 3d ed. Berkeley: University of California Press, 1985. A history and cultural interpretation of Spanish civilization from its beginning.

• Ganivet, Ángel. *Idearium español con el porvenir de España*. Madrid: Espasa-Calpe, 1990. An attempt to penetrate the character of Spain and Spaniards. Identi-

fies themes that later preoccupied writers of the Generation of 98.

• Michener, James A. *Iberia: Spanish Travels and Reflections*. New York: Random House, 1968. An old-fashioned travel book that thoroughly acquaints the reader with geographical, historical, and psychosocial nuances of Spain.

• Thomas, Hugh. *The Spanish Civil War*. Rev. ed. New York: Harper & Row, 1977. A rewriting and expansion of the original edition, which is a classic work on the subject.

• Way, Ruth. *A Geography of Spain and Portugal*. London: Methuen, 1962. A well-illustrated introduction to the physical and human geography of Spain and its regions.

Spanglish: Linguistic CODE SWITCHING between Spanish and English. *Spanglish* is a common phenomenon among bilingual individuals of Hispanic descent. Chicano poets such as ALURISTA, José MONTOYA, and Gloria ALZANDÚA have incorporated Spanglish into their writings, both to convey a realistic linguistic portrayal of their communities and to take advantage of the formal stylistic possibilities it offers. NUYORICAN writers such as Tato LAVIERA and Pedro PIETRI also make use of Spanglish. In Nuyorican literature, the presence of code switching is associated primarily with the urban experience of Puerto Rican immigrants to the United States.

Spanish American League Against Discrimination (SALAD): Organization dedicated to the advancement of Latinos. SALAD was established in 1974 in Miami, Florida. It participates in a broad range of programs with related goals of equal opportunity, advancement for Latinos, and fighting discrimination in such areas as employment, education, housing, social services, and the judicial system. SALAD works on many issues including immigration policy and retention of Spanish-language programs in public schools. It fights anti-bilingual ordinances and discrimination in the workplace, in housing, and in education. Its membership is based in Florida.

Spanish-American War: A dispute over Spain's suppression of a Cuban rebellion erupted into war between Spain and the United States from April to August of 1898. The war officially ended with the Peace of Paris, which was signed on December 10, 1898.

Background. The 1898 conflict between Spain and the United States was rooted in the Cuban rebellion for

Cuban troops line up to receive their pay during the Spanish-American War. (National Archives)

independence, which began on February 24, 1895. Longstanding defense considerations prompted by the proximity of CUBA to the United States, increasing U.S. trade with and investment in Cuba, reports of horrible hardships endured by the Cuban civilian population as a result of the Spanish general Valeriano Weyler y Nicolau's policies, and the lobbying of Cubans in the United States all served to focus American interest on the Cuban rebellion. Despite increasing pressure from both Congress and the public for U.S. intervention, both President Grover Cleveland and President William McKinley sought to use diplomacy to bring an end to the Cuban upheaval.

President McKinley welcomed reforms introduced by the liberal Spanish government of Práxedes M. Sagasta in October, 1897, including the recall of General Weyler and the establishment of an autonomous government for Cuba. The reforms, however, failed to gain the support of either the Cuban rebels or Spanish conservatives.

The February 9, 1898, publication in the *New York Journal* of a letter critical of President McKinley written by the Spanish minister in Washington, coupled with the sinking of the USS *Maine* in Havana harbor on February 15, inflamed American public opinion against Spain. A Spanish inquiry into the destruction of the USS *Maine* concluded that the battleship sank as the result of an internal explosion. The March 28 release of a U.S. Navy report placing the blame for the destruction of the USS *Maine* on an external explosion led to a public outcry against Spain, however, and the United States moved closer to war.

As a last effort to resolve the dispute with Spain over Cuba through diplomatic means, McKinley asked the government in Madrid to agree to a six-month armistice, during which negotiations for peace between Spain and the Cuban insurgents would take place through the offices of the United States. If no peace agreement had been reached by October 1, Spain was to accept the president of the United States as the final arbiter of the Cuban problem.

Public opinion in Spain made it impossible for the Spanish government to accept McKinley's terms, but the Spaniards did offer an armistice if the rebels would request one. Subsequently, the Spanish commander in Cuba was instructed to grant an armistice for such a length of time as he considered prudent. These responses did not meet McKinley's conditions.

On April 11, the president sent a message to Congress requesting authorization to use U.S. troops in Cuba. At the end of his message, McKinley mentioned that he hoped Congress would give the recent Spanish concessions due consideration.

The joint resolution passed by Congress on April 19 and signed by McKinley the next day recognized the independence of the Cuban people, demanded that Spain immediately withdraw from the island, and authorized the president to use the armed forces of the United States to secure those objectives. An amendment introduced by Senator Henry Teller of Colorado disclaimed any intention by the United States to exercise sovereignty over Cuba once Spain had been forced to withdraw. By April 25, Spain and the United States had declared war against each other.

War. The first military action of the war occurred far from Cuba. On May 1, the U.S. Navy's Asiatic squadron, under the command of Commodore George Dewey, destroyed the Spanish fleet anchored in Manila harbor.

In Cuba, military operations centered on the city of Santiago de Cuba. In mid-May, a Spanish fleet sailed into the Santiago harbor, which was shortly thereafter blockaded by a U.S. fleet under the command of Admiral William T. Sampson. Because the mouth of the harbor had been mined by the Spaniards, Sampson could not steam into the harbor and engage the Spanish fleet. Therefore, Army troops under the command of General William R. Shafter were instructed to land near Santiago to assist the Navy in capturing the forts that guarded the harbor's entrance and controlled the mines.

The landing began on June 22 at Daiquiri and Siboney Bay. Battles fought on June 30 and July 1 at El Caney and San Juan Hill allowed American troops to gain control of the heights overlooking Santiago. A Spanish attempt to break through the U.S. naval blockade on July 3 resulted in the destruction of the entire Spanish fleet. Thirteen days later, the Spanish army defending Santiago surrendered.

On July 25, a U.S. expedition under the command of General Nelson A. Miles invaded Puerto Rico. An armistice signed in Washington on August 12 ended the war before Miles's troops completed the conquest of the island. The invasion of Puerto Rico was both a logical consequence of the war against Spain and a natural outgrowth of U.S. strategic concerns. An attack anywhere on Spain's periphery could serve to weaken Spain's resolve to continue the war. In addition, U.S. control of Puerto Rico provided a vantage point for asserting U.S. mastery over the Caribbean.

Meanwhile, in the Pacific, the island of Guam was captured on June 22; on August 14, two days after the

U.S. troops prepare to assault San Juan Hill during a pivotal battle in the Spanish-American War. (Library of Congress)

signing of the armistice but before the end of the war was known in the Asian theater, Manila was captured by U.S. troops and elements of Philippine insurgent forces under the command of Emilio Aguinaldo.

Under the TREATY OF PARIS, signed on December 10, 1898, Spain relinquished sovereignty over Cuba and ceded Puerto Rico and other West Indies islands, the Philippines, and Guam to the United States. For its part, the United States agreed to occupy Cuba only temporarily, to pay Spain twenty million dollars for the Philippine Islands, and to recognize the rights of Spanish citizens living in the territories ceded to the United States.

Impact of the War. The Spanish-American War, which lasted three months and twenty-two days, marked the end of Spain's four hundred years as a colonial empire. The conflict saw the destruction of a large portion of Spain's fleet; from 1895 to 1898, moreover, Spain's military lost 9,413 men from battle-related injuries and 53,440 from disease. For the United States, the war marked the beginning of an overseas empire and announced the nation's entrance onto the stage of world affairs as a major power with global interests. The war cost the United States 698 deaths from battle-related injuries and 5,509 deaths from disease.

Immediately following the war, Cuba was placed under a U.S. military government. On May 20, 1902, the government of the island was turned over to President Tomás ESTRADA PALMA and a congress duly elected under the new Cuban constitution. The imposition by the United States of the PLATT AMENDMENT, a document that provided for, among other things, the right of the United States to intervene in Cuba and to acquire a naval base on the island, left Cuba's sovereignty impaired until the amendment's abrogation in 1934.

At the end of the war, Puerto Rico became a U.S. possession, with the political status and civil rights of its inhabitants to be determined by the U.S. Congress. From October 18, 1898, until May 1, 1900, the island was under a military government. On May 1, 1900, the FORAKER ACT, a law passed by the U.S. Congress, established civil government for the island with a governor appointed by the president of the United States, an executive council appointed by the governor, and an elected legislative assembly. Individuals born on the island were to be considered citizens of Puerto Rico, not citizens of the United States.   —*Glenn J. Kist*

SUGGESTED READINGS: • Carr, Raymond. *Puerto Rico: A Colonial Experiment.* New York: Vintage Books, 1984. • Foner, Philip S. *The Spanish-Cuban-American War and the Birth of American Imperialism, 1895-1902.* 2 vols. New York: Monthly Review Press, 1972. • May, Ernest R. *Imperial Democracy: The Emergence of America as a Great Power.* New York: Harcourt, Brace & World, 1961. • Milton, Joyce. *The Yellow Kids: Foreign Correspondents in the Heyday of Yellow Journalism.* New York: Harper & Row, 1989. • Prioli, Carmine. "The Second Sinking of the *Maine.*" *American Heritage* 41 (December, 1990): 94-101. • Thomas, Hugh. *Cuba: The Pursuit of Freedom.* New York: Harper & Row, 1971. • Trask, David F. *The War with Spain in 1898.* New York: Macmillan, 1981.

Spanish Americans: Most of the more than twenty million Spanish-speaking people in the United States as of 1990 had origins in Puerto Rico, Cuba, Mexico, and other Latin American countries. Only approximately 2 percent of the Spanish-speaking population in the United States had origins directly traceable to Spain. Spain, however, has influenced the Americas from the age of exploration through the end of the twentieth century.

Historical Perspective. Spanish soldiers or conquistadores, along with Catholic missionary priests, came to the Americas in search of gold and souls, imposing religion, language, and customs on the indigenous people. In the eighteenth century, Franciscan monks such as Father Junípero SERRA founded missions along the California coast. By the late 1700's, approximately six hundred Spaniards lived in California.

During the following two centuries, Spanish-speaking people from Mexico, Puerto Rico, Cuba, and various other Latin American countries added to the Hispanic influence in the United States. All of those countries had been influenced by Spanish explorers and settlers. By 1990, the Spanish-speaking populations of New York and Los Angeles were among the world's largest, surpassed only by those of Madrid, Barcelona, Mexico City, and Buenos Aires.

Immigration and Acculturation. It is difficult to compile accurate data on the number of people of direct Spanish descent in the United States because statistical data have often combined Spaniards with non-European Latino or Hispanic immigrants. Data for Canada's Spanish population are relatively clear, but that population is small. A small group of immigrants from Spain and the Canary Islands settled in Canada, along with other Spanish-speaking people escaping sociopolitical events in Latin American countries.

The U.S. Immigration and Naturalization Service reported a total of 250,000 immigrants from Spain between 1820 and 1976. In the first quarter of the twentieth century, approximately 175,000 emigrants from Spain arrived in the United States; about 50,000 eventually returned home. At that time, millions of Spaniards also immigrated to Argentina and Cuba. Immigration quotas instituted in 1924 severely limited Spanish migration to the United States.

As was true for other emigrants from Southern Europe, Spanish emigrants were predominantly men who later sent for their families. Many of the Spanish emigrants were searching for economic freedom and came from agricultural areas.

The Spanish introduced large-scale cattle ranching in the United States. Immigrants from the Basque region, an area between Spain and France, settled in the New York area and the Rocky Mountains. Basques are known for their skills and experience in SHEEP-HERDING, and during the 1950's, when the United States had a shortage of sheepherders, Basques were encouraged to enter the country through special immigration laws.

Spanish emigrants from Andalusia settled in Hawaii, working on sugar plantations. During the fascist regime of Francisco Franco in the 1940's and 1950's, many Spaniards left the country for political reasons. Many immigrants moved to Florida from Spain via Cuba. A major wave of Spanish immigration, approximately 100,000 people, occurred between 1960 and 1990.

Spanish Americans have not tried to maintain a separate ethnic identity or community; they often refer to themselves as Galicians, Basques, Asturians, or Catalonians, depending on the Spanish region of origin. Traditionally, Spanish Americans have emphasized the traditional family structure, in which the male head of household is considered to be the dominant figure and women are responsible for running the household and rearing the children. As more Spanish American women joined the work force, men began to share in household responsibilities.

Contributions. Spanish Americans have made numerous contributions to U.S. culture in terms of language, religion, science, art, literature, dance, music,

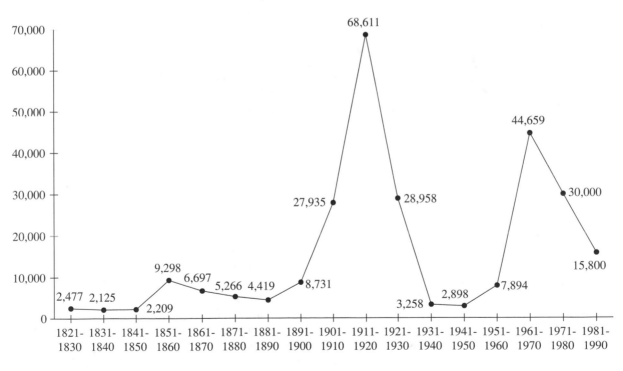

SPANISH IMMIGRATION TO THE UNITED STATES, 1821-1990

Source: Data are from "Spaniards," in Stephan Thernstrom, ed., *Harvard Encyclopedia of American Ethnic Groups* (Cambridge, Mass.: Harvard University Press, 1980), Table 1, p. 945; and Marlita A. Reddy, ed., *Statistical Record of Hispanic Americans* (Detroit: Gale Research, 1993), Tables 25 and 26.

Note: The numbers of immigrants for 1971-1980 and 1981-1990 are rounded.

These Spanish American girls celebrate their heritage with traditional costumes and sashes that proclaim their ancestral provinces. (Frances M. Roberts)

and foods. Their architectural influences can be found in homes, churches, and public buildings. Catholicism, one of the major Christian religions in the United States, was brought to the Americas by the Spanish. Spanish is becoming a second language in the United States, with street signs, billboards, magazines, newspapers, and radio and television programs catering to the Spanish-speaking population.

A few of the world-renowned Spanish Americans are architect Jose Luis Sert, scientist Severo Ochoa, and writers Juan Ramon Jimenez, Pedro Salinas, Ramon Sender, and Jorge Guillen. Julio Iglesias, the well-known Spanish singer, was born and reared in Madrid but lives part-time in Miami. Many other artists and professionals have enriched American culture with their contributions. —*Mario A. Pacino*

SUGGESTED READINGS: • Altrocchi, Julia Cooley. "The Spanish Basques in California." *The Catholic World* 146 (January, 1938): 417-424. • Fernandez-Shaw, Carlos M. *The Hispanic Presence in North America from 1492 to Today.* Translated by Alfonso Bertodano Stourton et al. New York: Facts on File, 1991. • Gomez, R. A. "Spanish Immigration to the United States." *The Americas* 19 (July, 1962): 59-78. • Martinez Cachero, Luis Alfonso. *La Emigracion Espanola a Examen.* Madrid: ASE, 1970. • Namias, June, comp. *First Generation: In the Words of Twentieth-Century American Immigrants.* Boston: Beacon Press, 1978. • Natella, Arthur A., Jr., ed. *The Spanish in America, 1513-1974.* Dobbs Ferry, N.Y.: Oceana, 1975. • Rips, Gladys Nadler. *Coming to America: Immigrants from Southern Europe.* New York: Delacorte Press, 1981.